Frommer's®

4th
Edition

Toronto

by Marilyn Wood

Macmillan • USA

ABOUT THE AUTHOR

Marilyn Wood came to the United States from England to study journalism at
Columbia University. The former editorial director of Prentice Hall Travel, she has also
worked as a reporter, ranch hand, press officer, and book reviewer. In addition, Marilyn is
the author of *Frommer's Wonderful Weekends from New York City* and *Frommer's London
from $55 a Day*, as well as a coauthor of *Frommer's Canada*.

MACMILLAN TRAVEL

A Simon & Schuster Macmillan Company
1633 Broadway
New York, NY 10019

Find us online at **http://www.mgr.com/travel** or
on America Online at Keyword: **Frommer's.**

ISBN 0-02-860892-5
ISSN 1047-7853

Editor: Erica Spaberg
Production Editor: Brian Robinson
Map Editor: Douglas Stallings
Design by Michele Laseau
Maps by Ortelius Design

SPECIAL SALES

Manufactured in the United States of America

Contents

List of Maps

AN INVITATION TO THE READER

In researching this book, I discovered many wonderful places—hotels, restaurants, shops, and more. I'm sure you'll find others. Please tell us about them, so we can share the information with your fellow travelers in upcoming editions. If you were disappointed with a recommendation, we'd love to know that, too. Please write to:

Marilyn Wood
Frommer's Toronto, 4th Edition
Macmillan Travel
1633 Broadway
New York, NY 10019

AN ADDITIONAL NOTE

Please be advised that travel information is subject to change at any time—and this is especially true of prices. We therefore suggest that you write or call ahead for confirmation when making your travel plans. The authors, editors, and publisher cannot be held responsible for the experiences of readers while traveling. Your safety is important to us, however, so we encourage you to stay alert and be aware of your surroundings. Keep a close eye on cameras, purses, and wallets—all favorite targets of thieves and pickpockets.

WHAT THE SYMBOL MEANS

✪ Frommer 's Favorites

Hotels, restaurants, attractions, and entertainment you should not miss.

The following abbreviations are used for credit cards:

AE	American Express	EU	Eurocard
CB	Carte Blanche	JCB	Japan Credit Bank
DC	Diners Club	MC	MasterCard
DISC	Discover	V	Visa
ER	enRoute		

Introducing Toronto, a Multicultural Mosaic

Once lampooned as a dull and ugly city, Toronto, now with a population of more than four million, has burst forth from its stodgy past and grabbed attention as one of North America's most exciting cities.

How did it happen? Toronto got a chance to change its image with a substantial blood transfusion from other cultures. A post–World War II influx of large numbers of Italians, Chinese, and Portuguese, plus Germans, Jews, Hungarians, Poles, Ukrainians, Greeks, East Indians, West Indians, and French Canadians infused this once quiet, conservative community with new energy. Now, there are neighborhoods where residents can eat an authentic Portuguese meal, see a Hong Kong action film, or catch a late-night reggae set—all within a few blocks of their doorstep. And many Torontonians do these things, regarding their incredible diversity as nothing particularly out of the ordinary.

In recent years, this cultural growth has been accompanied by new developments—from theaters and concert halls to sports stadiums and major projects like the BCE building and the new Canadian Broadcasting complex. Yet through it all, Toronto has managed to preserve the old while creating the new. Progress has not inevitably brought in the wrecker's ball; much has survived. When you see Holy Trinity Church and the Scadding House, one of the oldest residences in the city, standing proudly against the glass-galleried Eaton Centre, preserved because the people demanded it, you know that certain values and a great deal of thoughtful debate have gone into the making of this city.

In Toronto, people walk to work from their restored Victorian town houses (no developer can erect downtown commercial space without including living space), the subway positively gleams, and the streets are safe. Here, old buildings are saved and converted to other uses; architects design around the contours of nature instead of just bulldozing the trees. This is a city created with flair and imagination, but also a sense of traditional values.

1 Frommer's Favorite Toronto Experiences

- **Picnicking on the Toronto Islands:** A short ferry ride will transport you to another world of lagoons and rush-lined backwaters,

Metropolitan Toronto

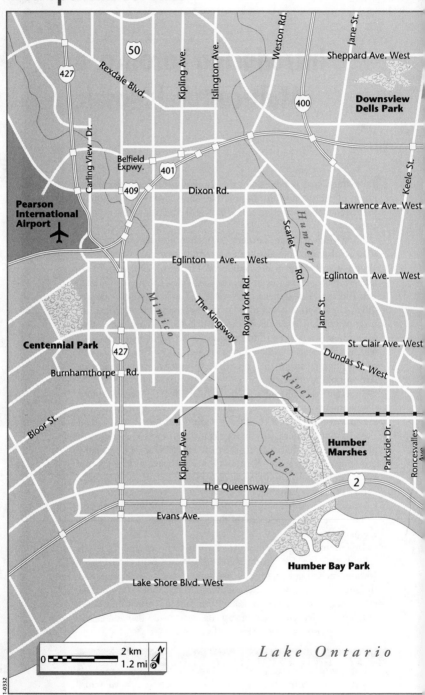

50

427

Rexdale Blvd.

Kipling Ave.

Islington Ave.

Weston Rd.

Jane St.

Sheppard Ave. West

400

Downsview Dells Park

Keele St.

Carling View Dr.

Belfield Expwy.

401

409

Dixon Rd.

Lawrence Ave. West

Pearson International Airport ✈

Humber Rd.

Scarlet Rd.

Eglinton Ave. West

Eglinton Ave. West

Mimico

The Kingsway

Royal York Rd.

Jane St.

Centennial Park

427

St. Clair Ave. West

Burnhamthorpe Rd.

Dundas St. West

River

Bloor St.

River

Humber Marshes

Parkside Dr.

Roncesvalles Ave.

Kipling Ave.

The Queensway

2

Evans Ave.

Humber Bay Park

Lake Shore Blvd. West

0   2 km
     1.2 mi

N

Lake Ontario

1-0332

2

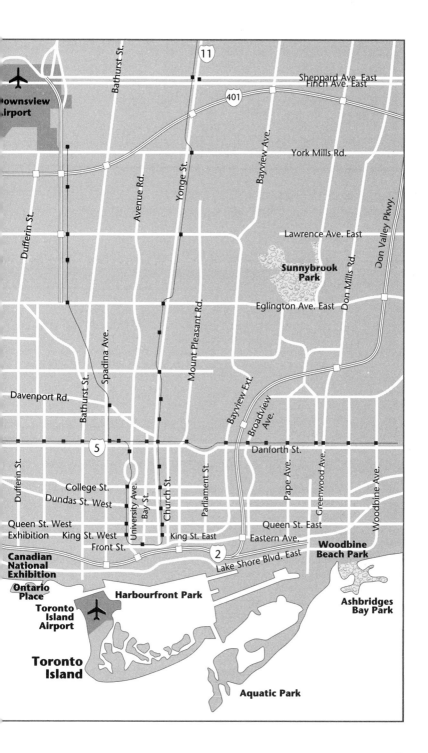

miles away from the urban tarmac—a world of houseboats and bicycles, a place to stroll beside the weeping willows.

- **Exploring Harbourfront:** Bring a model boat; watch artisans blowing glass; take a sailing lesson; tour the harbor; shop the quay and the antique mart—and this is just the beginning.

- **Relaxing in the Beaches:** Stroll or bike along the boardwalk, picnic in the adjacent parkland and gardens, and browse the stores one block from the beach.

- **Viewing the McMichael Collection at Kleinburg:** Kleinburg—a log and stone gallery amid quiet stands of pine trees—is a peaceful oasis that's completely appropriate for the famous Group of Seven landscape paintings, inspired by the Canadian wilderness of Northern Ontario, displayed inside. Well worth the 25-mile drive from downtown.

- **Playing and Learning at the Ontario Science Centre:** Here you can test your reaction time, play exotic musical instruments, experiment with the Internet, and play all kinds of interactive, enlightening, and fun games.

- **Strolling through Chinatown or Queen Street West:** The first is crowded, bustling, and lined with Chinese teashops, restaurants, bakeries, groceries, and herb stores; the second is a gathering place for the artsy crowd and a street that is known for its assortment of eclectic stores selling everything from funky junk and antique clothing to fabrics and antiquarian books.

- **Hanging Out in the Evening in the Two Hottest Neighborhoods in Town, Little Italy and Greektown:** In Little Italy, people crowd into the cafes and restaurants, as well as the bars that feature pool tables. In Greektown—the one area where you can dine after 11pm (to the strains of bouzouki music), sidewalk cafes are jammed until all hours.

- **Shopping St. Lawrence Market on Saturday Morning:** The St. Lawrence food hall is a veritable forest of edible delights. Here you can assemble all the ingredients for a picnic—cheeses and cold cuts of all kinds, breads, deli items, and desserts—or else enjoy a Canadian bacon sandwich at one of the stands.

- **Sipping Cocktails atop the CN Tower:** On a clear day, you can see at least as far as Lake Simcoe or, if you're lucky, all the way to Georgian Bay. If it's foggy, forget it.

- **Watching a Game at Maple Leaf Gardens:** Join the crowds of loyal fans watching their beloved Maple Leafs battle it out on the ice. In the world of hockey, it's hard to find a more dedicated bunch, especially when you consider the years of lackluster performance the team's had. This is one place to see Canadians verging on the out of control.

- **Seeing a Baseball Game at the SkyDome:** If you're a baseball fan, you owe yourself a look at SkyDome, the state-of-the-art home of the former world champion Blue Jays. If you want to go the luxury route, book one of the 70 rooms with field views at the complex's hotel. The retractable roof is nothing short of amazing.

- **Riding the Streetcar along College and Carlton Streets or along Queen Street West and East:** Enjoy the clang of the bell and the hiss of the air brakes as you glide along the rails. On the College route, you'll pass the University of Toronto, going through Little Italy and Little Portugal to the West End. The Queen Street car takes you through the funky area of Queen Street West or, if you're traveling in the opposite direction, to the Beaches, favorite residential neighborhood of young boomers and their families.

- **Viewing the Spectacular Collection of Henry Moore Sculptures at the Art Gallery of Ontario:** Henry Moore was so grateful to the citizens of Toronto for their support, he donated many of his works to this museum, giving it one of the better collections of his sculpture in North America.

- **Shopping in the Chic Complex of Hazelton Lanes:** Hazelton Lanes shelters all the big names of world retail, conveniently located under one roof. There are also a couple of fine places for an energizing snack. Once you're refreshed, check out a few galleries in surrounding Yorkville.
- **Cruising the Harbor aboard a Schooner:** Feel the wind in the ship's sails pushing you across the surface of the lake, as you weave in and out between the islands. The view of the Toronto skyline, dominated by the CN Tower, is superb.
- **Day Tripping to the Shaw Festival in Niagara-on-the-Lake or to the Stratford Festival:** Both are attractive historic towns. In Niagara-on-the Lake, there's the added advantage of tasting the region's increasingly fine wines, while Stratford offers some of the finest dining opportunities in Ontario at its top-notch restaurants.

2 Toronto Today

Today, the city's multiethnic mosaic continues to grow in richness with a steady flow of immigrants from around the world. The exodus from Hong Kong continues unabated as 1997's hand-over of that crown colony to the Chinese fast approaches, and has helped swell Toronto's Chinese population to more than 300,000. This has led to the development of several Chinatowns. The original downtown Chinatown has been largely taken over by Vietnamese families, while other, more recently minted Chinatowns with large shopping malls have developed around Kennedy and Lawrence. Asian immigrants from India, Pakistan, Korea, Thailand, and Vietnam have added new dimensions and flavor to the city's cultural life, as have newcomers from the Caribbean islands (most notably Trinidad and Tobago), and Central America.

It would be naive not to acknowledge the stresses and strains this rapid increase in population has etched into the social fabric of Toronto, and the city has had its share of problems. Overall, though, Toronto's quality of life is far higher than a comparably sized American city, and much less violent.

The most visible problems are the homeless on the streets, the squeegee kids who line up with pails at intersections to clean car windshields, the steady deterioration of Yonge Street into the Times Square of Toronto, and the increased reports of violent, drug-related crime, especially in Regent Park, a public housing development bounded by Parliament, Shuter, River, and Gerrard streets, near Allan Gardens.

The new Progressive Conservative Provincial Government, elected in June 1995 and headed by Mike Harris, has trimmed Ontario's social welfare budgets by 22%, which hasn't exactly ameliorated the situation. During the frigidly cold winter of 1995–96, several homeless people froze to death on city streets; with limited resources, nothing could be done. Finally, the Canadian army stepped in, establishing shelters at places like the Moss Park Armory.

Despite cuts in social services, money is being invested in the development of several major public facilities, most notably a new stadium for Toronto's basketball team, the Raptors. When they hit the courts as the first NBA team outside the United States, the Raptors created massive excitement. Basketball fever has swept the city, with fans packing the SkyDome for their games (the team's home until the new stadium is erected). Other major construction projects underway include the expansion of the Metro Toronto Convention Centre. When it reopens in mid-1997, it will have doubled in size. Also due to be unveiled in 1997 is a new National Trade Centre—

Canada's largest. Of Toronto's museums, The Royal Ontario Museum (ROM) has just completed a massive renovation, and the recently expanded Art Gallery of Ontario will host a large exhibition of works by Edvard Munch from late 1996 to early 1997.

When the sun goes down, the fashionable crowd continues to hang out along Queen Street, with new restaurants, boîtes, and jazz clubs pushing ever farther west; but other neighborhoods are also bursting forth with new life—Greektown and Little Italy, in particular. These last two are hot, hot, hot dining and late-night spots.

In the private sector, few office buildings are being constructed as, just as in most American cities, Canadian corporations downsize and move their headquarters to the suburbs or farther afield. The construction that is going on around town is primarily of condominiums, which will at least encourage residents to stay downtown and not flee to suburban satellites like North York, with its gigantic strip malls.

The biggest political issue at the moment is the planned reorganization of city government. Currently, Metro consists of the cities of Toronto, North York, Etobicoke, Scarborough, and York, and the borough of East York, each with its own city (or borough) hall. At present, Metro is responsible for public transportation, police services, social services, traffic control, and the borrowing and issuing of debentures. Fire, health, and some other services are provided by the local municipalities; still other responsibilities, including sewage disposal, water supply, and libraries, are shared. Everyone seems to agree that this inefficient tangle of overlapping responsibilities needs reforming, and that Metro needs to be expanded. Perhaps even a Greater Toronto regional government needs to be created, absorbing as many as 15 municipalities. Naturally, everyone disagrees about how this should be done, and so far, only reports and recommendations have been filed. Something does have to be done, however, and by the time the next edition of this book appears, Metro Toronto will most likely engulf a much greater area than it does at the moment.

3 History 101

Dateline

- **1615** Etienne Brûleé travels the Toronto Trail.
- **1720** France establishes post at Toronto.
- **1751** Fort Rouille built.
- **1763** Treaty of Paris effectively ends French rule in Canada.
- **1787** Lord Dorchester, British governor of Québec, purchases land from Scarborough to Etobicoke from the Mississauga tribe.
- **1791** British colony of Upper Canada formed.
- **1793** Governor of Upper Canada, Col. John Simcoe, arrives and names settlement York.

continues

FROM FUR TRADING POST TO MUDDY YORK   As with most cities, geography, trade, and communications are the influences that have shaped Toronto and its history. Although the city today possesses a downtown core, it also sprawls across a large area—a gift of geography, for there are no physical barriers to stop it. Initially, the flat broad plain rising from Lake Ontario to an inland ridge of hills (around St. Clair Avenue today) and stretching between the Don River in the east and the Humber in the west made an ideal location for a settlement.

Native Canadians had long stopped here at the entrance to the Toronto Trail—a short route between the Lower and Upper lakes. French fur trader Etienne Brûlé was the first European to travel this trail in 1615, but it wasn't until 1720 that the first trading post, known as Fort Toronto, was established by the French to intercept the furs that were being taken across Lake Ontario to New York State by English rivals. This trading post was replaced in

1751 by Fort Rouille, which was built on the site of today's CNE grounds. When the 1763 Treaty of Paris ended the Anglo-French War after the fall of Québec, French rule in North America was effectively ended and the city's French antecedents were all but forgotten.

Only 20 miles across the lake from the United States, Toronto has always been affected by what happens south of the border. When the American Revolution established a powerful and potentially hostile new nation, Toronto's location became strategically more important, or it certainly seemed so to John Graves Simcoe, lieutenant-governor of the newly formed province of Upper Canada, which had been established in 1791 to administer the frontiers—from Kingston and Quinte's Isle to Windsor and beyond—settled largely by Loyalists fleeing the Revolution. To Simcoe Toronto was more defensible than Fort Niagara and a natural arsenal for Lake Ontario, which also afforded easy access to Lake Huron and the interior.

The governor had already purchased a vast tract of land from the Mississauga tribe for the paltry sum of £1,700 plus such baubles as blankets, guns, rum, and tobacco. In 1793 Lieutenant-Governor Simcoe, his wife, Elizabeth, and the Queen's Rangers arrived to build a settlement. Simcoe ordered a garrison built, renamed the settlement York, and laid it out in a 10-block rectangle around King, Front, George, Duke, and Berkeley streets. Beyond stretched a series of 100-acre lots from Queen to Bloor, which were granted to government officials to mollify their resentment about having to move to this mosquito-plagued, marshy, muddy outpost. Its muddiness was indeed prodigious, and in fact there is a story told of a fellow who saw a hat lying in the middle of a street, went to pick it up, and found the head of a live man submerged below it! In 3 short years a small hamlet had grown, and Simcoe had laid out Yonge Street—then a 33-mile ox-cart trail—and 4 years later the first Parliament meeting confirmed York as the capital of Upper Canada.

FROM MUDDY YORK TO THE FAMILY COMPACT   The officials were a more demanding and finicky lot than the sturdy frontier farmers, and businesses sprang up to serve them. By 1812 the population had grown to 703 and included a brewer-baker, a blacksmith, a watchmaker, a chairmaker, an apothecary, a hatter, and a tailor.

During the War of 1812, despite initial victories at Queenston and Detroit, Canada was under siege,

- **1796** Yonge Street laid out, a 33-mile oxcart trail.
- **1797** Center of government transferred from Niagara to York.
- **1813** War of 1812: Americans invade, blow up Fort York, and burn Parliament buildings.
- **1820s** Immigration of Nonconformists and Irish Catholics fosters reform politics.
- **1828** Erie Canal extended to Oswego on Lake Ontario.
- **1830s** Orange Order becomes prominent influence in politics.
- **1832–34** Cholera epidemics.
- **1834** City named Toronto: City Council replaces magistrates; William Lyon Mackenzie becomes first mayor.
- **1837** Rebellion led by former mayor William Lyon Mackenzie, sparked by bad economic times.
- **1841** Act of Union establishes the United Province of Canada, with Kingston as ruling seat; Toronto loses status as a capital.
- **1842** Streets are gaslit.
- **1843** The university, King's College, opens.
- **1844** City hall built; George Brown founds the *Globe*.
- **1840s–50s** Mass Irish immigration.
- **1849** Great fire destroys much of city; Anglican King's College converts to secular University of Toronto.
- **1851** Population 30,000 (33% Irish); Anglican Trinity College founded; St. Lawrence Hall built.
- **1852** Toronto Stock Exchange opens; Grand

continues

Trunk Railroad charted, linking Québec-Montréal-Toronto-Guelph-Sarnia.

- **1853** St. James Cathedral completed at King and Church.
- **1858** Storm creates the Toronto Islands.
- **1861** Population 44,000; horse-powered street railway runs along Yonge to Yorkville.
- **1867** Canadian Confederation; Toronto becomes capital of new province of Ontario.
- **1868** Canada First movement begins.
- **1869** Eaton's opens.
- **1871** Population 56,000.
- **1872** Simpson's department store opens.
- **1876** John Ross Robertson starts *Evening Telegram*, which wields influence for next 90 years.
- **1884** Streets electrically lit.
- **1886** Provincial parliament buildings erected in Queen's Park.
- **1891** Population 181,000.
- **1893** First Stanley Cup played.
- **1896** *MacLean's* magazine started.
- **1901** Population 208,000.
- **1904** Great Fire burns much of downtown.
- **1906** First autos produced by Canada Cycle and Motor Company; Toronto Symphony founded.
- **1907** Bell strike broken; Royal Alexandra opens.
- **1911** Population 376,538.
- **1912** Garment workers' strike broken; Royal Ontario Museum founded.
- **1914** New Union Station built.
- **1914–18** World War 1; 70,000 Torontonians enlist. 13,000 die.

continues

and in April 1813, 14 ships carrying 1,700 American troops invaded York, blew up the uncompleted fort, burned the Parliament Buildings, and carried off the mace (which was not returned until 1934). The British general burned a 30-gun warship, the *Sir Isaac Brock,* which was being built, and retreated, leaving young John Strachan to negotiate the capitulation. This event did much to reinforce the town's pro-British, anti-American attitude—an attitude that persists to some extent to this day. In retaliation for the burning of Fort York, some Canadians went down and torched the American president's residence. (The Americans later whitewashed it to hide the charred wood—hence, the White House.)

A conservative pro-British outlook permeated the official political oligarchy that dominated York, and this group was dubbed the Family Compact. Many of the names that visitors will see on street signs, subway stops, and maps are derived from this august group of early government officers and their families. Among them were William Jarvis, a New England Loyalist who became provincial secretary; John Beverley Robinson, son of a Virginia Loyalist, who at age 22 became attorney general and later chief justice of Upper Canada; Scottish-educated Dr. John Strachan, who rose from being a schoolmaster to an Anglican rector and the most powerful figure in York; Anglo-Irish Dr. William Warren Baldwin, doctor, lawyer, architect, judge, and parliamentarian, who laid out Spadina Avenue as a thoroughfare leading to his house of that name in the country; and the Boultons, prominent lawyers, judges, and politicians—Judge D'Arcy Boulton built a mansion, The Grange, which later became the core of the art museum and still stands today.

These men, extremely conscious of rank, were conformist, conservative, pro-British, Tory, and Anglican. Their power would be broken only later in the 19th century as a larger and more diverse population gave reformers a chance to challenge their control. But even today their influence still lingers in the corporate world where a handful of companies and individuals control 80% of the companies on the Toronto Stock Exchange.

THE EARLY 19TH CENTURY—CANAL, RAILROAD & IMMIGRATION The changes that would eventually dilute their control began in the early 19th century, especially during the 1820s, 1830s, and 1840s, when immigrants—Irish Protestants and Catholics, Scots, Presbyterians, Methodists, and other Nonconformists—poured in to settle the frontier farmlands. By 1832 York had become the largest urban community in the province, with a population of 1,600. Already well established commercially as a supply center, York was given another boost when the Erie Canal was extended to Oswego on Lake Ontario, giving it direct access to New York, and the Welland Canal was built across the Niagara Peninsula, giving it access to Lake Erie and points beyond. In 1834 the city was incorporated and York became Toronto, a city bounded by Parliament Street to the east, Bathurst to the west, the lakefront to the south, and 400 yards north of current Queen Street (then called Lot) to the north. Outside this area—stretching west to Dufferin Street, east to the Don River, and north to Bloor Street—lay the "liberties," out of which new wards would later be carved. North of Bloor, local brewer Joseph Bloor and Sheriff Jarvis were already drawing up plans for the village of Yorkville.

As more immigrants arrived, the population grew more diverse and demands for democracy and reform were voiced. Among the reformers were such leaders as Francis Collins, who launched the radical paper *Canadian Freeman* in 1825; lawyer William Draper; and, perhaps most famous of all, fiery William Lyon Mackenzie, who was elected Toronto's first mayor in 1834.

Mackenzie had started his *Colonial Advocate* to crusade against the narrow-minded Family Compact, calling for reform and challenging their power to such an extent that some of them dumped his presses into the lake. Mackenzie was undaunted and by 1837 was calling for open rebellion.

A severe depression, financial turmoil, and the failure of some banks all contributed to the 1837 Rebellion, one of the most dramatic events in the city's history. On December 5 the rebels, a scruffy bunch of about 700, gathered at Montgomery's Tavern outside the city (near modern-day Eglinton Avenue). From here, led by Mackenzie on a white mare, they marched on the city. Two days later the city's militia, called out by Sheriff Jarvis, scattered the rebels at Carlton Street. Both sides then turned and ran. Reinforcements arrived and pursued the rebels and bombarded the tavern with cannon balls. Mackenzie fled to the United States and two other leaders—Lount and Matthews—were hanged. Their graves can be visited in the Necropolis cemetery.

Between 1834 and 1884 the foundations of an industrial city were laid: Water works, gas, and later, electrical lighting were installed, and public transportation was organized. Many municipal facilities were built, including a city hall, the Royal Lyceum Theatre (1848) on King near Bay, the Toronto Stock Exchange (1852), St. Lawrence Hall (1851), an asylum, and a jail.

- **1920** Group of Seven exhibit.
- **1921** Population 521,893.
- **1923** Chinese Exclusion Act.
- **1930s** Depression; thousands go on relief or ride the boxcars.
- **1931** Maple Leaf Gardens built.
- **1939** Canada enters World War II; thousands of troops leave from Union Station.
- **1940–45** Toronto functions as war supplier.
- **1947** Cocktail lounges approved.
- **1950** Sunday sports allowed.
- **1951** Population 31% foreign-born.
- **1953** Metro created.
- **1960** O'Keefe Centre opens.
- **1961** Population 42% foreign-born.
- **1965** New city hall built.
- **1971** Ontario Place built.
- **1972** Harbourfront under development.
- **1974** Metro Zoo and Ontario Science Centre open.
- **1975** CN Tower opens for business.
- **1984** City's 150th anniversary.
- **1989** SkyDome opens.
- **1992** Residents of Toronto Islands win 40-year struggle to retain their homes.
- **1993** Princess of Wales Theatre and CBC Building open.
- **1995** Progressive Conservative Government elected; focuses on budget cuts.

During the 1850s the building of the railroads accelerated the economic pace. By 1860 Toronto was at the center of a railroad web that linked the city north, south, east, and west. Toronto became the trading hub for lumber and grain imports and exports. Merchant empires were founded; railroad magnates emerged; and institutions like the Bank of Toronto were established.

Despite its growth and wealth Toronto still lagged behind Montréal—its population being only half of Montréal's in 1861—but increasingly Toronto took advantage of its superior links to the south, an advantage that would eventually help it overtake its rival. Under the Confederation of 1867 the city was guaranteed another advantage when it was made the capital of the newly created Ontario, which, in effect, gave it control over the minerals and timber of the north.

As the city grew it gobbled up the countryside and so, to compensate for this loss, recreational areas were developed. In 1857 G. W. Allan donated 5 acres (later enlarged to 10) for the laying out of a garden. In 1860 Queen's Park was laid out. But the real gem was architect John Howard's gift of High Park to the citizens of the west end in 1873. Riverdale Park and Zoo were developed later in the 1890s.

During this same mid-Victorian period the growth of a more diverse population continued. In 1847 Irish famine victims flooded into Toronto, and by 1851 and 1852 the Irish-born were the largest single ethnic group in Toronto. While many of them were Ulster Irish Protestants who did not threaten the Anglo-Protestant ascendancy, these newcomers were not always welcomed—a pattern that was to be repeated whenever a new immigrant group threatened to change the shape and order of society. As the gap between the number of Anglicans and Catholics closed, sectarian tensions increased and the old-country Orange and Green conflicts flared into mob violence.

LATE & HIGH VICTORIAN TORONTO   Between 1871 and 1891 the city's population more than tripled, shooting from 56,000 to 181,000. This increasingly large urban market helped spawn two great Toronto retailers—Timothy Eaton and Robert Simpson—who both moved to Toronto from Ontario towns to open stores at Queen and Yonge streets in 1869 and 1872, respectively. Eaton developed his reputation on fixed prices, cash sales only, and promises of refunds if the customer wasn't satisfied—all unique gambits at the time. Simpson copied Eaton and also competed by providing better service, such as two telephones to take orders instead of one. Both developed into full-fledged department stores, and both entered the mail-order business, conquering the country with their catalogs.

The business of the city was business, and amassing wealth was the pastime of such figures as Henry Pellatt, stockbroker and president of the Electrical Development Company and builder of Casa Loma; E. B. Osler; George Albertus Cox; and A. R. Ames. Although these men were self-made entrepreneurs, not Family Compact officials, they still formed a traditional socially conservative elite linked by money, taste, investments, and religious affiliation. And they were still British to a tee. They and the rest of the citizens celebrated the Queen's Jubilee in 1897 with gusto and gave Toronto boys a rousing send-off to fight in the Boer War in 1899. They also, like the British, had a fondness for clubs—the Albany Club for the Conservatives and the National Club for the Liberals. As in England, their sports clubs carried a certain cachet—notably the Royal Yacht Club, the Toronto Cricket Club, the Toronto Golf Club, and the Lawn Tennis Club.

As the city's financial power increased, many leading companies and organizations moved their headquarters to the city, and Toronto became a cultural-intellectual powerhouse. The Canadian Institute, the Ontario Society of Artists, and the Toronto Philharmonic Society were all founded in the 1870s or 1880s. On the sports front, the first Queen's Plate was run at Woodbine in 1883; the Stanley Cup competition was begun in 1893; baseball overtook cricket; and rowing was a red-hot sport, with Ned Hanlan holding the world title from 1880 to 1884.

The boom also spurred new commercial and residential construction, such as the first steel-frame building—the Board of Trade Building (1889) at Yonge and Front; George Gooderham's Romanesque-style mansion (1890) at St. George and Bloor (now the York Club); the provincial parliament buildings in Queen's Park (1886–92); and the city hall (1899) at Queen and Bay. Public transit was improved, and by 1891 people were traveling the 68 miles of horse-drawn tracks. Electric lights, telephones, and electrical streetcars also appeared in the 1890s.

FROM 1900 TO 1933   Between 1901 and 1921 the population more than doubled, climbing from 208,000 to 521,893, and the economy continued to expand, fueled by the lumber, mining, wholesale, and agricultural machinery industries, and after 1911 by hydroelectric power. Toronto began to seriously challenge Montréal. Much of the new wealth went into construction, and three marvelous buildings from this era can still be seen today: the Horticultural Building at the Exhibition Grounds (1907), the King Edward Hotel (1903), and Union Station (1914–19). Most of the earlier wooden structures had been destroyed in the Great Fire of 1904, which wiped out 14 acres of downtown.

The booming economy and its factories attracted a wave of new immigrants—mostly Italians and Jews from Russia and Eastern Europe. They were very different from the British and Irish who had come earlier. They settled in the city's emerging ethnic enclaves. By 1912 Kensington Market was well established, and the garment center and Jewish community were firmly ensconced around King and Spadina. Little Italy clustered around College and Grace. By 1911 more than 30,000 Torontonians were foreign-born, and the slow march to change the English character of the city had begun.

It was still a city of churches worthy of the name "Toronto the Good," with a population of staunch religious conservatives, who barely voted for Sunday streetcar service in 1897 and in 1912 banned tobogganing on Sundays. As late as 1936, 30 men were arrested at the lakeshore resort of Sunnyside because they exposed their chests—even though the temperature was 105°F! In 1947 cocktail lounges were approved, but it wasn't until 1950 that commercialized sports could be played on Sundays.

Increased industrialization brought social problems, largely concentrated in Cabbagetown and the Ward, a large area that stretched west of Yonge and north of Queen. Here, poor people lived in crowded, wretched conditions: Housing was inadequate, health conditions were poor, and rag-picking or sweatshop labor was the only employment.

As industry grew unionism also increased, but the movement, as in the United States, failed to organize politically. Two major strikes—at Bell in 1907 and in the garment industry in 1912—were easily broken.

As the city became larger and wealthier it also became an intellectual and cultural magnet. Artists like Charles Jefferys, J. H. MacDonald, Arthur Lismer, Tom Thomson, Lawren Harris, Frederick Varley, and A. Y. Jackson, most associated with the Group of Seven, set up studios in Toronto, their first and now-famous group show opening in 1920. Toronto also became the English-language publishing center of the nation, and national magazines like *Maclean's* (started in 1896) and *Saturday Night* were launched. The Art Gallery of Ontario, the Royal Ontario Museum, the Toronto Symphony Orchestra, and the Royal Alexandra Theatre all opened before 1914.

Women advanced, too, at the turn of the century. In 1880 Emily Jennings Stowe became the first Canadian woman authorized to practice medicine. In 1886 women were admitted to the university. Clara Brett Martin was the first woman admitted to the law courts, and the women's suffragist movement gained strength, led by Dr. Stowe, Flora McDonald Denison, and the Women's Christian Temperance Union.

During World War I, Toronto sent 70,000 men to the trenches; about 13,000 were killed. At home, the war had a great impact economically and socially: Toronto became Canada's chief aviation center; factories, shipyards, and power facilities expanded to meet the needs of war; and women entered the work force in great numbers.

After the war the city took on much more of the aspect and tone that is still recognizable today. Automobiles appeared on the streets—the Canadian Cycle and Motor Company had begun manufacturing them in 1906 (the first parking ticket was given in 1908); one or two skyscrapers appeared; and although 80% of the population still boasted British origin, ethnic enclaves were clearly defined.

The 1920s roared along, fueled by a mining boom, which saw Bay Street turned into a veritable gold-rush alley where everyone was pushing something hot. The Great Depression followed, racking up 30% unemployment in 1933. The only distraction from its bleakness was the opening of Maple Leaf Gardens in 1931, which besides being an ice-hockey center also hosted large protest rallies during the depression and later such diverse groups and personalities as the Jehovah's Witnesses, Billy Graham, the Ringling Bros. Circus, and the Metropolitan Opera.

As in the United States, hostility toward new immigrants was rife during the twenties, and it reached one of its peaks in 1923, when the Chinese Exclusion Act was passed, banning Chinese immigration. In the 1930s antagonism toward the Jews intensified. Signs such as NO JEWS, NIGGERS, OR DOGS were posted occasionally at Balmy and Kew beaches, and in August 1933, the display of a swastika at Christie Pits caused a battle between Nazis and Jews.

AFTER WORLD WAR II   In 1939 Torontonians again rallied to the British cause, sending thousands to fight in Europe. At home, plants turned out fighter bombers and Bren guns, and people endured rationing—one bottle of liquor a month and ration books for sugar and other staples—while they listened to the warfront news delivered by Lorne Greene.

Already prosperous by World War II, Toronto continued to expand during the 1940s. The suburbs alone added more than 200,000 to the population between 1940 and 1953. By the 1950s the urban area had grown so large, disputes between city and suburbs were so frequent, and the need for social and other services was so great that an effective administrative solution was needed. In 1953 the Metro Council was established, composed of equal numbers of representatives from the city and the suburbs.

Toronto became a major city in the 1950s, with Metro providing a structure for planning and growth. The Yonge subway opened, and a network of highways was constructed, linking the city to the affluent suburbs, which were populated by families who were buying cars, TVs, barbecues, refrigerators, and washing machines—all the

Impressions

Toronto is known as Toronto the Good, because of its alleged piety. My guess is that there's more polygamy in Toronto than Baghdad, only it's not called that in Toronto.
                                                                    —Austin F. Cross, *Cross Roads* (1936)

modern conveniences associated with house-and-backyard suburbia. Don Mills, the first new town, was built between 1952 and 1962; Yorkdale Center, a mammoth shopping center, followed in 1964. Much of this growth was also fueled by the location of branch plants by American companies that were attracted to the area.

The city also began to loosen up, and while the old social elite (still traditionally educated at Upper Canada College, Ridley, and Trinity College) continued to dominate the boardrooms, politics, at least, had become more accessible and fluid. In 1954 Nathan Phillips became the first Jewish mayor, signifying how greatly the population had changed from earlier days when immigrants were primarily British, American, or French. In 1947 the Chinese Exclusion Act of 1923 was repealed, opening the door to the relatives of Toronto's then-small Chinese community. After 1950 the door swung open further. Germans and Italians were allowed to enter, adding to the communities that were already established, and then, under United Nations pressure, Poles, Ukrainians, Central European and Russian Jews, Yugoslavs, Estonians, Latvians, and other East Europeans poured in. Most arrived at Union Station, having journeyed from the ports of Halifax, Québec City, and Montréal. At the beginning of the 1950s the foreign-born were 31% of the population; by 1961 they were 42%, and the number of people claiming British descent had fallen from 73% to 59%. The 1960s were to bring an even richer mix of people—Portuguese, Greeks, West Indians, South Asians, and Chinese, Vietnamese, and Chilean refugees—changing the city's character forever.

In the 1960s the focus shifted back from the suburbs to the city. People moved back downtown, renovating the handsome brick Victorians so characteristic of today's downtown. Yorkville emerged briefly as the hippie capital—the Haight-Ashbury of Canada. Gordon Lightfoot and Joni Mitchell sang in the coffeehouses, and anti-Vietnam protests took over the streets. Perhaps the failure of the experimental, alternative Rochdale College in 1968 marked the demise of that era. By the mid-1970s Yorkville had been transformed into a village of elegant boutiques and galleries and high-rent restaurants, and the funky village had moved to Queen Street West.

In the 1970s Toronto became the fastest-growing city in North America. For years the city had competed with Montréal for first-city status, and now the separatist issue and the election of the Parti Québécois in 1976 hastened Toronto's dash to the tape. It overtook Montréal as a financial center, boasting the greatest number of corporate headquarters. Its stock market was more important, and it was also the country's prime publishing center. A dramatically different new city hall opened in 1965, symbol of the city's equally new dynamism. Toronto also began reclaiming its waterfront with the development of Harbourfront. New skyscrapers and civic buildings reflected the city's new power and wealth—the Toronto Dominion, the 72-story First Canadian Place, Royal Bank Plaza, Roy Thomson Hall, the Eaton Centre, the CN Tower—all of which transformed the old 1930s skyline into an urban landscape worthy of world attention.

Unlike the rapid building of highways and other developments completed in the 1950s, these developments were achieved with some balance and attention to the city's heritage. From the late sixties through the early eighties the citizens fought to ensure that the city's heritage was saved and that development was not allowed to continue as wildly as it had in the fifties. The best examples of the success of this reform movement were the stopping of the proposed Spadina Expressway in 1971 and the fight against several urban renewal plans.

During the 1970s the provincial government also helped develop attractions that would polish Toronto's patina and lure visitors: Ontario Place in 1971,

Returning to Toronto was like finding a Jaguar parked in front of the vicarage and the padre inside with a pitcher of vodka martinis reading Lolita.
—Article in *Maclean's,* January 1959

Harbourfront in 1972, and the Metro Zoo and the Ontario Science Centre in 1974. Government financing also supported the arts and helped turn Toronto from a city with four theaters in 1965 to one boasting 22 in 1976 and more than 40 today. The growth has continued with the 1989 downtown opening of SkyDome—the first stadium in the world with a fully retractable roof—and the planned opening of a brand-new stadium in 1997.

4 Recommended Reading

There are plenty of books that deal with all aspects of Canada's history and society. Canada is also blessed with several world-renowned writers of fiction.

GENERAL   Anything by Pierre Berton is great reading. George Woodcock's *The Canadians* (Harvard University Press, 1979) is a lively, honest appraisal of his fellow nationals and national culture. Edmund Wilson's *O Canada: An American's Notes on Canadian Culture* (Noonday Press, 1965) provides an outsider's vision of what the culture's about. And Donald Creighton has written many books about specific issues in Canadian history as well as his *Canada's First Century* (Macmillan, 1976).

For a general sociological history of the growth of Toronto, complete with statistics and historical photographs, there's the two-volume *Toronto: An Illustrated History* (Lorimer & Company, 1985). The first volume (to 1918) is by J. M. S. Careless; the second volume (after 1918) is by James Lemon.

William Kilbourn's *Toronto Remembered* (Stoddart, 1984) is, as the subtitle states, "a celebration of the city" by the author himself and many other fine writers, all of whom provide insights into the city's life and history. It's made even livelier by the quotations and illustrations that accompany the text—a delightful read.

Other general city and provincial histories include G. P. de T. Glazebrook's *The Story of Toronto* (Toronto, 1971) and Robert Bothwell's *A Short History of Ontario* (Hurtig, 1986).

ART & ARCHITECTURE   *A Concise History of Canadian Painting* by Dennis Reid (Oxford University Press, 1988) is a well-written, well-illustrated, and informative history that has chapters on significant periods of art in Toronto, including the Group of Seven and the Painters Eleven. It's entertaining and anecdotal, too.

David Burnett and Marilyn Schiff's *Contemporary Canadian Art* (Hurtig, 1983) is a well-written, concise, and liberally illustrated history of Canadian art from the 1940s to the 1980s.

Edith G. Firth's *Toronto in Art* (Fitzhenry & Whiteside, 1983) provides a pictorial history of the city as viewed by artists from the early 19th century through the 1980s. It contains more than 170 delightful illustrations.

The book on Toronto's architecture is Eric Arthur's *Toronto, No Mean City,* which, in its 1986 edition by the University of Toronto Press, has been revised by Stephen Otto. Arthur conveys his great love for the city and the history of its buildings, many of which he helped to save.

Toronto Observed by William Dendy and William Kilbourn (Oxford University Press, 1986) focuses on the many architectural treasures that still stand in the city.

It's a large-format volume with elegant black-and-white photographs of each of the 77 buildings and architectural groupings discussed.

For more of a walking-tour approach, complete with maps referenced to the text, there's Patricia McHugh's *Toronto Architecture* (McClelland & Stewart, 1989).

William Dendy's *Lost Toronto* (Toronto, 1978) recovers in words and pictures the great buildings that have been demolished.

Lucy Martyn's *Toronto: A Hundred Years of Grandeur—The Inside Story of Toronto's Great Homes* (Toronto, 1978) gives a glimpse into the lives of the wealthy— the era of millionaires and Toronto aristocrats. The life of one such self-made man is described in Carlie Oreskovich's *Sir Henry Pellatt: The King of Casa Loma* (McGraw-Hill Ryerson, 1982). Other titles to look for are A. S. Thompson's *Spadina: A Story of Old Toronto* (Paguarian Press, 1988) and *Jarvis Street* (Toronto, 1980).

FICTION   Until his death in 1995, Robertson Davies was perhaps Canada's pre-eminent man of letters. He began his literary career as a playwright and newspaper editor, working in the small Ontario town of Peterborough. His two trilogies are considered among the great works of Canadian literature. The first, the Salterton Trilogy (*Tempest-Tost, Leaven of Malice,* and *A Mixture of Frailties*) was written in the 1950s and paints a satirical portrait of a small Ontario town. The second, the Deptford Trilogy, consisting of *Fifth Business, The Manticore,* and *The World of Wonders,* is about myth, magic, and illusion. For anyone interested in psychology, *The Manticore* provides an accurate description of the experience of Jungian analysis. A later novel, *The Rebel Angels,* is a witty tale of murder, thievery, and love set at the University of Toronto, where Davies was Master of Massey College and taught for so many years.

Many of Margaret Atwood's novels are set in Toronto, including *Life Before Man* (1980), which examines the redefinition of sexual roles that occurred in the 1960s and 1970s; *Cat's Eye* (1989), in which an artist returns to the city for an exhibition of her work and recalls her years as a child in Toronto; and *The Robber Bride* (1993), in which three Toronto friends recall in flashbacks how one woman shattered each of their lives in turn.

Austin Clarke's trilogy—*The Meeting Point* (1967), *Storm of Fortune* (1971), and *The Bigger Light* (1975)—portrays the life of a family of Caribbean immigrants in Toronto.

Marian Engel's *The Year of the Child* (1981) portrays the life of a family on one particular street in Toronto. Other novels include *Honeyman Festival* and *No Clouds of Glory.*

Several of Timothy Findley's books are also set in the city, the most recent being his Canadian bestseller, *Headhunter.*

Hugh Garner's *Cabbagetown* (1950) paints what the author described as an Anglo-Saxon slum. *The Silence on the Shore* (1962) and *The Intruders* (1978) are also set in Toronto, as are several of the mysteries he wrote.

Katherine Govier's stories, *Fables of Brunswick Avenue* (1985) for example, depict the era and social scene of Toronto's young urban professionals.

2

Planning a Trip to Toronto

This chapter is devoted to the where, when, and how of your trip—the advance-planning issues required to get it together and take it on the road.

After deciding where to go, most people have two fundamental questions: What will it cost? and How do I get there? This chapter will answer both of these questions and also resolve other important issues, such as when to go, and where to obtain more information about Toronto.

1 Visitor Information & Entry Requirements

VISITOR INFORMATION

General information on travel to Canada can be obtained from the following offices in the United States: **Atlanta,** Canadian Consulate General, 400 South Tower, One CNN Center, Atlanta, GA 30303-2705 (☎ **404/577-6810**); **Boston,** Canadian Consulate General, Three Copley Place, Suite 400, Boston, MA 02116 (☎ **617/262-3760**); **Buffalo,** Canadian Consulate, Marine Midland Center, Suite 3000, Buffalo, NY 14203-2884 (☎ **716/852-1247**); **Chicago,** Canadian Consulate General, 2 Prudential Plaza, 180 N. Stetson Ave., Chicago, IL 60601 (☎ **312/616-1860**); **Dallas,** Canadian Consulate General, 750 N. St. Paul, Suite 1700, Dallas, TX 75201 (☎ **214/922-9806**); **Detroit,** Canadian Consulate General, 600 Renaissance Center, Suite 1100, Detroit, MI 48243-1798 (☎ **313/567-2340**); **Los Angeles,** Canadian Consulate General, 550 S. Hope St., 9th floor, Los Angeles, CA 90071 (☎ **213/346-2700**); **Miami,** Canadian Consulate General, 200 S. Biscayne Blvd., Suite 1600, Miami, FL 33131 (☎ **305/372-2352**); **Minneapolis,** Canadian Consulate General, 701 Fourth Ave., Suite 900, Minneapolis, MN 55415-1899 (☎ **612/333-4641**); **New York,** Canadian Consulate General, Exxon Building, 16th floor, 1251 Avenue of the Americas, New York, NY 10020-1175 (☎ **212/596-1600**); **Seattle,** Canadian Consulate General, 412 Plaza 600, Sixth and Stewart, Seattle, WA 98101-1286 (☎ **206/443-1777**); and **Washington, D.C.,** Canadian Embassy, Tourism Section, 501 Pennsylvania Ave. NW, Washington, DC 20001 (☎ **202/682-1740**).

The best source for information specific to Toronto is Tourism Toronto, **Metropolitan Toronto Convention & Visitors Association,** Queen's Quay Terminal at Harbourfront, 207 Queen's Quay West, Toronto (☎ **800/363-1990** from the continental U.S., or 416/203-2500). Call them before you leave and request the kind of information you want.

For information about Ontario, contact **Ontario Travel,** Queen's Park, Toronto (☎ **800/ONTARIO** or 416/314-0944), or go to their travel center in the Eaton Centre.

ENTRY REQUIREMENTS

DOCUMENTS   U.S. citizens and legal residents do not need passports or visas, but must show proof of citizenship (birth or voter's certificate, naturalization certificates or green card). Every person under 19 years of age is required to produce a letter from a parent or guardian granting him or her permission to travel to Canada. The letter must state the traveler's name and the duration of the trip. It is therefore essential that teenagers also carry proof of citizenship; otherwise their letter is useless at the border.

Citizens of Australia, New Zealand, the United Kingdom, and Ireland must have valid passports. Citizens of many other countries will need visas, which must be applied for in advance at the local Canadian embassy or consulate. For detailed information, call your local Canadian consulate or embassy.

CUSTOMS   Customs regulations are generous in most respects, but they get pretty complicated when it comes to firearms, plants, meats, and pets. Fishing tackle poses no problem (provided the lures are not made of restricted materials—specific feathers, for example), but the bearer must possess a nonresident license for the province or territory where he or she plans to use it. You can bring in free of duty up to 50 cigars, 200 cigarettes, and 2 pounds of tobacco, providing you're at least 18 years of age. You are also allowed 40 ounces (1.14l) of liquor or wine as long as you're over the minimum drinking age of the province you're visiting (19 in Ontario).

For more detailed information about customs regulations, write to Revenue Canada, 875 Heron Rd., Ottawa, ON, K1A 0L8.

2 Money

Canadians use dollars and cents, but with a distinct advantage for U.S. visitors—the Canadian dollar is worth 73¢ in U.S. money (give or take a couple of points' daily variation). So, in effect, your American money gets you 27% more the moment you exchange it into local currency. That makes quite a difference in your budget, and since the prices of many goods are roughly on a par with those in the United States, the difference is real, not imaginary. (Before you get too excited, though, keep in mind that sales taxes are astronomical.) You can bring in or take out any amount of money, but if you are importing or exporting sums of $5,000 or more, you must file a report of the transaction with U.S. Customs. Most tourist establishments in Canada will take U.S. cash, but for the best rate, exchange your funds into Canadian currency.

If you do spend American money at Canadian establishments, you should understand how the conversion is calculated. Often there will be a sign at the cash register that reads "U.S. Currency 20%." This 20% is the "premium," which means that for every U.S. greenback you hand over, the cashier will consider it $1.20 in Canadian dollars. For example, for an $8 tab you need pay only $6.40 in U.S. bills.

What Things Cost in Toronto	U.S. $
Taxi from the airport to downtown	29.60
Subway/bus from the airport to downtown	5.75
Local telephone call	.18
Double at the Four Seasons (expensive)	207.00
Double at Bond Place (moderate)	60.00
Double at Victoria University (budget)	45.90
Two-course prix-fixe lunch for one at La Bodega (moderate)*	12.40
Two-course lunch for one at Kensington (budget)*	7.70
Three-course dinner for one at Scaramouche (expensive)*	47.65
Three-course dinner for one at Grano (moderate)*	30.80
Three-course dinner for one at Jerusalem (budget)*	16.70
Pint of beer	3.50
Coca-Cola	.90
Cup of coffee	.75
Roll of ASA 100 Kodacolor film, 36 exposures	4.85
Admission to the Royal Ontario Museum	5.20
Movie ticket	6.30
Theater ticket at the Royal Alex	18.50–70.35

*Includes tax and tip but not wine.

Note: Prices are listed here in U.S. dollars; all other prices in the book are quoted in Canadian dollars.

It used to be that before leaving home, you were well-advised to purchase traveler's checks and arrange to carry some ready cash (usually about $200), but now that **ATMs** are virtually everywhere in the world, and often deliver a better exchange rate, I now recommend obtaining money from them. You can find them at most banks. For the location of the nearest ATM that services the **Cirrus** network, dial **800/424-7787** (a global access number). If you're reading this before you've left home, you can obtain the locations of ATMs in the **Plus** network by calling **800/843-7587** (the number can only be dialed from within the U.S.). Alternately, if you have access to the Web, you can scroll over to **http://www.visa.com** or **http://www.mastercard.com** for the location of the nearest ATM that's linked to the Plus network. Most ATMs will make cash advances against MasterCard and Visa, but make sure you have your personal identification number with you.

For those who prefer the extra security of **traveler's checks,** U.S. dollar traveler's checks and credit cards are accepted in almost all hotels, restaurants, shops, and attractions; and they can be exchanged for cash at banks. You're best off cashing them at banks. As in the United States, most small businesses will not cash traveler's checks in a denomination greater than $50, or perhaps even $20.

American Express (☎ 800/221-7282 in the U.S. and Canada) is the most widely recognized traveler's check; depending on where you purchase them, expect to pay between 1% and 4% commission. Checks are free to members of the American Automobile Association (AAA).

The Canadian Dollar & the U.S. Dollar

Unless stated otherwise, the prices cited in this guide are given in Canadian dollars, which is good news for U.S. travelers because the Canadian dollar is worth 27% less than the American dollar, but buys nearly as much. As we go to press, $1 Canadian is 73% U.S., which means that your $100-a-night hotel room will cost only U.S. $73, and your $6 breakfast costs only U.S. $4.38.

Here's a quick table of equivalents:

Canada $	U.S. $
1	0.73
5	3.65
10	7.30
20	14.60
50	36.50
80	58.40
100	73.00

Citicorp (☎ **800/645-6556** in the U.S., or **813/623-1709** collect in Canada) issues checks in U.S. dollars or British pounds.

MasterCard International (☎ **800/223-9920** in the U.S.) issues checks in about a dozen currencies.

Thomas Cook (☎ **800/223-7373** in the U.S.) issues checks in U.S. or Canadian dollars.

3 When to Go

THE CLIMATE

As a general rule, you can say that spring runs from late March to mid-May (though occasionally there'll be snow in mid-April); summer, from mid-May to mid-September; fall, from mid-September to mid-November; and winter, from mid-November to late March. The highest recorded temperature was 105°F; the lowest, -27°F. The average date of first frost is October 29; the average date of last frost is April 20. The blasts from Lake Ontario can sometimes be fierce, even in June. Bring a windbreaker or something similar.

Toronto's Average Temperatures (°F)

	Jan	Feb	Mar	Apr	May	June	July	Aug	Sept	Oct	Nov	Dec
High	30	31	39	53	64	75	80	79	71	59	46	34
Low	18	19	27	38	48	57	62	61	54	45	35	23

HOLIDAYS

Toronto celebrates the following holidays: New Year's Day (January 1), Good Friday and/or Easter Monday (variable; in March or April), Victoria Day (last Monday in May), Canada Day (July 1), Civic Holiday (first Monday in August), Labour Day (first Monday in September), Thanksgiving (second Monday in October), Remembrance Day (November 11), Christmas Day (December 25), and Boxing Day (December 26).

On Good Friday and Easter Monday, both schools and government offices are closed; most corporations are closed on one or the other, and some are closed on both. Only banks and government offices close on Remembrance Day (November 11).

TORONTO CALENDAR OF EVENTS

May
- **Milk International Children's Festival,** Harbourfront. A 9-day celebration of the arts for kids—from theater and music to dance, comedy, and storytelling. For information, call **416/973-3000.** Usually starts on Mother's Day.
- **Toronto International Pow Wow,** SkyDome. A weekend celebration attended by more than 1,500 Native American dancers, drummers, and singers. There's also an arts-and-crafts marketplace and traditional foods to savor. Call **519/751-0040.** Usually third weekend.

June
- ✪ **Metro International Caravan,** citywide. This popular 9-day event (North America's largest international festival) features craft demonstrations, opportunities to sample authentic dishes, and traditional dance performances by 100 different cultural groups with a tie to Toronto. Usually third and fourth weekends.
- **Du Maurier Ltd. Downtown Jazz Festival,** citywide. Begun in 1987, this 10-day festival showcases more than 1,600 artists playing in every jazz style conceivable—blues, gospel, Latin, African, traditional, and more—at more than 50 venues throughout town. For **information,** call **416/363-8717.** For **tickets,** call **416/973-3000.** Usually the last 11 days in June.
- **Benson & Hedges, Inc. International Fireworks Festival,** Ontario Place. Boats fill the harbor and people flock to the waterfront to view this spectacular display of gunpowder art. Six shows are given on several Saturdays and Wednesdays. For information, call **416/442-3667.** Ongoing all month.
- **Fringe of Toronto Festival,** citywide. A 10-day celebration of new and challenging theater performed by as many as 80 different artists/groups. Each performance lasts no more than an hour. Shows are given on several different stages and ticket prices are low (the most expensive ticket at the time of this writing is $8). Every evening at the Fringe Club (292 Brunswick Ave.), a free cabaret that combines comedy, clowning, music, dance, and literary presentations is held. For information, call **416/534-5919.** Usually the last week in June and the first week in July.

July
- **Molson Indy,** the Exhibition Place Street circuit. A major IndyCar race. Call **416/872-4639.** Usually third weekend in July.
- ✪ **Caribana,** citywide. Toronto's version of Carnival, complete with traditional foods from the Caribbean and Latin America, ferry cruises, island picnics, concerts, and arts-and-crafts exhibits. Call **416/465-4884** for more information. Last week in July and first week in August.

August
- ✪ **Canadian National Exhibition,** Exhibition Place. One of the world's largest exhibitions, this 18-day extravaganza features midway rides, display buildings, free shows, and grandstand performers. The Canadian International Air Show (first staged in 1878) is an added bonus. Call **416/393-6000** for information. Mid-August to Labor Day.

- **Du Maurier Ltd. Open,** National Tennis Centre at York University. Canada's international tennis championship. An important stop on the pro-tennis tour that attracts players such as Becker, Agassi, and Sanchez Vicario, the Du Maurier Ltd. Open is run in conjunction with a tournament in Montréal during the middle of August. In 1997, women play in Toronto; men play in Montréal. In 1998, they alternate, and so on in subsequent years. Call **416/665-9777.** Usually third to fourth weekend in July.

September
- **Toronto International Film Festival,** citywide. The second-largest film festival in the world, showing more than 250 films in 10 days. For information, call **416/967-7371.** Early September.
- **Bell Canadian Open,** the Glen Abbey Golf Club in Oakville. Canada's national golf tournament (☎ **905/844-1800**). Usually held over Labor Day weekend.

October
- **Oktoberfest,** in Kitchener-Waterloo, about 1 hour (60 miles) from Toronto. Features cultural events plus a pageant and parade. For information, call **519/570-4267.** Oct 10–18 (1997).
- **International Festival of Authors,** at the Harbourfront. A prestigious 11-day literary festival that draws more than 100 participants from 25 countries to readings and on-stage interviews. Among the literary luminaries who have appeared are Margaret Drabble, Thomas Kenneally, Joyce Carol Oates, A. S. Byatt, and Margaret Atwood. For information, call Harbourfront at **416/973-4000.** Usually starts the third weekend of October.

November
- ✪ **Royal Agricultural Winter Fair and Royal Horse Show,** Exhibition Place. At this 12-day show, the largest indoor agricultural and equestrian competition in the world, vegetables and fruits are on display, along with crafts, farm machinery, livestock, and more. The horse show is traditionally attended by a member of the British royal family. Call **416/393-6400** for information. Usually second and third weekends of November.

4   Travel Insurance

Before you decide to purchase travel insurance, check your existing policies to see if they'll cover you while you're traveling. Check with your health-insurance company to make sure that your coverage extends to Canada. Some credit cards offer automatic flight insurance when you purchase an airline ticket with that credit card. These policies insure against death or dismemberment in the event of a plane crash. Also, check your credit cards to see if any of them pick up the collision damage waiver (CDW) if you plan to rent a car. The CDW can run as much as $14 a day and add as much as 50% to the cost of renting a car. Check your automobile insurance policy, too; it might cover the CDW as well. If you own a home or have renter's insurance, see if that policy covers off-premises theft and loss wherever it occurs. Find out what procedures you need to follow to make a claim. If you're traveling on a tour or package deal and have prepaid a large chunk of your travel expenses, you might want to ask a travel agent about trip-cancellation insurance.

If, after checking all your existing insurance policies, you decide that you need additional insurance, a good travel agent can give you information on a variety of different options. Or you can contact **Wallach & Company,** 107 W. Federal

St., P.O. Box 480, Middleburg, VA 22117-0480 (☎ **800/237-6615** or 540/
687-3166). They provide a comprehensive travel policy that covers all contingencies—cancellation, health, emergency assistance, and loss.

5 Tips for Travelers with Special Needs

FOR TRAVELERS WITH DISABILITIES

Toronto is a very accessible city. Curb cuts are well made and common throughout
the downtown area; special parking privileges are extended to people with disabilities who have disabled plates or a special pass that allows parking in "No Parking"
zones. The subway and trolleys are, unfortunately, not accessible, but the city operates a special service for those with disabilities, called **Wheel-Trans.** Visitors can
register for this service. For information, call **416/393-4111.**

For more information, contact **Disabled Information on Community Services,**
Community Information Centre of Metropolitan Toronto, 425 Adelaide St. West,
at Spadina, Toronto, ON, M5V 3C1 (☎ **416/392-0505,** weekdays 7am–10pm;
weekends 10am–10pm).

FOR SENIORS

Bring some form of photo ID, as many city attractions grant special senior discounts.
Some hotels, too, will offer special discounted rates.

If you haven't already done so, think about joining the **American Association
of Retired Persons (AARP),** 601 E St. NW, Washington, DC 20049 (☎ **202/
434-2277**).

Also look into the fun courses that are offered at incredibly low prices by
Elderhostel, 75 Federal St., Boston, MA 02110 (☎ **617/426-7788**).

FOR STUDENTS

The key to securing discounts and other special favors is the **International Student
Identity Card (ISIC),** available to any bona fide full-time high school or university
student. Contact the **Council on International Educational Exchange (CIEE),**
205 E. 42nd St., New York, NY 10017 (☎ **212/822-2700**). The card is available
from all Council Travel offices in the United States. To find the office nearest you,
call **800/GETANID** (800/438-2643).

If you'd like to meet other students, you've come to the right place: Toronto has
several major colleges in addition to the large and sprawling **University of Toronto.**
The largest university in Canada, with 52,500 students (41,000 full-time), the University of Toronto offers many year-round activities and events that any visitor can
attend—lectures, seminars, concerts, and more. U of T Day is usually celebrated in
the middle of October, when the university holds an open house to the community
and also celebrates with a children's fair and the annual homecoming football game
and parade. Call **416/978-8342** for more information.

FOR GAY & LESBIAN TRAVELERS

Toronto has a large gay population estimated at about 250,000. This community is
centered on the intersection of Church and Wellesley streets. Any gay man or lesbian
will find the following resources useful. First, pick up a copy of the biweekly *Xtra!,*
available free at many bookstores, including the **Gay Liberation Bookstore/
Glad Day Bookshop,** 598A Yonge St., 2nd floor (☎ **416/961-4161**), open Monday to Friday from 10am to 9pm, Saturday until 7pm, and Sunday from noon
until 6pm. If you want to secure a copy of *Xtra!* ahead of time, contact *Xtra!* at Box
7289, Station A, Toronto, ON, M5W 1X9 (☎ **416/925-6665**).

For information on upcoming events, call the **Gay Phone Line** (☎ 416/ 964-6600) or **Tel-Xtra** (☎ 416/925-9872).

FOR WOMEN

For books and information on the feminist scene, stop by the **Toronto Women's Bookstore,** 73 Harbord St., at Spadina (☎ 416/922-8744). It's open Monday through Thursday and Saturday from 10:30am to 6pm, Friday until 7pm, and Sunday from noon to 5pm.

6 Getting There

BY PLANE

Air Canada (☎ 800/776-3000) operates direct flights to Toronto from most major American cities, including Atlanta, Baltimore/Washington, Boston, Chicago, Cleveland, Columbus, Denver, Hartford, Houston, Los Angeles, Miami, Minneapolis, New York, Newark, Orlando, Philadelphia, St. Louis, San Francisco, and Tampa. It also flies from major cities around the world and operates indirectly from other U.S. cities.

The other Canadian airline, **Canadian Airlines International** (☎ 800/ 426-7000), operates direct flights into Toronto from Boston, Chicago, Dallas, Miami, Los Angeles, New York City, Orlando, and Tampa.

Among U.S. airlines, **USAir** (☎ 800/842-5374) operates directly into Toronto from a number of U.S. cities, notably Baltimore, Boston, Cleveland, Indianapolis, Philadelphia, Pittsburgh, and Washington, D.C. **American** (☎ 800/433-7300) has daily direct flights from Chicago, Dallas, Miami, and New York. **United** (☎ 800/ 241-6522) has direct flights from Chicago and San Francisco. **Northwest** (☎ 800/ 225-2525) flies directly from Detroit only. **Delta** (☎ 800/221-1212) flies direct from Atlanta, Cincinnati, and Syracuse.

Wherever you're traveling from, always shop the different airlines and ask for the lowest fare, if price is a factor. You may be able to fly for less than the standard APEX fare by contacting a ticket broker or consolidator. These companies, which buy tickets in bulk and then sell them at a discount, advertise in the Sunday travel sections of major city newspapers. You may not be able to get the lowest price they advertise, but you're likely to pay less than the price quoted by the major airlines. Bear in mind that tickets purchased through a consolidator are often nonrefundable tickets. If you change your itinerary after purchase, chances are you'll pay a stiff penalty.

Most flights arrive at **Pearson International Airport,** located in the northwest corner of Metro Toronto approximately 30 minutes (17 miles) from downtown, although a few (mostly commuter flights) land at the **Toronto Island Airport,** a short ferry ride from downtown.

Three terminals, serviced by more than 50 airlines, cater to the traveler at Pearson. The most spectacular is the new **Trilium Terminal 3** (☎ 905/612-5100) used by American, Canadian Airlines, British Airways, KLM, Lufthansa, and United, among others. This is a supermodern facility with moving walkways, a huge food court, and hundreds of stores.

The most convenient way to get into the city from the airport is **by taxi,** which will cost about $40 to $45 to downtown. In addition, most first-class hotels run their own hotel limousine services, so check when you make your reservation.

Also convenient is Pacific Western's **Airport Express bus** (☎ 905/564-6333), which travels between the airport and downtown hotels—Harbour Castle Westin, the Royal York, L'Hôtel, the Sheraton Centre, the Holiday Inn, and the Chelsea

Inn—every 20 minutes from early morning until late at night. Fare is $11.10 for adults, free for two children under 11 accompanied by an adult; additional children pay $11.10. It takes from 35 minutes to 1¼ hours depending on the traffic.

The cheapest way to go is **by bus and subway,** which will take about an hour. Buses travel between the airport and the Islington subway stop about every 30 minutes for a fare of $6.20. Buses also travel between the airport and the Yorkdale and York Mills subway stations about every 40 minutes for a fare of $6.70 to Yorkdale, $7.75 to York Mills. On both routes two children under 11 travel free if accompanied by an adult. For information, call **905/564-6333** from 7am to 11pm.

BY TRAIN

Amtrak's *Maple Leaf* links New York City and Toronto via Albany, Buffalo, and Niagara Falls, departing daily from Penn Station. The journey takes 11¾ hours. From Chicago, the *International* carries passengers to Toronto via Port Huron, Michigan (a 12½-hr. trip). With either routing, you'll arrive in Toronto at Union Station on Front Street, one block west of Yonge Street, opposite the Royal York Hotel. The station has direct access to the subway, so you can easily reach any Toronto destination from here.

To secure the lowest round-trip fares, book as far in advance as possible and try to travel midweek. Seat availability determines price levels; the earlier you book the more likely you are to secure a lower fare. Here though are a few sample one-way fares for use as guidelines only: New York to Toronto, $65 one way; from Chicago, $98. Meals are not included in these prices. Depending on when you book, remember that round-trip fares could be double the fares quoted here if you leave it to the last minute, or as little as $20 extra. Always ask about the availability of discounted fares, companion fares, and other special tickets. Call **Amtrak** at **800/USA-RAIL** or 800/872-7245.

From Buffalo's Exchange Street Station, you can also make the trip to Toronto's Union Station on the **Toronto/Hamilton/Buffalo Railway (THB)**. Connecting services are also available from other major cities along the border.

BY BUS

Greyhound/Trailways (☎ **800/231-2222**) is the only bus company that crosses the border into Canada from the United States. You can travel from almost anywhere in the United States, changing buses along the way until you reach Toronto. You'll arrive at the Metro Coach Terminal downtown at 610 Bay St., near the corner of Dundas Street.

The bus may be faster and cheaper than the train, and its routes may be more flexible if you want to stop along the way, but it's also more cramped, toilet facilities are meager, and meals are taken at somewhat depressing rest stops along the way.

Depending on where you are coming from, you should check into Greyhound/Trailways' special unlimited-travel passes as well as into any discount fares that might be offered. It's hard to provide sample fares because bus companies, like the airlines, are adopting yield management strategies, causing prices to change from one day to the next depending on demand.

BY CAR

Hopping across the border by car is no problem as the U.S. highway system leads directly into Canada at 13 points. If you're driving from Michigan, you'll either enter at Detroit-Windsor (via I-75 and the Ambassador Bridge) or Port Huron–Sarnia (via I-94 and the Bluewater Bridge). If you're coming from New York, you have more options. Via I-190, you can enter at one of three places: Buffalo–Fort Erie; Niagara Falls, N.Y. –Niagara Falls, Ont.; or Niagara Falls, N.Y. –Lewiston. Via I-81, you'll cross the Canadian border at Hill Island; and via Rte. 37, you'll enter at either Ogdensburg-Johnstown or Rooseveltown-Cornwall.

From the United States you are most likely to enter Toronto via either Hwy. 401 or Hwy. 2 and the Queen Elizabeth Way if you come from the west. If you come from the east via Montréal, you'll also use Hwys. 401 and 2. Here are a few approximate driving distances in miles to Toronto: from Atlanta, 977; from Boston, 566; from Buffalo, 96; from Chicago, 534; from Cincinnati, 501; from Dallas, 1,452; from Detroit, 236; from Minneapolis, 972; and from New York, 495.

Obviously, be sure you are carrying your driver's license and car registration if you plan to drive your own vehicle into Canada. It isn't a bad idea to carry proof of your automobile liability insurance, either.

If you are a member of the American Automobile Association (AAA) and your car breaks down once you've crossed the border, the **Canadian Automobile Association (CAA),** 60 Commerce Valley Dr., E., Thornhill (☎ **905/771-3111**), provides emergency road service.

3

Getting to Know Toronto

This chapter helps you get your bearings in Toronto by describing the city's layout, offering options for getting around, and listing useful resources to assist you in handling any contingency that might crop up during your trip—from hiring a baby-sitter to removing a stain from your favorite shirt.

1 Orientation

VISITOR INFORMATION

For tourist information about Toronto, go to (or write) **Tourism Toronto,** 207 Queens Quay West, Suite 590, in the Queens Quay Terminal at Harbourfront (P.O. Box 126), Toronto, ON, M5J 1A7 (☎ **800/363-1990** or 416/203-2500), open Monday through Friday from 9am to 5pm. Take the LRT from Union Station to the York Street stop.

More conveniently located is the drop-in **Visitor Information Centre** in the Eaton Centre, on Yonge Street at Dundas Street. It's located on "Level 1 Below" and is open year-round Monday through Friday, 10am to 9pm, Saturday from 9am to 6pm, and Sunday from noon to 5pm.

If you happen to be in the neighborhood, the **Community Information Centre,** 425 Adelaide St. West (☎ **416/392-0505**), specializes in social, government, and health-service information, but will try to answer any question, and if they can't, they will direct you to someone who can.

If you want to pick up a few brochures and a map before you leave **Pearson International Airport,** stop by the **Transport Canada Information Centre** in your terminal (there's one in each), where a staff fluent in 10 languages can also answer questions about tourist attractions, ground transportation, and more (☎ **905/ 676-3506**).

CITY LAYOUT

Toronto is laid out in a grid system. **Yonge** (pronounced Young) **Street** is the main north-south street, stretching from Lake Ontario in the south well beyond Hwy. 401 in the north; the main east-west artery is **Bloor Street,** which cuts right through the heart of downtown. Yonge Street divides western cross streets from eastern cross streets.

"Downtown" usually refers to the area stretching south from Eglinton Avenue to the lake between Spadina Avenue in the west and Jarvis Street in the east. Because this is such a large area, I have divided it into **downtown** (from the lake north to College/Carlton Street), **midtown** (College/Carlton Street north to Davenport Road), and **uptown** (north from Davenport Road). In the first area you'll find all the lakeshore attractions—Harbourfront, Ontario Place, Fort York, Exhibition Place, the Toronto Islands, plus the CN Tower, City Hall, SkyDome, Chinatown, the Art Gallery, and the Eaton Centre. Midtown includes the Royal Ontario Museum, the University of Toronto, Markham Village, and chic Yorkville, a prime area for browsing and dining alfresco. Uptown is a fast-growing residential and entertainment area for the young, hip, and well heeled.

Metropolitan Toronto is spread over 634 square kilometers (245 sq. miles) and includes East York and the cities of (from west to east) Etobicoke, York, North York, and Scarborough. Some of its primary attractions exist outside the core, such as the Ontario Science Centre, the Metropolitan Zoo, Canada's Wonderland, and the McMichael collection. Be prepared to journey somewhat.

UNDERGROUND TORONTO   It is not enough to know the streets of Toronto; you also need to know the warren of subterranean walkways that enable you to go from Union Station in the south to Atrium on Bay at Dundas.

Currently, you can walk from the Queen Street subway station west to the Sheraton Centre, then south through the Richmond-Adelaide Centre, First Canadian Place, and Toronto Dominion Centre all the way (through the dramatic Royal Bank Plaza) to Union Station. En route, branches lead off to the stock exchange, Sun Life Centre, and Metro Hall. Additional walkways also link Simcoe Plaza to 200 Wellington West and to the CBC Broadcast Centre.

Other walkways exist around Bloor Street and Yonge Street and elsewhere in the city (ask for a map at the tourist information office). So if the weather's bad, you can eat, sleep, dance, shop, and go to the theater without even donning a coat.

NEIGHBORHOODS IN BRIEF

Metropolitan Toronto consists of five cities and one borough under one administrative umbrella. What follows, with a few exceptions, are in the downtown city center:

The Toronto Islands   These three islands in Lake Ontario—Ward's, Algonquin, and Centre—are home to a handful of residents and also a welcome summer haven to Torontonians where they can go to in-line skate, bicycle, boat, and picnic. Centre Island is the most visited. Catch the ferry at the foot of Bay Street by the Westin Hotel.

Harbourfront/Lakefront   The landfill on which the railroad yards and dock facilities were built. Now a glorious playground opening onto the lake.

Financial District   Toronto's major banks and insurance companies have their headquarters here, from Front Street north to Queen Street, between Yonge and York streets. It's where Toronto's first skyscrapers were built.

Old Town/St. Lawrence Market   During the 19th century, this area, east of Yonge Street between the Esplanade and Adelaide Street, was the focal point of the community. Today the market's still going strong and a stroll around the surrounding area will recapture an earlier era.

New Town/King Street West Theater District   An area of dense cultural development, this area stretches from Front Street north to Queen Street, and from Bay

Underground Toronto

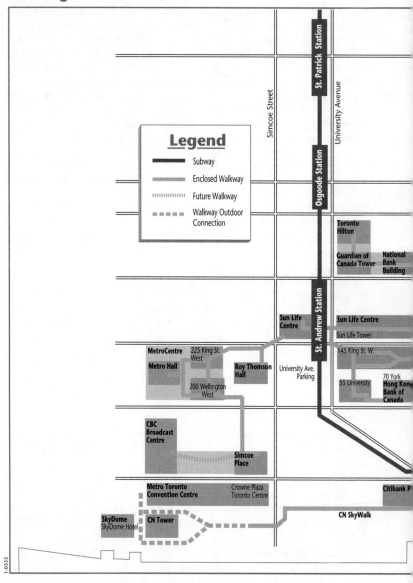

Street west to Bathurst Street. It contains the Royal Alex, Princess of Wales Theatre, Roy Thomson Hall, the CBC building, the Convention Centre, and the CN Tower.

Chinatown Dundas Street West from University Avenue to Spadina Avenue, and north to College Street are the boundaries of Chinatown. As the Chinese community has grown, it has extended along Dundas Street and north along Spadina Avenue. Here, you'll see a fascinating mixture of the old and the new, as tiny hole-in-the-wall restaurants that have been in business for years share the sidewalks with glitzy shopping centers built with new Hong Kong money.

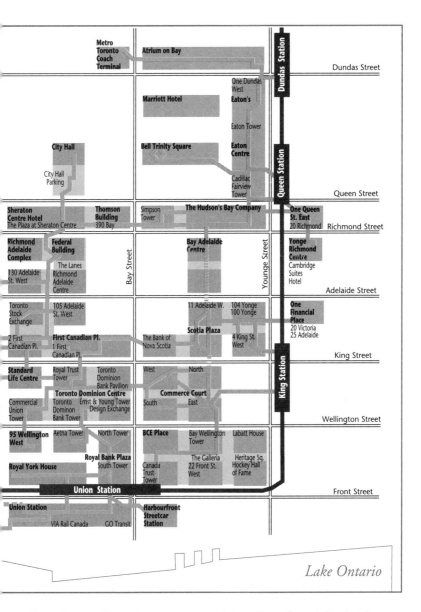

Yonge Street   Toronto's main commercial drag, Yonge Street is lined with stores and restaurants of all sorts. It's seedy in many places, but especially around College and Dundas streets, where there's a section of strip and porno joints.

Queen Street West   This stretch of Queen Street from University Avenue to Bathurst Street is youthful and hot. It offers an eclectic mix—antiques stores, second-hand bookshops, reasonably priced dining, and more. Despite the relatively new presence of such mega-retailers as the Gap, independently owned boutiques are still hanging on, lending a decidedly local funk to the scene.

Queen's Park and the University   Home to the Ontario Legislature and many of the colleges and buildings that make up the University of Toronto, this neighborhood extends from College Street to Bloor Street between Spadina Avenue and Queen's Park Crescent.

Cabbagetown   Once described by writer Hugh Garner as the largest Anglo-Saxon slum in North America, this area stretching east of Parliament Street to the Don Valley between Gerrard Street and Bloor Street has been gentrified and is now a sought-after residential district. It's so named because the front lawns of the homes occupied by the Irish immigrants who settled here in the late 1800s were covered with row upon row of cabbages.

Yorkville   Originally a village outside the city, this area north and west of Bloor Street and Yonge Street became Toronto's Haight-Ashbury in the 1960s. Now, it's a fashionable enclave of designer boutiques, galleries, cafes, and restaurants.

The Annex   An architecturally unique residential community, the Annex stretches from Bedford Road to Bathurst Street, and from Bloor Street to Bernard Street. Its residents led the fight against the Spadina Expressway, which would have put an expressway through downtown Toronto.

Rosedale   Curving tree-lined streets and elegant homes are the hallmarks of this leafy suburb, northeast of Yonge Street and Bloor Street to Castle Frank and the Moore Park Ravine. Named after Sheriff Jarvis's residence, its name alone is synonymous with Toronto's wealthy elite.

Forest Hill   After Rosedale, the second prime residential area in Toronto. Forest Hill is home to Upper Canada College and Bishop Strachan School for girls, and stretches west of Avenue Road between St. Clair Avenue and Eglinton Avenue.

Little Italy   A thriving, lively neighborhood filled with authentic Italian coffee bars, trattorias, and other stores serving the Italian community along College Street between Euclid and Shaw. It positively hums at night.

The Beaches   Communal, youthful, and cozy. These adjectives best describe the Beaches, just 15 minutes from downtown at the end of the Queen Street East streetcar line. A summer resort in the mid-1800s, its boardwalk and beach continue to make it a relaxing, casual neighborhood.

The East End—the Danforth   This continuation of Bloor Street across the Don Valley Viaduct is largely a Greek neighborhood, lined with old-style Greek tavernas and new, happening designer bars and restaurants that are crowded from early evening until early morning. The most concentrated Greek area starts in the 400 block.

North York   The redevelopment of this community about 8 miles north of Toronto's Queen Street has made it one of the hottest real-estate markets in the country. There's very little here for the visitor, other than the Ford Centre for the Performing Arts.

2 Getting Around

BY PUBLIC TRANSPORTATION

Public transit is operated by the **Toronto Transit Commission (TTC)** (☎ 416/ 393-4636 daily from 7am to 10pm for information), which provides an overall interconnecting subway, bus, and streetcar system.

   Fares (including transfers to buses or streetcars) are $2 (or 10 tickets for $15) for adults, $1 (10 tickets for $7.50) for students 19 and under and seniors, and 50¢

(eight tickets for $3.75) for children under 12. You can purchase a special $6 day pass good for unlimited travel Monday to Friday after 9:30am and all day Saturday from any subway collector. On Sundays or holidays, a similar $6 pass may be used by up to six people (a maximum of two adults).

For surface transportation, you need a ticket, a token, or exact change. Tickets and tokens may be obtained at subway entrances or authorized stores that display the sign TTC TICKETS MAY BE PURCHASED HERE. Always obtain a transfer, just in case you need it. They are obtainable free of charge in the subways from a push-button machine just inside the entrance or directly from drivers on streetcars and buses.

THE SUBWAY   It's a joy to ride—fast, quiet, and clean. It's a very simple system to use, too, consisting of two lines—Bloor-Danforth and Yonge-University-Spadina—designed basically in the form of a cross: The Bloor Street east-west line runs from Kipling Avenue in the west to Kennedy Road in the east, where it connects with Scarborough Rapid Transit traveling to Scarborough Centre and McCowan Road. The Yonge Street north-south line runs from Finch Avenue in the north to Union Station (Front Street) in the south. From here, it loops north along University Avenue and connects with the Bloor line at the St. George station. A Spadina extension runs north from St. George to Wilson Avenue.

A light rapid transit system connects downtown to Harbourfront, running from Union Station along Queen's Quay to Spadina with stops at Queen's Quay ferry docks, York Street, Simcoe Street, and Rees Street. No transfer is needed from subway to LRT and vice versa.

The subway operates Monday through Friday from around 6am to around 1:30am and Sunday from 9am to 1:30am. From 1am to 5:30am a Blue Night Network operates on basic surface routes running about every 30 minutes. For route information, pick up a Ride Guide at subway entrances or call **416/393-4636.** Multilingual information is available. You can also use the automated information service at **416/393-8663.**

Smart commuters park their cars at subway terminal stations at Kipling, Islington, Finch, Wilson, Warden, Kennedy, York Mills, Victoria Park, and Keele. Certain conditions apply. Call **416/393-8663** for details. You'll have to get there very early, though.

BUSES & STREETCARS   Where the subway leaves off, buses and streetcars take over to carry you east-west or north-south along the city's arteries. When you pay your fare (on bus, streetcar, or subway), always pick up a transfer, so that if you want to transfer to another mode of transportation, you won't have to pay another fare. For complete TTC information, call 416/393-4636.

BY TAXI

As usual, this is an expensive mode of transportation: It's $2.50 the minute you step in, and $1 for every additional kilometer. There's also a 10¢ charge for each bag. Cab fares can quickly mount up, especially during rush hours. Nevertheless, if you need a cab you can hail one on the street (they also line up in front of the big hotels), or call one of the major companies: **Diamond** (☎ **416/366-6868**), **Yellow** (☎ **416/504-4141**), or **Metro** (☎ **416/504-8294**). If you experience any problems with cab service, call the **Metro Licensing Commission** at **416/392-3000.**

BY CAR

Toronto may be spread out, but that doesn't necessarily mean that a car is the best way to get around. Driving in the city can be very frustrating because there's lots of

The TTC Subway System

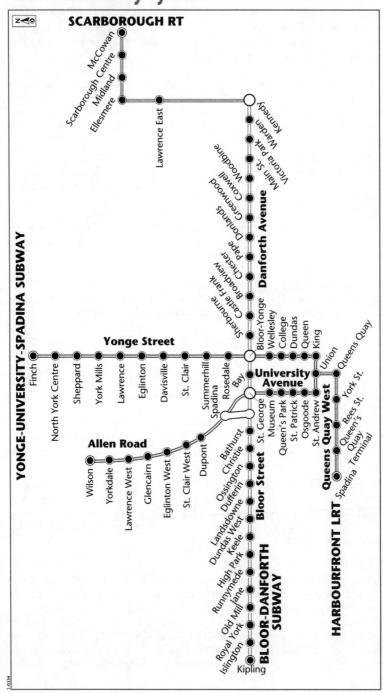

SCARBOROUGH RT

McCowan
Scarborough Centre
Midland
Ellesmere
Lawrence East
Kennedy
Warden
Main St.
Victoria Park
Woodbine
Coxwell
Greenwood
Donlands
Pape
Chester
Broadview
Castle Frank
Sherbourne

Danforth Avenue

YONGE-UNIVERSITY-SPADINA SUBWAY

Yonge Street

Finch
North York Centre
Sheppard
York Mills
Lawrence
Eglinton
Davisville
St. Clair
Summerhill
Rosedale
Bay
Spadina

Bloor-Yonge
Wellesley
College
Dundas
Queen
King
Union
Queens Quay

University Avenue

St. George
Museum
Queen's Park
St. Patrick
Osgoode
St. Andrew

Allen Road

Wilson
Yorkdale
Lawrence West
Glencairn
Eglinton West
St. Clair West
Dupont
Bathurst
Christie
Ossington
Dufferin
Landsdowne
Dundas West
Keele
High Park
Runnymede
Jane
Old Mill
Royal York
Islington
Kipling

Bloor Street

BLOOR-DANFORTH SUBWAY

Queens Quay West

York St.
Rees St.
Queen's Quay
Spadina Terminal

HARBOURFRONT LRT

traffic and parking is expensive. This is particularly true downtown, where traffic moves slowly, and parking lots are scarce.

RENTAL CARS   Prices on car rentals change so frequently and vary so widely that your best bet is to shop around before you make your reservations. At the time of this writing, **Budget,** 171 Bay St. (☎ **416/364-7104**), charges $37 (including 200km/124 miles free) per day plus 12¢ per kilometer, or $190 per week (including 1,400km/870 miles free), for a compact car. **Tilden,** 930 Yonge St. (☎ **416/925-4551**), charges $40 per day (including 200km/124 miles free) plus 15¢ per kilometer, or $234 per week, for a small car. If saving money is important to you, always ask about special weekend rates and other discounts.

Note: If you're under 25, check with the company—many will rent on a cash-only basis, some only if you have a credit card, and others will not rent to you at all.

Parking   Parking lots downtown run about $2 per half hour, with a $15 to $17 maximum. After 6pm and on Sunday, rates go down to around $6. Generally the city-owned lots, marked with a big green "P," are slightly cheaper. Observe the parking restrictions—otherwise the city will tow your car away.

Driving Rules   A right turn at a red light is permitted after coming to a full stop, unless posted otherwise. The driver and front-seat passenger must wear seat belts (if you're caught not wearing one, you'll pay a substantial fine). The speed limit within the city is 30 miles per hour (50kmph). You must stop at pedestrian crosswalks. If you are following a streetcar and it stops, you must stop well back from the rear doors so that passengers can exit easily and safely. (Where there are concrete safety islands in the middle of the street for streetcar stops, this rule does not apply, but exercise care nonetheless.) Radar detectors are illegal.

BY FERRY

Metro Parks operates ferries that travel to the Toronto Islands. Call **416/392-8193** for schedules and information.

BY BICYCLE

You can secure a pamphlet outlining biking routes from the Toronto Convention and Visitor's Office. The Toronto Islands, the Beaches, Harbourfront/Lakefront/Sunnyside, and High Park are all great biking areas.

You can **rent bicycles** at Harbourfront right across from Queen's Quay; on Centre Island from **Toronto Island Bicycle Rental** (☎ **416/203-0009**); and at **High Park Cycle and Sports,** 24 Ronson Dr. (☎ **416/614-6689**).

FAST FACTS: Toronto

Airport   See "Getting There," in chapter 2.

Area Code   Toronto's area code is **416;** Mississauga is now **905.**

Business Hours   Banks are generally open Monday through Thursday from 10am to 3pm and Friday from 10am to 6pm. Stores are generally open Monday through Wednesday from 9:30 or 10am to 6pm and Saturday and Sunday from 10am to 5pm, with extended hours (until 8 to 9:30pm) on Thursday and usually Friday.

Camera Repair   For major repairs, there's the **Camera Repair Centre,** 1162 Yonge St., north of the Rosedale subway station (☎ **416/923-8143**); otherwise, **Vistek,** 496 Queen St. East (☎ **416/365-1777**), is good for routine repairs.

Car Rentals See "Getting Around," earlier in this chapter.

Climate See "When to Go," in chapter 2.

Currency See "Visitor Information & Entry Requirements," in chapter 2.

Currency Exchange Generally, the best place to exchange your currency is at an ATM or bank. Currency can also be exchanged at the airport, but at a less favorable rate.

Dentist If you should need to see a dentist while traveling, **The Royal College of Dental Surgeons** (☎ 416/961-6555) offers emergency after-hours dental care. Otherwise, ask at the front desk or the concierge at your hotel.

Doctor If you need the services of a doctor while in Toronto, **The College of Physicians and Surgeons,** 80 College St. (☎ 416/961-1711), operates a referral service from 9am to 5pm. See also "Emergencies," below.

Documents Required See "Visitor Information & Entry Requirements," in chapter 2.

Driving Rules See "Getting Around," earlier in this chapter.

Electricity It's the same as in the United States—110 volts, 50 cycles, AC.

Embassies/Consulates All embassies are in Ottawa, the national capital. However, many nations maintain consulates in Toronto, including the following: **Australian Consulate-General,** 175 Bloor St. East (☎ 416/323-1155, or 416/323-3919); **British Consulate-General,** 777 Bay St. at College (☎ 416/593-1267); and the **U.S. Consulate,** 360 University Ave. (☎ 416/595-1700).

Emergencies Call **911** for fire, police, and ambulance. The **Toronto General Hospital** provides 24-hour emergency service (☎ 416/340-3948). There are two entrances: the main entrance at **200 Elizabeth St.,** and a second entrance at **150 Gerrard St. West.**

Eyeglass Repair If you have a problem with your glasses, or lose them, the two offices of **A-1 Public Optical,** 60 Queen St. East, at Church Street (☎ 416/364-0740) and 750 Dundas St. West, at Bathurst Street (☎ 416/603-1550), offer 1-hour service, depending on the prescription.

Hospitals Try **Toronto General Hospital,** 200 Elizabeth St. (emergency ☎ 416/340-3948). There's another entrance at 150 Gerrard St. West.

Hot Lines To reach the **rape crisis** hot line, call **416/597-8808;** the **victim assault** line is **416/863-0511;** and the **suicide prevention** line is **416/285-0100,** or 416/598-1121.

Information See "Visitor Information & Entry Requirements," in chapter 2 and also "Orientation," earlier in this chapter.

Laundry/Dry Cleaning The following are conveniently located self-service Laundromats: **Bloor Laundromat,** 598 Bloor St. West, at Bathurst Street (☎ 416/588-6600) and **Speedy Automatic Coin Wash,** 568 Church St., at Wellesley Street (☎ 416/922-1147). At the **Laundry Lounge,** 531 Yonge St., at Wellesley Street (☎ 416/975-4747), you can do your wash while sipping a cappuccino and watching TV or listening to music in their lounge. It's open from 7am to 6pm Monday through Saturday.

For 1-hour dry cleaning, try **Parliament One-Hour Cleaning,** 436 Parliament St., at Spruce Street, near Carlton Street (☎ 416/923-5276); **One-hour Dry Cleaner,** 987 Bay St. (☎ 416/966-6868); or **The Laundry Lounge** (see above), which provides this service until 10am.

Liquor Laws   The minimum drinking age is 19. Drinking hours are 11am to 1am Monday through Saturday and noon to 11pm Sunday (cocktail lounges are not usually licensed to sell liquor on Sunday; dining rooms are). Liquor, wine, and some beers are sold at **Liquor Control Board of Ontario (LCBO)** stores, open Monday through Saturday. Most are open from 10am to 6pm, but some stay open evenings. Convenient locations include: College Park, First Canadian Place, Manulife Centre, Eaton Centre, Union Station, and Yonge and Wellesley. Call **416/365-5900** for more.

True wine lovers will want to check out **Vintages** stores (also operated by the LCBO), which carry a more extensive and more specialized selection of wines. The most convenient downtown location is in the lower-level concourse of **Hazelton Lanes** (☎ **416/924-9463**). Look also for the **Wine Rack** at 560 Queen St. West (☎ **416/504-3647**) and at Wellesley and Church (☎ **416/923-9393**). This last chain specializes in Ontario wines only.

Beer is sold at **Brewers Retail Stores,** most of which are open Monday through Friday from 10am to 10pm and Saturday from 10am to 8pm. Convenient downtown locations include: Church and Wellesley, College and Bathurst, and Bloor and Spadina.

Lost Property   If you left something on a bus, streetcar, or the subway, call the **TTC Lost Articles Office** (☎ **416/393-4100**) at the Bay Street subway station. They're open Monday through Friday from 8am to 5:30pm.

Luggage Storage/Lockers   Lockers are available at Union Station.

Mail   Postage for letters and postcards to the United States costs 52¢; overseas, 90¢. Mailing letters and postcards within Canada costs 45¢.

Maps   Free maps of Toronto are available in every terminal at **Pearson International Airport** (look for signs directing you to the nearest Transport Canada Information Centre), the Metropolitan Toronto Convention & Visitors Association at **Harbourfront,** and the Visitor Information Centre in the **Eaton Centre,** on Yonge Street at Dundas Street. You can purchase a greater variety of maps at all convenience stores and bookstores, or try **Canada Map Company,** 63 Adelaide East between Yonge and Church (☎ **416/362-9297**) or **Open-Air Books and Maps**, 25 Toronto St., near Yonge and Adelaide streets (☎ **416/363-0719**).

Newspapers/Magazines   The three daily newspapers are the *Globe and Mail,* the *Toronto Star,* and the *Toronto Sun. Eye* and *Now* are the arts-and-entertainment weeklies of the moment. In addition, there are many English-language ethnic Toronto newspapers serving the Portuguese, Hungarian, Italian, East Indian, Korean, Chinese, and Caribbean communities. *Toronto Life* is the major monthly city magazine. *Where Toronto* is usually provided free in your hotel room.

Some of the best magazine selections can be found at the **Book Cellar** and **Maison de la Presse,** both in Yorkville; **Coles, the World's Biggest Bookstore** on Edward Street and **Pages** on Queen Street West; and **Lichtman's News and Books,** at Yonge and Bloor streets, Yonge and Richmond streets, the Atrium on Bay Street, Yonge Street and Eglinton Avenue, and Yonge and St. Clair.

Pharmacies (Late-Night)   **Shoppers Drug Mart,** at 360 Bloor St. West, at Spadina Avenue, stays open daily until midnight. They have several other branches around Toronto; for the location of the late-night branch closest to you, call **800/363-1040.** The other big chain is **Pharma Plus,** with a store at 68 Wellesley St., at Church Street (☎ **416/924-7760**), which is open daily from 8am to midnight. Other Pharma Plus branches are in College Park, Manulife Centre,

Commerce Court, and First Canadian Place.

Police   In a life-threatening emergency, call **911.** For all other matters, you can reach the Metro police (40 College St.) at **416/324-2222.**

Post Office   The post office has been withdrawing from direct customer service. Postal services can now be found at convenience and drug stores like **Shopper's Drug Mart,** and others. Look for the sign in the window indicating such services. There are also post-office windows open throughout the city in **Atrium on Bay** (☎ **416/506-0911**), **Commerce Court** (☎ **416/956-7452**), the **TD Centre** (☎ **416/360-7105**), and **First Canadian Place** (☎ **416/364-0540**).

Radio   The programming of the Canadian Broadcasting Corporation is one of the joys, as far as I'm concerned, of traveling in Canada. It offers a great mix of intelligent discussion and commentary as well as drama and music. In Toronto, the CBC broadcasts on 740 AM and 94.1 FM.

CHIN, at 1540 AM and 100.7 FM, will get you in touch with the ethnic/multicultural scene in the city, broadcasting in more than 30 different languages.

Rest Rooms   Public rest rooms are found in major shopping complexes like Eatons, the Manulife Centre, the Holt Renfrew Centre, the Colonnade, and similarly convenient locations. They are invariably clean and well kept. You can also use hotel and restaurant facilities.

Safety   As large cities go, Toronto is generally safe, but be alert and use your common sense, particularly at night. In the downtown area, Moss Park is considered one of the toughest areas to police.

Taxes   The provincial retail sales tax is 8%; there's also a 5% tax on hotel/motel rooms and a national 7% goods-and-services tax (GST).

In general, nonresidents may apply for a refund of these taxes for nondisposable merchandise that will be exported for use provided they were removed from Canada within 60 days of purchase. Note, though, that the following do not qualify for rebate: meals and restaurant charges, alcohol, tobacco, gas, car rentals, and such services as dry cleaning and shoe repair. The quickest and easiest way to secure the refund is to stop in at a duty-free shop at the border. You must have proper receipts with GST registration numbers. Or you can apply through the mail, but it will take about 4 weeks to receive your refund. For an application form and information, write or call **Revenue Canada,** Customs and Excise, Visitor Rebate Program, Ottawa, Canada K1A 1J5 (☎ **613/991-3346**), *well in advance* of your trip. You can also contact **Ontario Travel,** 77 Bloor St. West, Queen's Park, Toronto, ON, M7A 2R9 (☎ **800/668-2746** or 416/314-0944).

Taxis   See "Getting Around," earlier in this chapter.

Telephone   A local call from a telephone booth costs 25¢. Watch out for hotel surcharges on local and long-distance calls; often a local call will cost at least $1 from a hotel room.

Time   Toronto is on eastern standard time. Daylight saving time is in effect from April through October.

Tipping   Basically it's the same as in the United States: 15% in restaurants, 15% to 20% for taxis, and $1 per bag for porters.

Transit Information   For information on the subway, bus, and streetcar system, call **416/393-4636.**

Weather   Call **416/292-1010** for a current weather report.

Accommodations

Although Toronto has many fine hotels, it's not easy to find good-value accommodations downtown. The city is expensive. Most of the top hotels are pricey and cater to a business clientele; and even at the more moderate establishments, you can expect to pay $100 per day. The few budget hotels charge under $90 a night, while nonhotel accommodations, such as university dorms, start at $45 to $50 per night. Bed-and-breakfasts are a good bet for frugal travelers, but even they are creeping upward in price. The situation is not helped by a 5% accommodations tax and the new national 7% GST.

There are some things you can do to combat the situation. I cannot stress enough how important it is to ask for a discount. Just like the airlines, hotels practice yield-management strategies, and adjust the cost of a room depending on occupancy. This means that the official rack rate has virtually disappeared. For example, a single room with a rack rate of $199 could rent for as little as $130 or even lower. In fact, it's pretty standard today to sell rooms at 30% to 40% off the rack rate. If a room goes unsold, that revenue is lost forever, thus creating a nice incentive for a hotel's management to move to flexible room rates. If you're lucky and the market is slow, asking for a discount or stating simply what you're prepared to pay will certainly secure you a rate much lower than the published rack rate.

No matter what, always ask about discounts for special groups of people—corporate personnel, government employees, the military, seniors, students—whatever group to which you legitimately belong. These will be substantially lower than rack rates. Also ask about seasonal discounts, especially summer rates and weekend packages, which can help you secure some great bargains at even the most luxurious establishments. In addition, always ask about parking charges and surcharges on local and long-distance phone calls. Both can make a big difference in your bill.

In the pages that follow I have categorized my favorites according to price and location. **Downtown** runs from the lakeshore to College/Carlton Street between Spadina Avenue and Jarvis Street; **midtown** refers to the area north of College/Carlton Street to where Dupont crosses Yonge Street, also between Spadina and Jarvis; **uptown, west,** and **east** designate areas outside the city core. I have also included a few hotels close to **Pearson International Airport.**

AN IMPORTANT NOTE ON PRICES The prices quoted here are rack rates. The price brackets for a double room are roughly as follows: **very expensive,** $200 and up per day; **expensive,** from $110 to $200; **moderate,** from $80 to $110; **inexpensive,** less than $80. I emphasize that these are only very rough categories, and subtle distinctions of taste, clientele, and reputation must also be taken into account.

Unless stated otherwise, *the prices cited in this guide are given in Canadian dollars,* which is good news for you because the Canadian dollar is worth 27% less than the American dollar but buys just about as much. As we go to press, $1 Canadian is worth 73¢ U.S., which means that your $100-a-night hotel room will cost only $73 U.S. a night, your $50 dinner for two will cost only $36.50 U.S., and your $5 breakfast will cost only $3.65 U.S.

Note: The accommodations tax is 5%, and the goods and services tax is 7%, but both are refunded to nonresidents upon application (see "Taxes" under "Fast Facts: Toronto," in chapter 3).

BED-AND-BREAKFASTS For interesting, truly personal accommodations, contact **Toronto Bed & Breakfast,** Box 269, 253 College St. (P.O. Box 269), Toronto, ON, M5T 1R5 (☎ **416/588-8800** or 416/690-1407; Mon–Fri 9am–noon and 2–7pm), for their list of homes offering bed-and-breakfast accommodations within the city for an average of $60 to $90 per night double. The association will reserve for you, or you can choose an establishment and make all the arrangements yourself.

Other organizations to try include the **Downtown Toronto Association of Bed-and-Breakfast Guesthouses,** P.O. Box 190, Station B, Toronto, ON, M5T 2W1 (☎ **416/368-1420;** fax 416/368-1653). This association represents about 30 bed-and-breakfasts and is operated by Linda Lippa, an enthusiastic bed-and-breakfast host herself, who has a spacious Victorian home where she welcomes guests. The best time to call is between 8:30am and 7pm. All homes are nonsmoking. Room prices range from $45 to $65 single and $55 to $80 double.

1 Best Bets

- **Best Historic Hotel:** Once the tallest building in the city and the largest hotel in the British Empire, **The Royal York,** 100 Front St. West (☎ **416/368-2511**), is one of the most historically significant structures in all of Toronto. The lobby is vast, impressive, and crowned by an incredible inlay coffered ceiling that is lit by large cast-bronze chandeliers. Considering its size, the service is okay.
- **Best for Business Travelers:** There are three winners in this category: **The Four Seasons Hotel,** 21 Avenue Rd. (☎ **416/964-0411**), the **Inter-Continental,** 220 Bloor St. West (☎ **416/960-5200**), and **The Sheraton Centre,** 123 Queen St. West (☎ **416/361-1000**). The Four Seasons and the Inter-Continental take top honors because they are small enough to deliver great service to their business clientele. The Sheraton is noteworthy for its convenient location, close to the financial district, and its ability to deliver service with speed and grace—even while hosting multiple conventions, as it often does.
- **Best for a Romantic Getaway:** In town, the waterfront **Radisson Plaza Hotel Admiral,** 249 Queen's Quay West (☎ **416/203-3333**), is small enough to make you feel like you're in a romantic hostelry, while the outdoor rooftop pool provides a resortlike atmosphere. Out of town, luxury abounds at **Langdon Hall,** RR 3, Cambridge, Ontario (☎ **519/740-2100**), an accommodation that transports visitors as close as they can come to a romantic English country experience near Toronto (see chapter 10).

- **Best for Families:** The **Delta Chelsea Inn,** 33 Gerrard St. West (☎ 416/ 595-1975), has been catering to families for years. The special children's programs, the day-care center, and the separate health club for adults only all help smooth the way for family vacationers.
- **Best Moderately Priced Hotel:** The **Holiday Inn on King,** 370 King St. West (☎ 416/599-4000), has a great location near the SkyDome and the theater and entertainment district. It's only 4 years old, and has a fine jazz bar below ground level.
- **Best Budget Hotel:** The **Venture Inn,** 89 Avenue Rd. (☎ 416/964-1220), can't be beaten for its location in expensive Yorkville. It has no-frills rooms, and lacks a restaurant and other services, but that's precisely why it can charge the prices it does.
- **Best Alternative Accommodation: Victoria University,** 140 Charles St. West (☎ 416/585-4524), wins this category hands down because of its excellent downtown location, right across from the Royal Ontario Museum (ROM), and the facilities it offers—a pool, tennis courts, and a fitness center. Not to mention the simply furnished, but clean room with fresh linens you'll receive for just $62 a night.
- **Best Service:** No matter what you ask for at **The Four Seasons,** 21 Avenue Rd. (☎ 416/964-0411), it will be delivered to you graciously. Such personal attention can be lavished on guests because the hotel is relatively small and has a very high staff-to-guest ratio.
- **Best Location:** If you're in Toronto on vacation, the **Westin Harbour Castle,** 1 Harbour Sq. (☎ 416/869-1600), on the lake, is a very alluring summer location, even if it is a convention hotel. For the business traveler, the **Sheraton Centre,** 123 Queen St. West (☎ 416/361-1000), or the **Toronto Marriott Eaton Centre,** 525 Bay St., at Dundas (☎ 416/597-9200), are well-located, within walking distance of the financial district and City Hall.
- **Best Hotel Pool:** There are three delightful choices: The **Radisson Plaza Hotel Admiral,** 249 Queen's Quay West (☎ 416/203-3333), with its outdoor rooftop pool overlooking the lake, gives your afternoon swim a Caribbean resort air; the **Royal York,** 100 Front St. West (☎ 416/368-2511), with its beautifully decorated pool complete with classical murals, lends a touch of elegance; and the **Delta Chelsea Inn,** 33 Gerrard St. West (☎ 416/595-1975), with its two pools—one for adults, the other for everyone—offers a delightful luxury of choice.
- **Best Views:** Every room that faces south at the **Westin Harbor Castle,** 1 Harbour Sq. (☎ 416/869-1600), has a view of the lake.
- **Best for Sports Fans:** It's hard to be closer to the action than at the **SkyDome Hotel,** 1 Blue Jays Way, (☎ 416/341-7100), where more than half of the rooms have views of the diamond where the Toronto Blue Jays play their home games.

2 Downtown

The downtown area runs from the lakefront to College/Carlton Street between Spadina Avenue and Jarvis Street.

VERY EXPENSIVE

Cambridge Suites Hotel. 15 Richmond St. E. (close to the corner of Yonge St.), Toronto, ON, M5C 1N2. ☎ 800/463-1990 or 416/368-1990. Fax 416/601-3751. 230 suites. A/C MINIBAR TV TEL. $270 double, $285 for Gold Club Service. Rates include continental breakfast. AE, DC, DISC, ER, MC, V. Parking $17. Subway: Queen.

Downtown Toronto Accommodations

Best Western
  Primrose Hotel **2**
Bond Place Hotel **9**
Cambridge Suites **13**
Clarion Essex Park Hotel **3**
Crowne Plaza
  Toronto Centre **22**
Days Inn Carlton Inn **1**
Delta Chelsea Inn **5**
Hilton International **12**
Holiday Inn on King **24**
Hostelling International **10**
Hotel Victoria **16**
King Edward Hotel **15**
Metropolitan Hotel **7**
Neil Wycik College Hotel **4**
Novotel **19**
Quality Hotel **14**
Radisson Plaza
  Hotel Admiral **21**
Royal York **18**
Sheraton Centre **11**
SkyDome **23**
Strathcona **17**
Toronto Colony **8**
Toronto Marriott
  Eaton Centre **6**
Westin Harbour Castle **20**

LEGEND
✝ Church
✉ Post Office
TTC Subway stop

1-0335

40

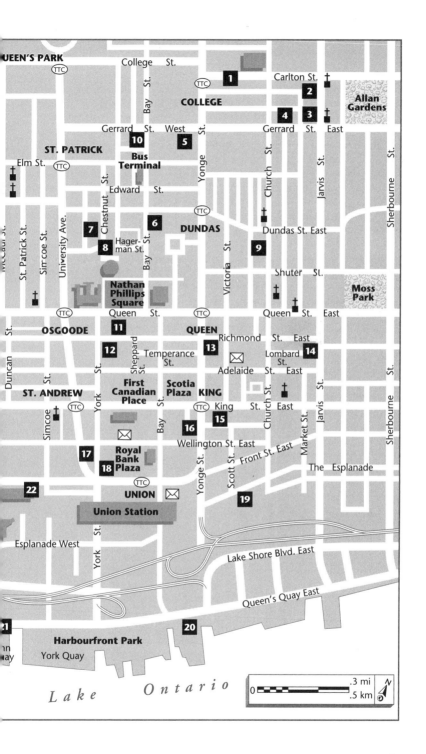

QUEEN'S PARK

College St.

Carlton St.

1

2

COLLEGE

4 **3**

Gerrard St. West

Yonge St.

10

5

Gerrard St. East

Allan Gardens

ST. PATRICK

Elm St.

Bus Terminal

Church St.

Jarvis St.

Sherbourne St.

Edward St.

Chestnut St.

7

6

DUNDAS

8

Hager-man St.

Bay St.

Dundas St. East

University Ave.

Simcoe St.

St. Patrick St.

McCaul St.

Victoria St.

9

Shuter St.

Nathan Phillips Square

Moss Park

Queen St.

Queen St. East

OSGOODE

11

QUEEN

12

Sheppard St.

Temperance St.

Richmond St. East

13

Lombard St.

14

Adelaide St. East

Duncan St.

York St.

First Canadian Place

Scotia Plaza

KING

Church St.

Jarvis St.

Sherbourne St.

ST. ANDREW

Simcoe St.

King St. East

15

16

Bay St.

Wellington St. East

17

Royal Bank Plaza

Yonge St.

Scott St.

Front St. East

Market St.

The Esplanade

18

22

UNION

19

Union Station

Esplanade West

York St.

Lake Shore Blvd. East

Queen's Quay East

21

20

Harbourfront Park

York Quay

Lake   Ontario

0   .3 mi
         .5 km

N

Ideally situated for the business traveler in the financial district, this all-suites hotel features comfortable accommodations and the extra-special conveniences that make all the difference. Each large 550-square-foot suite has a refrigerator, a microwave, and dishes, along with a supply of coffee, tea, and cookies, plus a sizable working area with a desk, two two-line telephones, and a fax. If you like, you can leave a list and your grocery shopping will be done for you. The furnishings are extremely comfortable and include a couch, armchairs, and a coffee table. There's also a dressing area with a full-length mirror, and a marble bathroom equipped with a hair dryer and a full complement of amenities. The penthouse luxury suites are duplexes that have Jacuzzis. Gold Club suites have everything the standard suites have, plus free local calls, complimentary shoe-shine, and complimentary breakfast and snacks.

Dining/Entertainment: Facilities include a small, comfortable bar and a fine dining room that serves reasonably priced entrees at dinner, such as salmon teriyaki or breast of chicken with cilantro and lime beurre blanc.

Services: Room service 11am to 11pm; daily maid service, valet, concierge.

Facilities: Business center; laundry; convenience store; fitness center, boasting a fine view of the city and equipped with whirlpool; exercise room and sauna.

Hilton International. 145 Richmond St. W., Toronto, ON, M5H 3M6. ☎ **800/445-8667** or 416/869-3456. Fax 416/869-1478. 601 rms and suites. A/C MINIBAR TV TEL. $290 double. Extra person $20. One child under 18 stays free in parents' room. Weekend packages available. AE, DC, ER, EU, JCB, MC, V. Parking $17 overnight. Subway: Osgoode.

Conveniently located near the Convention Centre and financial district, this 32-story hotel has all the facilities one expects from the Hilton chain. The refurbished rooms are large and well decorated, and have phones, color TVs, AM/FM radios, scales, alarm clocks, and individual temperature control.

Dining/Entertainment: Trees 20 feet tall separate the lobby from the Garden Court restaurant, where you can enjoy breakfast, lunch, afternoon tea, or dinner while seated on a cushioned rattan chair. Barristers has a clubby atmosphere, with wonderful leather armchairs and couches.

Services: 24-hour room service, concierge, laundry/valet, baby-sitting.

Facilities: Heated indoor/outdoor pool, sauna, whirlpool, exercise room, massage specialist, executive business center.

King Edward Hotel. 37 King St. E., Toronto, ON, M5C 2E9. ☎ **416/863-9700.** Fax 416/367-5515. 299 rms and suites. A/C MINIBAR TV TEL. $170–$279 double; from $325 suite. AE, DC, MC, V. Parking $24. Subway: King.

Affectionately known as The King Eddy, this is the city's oldest hotel. In its heyday, it welcomed such guests as Edward, Prince of Wales, Rudolph Valentino, Charles de Gaulle, Richard Burton and Liz Taylor, and the Beatles. Built in 1903 by distiller George Gooderham, the richest man in Toronto, it underwent a $40 million renovation in 1981 that restored all of its architectural features—marble Corinthian columns, sculpted stucco, and a glass-domed rotunda above the lobby.

The 299 rooms are extremely spacious and beautifully decorated. Each comes fully equipped with a remote-control color TV; telephones in the bedroom and bathroom; a clock radio; and such niceties as complimentary newspaper delivery, bathrobes, super-fluffy towels without monogram, shampoo, perfume, and marble bathtubs.

Dining/Entertainment: Traditional English afternoon tea—complete with clotted cream, strawberry preserves, and cucumber finger sandwiches—is served in the Lobby lounge. The famous old Victoria Room has been turned into the Café Victoria, where baroque plasterwork and etched glass is matched with extravagant potted shrubs. Eight-foot-high windows in the main floor Consort Bar look out onto

King Street. For formal dining, Chiaro's specializes in fine continental cuisine with main dishes priced from $21 to $30.

Services: 24-hour room service, concierge, laundry/valet, complimentary shoe-shine and newspaper, nightly turndown.

Facilities: Health club.

Royal York. 100 Front St. W., Toronto, ON, M5J 1E3. ☎ **800/441-1414** in the U.S., or 416/368-2511; 416/863-6333 for reservations only. 1,157 rms, 191 suites. A/C MINIBAR TV TEL. $179 double, from $220 suites and Entree Gold service. Many special packages available. AE, DC, DISC, MC, V. Parking $21.50. Subway: Union.

To many citizens and regular visitors, the Royal York *is* Toronto, because in its 34 banquet and meeting rooms, many of the city's historical and social events have taken place. Today, it's a major convention hotel and, as such, not to everyone's taste. Still, there is a magnificence to this hotel, which opened in 1929 and has hosted a raft of royalty, heads of state, and celebrities. The lobby itself is vast, impressive, and crowned by an incredible inlay coffered ceiling that is lit by large cast-bronze chandeliers. If you stay here, do go down and look at some of the banquet rooms, several of which have splendid ceiling murals, and the series of provincial meeting rooms, each with a unique decor.

The Royal York is a huge enterprise, and the statistics describing its capacity and use are mind-boggling. It can sleep 2,800 guests; it contains an eighth of a mile of carpeting; and it can accommodate 10,000 people at one meal sitting. The kitchen bakes 10,000 rolls daily, uses 18,000 eggs per week, and washes 25,000 pieces of china and 45,000 pieces of silverware daily.

The hotel has recently undergone major renovations. Rooms vary in size, but a standard room will have a king-size bed. The decor varies, but tends toward warm florals or a combination of jade and rose with antique reproduction furnishings that always include an armchair and a well-lit desk. Nice features are solid-wood doors, windows that open, and wall moldings. Rooms for travelers with disabilities are exceptionally well equipped for wheelchair guests and for the deaf and blind. Entree Gold-level rooms are superior rooms on a private floor with separate check-in, a private lounge, complimentary breakfast and newspaper, and nightly turndown.

Dining/Entertainment: The Royal York boasts an incredible 10 restaurants and lounges. The Acadian Room offers Canadian cuisine in an elegant atmosphere. The wine list features the most extensive selection of Ontario wines anywhere. For a show of Japanese finesse, there's a Benihana steak house. The Gazebo affords a gardenlike setting for lunch, York's Kitchen is open for breakfast and lunch featuring buffets, and York's Deli and Bakery offers an array of salads, soups, hot dishes, and super-sized sandwiches. Muffin on the Run has an extensive selection of muffins. Piper's Bar & Eatz has a full range of drinks, a tavern menu, and singing waiters. The Lobby Bar features a sports screen; the Library Bar is a more intimate and cozy meeting spot that's rated highly for the quality and selection of its martinis. Downstairs, you'll find the Black Knight karaoke bar, Dick Turpin's, an English-style pub with sing-along entertainment, and the small York Station bar.

Services: 24-hour room service, laundry/valet, concierge.

Facilities: Skylit indoor lap pool with hand-painted trompe l'oeil murals and potted palms, exercise room, saunas, steam rooms and whirlpool, barbershop and beauty salon, shopping arcade with an American Express Travel Centre, business center.

The Sheraton Centre. 123 Queen St. W., Toronto, ON, M5H 2M9. ☎ **800/325-3535** or 416/361-1000. Fax 416/947-4854. 1,382 rms, 79 suites. A/C MINIBAR TV TEL. $230 double. Extra person $20; rollaway bed $10. Two children under 18 stay free in parents' room. Various packages available. AE, CB, DC, ER, EU, JCB, MC, V. Parking $22 a day. Subway: Osgoode.

A very large convention hotel that nevertheless provides prompt service, the Sheraton Centre is located right across from City Hall in a 43-story shopping complex with six restaurants and bars and two movie theaters. In the lobby, there are 2 acres of landscaped gardens with a waterfall and summer terrace enclosed behind glass walls.

All of the Sheraton Centre's more than 1,000 spacious rooms are attractively furnished and well equipped, having gone through a $47 million renovation in the last few years. Nice amenities in the standard rooms include coffeemakers and irons and ironing boards. The Towers rooms, which are more expensive, offer additional amenities—bathrobes, an additional telephone in the bathroom, a private elevator and reception area, and complimentary continental breakfast and evening hors d'oeuvres.

Dining/Entertainment: In the shopping concourse, you'll find an authentic-looking English pub (shipped from England in sections) called Good Queen Bess, complete with toby mugs, cozy fireplaces, and mugs of Newcastle brown. At the Reunion Billiard Lounge in the lobby, where great drinks and snacks are served, there's a dance floor, foozball, and 13 30-inch video monitors. The Long Bar provides off-track betting and a great view of City Hall. Postcards Grill presents regional Canadian cuisine showcasing the country's finest ingredients.

Services: 24-hour room service, laundry/valet, baby-sitting available.

Facilities: Large indoor/outdoor pool with sundeck, sauna, game room, hot tub, exercise room, shopping mall, two movie theaters.

SkyDome. 1 Blue Jays Way, Toronto, ON, M5V 1J4. ☎ **416/341-7100.** Fax 416/341-5090. 346 rms. A/C MINIBAR TV TEL. City view, from $139 double; field side, from $289. AE, DC, DISC, JCB, MC, V. Subway: Union.

For sports fans (baseball fans in particular), this is hotel heaven. Imagine having a room that overlooks the bullpen and the splendid green of the field, as 70 rooms of this hotel located right inside the SkyDome stadium do.

Standard rooms come with a view window, more expensive field-side rooms have raised living areas, and then there are the suites. The city-view rooms are the least expensive. Each unit has modern furnishings and is equipped with full amenities, including a hair dryer, coffeemaker, and clock radio.

Dining/Entertainment: Cafe on the Green overlooks the field, and, adjacent to the hotel, so do Sightlines and the Hard Rock Café.

Services: 24-hour room service, laundry/valet, concierge.

Facilities: Fitness center with pool, squash courts, sauna, and exercise room.

✪ Westin Harbour Castle. 1 Harbour Sq., Toronto, ON, M5J 1A6. ☎ **800/228-3000** or 416/869-1600. Fax 416/869-0573. 922 rms, 56 suites. A/C MINIBAR TV TEL. $240–$230 double. Extra person $20. Children stay free in parents' room. Weekend packages (double occupancy) and special long-term rates available. Parking $19. AE, DC, DISC, ER, MC, V. Subway: Union; then LRT to the hotel.

A popular convention hotel, the Harbour Castle is located right on the lakefront, ideally situated for those who want to explore the Harbourfront. It's also conveniently linked to downtown by the LRT. The rooms are located in two towers joined at the base by a five-story podium. Marble, oak, and crystal adorn the spacious lobby, which commands a great harbor view.

Each room has a view of the lake and is furnished with a remote-control color TV featuring in-room movies, a bathroom telephone, a marble-top desk and night table, a table and floor lamps, and color-coordinated fabrics. There are 442 nonsmoking rooms.

Dining/Entertainment: The moderately priced Lobby Lounge overlooking the harbor serves breakfast, lunch, and dinner. The Lighthouse, a revolving restaurant on

An Important Note on Prices

Unless stated otherwise, the prices cited in this guide are given in Canadian dollars, which is good news for U.S. travelers because the Canadian dollar is worth 27% less than the American dollar, but buys nearly as much. As we go to press, $1 Canadian is worth 73¢ U.S., which means that your $100-a-night hotel room will cost only U.S. $73, and your $6 breakfast costs only U.S. $4.38.

Here's a quick table of equivalents:

Canadian $	U.S. $
$1	$0.73
$5	$3.65
$10	$7.30
$20	$14.60
$50	$36.50
$100	$73.00
$200	$146.00

the 37th floor, reached via a glass-walled elevator, provides fabulous views during lunch, brunch, or dinner. There's also a Chinese restaurant called Grand Yatt Dynasty.

Services: 24-hour room service, concierge, laundry/valet, guest-room voice mail, beauty shop.

Facilities: Fitness center with indoor pool, whirlpool, sauna, steam room, two squash courts, tennis court, massage clinic, shopping arcade.

EXPENSIVE

Clarion Essex Park Hotel. 300 Jarvis St. (just south of Carlton), Toronto, ON, M5B 2C5. ☎ **800/567-2233** or 416/977-4823. Fax 416/977-4830. 58 rms, 44 suites. A/C TV TEL. $130–$145 double. AE, DISC, ER, JCB. Parking $12.

Conveniently located within walking distance of the Eaton Centre, Pantages Theatre, and City Hall, the Clarion Essex Park is a comfortable, moderately priced hotel that's used by a lot of tour groups and is located in a slightly dubious neighborhood. All rooms have queen- or king-size beds, and each is nicely furnished with a sofa, a desk, and a coffee table. Amenities include phones, cable color TVs, refrigerators, and a fully tiled bathroom with a hair dryer. Closets are large.

There's a bistro with a bar, Clarion, that's open for lunch and dinner, and room service is available from 7am to 10pm. Facilities include an indoor pool, sauna, whirlpool, fitness center, squash courts, and billiards room.

Crowne Plaza Toronto Centre. 225 Front St. W., Toronto, ON, M5V 2X3. ☎ **800/HOLIDAY** or 416/597-1400. Fax 416/597-8128. 549 rms, 38 suites. A/C MINIBAR TV TEL. $209 double. Extra person $20. Weekend packages available. AE, DC, DISC, MC, V. Parking $19.50. Subway: Union.

The Crowne Plaza Toronto Centre, attached to the Convention Centre, is ideally located for the CN Tower, SkyDome, Roy Thomson Hall, and the theater district. Rose marble, cherry wood, and polished bronze are used throughout the lobby. The 25-story tower slopes back and upward from the main entrance, creating a garden court, which accommodates a lounge and cafe.

The rooms, decorated in dusky rose or muted green, are finely appointed, with marble bathroom counters, writing desks, elegant table lamps, draped tables, and matching window valances. All feature color TVs, clock radios, individual climate control, two telephone lines, and hair dryers. Nonsmoking rooms are available.

Entree Gold accommodations offer additional amenities—complimentary breakfast, cocktail canapés, a shoe-shine, as well as private check-in, an honor bar, and nightly turndown.

The Trellis Lounge, decorated with trees and plants, is well known for its Sunday brunch and after-theater menu. The elegant Chanterelles serves imaginative main courses ranging from $20 to $33.50. For casual dining, there's the Trellis Bistro. Twenty-four–hour room service, a concierge, and laundry/valet service are all available. Facilities include an indoor pool, whirlpool, saunas, a well-equipped exercise room, squash courts, and a sundeck.

Days Inn Carlton Inn. 30 Carlton St., Toronto, ON, M5B 2E9. ☎ **800/329-7466** or 416/977-6655. Fax 416/977-0502. 536 rms and suites. A/C TV TEL. $99–$160 double. Extra person $15. Children under 18 stay free in parents' room. Summer discounts available. AE, DC, DISC, MC, V. Parking $12. Subway: College.

Nicely furnished rooms with modern conveniences at fair prices are the hallmark of the Carlton Inn, a modern, centrally air-conditioned high-rise. Besides offering reasonably priced (for Toronto) accommodations, the inn is well located, only a few steps from Yonge Street, right next door to Maple Leaf Gardens.

All rooms contain color TVs with in-house movies. Refrigerators are available on request. There is a lounge, a sports bar, and a restaurant. Laundry and valet services are available. Facilities include an indoor pool, saunas, and a hair salon. If you book a room here, you may obtain a discount on a car rental with Alamo.

Delta Chelsea Inn. 33 Gerrard St. W., Toronto, ON, M5G 1Z4. ☎ **800/243-5732** or 416/595-1975. Fax 416/585-4362. 1,547 rms, 47 suites. A/C TV TEL. $199 double with standard service; $210 double with signature service; $214 double on business floor; from $275 suite. Extra person $20. Children under 18 share parents' room free. Weekend packages available. AE, DC, DISC, MC, V. Parking $18–but only 300 spaces. Subway: College.

The Delta Chelsea, located between Yonge and Bay streets, is still one of Toronto's best buys—particularly for families and on weekends—although prices have risen considerably in recent years. The crowded scene in the lobby, though, testifies to its continued popularity.

All rooms have color TVs with in-room movies, phones, and bright, modern furnishings. Some rooms have kitchenettes. The south tower has 600 rooms featuring dual phones with data jacks, call waiting, and conference-call features. This tower also contains a penthouse lounge, a business center, and more dining facilities.

All rooms have 24-hour room service, baby-sitting, and laundry and valet service. For $10 more, you can have a signature service room, with complimentary tea and coffee service, a minibar, a terry-cloth bathrobe, and an iron and ironing board.

The hotel also offers a special business floor, where rooms contain ergonomic chairs; cordless speaker phones, with a speaker in the bathroom; desks with supplies; in-room faxes with confidential numbers; terry-cloth bathrobes, minibars, and irons and ironing boards. Guests staying here also receive such amenities as free local calls, complimentary copies of the *Globe and Mail*, and access to a business center located on the same floor—all for just under $15 more than regular room rates.

Wittles offers casual but elegant dining, while the Market Garden is an attractive self-service cafeteria with an outdoor courtyard that sells salads, sandwiches, and grilled items at reasonable prices. The restaurants offer a good-value children's menu, and children under 7 eat free. The Chelsea Bun, which serves lunch buffets and Sunday brunch, offers live entertainment daily and Dixieland jazz on Saturday afternoon. For a relaxing drink, there's the Elm Street Lounge or Deck 27, which offers a great view of the skyline.

Facilities include: two swimming pools, whirlpool, sauna, exercise room, lounge, game room with three pool tables, beauty salon, business center, and—a blessing for parents—a children's creative center where 3 to 8 year-olds can play under expert supervision (it's open until 10pm on Friday and Saturday, and there's a nominal charge).

Holiday Inn on King. 370 King St. W. (at Peter), Toronto, ON, M5V 1J9. ☎ **416/599-4000.** 405 rms, 20 suites. A/C TV TEL. From $110 double. Extra person $15. AE, DISC, ER, MC, V. Parking $11. Subway: St. Andrew.

Housed in an odd-looking Miami-style building, the Holiday Inn is close to the theater district, the CN Tower, and SkyDome. The rooms are pleasantly furnished in pastels, with sage-green carpeting and floral bedspreads; each is fully equipped with a phone, clock radio, TV on a stand, wet bar, and a decently lit desk. Many have balconies. The bathrooms have a number of amenities, including hair dryers. There's a restaurant, a lounge that's famous for its live jazz, and a deli.

An outdoor pool, sauna, and fitness center round out the facilities.

The Metropolitan Hotel. 108 Chestnut St., Toronto, ON, M5G 1R3. ☎ **416/977-5000.** Fax 416/977-9513. 463 rms, 18 suites. A/C MINIBAR TV TEL. $230 double. Children under 16 stay free in parents' room. AE, CB, DC, DISC, ER, EU, JCB, MC, V. Parking $18.25. Subway: St. Patrick.

Previously owned by the Best Western chain, the Metropolitan was recently purchased by a Hong Kong hotel company which has invested a lot of money in it. The decor has been enhanced, but so have the dining facilities, with the help of one of Toronto's star chefs—Susur Lee. The ambiance is sleek and modern, with some Oriental accents throughout. At the time of writing, though, service was not as swift or smooth as it should be.

The rooms are spiffily furnished and well equipped for the business traveler—with large desks, telephones with computer- and fax-compatible jacks, and in-closet safes. Bathroom amenities include lighted swing mirrors, massage showerheads, bathrobes, and hair dryers. The luxury and executive suites have Jacuzzis, Dolby surround sound TVs, stereos and CD players.

When it comes to dining, Hemispheres, with its Kandinsky-inspired painting and curvaceous glass walls, has to be one of the most attractive all-day dining rooms in the city, and one of the few with a special chef's table. The Alibi bar and restaurant overlooking the lobby serves casual fare. Lai Wah Heen is an elegant contemporary Chinese restaurant serving really fine Cantonese cuisine (see chapter 5 for a review). Facilities include an indoor swimming pool, fitness center with sauna, whirlpool, and massage therapy services, as well as a business center. There's 24-hour room-service, concierge, and valet service.

The Metropolitan is conveniently located two blocks from the Eaton Centre on Chestnut Street, just off Dundas Street between Bay Street and University Avenue.

Novotel. 45 The Esplanade, Toronto, ON, M5E 1W2. ☎ **800/668-6835** or 416/367-8900. Fax 416/360-8285. 262 rms, 8 suites. A/C MINIBAR TV TEL. From $135 double. AE, DC, ER, EU, MC, V. Parking $11.75. Subway: Union.

Located just off Yonge Street near the St. Lawrence Centre and O'Keefe Centre, the Novotel is an ultramodern hotel, built in French Renaissance–style with a Palladian entrance leading to a marble lobby with oak and Oriental decorative accents.

The rooms are nicely appointed with all the expected conveniences, including remote-control TVs, two telephones, hair dryers, minibars, radio and TV speakers in the bathrooms, and skirt hangers. The Café Nicole serves breakfast, lunch, and dinner. Room service is available from 6am to midnight; there's also a concierge, laundry and valet service, and airport shuttle service.

Facilities include an indoor pool, sauna, whirlpool, and exercise room.

✪ **Radisson Plaza Hotel Admiral.** 249 Queen's Quay W., Toronto, ON, M5J 2N5. ☎ **800/ 333-3333** or 416/203-3333. Fax 416/203-3100. 140 rms, 17 suites. A/C MINIBAR TV TEL. $165–$205 double. Extra person $20. Weekend packages available. AE, DC, MC, V. Parking $12.50. Subway: Union.

As the name and the harborfront location suggest, the Hotel Admiral has a strong nautical flavor. The lobby combines polished woods and downtown Toronto brass with nautical paintings. The horseshoe-shaped roofdeck comes complete with a pool and cabana-style bar and terrace.

The rooms are elegantly furnished with a campaign-style chests of drawers with brass trimmings, marble-top side tables, and desks, all set on jade carpets. Extra amenities include two phones, a hair dryer and clothesline in the bathroom, a clock radio, a minibar, and a complimentary newspaper.

The Commodore's Dining Room, which looks out onto Lake Ontario and the waterfront, serves classic continental cuisine, with main courses ranging from $30 to $40. The Galley serves a more modest menu, priced from $15 to $25. The adjacent Bosun's Bar also offers light snacks.

There's 24-hour room service, a concierge, and complimentary newspaper delivery. Facilities include an outdoor swimming pool, whirlpool, and squash court.

Toronto Colony. 89 Chestnut St., Toronto, ON, M5G 1R1. ☎ **416/977-0707.** Fax 416/ 977-1136. 717 rms and suites. A/C TV TEL. $170 double. Extra person $15. Children under 19 stay free in parents' room. AE, DC, DISC, JCB, MC, V. Parking $15. Subway: Dundas or University.

The Toronto Colony (formerly the Ramada Hotel City Hall—it's located right behind City Hall) still retains many of the earmarks of the Ramada chain, even though the hotel is no longer affiliated with it. The rooms have recently been upgraded, and such nice amenities as hair dryers have been added. Each room is large and well furnished, with a console control panel by the bed for the color TV and radio, a vanity mirror or sink outside the bathroom, and individual climate control. Dewey's Lounge offers billiards and snacks in the evening, while the Chestnut Tree restaurant on the main floor offers all-day dining. Room service is available from 6am to 11pm, a concierge is on call, and baby-sitting can be arranged. Facilities include indoor and outdoor pools, a sauna, exercise room, sun terrace, and business center.

Toronto Marriott Eaton Centre. 525 Bay St., at Dundas, Toronto, ON, M5G 2L2. ☎ **416/ 597-9200.** Fax 416/597-9211. 459 rms and suites. A/C MINIBAR TV TEL. $250 double. AE, DC, MC, V. Subway: Dundas.

This is a modern hotel with all the hallmarks of the Marriott chain that's conveniently located alongside Eaton Centre. In addition to the amenities listed above, rooms contain clock radios and attractive furnishings. Nonsmoking rooms and rooms for travelers with disabilities are available, too.

The Parkside restaurant offers all-day dining. Characters, a bar, features billiards and table games as well as music and sporting events.

Services include: 24-hour room service, laundry and valet, a concierge, and baby-sitting. It's refreshing that the staff (porters, car valets, and others) do not expect or accept tips. An indoor rooftop swimming pool, whirlpool, sauna, and health club round out the facilities.

MODERATE

Best Western Primrose Hotel. 111 Carlton St. (between Church and Jarvis sts.), Toronto, ON, M5B 2G3. ☎ **800/268-8082** or 416/977-8000. Fax 416/977-6323. 338 rms, 4 suites. A/C TV TEL. $159 double. Extra person $10. Weekend packages available (except July–Sept). AE, DC, MC, V. Parking $10. Subway: College.

The Primrose offers spacious rooms, all with wall-to-wall carpeting and color-coordinated furnishings, color TVs, and individual climate control. About 25% contain king-size beds and sofas; the rest have two double beds. The downstairs coffee shop charmingly evokes the atmosphere of a Viennese cafe with its painted-wood decor. For relaxing, there's the One Eleven Lounge. Room service is available from 7am to 10pm, and there's also laundry and valet service, as well as a complimentary newspaper every morning. An outdoor pool and sauna are available for guests' use.

Bond Place Hotel. 65 Dundas St. E., Toronto, ON, M5B 2G8. ☎ **416/362-6061.** Fax 416/360-6406. 286 rms and suites. A/C TV TEL. $80–$130 double. Extra person $15. Weekend packages available. AE, DC, DISC, ER, MC, V. Parking $11. Subway: Dundas.

Ideally located just a block from the Eaton Centre and adjacent to the Pantages and Elgin theatres, the Bond Place Hotel is an independently owned, medium-size modern establishment offering all the features of a first-class hotel at reasonable prices.

The rooms, all pleasantly decorated in pastel colors, with Scandinavian-style furnishings and wall-to-wall carpeting, contain color TVs with in-house movies, individual climate control, and direct-dial phones.

Off the lobby, the Garden Café serves breakfast, lunch, and dinner from 7am to 11pm daily. Downstairs, Freddy's Lounge is a quiet bar.

There's laundry and valet service, and room service from 7am to 10pm.

Hotel Victoria. 56 Yonge St., Toronto, ON, M5E 1G5. ☎ **416/363-1666.** Fax 416/363-7327. 48 rms and suites. A/C TV TEL. $150 double. Extra person $15. Ask about special summer discounts. AE, DC, DISC, ER, MC, V. Subway: King.

In search of a small, personal hotel? Try the Hotel Victoria, with only 48 rooms spread over six floors. It's only two blocks from the O'Keefe Centre. The lobby is small and elegant, and retains the marble columns, staircase, and decorative moldings of an earlier era.

The rooms are either standard or select (the latter are larger). Furnishings are modern and combined with a green-and-beige decor. Each room contains a color TV, a private bath, and a clock radio. Some have coffeemakers and minirefrigerators. A complimentary *Globe and Mail* is delivered to all rooms.

In addition to an attractive restaurant and lounge, as well as a lobby bar, room service is available from 7am to 2pm; laundry and valet service is also available.

Quality Hotel. 111 Lombard St. (between Adelaide and Richmond sts.), Toronto, ON, M5C 2T9. ☎ **416/367-5555.** Fax 416/367-3470. 195 rms and suites. A/C TV TEL. $109 double. AE, DC, DISC, MC, V. Parking $9.75 Subway: King or Queen.

Formerly a Journey's End, the Quality Hotel has modern rooms fully appointed with color TVs and jade-and-rose or gray-blue decor. Features include complimentary local phone calls, and a newspaper.

INEXPENSIVE

Hostelling International. 90 Gerrard St. W., Toronto, ON, M5G 1J6. ☎ **416/971-4440.** Fax 416/971-4088. 175 beds. A/C. $22.50 per person in a two-bedded room MC, V. Subway: College/Queen's ParkDundas.

This downtown youth hostel contains 175 beds, all in either two- or four-bedded rooms. There's a comfortable lounge with a couch and TV, a kitchen, and laundry facilities. Washrooms are on every floor. Other facilities include an indoor pool, two tennis courts, gymnasium with weight room, exercise machines, and basketball courts. The hostel is open 24 hours.

Neil Wxycik College Hotel. 96 Gerrard St. E. (1 block east of Yonge), Toronto, ON, M5B 1G7. ☎ **800/268-4358** in Canada and the northeastern U.S., or 416/977-2320. Fax 416/977-2809. 300 rms. $53–$57 double (10% discount for 7 days or more). MC, V. Mid-May to late Aug. Parking $8 nearby. Subway: College.

From mid-May to late August, the Neil Wycik College Hotel offers modern, clean accommodations to travelers at extremely reasonable rates. Since these are primarily student accommodations, rooms have no air-conditioning and no TVs, and contain only the most essential furnishings—a bed, chair, and desk. Each unit contains five bedrooms (singles, twins, and a family room), two washrooms, a kitchen (with fridge and stove but no utensils), and a common room. Linen, towels, and daily housekeeping are provided. The facilities include a TV lounge, a rooftop sundeck, a sauna, a laundry room, and a cafeteria in which you can secure a full breakfast for $4 or less.

The Strathcona. 60 York St., Toronto, ON, M5J 1S8. ☎ **416/363-3321.** Fax 416/363-4679. 196 rms and suites. A/C TV TEL. $90 double. AE, DC, ER, MC, V. Parking: $12.50 Subway: Union.

Currently one of Toronto's best buys, the Strathcona is located right across from the Royal York Hotel, within easy reach of all downtown attractions. Although the rooms are small, they are decently furnished with modern blond-wood furniture, gray carpeting, and brass floor lamps. Each has a phone, a color TV, and a private bath.

The coffee shop/restaurant is open daily; there's also a luncheon snack bar and a lounge with a large-screen TV for sports watching. Room service is offered from 6am to 7pm. The Stratcona offers a great location at a great price.

3 Midtown

The midtown area runs north from College/Carlton Street between Spadina Avenue and Jarvis Street to where Dupont crosses Yonge Street.

VERY EXPENSIVE

Inter-Continental. 220 Bloor St. W., Toronto, ON, M5S 1T8. ☎ **416/960-5200.** Fax 416/960-8269. 209 rms. A/C MINIBAR TV TEL. $210–$285 double. AE, DC, JCB, MC, V. Parking $22 valet. Subway: St. George.

The Inter-Continental, conveniently located on Bloor Street at St. George, is small enough to provide excellent, very personal service from the minute you enter the small but rich-looking marble lobby. The rooms are spacious and well furnished with comfortable French-style armchairs and love seats. The marble bathrooms, with separate showers, are large and equipped with every imaginable amenity—each has a dual-line telephone with a personal computer/fax hookup; a clothesline; large fluffy towels; a bathrobe; a scale; and a full range of soaps, lotions, and more. Extra special room features include closet lights, a large desk-table, a clock radio, a full-length mirror, and windows that open.

Dining/Entertainment: Signatures offers fine dining with dinner entrees priced from $21 to $25. The attractive, comfortable Harmony Lounge, with its marble bar, fireplace, and cherry paneling, is a pleasant retreat for afternoon tea or cocktails accompanied by piano entertainment. From here, French doors lead out to an inviting patio.

👪 Family-Friendly Hotels

Delta Chelsea Inn *(see p.46)*   This hotel has always been on the cutting edge of the hospitality industry, and their Family Fun rooms attest to this. They're jam-packed with lots to do: in-room family movies, Super Nintendo, bubble bath, and such extras as a nighttime gift, night-light, and a cookie jar with a supply of cookies that's refreshed daily. The Delta Kids Have Fun program for kids aged 3 to 12 sponsors special activities in the Children's Creative Centre and throughout the hotel. When kids check in at the life-size gingerbread house, they get a registration card and passport. Children 6 and under eat free; kids 7 to 12 eat for half-price. All this goes a long way toward creating a smooth and more economical family stay.

The Four Seasons *(see p.56)*   Free bicycles, video games, and the pool should keep most kids occupied. The meals served in Animal World wicker baskets or on Sesame Street plates, and the complimentary room-service cookies and milk on arrival make them feel special. To top it all off, housekeeping provides all the amenities parents need.

Services: 24-hour room service, laundry/valet, twice-daily maid service, nightly turndown, concierge, complimentary shoe-shine and newspaper.

Facilities: Lap pool with adjacent patio; fitness room with treadmill, bikes, Stairmaster, and Paramount equipment; sauna and massage room; business center.

The Park Plaza. 4 Avenue Rd., Toronto, ON, M5R 2E8. ☎ **416/924-5471** or 416/977-4197. Fax 416/924-4933. 224 rms, 40 suites. A/C MINIBAR TV TEL. Prince Arthur Tower, $190 double; Plaza Tower, $215 double. Extra person $15. Weekend and other packages available. Children under 18 stay free in parents' room. AE, DC, DISC, MC, V. Parking $17. Subway: Museum or Bay.

The Park Plaza, located in fashionable Yorkville, is close to the ROM and the planetarium. All 64 rooms and 20 suites in the original Plaza Tower, built in 1935, were recently renovated and have been redecorated to exceptionally high standards. The rooms are very tastefully furnished in a candy-stripe style, with brass and glass accents. Each is fully equipped with the latest conveniences, including a clock radio, two phones (one in the bathroom), louvered closets, and full-length mirror. The marble bathroom has a hair dryer, makeup mirror, bathrobe, and full amenities. Suites have additional features such as scales and two-line telephones that can be hooked up to faxes and personal computers. The Plaza Tower rooms are more expensive than the 180 rooms in the Prince Arthur Tower because they are more lavish. The latter rooms, though, are large and well furnished, with full facilities, including TVs, push-button phones, hair dryers, and minibars.

Dining/Entertainment: The Prince Arthur Garden Restaurant is a popular city brunch and lunch spot. Chandeliers ring the room, and there's always a brilliant floral centerpiece. The main dining room, the Roof Restaurant, is on the 18th floor, adjacent to the lounge that has attracted so many Toronto literati. Their books are showcased and portrait sketches of them grace the walls of this comfortable room. The inviting couches, wood-burning fireplace, and marble-top tables make it a perfect venue for viewing the city's skyline. In summer, the outdoor terrace is great for twilight dining. Main dishes in the dining room range from $20 to $30.

Midtown Toronto Accommodations

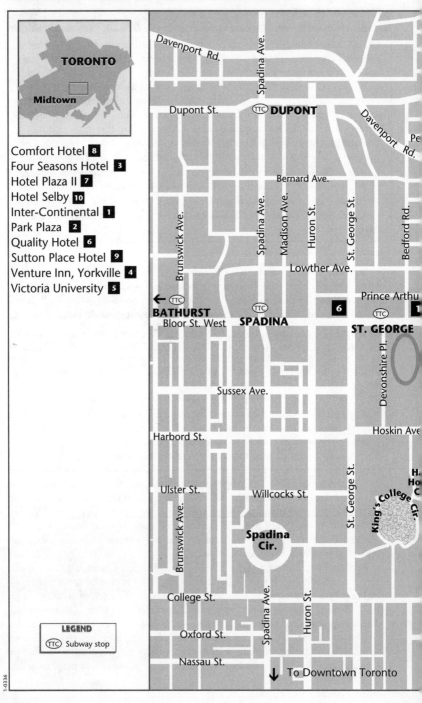

Comfort Hotel **8**
Four Seasons Hotel **3**
Hotel Plaza II **7**
Hotel Selby **10**
Inter-Continental **1**
Park Plaza **2**
Quality Hotel **6**
Sutton Place Hotel **9**
Venture Inn, Yorkville **4**
Victoria University **5**

LEGEND
TTC Subway stop

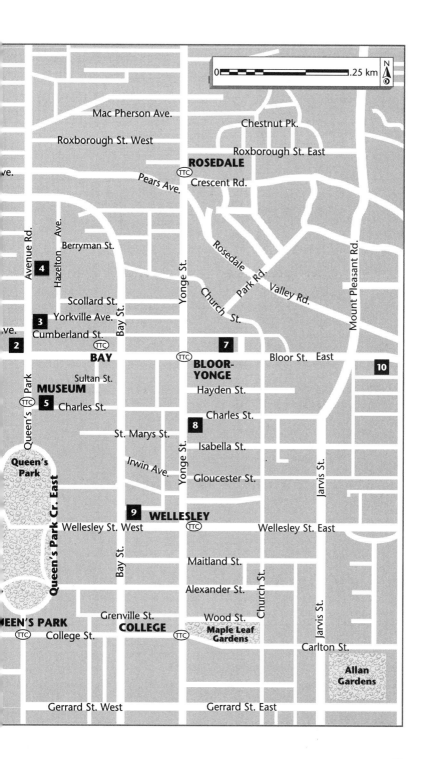

Services: 24-hour room service, laundry/valet, complimentary newspaper and shoe-shine, concierge.

Facilities: Business center; off-site fitness privileges.

The Sutton Place Hotel. 955 Bay St., Toronto, ON, M5S 2A2. ☎ **800/268-3790** or 416/924-9221. Fax 416/924-1778. 292 rms, 62 suites. A/C MINIBAR TV TEL. $215 double; from $290 suite. Extra person $20. Children under 18 stay free in parents' room. Weekend rates available. AE, DC, JCB, MC, V. Parking $19. Subway: Museum or Wellesley.

A small luxury hotel, the Sutton Place attracts a celebrity and business clientele. It has a European flair that is exhibited in the decor and the service. Throughout the public areas you will find antiques, old-master paintings, 18th-century Gobelins, Oriental carpets, and crystal chandeliers. The very spacious rooms are luxuriously furnished in a French style and each contains a couch and desk. All have remote-control color TVs and hair dryers. The suites have bathrobes and also, for business travelers, two telephones allowing hookup to a fax or PC.

Dining/Entertainment: Accents Restaurant is a relaxed bistro-style restaurant and bar that's also a popular Sunday brunch spot, where you can choose your main dish from an à la carte menu or combine it with selections from the salad and dessert buffets. My favorite brunch selection has to be the French toast with cinammon and nutmeg drizzled with honey, lime, and sliced bananas. At dinner, prices range from $17 to $22 for such dishes as grilled veal medallions wrapped in prosciutto in a black olive jus with potato basil beignets, or the casserole of sea scallops with leek and black truffle fondue and smoked tomato sauce. Breakfast and lunch are served, as well as a special light menu in the bar. A late afternoon tapas menu and jazz are offered on weekends.

Services: 24-hour room service, valet pickup, complimentary newspaper and shoe-shine, twice-daily maid service, concierge, beauty salon, limousine to the financial district.

Facilities: Indoor pool with sundeck, sauna, massage, fully equipped fitness center, business center.

EXPENSIVE

Comfort Hotel. 15 Charles St. E., Toronto, ON, M4Y 1S1. ☎ **800/228-5150** in the U.S. and Canada, or 416/924-7381. Fax 416/927-1369. 113 rms. A/C TV TEL. $99 double. Weekend rates available. AE, DISC, MC, V. Parking $9. Subway: Bloor.

The Comfort Hotel is a small, pleasant place. The rooms are large; they're furnished with light-oak pieces and have full amenities.

The restaurant, which is plush and comfortable day or night, serves a continental dinner menu. Prices begin at $11.50. Piano entertainment is provided on weekends. The hotel is ideally situated less than 100 yards off Yonge Street and only two blocks south of Bloor. A fully equipped health club is nearby and open to hotel guests for $10 a day.

Hotel Plaza II. 90 Bloor St. E., Toronto, ON, M4W 1A7. ☎ **800/267-6116** or 416/961-8000. Fax 416/961-4635. 238 rms, 18 suites. A/C MINIBAR TV TEL. From $175 double; from $270 suite. Extra person $15. Children under 18 stay free in parents' room. Weekend packages available. AE, DC, DISC, JCB, MC, V. Parking $18. Subway: Bloor.

Occupying the 7th to 12th floors of a multiuse complex, the Hotel Plaza II is designed around an inner cobblestone courtyard with flowers, shrubbery, and trees. The lobby is on the street level.

All the rooms have double beds and are tastefully decorated. Appointments include the standard ones listed above as well as clock radios, makeup mirrors, hair dryers, and in-house movies. Plaza Club rooms have a concierge and private lounge.

The restaurant, Matisse, pays homage to the artist with floor-to-ceiling replicas of his paintings. It serves all day, featuring California-style cuisine with Asian/European accents—roast salmon with a wasabi cream, all spiced pork chop with corn fritters and maple and apple glazed squash—priced from $14 to $22. There's also a bar.

Room service is available from 7am to 11pm; twice daily maid service, laundry and valet service, a concierge, complimentary shoe-shine, and nightly turndown are also offered. Squash, sauna, and whirlpool facilities are in the Bloor Park Club in the building.

Quality Hotel. 280 Bloor St. W. (at St. George), Toronto, ON, M5S 1V8. ☎ **416/968-0010.** 212 rms. A/C TV TEL. $130 double. Weekend and other packages available. AE, DC, DISC, MC, V. Parking $11.50.

Part of the well-known chain, this hotel is only a few blocks west of the Inter-Continental and represents a great value for the location. Rooms are modern and well equipped, with remote-control cable TVs and modern light furnishings, including useful well-lit work tables. There's a restaurant and coffee shop, too.

Venture Inn, Yorkville. 89 Avenue Rd., Toronto, ON, M5R 2G3. ☎ **800/387 3933** or 416/964-1220. Fax 416/964-8692. 71 rms. A/C TV TEL. $110 double. Extra person $10. Rate includes continental breakfast. AE, DC, DISC, MC, V. Parking $6. Subway: Bloor, Bay or St. George.

A clean, no-frills hotel in exclusive Yorkville, the Venture Inn is a good value. The modern rooms are attractively furnished in pine. Laundry and dry-cleaning services are available.

INEXPENSIVE

Hotel Selby. 592 Sherbourne St., Toronto, ON, M4X 1L4. ☎ **800/387-4788** or 416/921-3142. Fax 416/923-3177. 67 rms (59 with bath). A/C TV TEL. $75–$95 double; $100–$125 suite. All rates include continental breakfast. AE, MC, V. Limited free parking on first-come first-serve basis; otherwise $8.

This hotel, located in a large heritage Victorian, represents a great downtown bargain. The clientele, a mixture of gay and straight couples, seems to enjoy the comfortable lobby/sitting area with a chandelier and a fireplace near the front desk downstairs. The rooms are individually decorated with an eclectic mix of furniture. Ceilings are high, making the rooms airy and dramatic; many have stucco decoration and moldings. In several rooms, the old bathroom fixtures have been retained. Furnishings include a couch, a TV, and a phone. There's a large walk-in closet, and the bathroom has a claw-foot tub and pedestal sink. Notable rooms include the very large Hadley-Hemingway Suite, which boasts a fireplace; the Gooderham Suite, with a brass-hooded fireplace, an oak dresser, a couple of wingbacks, and a small tub with a shower in the bathroom; and room 401, with an old-fashioned burled-wood bed, angled ceilings, track lighting, and a pair of leatherette wingbacks. There's also a coin laundry on premises. Guests have access to a nearby health club for a small charge.

Victoria University. 140 Charles St. W., Toronto, ON, M5S 1K9. ☎ **416/585-4524.** 425 rms (none with bath). $62 double. Rate includes breakfast. MC, V. Discounts available for seniors and students. Early May to late Aug. Subway: Museum.

Summer visitors can stay at Victoria University, right across from the Royal Ontario Museum, in a 425-room university residence. Each accommodation is furnished as a study/bedroom and is supplied with fresh linen, towels, and soap. Bathrooms are down the hall. Guests enjoy free local calls and use of laundry facilities as well as access to the dining and athletic facilities, which include tennis courts.

4 Uptown

VERY EXPENSIVE

✪ **The Four Seasons Hotel.** 21 Avenue Rd., Toronto, ON, M5R 2G1. ☎ **800/268-6282** or 416/964-0411. Fax 416/964-2301. 210 rms, 170 suites. A/C MINIBAR TV TEL. $280–$350 double; from $370 suite. Weekend rates available. AE, DC, JCB, MC, V.Parking $19. Subway: Bay.

Located in the heart of the Bloor-Yorkville area, the Four Seasons has a well-deserved reputation for consistently fine and highly personal service, attention to detail, quiet but unimpeachable style, and total comfort. The lobby, with its marble and granite floors, Savonnerie carpets, and stunning fresh-flower arrangements, epitomizes this style.

The spacious rooms are furnished with king-size, queen-size, or twin beds and boast dressing rooms and marble bathrooms. The table lamps are porcelain, the furnishings elegant, and the fabrics plush. All rooms are air-conditioned and have re-mote-control color TVs, AM/FM radios, and terry-cloth bathrobes. Extra amenities include hair dryers, makeup and full-length mirrors, tie bars, closet safes, and windows that open. Corner rooms have balconies. Four Seasons Executive Suites each have an additional seating area separated from the bedroom by French doors, two TVs, and a deluxe telephone with two lines and conference-call capacity. Nonsmoking rooms and special rooms for those with disabilities are available.

Dining/Entertainment: Truffles, on the second floor, has been named one of the world's 10 great hotel restaurants (see chapter 5 for a review). Two sculptures of Uffizi wild boars adorn the entrance to the lavish dining area which features murals, ceramics, and furniture designed by Canadian artists. Only the finest materials have been used in the design elements, such as the curly maple walls and the magnificent mar-quetry floor crafted from 11,000 pieces of walnut, oak, jojoba, and purple-heart wood. The tables are amply spaced and the cuisine is extraordinary.

The Studio Cafe, which has become the city's place to see and be seen, serves meals all day. It features an open kitchen, and is filled with light. The modern Italian de-cor and furnishings include gorgeous Gianni Versace fabrics on the tables and display cases filled with original glass artworks, all of which are for sale. The menu is inspired by the Mediterranean and offers several gourmet pizzas (delicious!), pastas, salads, and light entrees—such as black tiger shrimp stir-fry with hoisin sauce or grilled double lamb chops with roasted garlic aioli, all priced from $10 to $22. A luncheon buffet and evening hors d'oeuvres are served in La Serre, which also features entertainment in the evenings. The Lobby Bar serves a traditional afternoon tea. There are special kids' menus, too, with meals served either in Animal World wicker baskets or on Sesame Street plates.

Services: 24-hour concierge, 24-hour room service and valet pickup, 1-hour pressing, complimentary shoe-shine, twice-daily maid service, baby-sitting, doctor on call, children's activities, weekday courtesy limo to downtown, complimentary coffee and newspaper.

Facilities: Business center; health club with indoor/outdoor pool, whirlpool, Universal equipment, and massage; free bicycles and video-game units for children.

Best Western Roehampton Hotel. 808 Mount Pleasant Rd., Toronto, ON, M4P 2L2. ☎ **800/387-8899** or 416/487-5101. Fax 416/487-5390. 110 rms and suites. A/C TV TEL. From $105 double. Special discount packages available. AE, DC, DISC, ER, MC, V. Parking $6.45. Subway: Eglinton.

Situated at the center of the Eglinton Avenue business district, the Roehampton has spacious, recently renovated rooms. The corner rooms are especially large and attractive, with pleasant views. All units are well equipped with color TVs and individual climate control; some have refrigerators. Champs sports lounge/restaurant serves an all-day menu; room service is available from 11am to 11pm. Laundry and valet service and an outdoor rooftop pool and sundeck on the third floor round out the hotel's features.

5 At the Airport

VERY EXPENSIVE

Bristol Place Hotel. 950 Dixon Rd., Rexdale, ON, M9W 5N4. ☎ **416/675-9444.** Fax 416/675-4426. 287 rms and suites. A/C MINIBAR TV TEL. $220 double; from $285 suite. Extra person $15. Children under 18 stay free in parents' room. Special packages available. AE, DC, DISC, JCB, MC, V. Free parking. Subway: Kipling.

For really personal service—the kind that caters to the idiosyncrasies of each guest—and ultrachic surroundings, try the Bristol Place, a select hotel where contemporary architecture and facilities blend with old-fashioned attention to detail and service. Outside, the redbrick building is striking enough, but step into the lobby and it's stunning. It soars three stories to a skylit ceiling through which the sun dances on the trees, sculptures, mosaics, and contemporary wall hangings. The sound of the waterfall alone made me want to stay.

The standard rooms are beautifully designed, decorated, and appointed. Each has custom-made contemporary furniture, double or king-size beds, geometric design throws, two telephones, a color TV, a bedside console, an alarm clock, and large parlor lights in the bathroom.

Dining/Entertainment: Le Café, raised slightly to overlook the lobby, is a plush coffee shop with comfortable banquettes and handmade ceramic tiles. Zachary's dining room is delightfully contemporary and graced with a kaleidoscopic tapestry hung over white tile. The dinner specialties range from $25 to $30, and may include monkfish on yellow squash ratatouille and white wine tomato coulis or medallions of veal on wild mushroom strudel with Madeira wine glaze.

Services: 24-hour room service, laundry/valet, concierge, supervised kids' program.

Facilities: Indoor/outdoor pool with skylight dome and sundeck; flower gardens; reflecting pools; children's play area; health club with exercise room, sunroom, sauna.

EXPENSIVE

Regal Constellation Hotel. 900 Dixon Rd., Etobicoke, ON, M9W 1J7. ☎ **416/675-1500.** Fax 905/675-4611. 708 rms and suites. A/C TV TEL. $130–$160 double. Extra person $15. Children under 16 stay free in parents' room. Weekend and honeymoon packages available. AE, DC, DISC, MC, V. Free parking. Subway: Kipling.

Even though it's an old and very large hotel, the Constellation still has a certain elegance—former Prime Minister Lester Pearson liked to stay here when he came to Toronto, and many celebrities still do.

Although built almost 35 years ago, the Constellation has expanded so often that its rooms offer a myriad of different styles. Color schemes run from beige to green. Every room is a minisuite featuring L-shaped sofas, large desks, king-size or twin/double-bed arrangements, and a color TV with in-house movies.

The hotel is a veritable entertainment and dining complex, with the Atrium off the main lobby for all-day buffet dining, the Grill specializing in steaks and other grilled items, the Mikasa offering Japanese fare, and even a Chinese restaurant. At night, you can sit under a spreading banyan tree overlooking a tropical garden and enjoy a cocktail or dance to live entertainment in the Banyan Tree bar.

There's 24-hour room service; other services include a concierge, dry cleaning, and baby-sitting. An unusual indoor/outdoor pool (it's shaped like a river around a tropical island and reached by small wooden footbridges), a bank, a hair salon, and a full recreation complex with exercise room and saunas round out the hotel's facilities.

Sheraton Gateway at Terminal Three. Toronto AMF, Box 3000, Toronto, ON, L5P 1C4. ☎ **800/565-0010** or 905/672-7000. Fax 905/672-7100. 474 rms, 6 suites. A/C MINIBAR TV TEL. $190–$210 double. AE, DC, DISC, ER, MC, V. Parking: $4.

Connected by skywalk to Terminal 3, this is the most convenient place to stay at the airport. All rooms are soundproofed and luxuriously decorated, containing all the expected amenities, including hair dryers. For travelers it's also convenient to be able to view flight departure and arrival times on your own personal TV.

Three buffets are served daily in the Café Suisse while the Mahogany Grill is reserved for fine dining (main dishes $16–$30). There's also a bar featuring nightly piano entertainment. Room service is available from 5am to 1am. Other facilities include a hair salon, indoor pool, whirlpool, and exercise center.

Toronto Airport Hilton International. 5875 Airport Rd., Mississauga, ON, L4V 1N1. ☎ **800/567-9999** or 905/677-9900. Fax 905/677-7782. 413 rms, 154 minisuites. A/C MINIBAR TV TEL. $219 double; minisuites from $229 double. Extra person $20. Children stay free in parents' room. Weekend packages available. AE, CB, DC, DISC, ER, MC, V. Free parking. Take the Gardiner Expressway west to Hwy. 427 north, to Airport Expressway (Dixon Rd. exit).

The Airport Hilton has all the comfort and conveniences associated with the Hilton name. A 12-story tower added to the hotel contains minisuites, each featuring separate bedroom, bathroom, and parlor areas. Each minisuite comes fully equipped with a king-size bed, a sofa bed, two color TVs, three telephones, a table for working or dining, a minibar, a hair dryer, a bathrobe, and individually controlled air-conditioning and heating. The rest of the hotel's 259 rooms contain all the expected appurtenances: queen-size beds, bedside remote-control consoles, color TVs with in-house movies, louvered closets, bathrooms with telephones, and minibars.

The Harvest Restaurant/Café features international cuisine; Latte Seattle offers coffee and snacks. Misty's club is well known for its musically themed evenings—from country to reggae (Wed to Sun). There's 24-hour room service, laundry and valet service; baby-sitting can be arranged. An outdoor heated pool with poolside deck, squash and racquetball courts, an exercise room, and business services are available for guests' use.

MODERATE

Best Western Carlton Place Hotel. 33 Carlson Court, Toronto, ON, M9W 6H5. ☎ **800/528-1234** or 416/675-1234. Fax 416/675-3436. 524 rms. A/C TV TEL. $135–$150 double. Extra person $15. AE, DC, DISC, ER, MC, V. Subway: Kipling.

Best Western's Carlton Place Hotel offers modern rooms, each equipped with two telephones and a hair dryer, among other expected amenities from this chain; some rooms have minibars. The public areas have that light-pine, wicker, and tile look. Willow Tree restaurant offers all-day dining. There's also 24-hour room service, an indoor swimming pool, a sauna and whirlpool, exercise room, and laundry room.

Days Inn—Toronto Airport. 6257 Airport Rd., Mississauga, ON, L4V 1N1. ☎ **800/325-2525,** or 905/678-1400 in the northeastern U.S. and eastern Canada. Fax 905/678-9130. 200 rms. A/C TV TEL. $107 double. Extra person $10. Children under 18 stay free in parents' room. Weekend packages available. AE, DC, DISC, ER, JCB, MC, V. Free parking. Subway: Kipling.

The Days Inn offers facilities similar to those of the larger hotels on the airport strip, but at lower prices. It's a small, friendly place set in a streamlined seven-story block. The lobby has a comfy air with its natural-stone fireplace. The rooms are bright and airy and feature natural-pine furniture, beige-and-brown color schemes, color TVs, phones, individual climate control, and a vanity outside each bathroom.

In the Steak and Burger, carefully tended plants and flowers are set in an actual greenhouse wall and are complemented by exposed brick and a host of Canadian artifacts—a steeple clock, Staffordshire figures, and other ceramics. Room service is available from 6am to 11pm; there's an indoor pool and exercise room, and squash courts are available at an affiliated health club.

Delta's Meadowvale Inn. 6750 Mississauga Rd. (at Hwy. 401), Mississauga, ON, L5N 2L3. ☎ **905/821-1981.** Fax 905/542-4036. 374 rms, 5 suites. A/C TV TEL. $190 double. Weekend packages available. AE, DC, DISC, MC, V. Free parking. Subway: Yorkdale; then GO bus to the hotel.

The Meadowvale has a cozy, rustic ambiance that's brought about by the use of wood and brass in the hotel's decor, and the fireplace in the lobby. Here you'll find 374 fully appointed rooms with balconies. Fifteen executive rooms have turndown service, complimentary newspapers, bathrobes, and other extra amenities. All rooms have 24-hour room service, and laundry and valet service. There's also an indoor pool; indoor tennis, racquetball, and squash courts; an exercise room; and a creative center for children.

Four Points Hotel. 5444 Dixie Rd. (at Hwy. 401), Mississauga, ON, L4W 2L2. ☎ **800/737-3211** or 905/624-1144. Fax 416/624-9477. 289 rms, 8 suites. A/C TV TEL. $188 double. Extra person $12. Weekend rates are lower. AE, DC, DISC, ER, MC, V. Free parking. Subway: Kipling.

Located on a 6-acre woodland site 10 minutes from the airport, the Four Points Hotel has natural-oak walls and trim in the lobby, plenty of plants scattered throughout, and clean, comfortable rooms. There's a restaurant on the premises, as well as 24-hour room service and laundry/valet service; baby-sitting can also be arranged. An indoor pool, sauna, and exercise room round out the facilities.

Venture Inn at the Airport. 925 Dixon Rd., Etobicoke, ON, M9W 1J8. ☎ **800/387-3933** or 416/674-2222. Fax 416/674-5757. 283 rms. A/C TV TEL. $100 double. Extra person $10. Rate includes breakfast. AE, DC, ER, MC, V. Free parking. Take the Gardiner Expressway west to Hwy. 427 north, to Airport Expressway (Dixon Rd. exit).

This hotel is part of the moderately priced Venture Inn chain, which features modern rooms furnished in a country style. Complimentary breakfast is available, but there is no restaurant on the premises. Pat and Mario's is connected to the hotel, however, and there are plenty of other choices nearby. Facilities include an indoor pool, sauna, and whirlpool.

INEXPENSIVE

Comfort Inn—Airport. 240 Belfield Rd., Rexdale, ON, M9W 1H3. ☎ **416/241-8513.** Fax 416/249-4203. 122 rms. A/C TV TEL. $80 double. Extra person $8. AE, DC, MC, V. Free parking. Take Hwy. 27 north to Belfield Rd.

Off the airport strip, but close enough to be convenient, the Comfort Inn—Airport has modern rooms with up-to-date, color-coordinated decor and pine furnishings, plus individual climate control, color TVs, and phones.

6 Metro West

While this is not the most salubrious area in which to stay, it does have some low-cost motels. The best of the lot is the **Silver Moon,** 2157 Lakeshore Blvd. West (☎ 416/252-5051). It's situated in a row of motels along Lakeshore Boulevard that saw their heyday when Hwy. 2 was the main route into the city. The Silver Moon has 24 clean but basic rooms, all with air-conditioning, TVs, and telephones (local calls are free). A double costs $60 a night; parking is free.

7 Metro East

Accommodations here are conveniently located to the Metro Zoo, the science center, and Scarborough Town Centre, a vast shopping mall. Most charge in excess of $100 a night for a double room, and have few exceptional features. A couple accommodations have moderately priced rooms, and, as such, are a good value option.

There are a number of chain hotels in this area, including: **Embassy Suites,** 8500 Warden Ave., Markham, ON L6G 1A5 (☎ **905/470-8500**); **Holiday Inn,** 50 Estate Dr., Scarborough, ON M1H 2Z1 (☎ **416/439-9666**); **Radisson,** 1250 Eglinton Ave. East, Don Mills, ON M3C 1J3 (☎ **416/449-4111**); and **Sheraton,** 2035 Kennedy Rd., Scarborough, ON M1T 3G2 (☎ **416/299-1500**).

VERY EXPENSIVE

Prince Hotel. 900 York Mills Rd., Don Mills, ON, M3B 3H2. ☎ **800/323-7500** in the U.S., 800/268-7677 in Canada, or 416/444-2511. Fax 416/444-9597. 406 rms and suites. A/C MINIBAR TV TEL. $130–$175 double. Extra person $20. Children under 18 stay free in parents' room. Weekend packages available. AE, DX, MC, V. Free parking. Subway: York Mills.

Located 20 minutes from downtown, this luxury Japanese-owned resort hotel offers a quiet ambiance. It is set on 15 acres of private parkland where you can wander marked nature trails.

A warm, soft decor is found in the rooms, many of which have handsome bay windows or appealing balconies. Each of the oversize rooms has a marble bathroom with a hair dryer, a color TV with in-house movies, two telephones, and an in-room safe.

Dining/Entertainment: Le Continental features a walk-in cellar and fine cuisine with main courses priced from $19.50 to $27. Katsura, the specialty restaurant, has four separate dining areas, a tempura counter and sushi bar, tatami-style dining, teppanyaki-style cuisine, and a robata bar. Complete dinners range from $35 to $45. The Coffee Garden restaurant overlooks a grove of 30-foot-tall trees, as does the Brandy Tree, a sophisticated piano bar, restfully decorated in gray and plum.

Services: 24-hour room service, laundry/valet, nightly turndown, concierge, babysitting.

Facilities: Outdoor heated pool, sauna, tennis courts, fitness center, game room, putting green, nature trails.

MODERATE

Travelodge Scarborough. 20 Milner Business Court, Scarborough, ON, M1B 3C6. ☎ **800/578-7878** or 416/299-9500. Fax 416/299-6172. 160 rms. A/C TV TEL. $70 double. AE, DC, DISC, MC, V. Free parking. Subway: Scarborough Town Center.

The Travelodge has rooms containing color TVs with in-room movies, individual climate control, and attractive furnishings. There's a restaurant/lounge and an indoor pool and whirlpool.

Holiday Inn—Toronto East. 50 Estate Dr. (Markham Rd. and Hwy. 401), Scarborough, ON, M1H 2Z1. ☎ **800/387-3933** or 416/439-9666. Fax 416/439-4295 136 rms. A/C TV TEL. $80 double. Rate includes continental breakfast. Children under 19 stay free in parents' room. AE, DC, DISC, MC, V. Free parking. Subway: McCowan.

The Holiday Inn has pleasantly decorated rooms.

INEXPENSIVE

University of Toronto in Scarborough, Student Village. Scarborough Campus, University of Toronto, 1265 Military Trail, Scarborough, ON, M1C 1A4. ☎ **416/287-7369.** $148 for 2-night minimum stay per town house. Family rates available. Mid-May to the end of Aug. Free parking. Take the subway to Kennedy, then the Scarborough Rapid Transit to Ellesmere, then bus no. 95 or 95B to the college entrance.

From mid-May to the end of August, the University of Toronto in Scarborough, Student Village, has accommodations available in town houses that sleep four to six people and contain equipped kitchens. None has air-conditioning, a TV, or a telephone. There is a cafeteria, a recreation center (with squash and tennis courts, a gym, and an exercise room), as well as a laundry, a bank, and a bookstore on campus. The parklike setting is appealing.

A LOVELY RURAL RETREAT

The Guild Inn. 201 Guildwood Pkwy., Scarborough, ON, M1E 1P6. ☎ **416/261-3331.** Fax 416/261-5675. 80 rms, 6 suites. A/C TV TEL. $150 double, Extra person $10; children under 12 stay free in parents' room. Special packages available. AE, DC, ER, EU, MC, V. Free parking. Subway: Kennedy.

If you want to stay in a unique and beautiful setting, then try the Guild Inn, just 10 miles (about 20 minutes) outside the city. Enter through the broad iron gates and follow the circular drive, which is shaded by trees and bordered with flowers. The original entrance hall retains the character of an English manor, with its broad staircase, oak beams, and wrought-iron chandeliers.

The 90-acre grounds are dotted with historic architectural fragments, remnants from the Guild of All Arts, which once occupied the property. So many visitors were attracted by the Guild's collections and workshops that dining facilities and guest rooms were added, until the Guild became a flourishing country inn. During these halcyon years many notables visited, including Queen Juliana of the Netherlands, Dorothy and Lillian Gish, Moira Shearer, Rex Harrison, Sir John Gielgud, and Lilli Palmer.

The gardens at the rear sweep down to the Scarborough Bluffs, rising 200 feet above Lake Ontario, and for a room with this view you'll pay a little extra. The original central section of the inn was built in 1914, and the rooms here have been renovated. All 86 rooms have air-conditioning, AM/FM radios, color TVs, and private balconies.

Dining/Entertainment: The dining room is still a popular gathering place for Sunday brunch ($18), and it serves primarily grills, roasts, and seafood, priced from $17 to $26. In summer, cocktails are served outside on a lovely veranda.

Facilities: Outdoor swimming pool, tennis court, fitness room, nature trails.

5 Dining

The city's palate is wide-ranging and adventurous, making dining in Toronto a delightful round-the-world experience that can be enjoyed for a moderate price. Current trends seem to lean toward Latin and Mediterranean cuisine, with ever more concentrated doses of Southeast Asian and Pacific Rim flavors. You can eat at the fashionable hot spots, and by all means do so, but more fun, in my opinion, is to explore the city's neighborhoods and visit the ethnic dining spots in Little Italy, Little Portugal, Chinatown, and Greektown.

Another charming and welcome aspect of the city's dining scene is the incredible number of outdoor dining spots, and the tolerance extended to those of us who just want to linger for a few hours over an iced coffee or a lemonade. It's refreshing and very European in flavor. Supposedly there are 5,000-plus restaurants in the city. Below is a quick-reference list of 130 or so of my favorites organized by cuisine (with the neighborhood and an abbreviation of the price category in parentheses), followed by write-ups of each establishment, categorized by location and price.

SOME DINING NOTES   Although dining in Toronto can be expensive, it usually seems that way not so much because of the food, but because of the extras—like the 8% provincial sales tax on meals and the 7% GST. In addition, wine prices are higher than those in the United States, largely because of the tax on all imported wines. You will pay as much as $6 for a glass of house wine in the better restaurants, and as much as $25 for a 1-liter (1.1 qt.) carafe. Most wine lists start at around $25. There's also a 10% tax on all alcohol—keep in mind that the prices quoted often do not reflect that tax.

The price categories used here are rather broad: At luxury (or very expensive) establishments, expect to pay $120 and up for dinner for two without wine; expensive, $90 to $110; moderate, $60 to $90; and at inexpensive establishments, under $50. These, I stress, are only rough guidelines, and at many of the moderately and inexpensively priced establishments, you can pay much less by choosing carefully.

Unless stated otherwise, *the prices cited here are given in Canadian dollars*—good news for Americans because the Canadian dollar is worth 27% less than the American dollar but buys just about as much. As we go to press, $1 Canadian is worth 73¢ U.S., which means that your $50 dinner for two will cost only $36.50 U.S., and your $5 breakfast will cost only $3.65 U.S.

Locations are as follows: **Downtown** refers roughly to streets from the waterfront to and including College/Carlton Street between Spadina Avenue and Jarvis Street; **Midtown** refers to the area north of College/Carlton Street to Davenport and Yonge streets and also between Spadina and Jarvis; I have also further subdivided both of these sections into west and east. **Uptown** covers Yonge/Davenport Street and north.

1 Best Bets

- **Best for a Romantic Dinner:** Securing a table at **Lotus,** 96 Tecumseh St. (☎ 416/504-7620), is romance enough. What appears on your plate just enhances the experience—especially for couples who are as romantically attached to food as they are to each other.
- **Best for a Business Lunch: Jump Cafe and Bar,** 1 Wellington St. West (☎ 416/363-3400), is right in the heart of the financial district. Its patrons appreciate the well-spaced tables, the handsome surroundings, the up-to-the minute service and food, and the extensive selection of single malts and grappas at the bar.
- **Best for a Celebration:** At **N 44,** 2537 Yonge St. (☎ 416/487-4897), the room positively glows at night. Whatever you choose on the menu will be beautifully presented and taste exquisite. Accompany it with a selection from the extensive wine list (more than 300 choices), and then, when you've finished, take the party upstairs to the piano bar.
- **Best Decor: Palavrion,** 270 Front St. West (☎ 416/979-0060), has to be one of the most dramatic restaurants in the city for the way its decor combines colors and textures. Wall colors are brilliant—orange, yellow, and turquoise—and further illuminated with trompe l'oeil art—while the floors are studded with individually crafted art tiles.
- **Best View:** The 360° view from the **revolving restaurant** atop the **CN Tower,** 301 Front St. West (☎ 416/362-5411), is nothing short of amazing, and the food is somewhat better than most similarly located restaurants. Another contender is **Canoe,** on the 54th floor of the Toronto Dominion Bank Tower, 66 Wellington St. West (☎ 416/364-0054), which has terrific views and great food, but the views remain the same throughout your meal.
- **Best Wine List: The Acadian Room** at the Royal York hotel, 100 Front St. West (☎ 416/368-2511), has the best VQOA Canadian wine list; **Jump Cafe and Bar,** 1 Wellington St. West (☎ 416/363-3400), has the most eclectic and unique selection, including wines from South Africa; but **N 44,** 2537 Yonge St. (☎ 416/487-4897), offers the most well-rounded list, with more than 300 wines, 20 of which are available by the glass.
- **Best Bistro:** For honest, comforting bistro food, go to **Brownes Bistro,** 4 Woodlawn Ave. East (☎ 416/924-8132), along with the mink-coat crowd from Rosedale. Personally, I love the less traditional but much more exciting cuisine and decor at **Indulge,** 676 Queen St. West (☎ 416/504-5514).
- **Best Greek: Pan on the Danforth,** 516 Danforth Ave. (☎ 416/466-8158), offers contemporary Greek cuisine that goes far beyond the typical kebab house basics.
- **Best Italian:** The risottos and other Italian fare offered at **Biagio,** 157 King St. East (☎ 416/366-4040) are quite extraordinary, and the well-spaced tables make for a gracious dining experience. For a less imposing experience, I like **Trattoria**

Giancarlo, 41–43 Clinton St. at College (☎ 416/533-9619), where any grilled item will be perfectly done—without a hint of dryness—regardless of whether it's fish or meat. Uptown, **Pronto,** 692 Mount Pleasant Rd. (☎ 416/486-1111) is the best, with **Centro,** 2472 Yonge St. (☎ 416/483-2211) close at its heels.

- **Best Latin:** At **Xango,** 106 John St. (☎ 416/593-4407), diners can taste a full range of South American cuisines—from Ecuador, Chile, Peru, and Argentina. The flavors are tongue-tingling and fiery, though not distastefully so. There are beautifully served tropical drinks, too.

- **Best Portuguese:** At **Chiado,** 864 College St. at Concord Avenue (☎ 416/538-1910), diners will discover authentic Portuguese cuisine—fish dishes such as grilled filet of salted cod or *parrilhada* of seafood, and desserts like *natas do ceu,* a very rich cream dessert served over lady fingers and soaked with bitter almond liqueur.

- **Best Seafood:** Toronto is not a great city for fresh seafood, but at **Joso's,** 202 Davenport, just east of Avenue Road (☎ 416/925-1903), you'll always be presented with a good selection of fresh fish on a board, so you can select the freshest for cooking. The chef at Chiado also knows how to retain the subtlety and moisture of every fish he cooks, regardless of the preparation. Just as long as you don't mind the breast-and-buttocks decor.

- **Best Steak House: Barberian's,** 7 Elm St. (☎ 416/597-0225, or 416/597-0335), has been a Toronto institution for years, and still rates among the city's best places for a thick, juicy steak.

- **Best Desserts: Dufflet Pastries,** 787 Queen St. West (☎ 416/504-2870), is great for tarts and cakes, and in fact, supplies many of the city's restaurants; **Sicilian Ice Cream Company,** 710-712 College St. (☎ 416/531-7716), scoops the best ice cream and gelati. As far as restaurants go, there are many great places for dessert, but **Scaramouche,** 1 Benvenuto Place (☎ 416/961-8011), stands out for its wonderful crème brûlée, chocolate cake, and bread pudding. Innovative desserts, like coconut custard served with chocolate-dipped plantain chips, can found at **Xango,** 106 John St. (☎ 416/593-4407).

- **Best Late-Night Dining:** Greektown is the only place in Toronto where you can dine after midnight, until 3am or so, and there are several places along the strip that serve a full range of delicious, small dishes—**Ouzeri,** 500A Danforth Ave. (☎ 416/778-0500), **Myth,** 417 Danforth Ave. between Logan and Chester (☎ 416/461-8383), and **Christina's/Byzas,** 535 Danforth Ave. (☎ 416/778-1100), are the most popular.

- **Best People-Watching:** There's a very good chance you'll see some major visiting celebrities in the **Studio Cafe** at The Four Seasons Hotel, 21 Avenue Rd. (☎ 416/964-0411), or in **Bistro 990,** 990 Bay St. at St. Joseph (☎ 416/921-9990), near the Sutton Place hotel. Other good spying places are the restaurants along King Street in the theater district (especially **KitKat Bar & Grill,** 297 King St. West, ☎ 416/977-4461), or the private dining room at the **Left Bank,** 567 Queen St. West (☎ 416/504-1626).

- **Best Brunch:** Among Toronto's hotels, the two standouts for weekend brunch are **The Four Seasons,** 21 Avenue Rd. (☎ 416/964-0411), and Accents at **The Sutton Place,** 955 Bay St. (☎ 416/924-9221). The king of the restaurant Sunday brunch scene is **Mildred Pierce,** 99 Sudbury St. (☎ 416/588-5695). Their version of eggs Benedict—poached eggs with smoked salmon on a croissant, served with a Gorgonzola cream sauce—and their banana pecan pancakes with honey-bourbon butter sauce are especially good. For an old-fashioned honest-to-goodness egg breakfast, you can't beat **The Senator,** 99 Sudbury St. (☎ 416/588-5695).

2 Restaurants by Cuisine

ASIAN

Lotus (Downtown West, *VE*)
Tiger Lily's (Downtown West, *I*)

BURGERS

Hughie's Burgers
(Downtown West, *I*)
Toby's Goodeats (Midtown West, *I*)

CAJUN

Bayou Bistro (Downtown West, *M*)
N'Awlins (Downtown West, M)
Southern Accent
(Midtown West, *M*)

CANADIAN

Canoe (Downtown West, *E*)
Fred's Not Here Smokehouse and
Grill (Downtown West, *M*)
Red Tomato (Downtown West, *M*)

CHINESE

Kowloon Dim Sum
(Downtown West, *I*)
The Eating Counter
(Downtown West, *I*)
Lai Wah Heen
(Downtown West, *E*)
Lee Garden (Downtown West, *I*)
Pink Pearl (Downtown West, *M*)
Saigon Palace (Downtown West, *I*)
Wah Sing (Downtown West, *I*)
Young Lok Gardens
(Downtown West, *I*)

CONTINENTAL

Arlequin (Midtown West, *M*)
Chiaro's (Uptown, *VE*)
Herbs (Uptown, *M*)
Jacques Bistro du Park
(Midtown West, *M*)
Lakes (Midtown West, *M*)
La Maquette (Downtown East, *E*)
Mildred Pierce
(Downtown West, *M*)
Movenpick Bistretto
(Midtown West, *M*)

Movenpick Marche
(Downtown East, *I*)
Palavrion (Downtown West, *I*)
Rivoli (Downtown West, *I*)
Scaramouche (Uptown, *E*)
360 Revolving Restaurant
(Downtown West, *E*)
Trapper's (Uptown, *M*)
Truffles (Uptown, *VE*)

CREPES

Le Papillon (Downtown East, *I*)

DELI

The Bagel (Downtown West, *I*)
Shopsy's (Downtown East, *I*)

ECLECTIC

Avalon (Downtown West, *E*)
Cities (Downtown West, *M*)
Mildred Pierce
(Downtown West, *M*)
Jump Cafe and Bar
(Downtown West, *E*)
Zachary's (Uptown, *E*)

FRENCH

Azalea (Midtown West, *M*)
Bistro 990 (Midtown West, *E*)
Brasserie Les Artistes
(Downtown East, *M*)
Brownes Bistro (Uptown, *M*)
Centro (Uptown, *E*)
Chiaro's (Uptown, *VE*)
La Bodega (Downtown West, *M*)
La Grenouille (Uptown, *M*)
Left Bank (Downtown West, *M*)
Le Paradis (Uptown, *M*)
Le Rendez-Vous
(Midtown West, *M*)
Le Select (Downtown West, *M*)
Mildred Pierce
(Downtown West, *M*)
Opus (Midtown West, *E*)
St. Tropez (Downtown West, *M*)
Taro Grill (Downtown West, *M*)

Key to abbreviations: *I* = Inexpensive, *M* = Moderate, *E* = Expensive, and *VE* = Very Expensive

FUSION

Boba (Midtown West, *E*)
Indulge (Downtown West, *M*)
Lotus (Downtown West, *VE*)
Mercer Street Grill
(Downtown West, *E*)
Peter Pan (Downtown West, *M*)

GREEK

Astoria (Midtown East/
The East End, *I*)
Christina's/Byzas (Midtown East/
The East End, *I*)
Lolita's Lust (Midtown East/
The East End, *I*)
Myth (Midtown East/
The East End, *I*)
Omonia (Midtown East/
The East End, *I*)
Ouzeri (Midtown East/
The East End, *I*)
Pan on the Danforth (Midtown East/
The East End, *I*)

INDIAN

The Bombay Palace
(Downtown East, *I*)
Indian Rice Factory
(Midtown West, *I*)

INTERNATIONAL

N 44 (Uptown, *E*)
Queen Mother Cafe
(Downtown West, *I*)

ITALIAN

Acqua (Downtown East, *E*)
Biagio (Downtown East, *E*)
Centro (Uptown, *E*)
Coppi (Uptown, *M*)
Galileo (Downtown East, *E*)
Grano (Uptown, *M*)
Grappa (Midtown West, *M*)
Il Fornello (Downtown West, *I*)
Il Posto (Midtown West, *M*)
KitKat Bar & Grill
(Downtown West, *M*)
La Fenice (Downtown West, *E*)
Maccheroni (Downtown East, *I*)
Myth (Midtown East/
The East End, *I*)

N'Awlins (Downtown West, *M*)
Pronto (Uptown, *E*)
Spiaggia (Downtown East, *M*)
Splendido Bar and Grill
(Midtown West, *E*)
Trattoria Giancarlo
(Midtown West, *M*)

JAPANESE

Masa (Downtown West, *M*)
Mori (Midtown West, *I*)
Nami Japanese Seafood
(Downtown East, *E*)
Takesushi (Downtown East, *M*)

LIGHT FARE

Bloor Street Diner (Midtown East/
The East End, *I*)
Brownes Bistro (Uptown, *M*)

LAOTIAN

Vanipha (Downtown West, *I*)

LATIN AMERICAN

The Boulevard Café
(Midtown West, *I*)
Xango (Downtown West, *E*)

MEDITERRANEAN

Lolita's Lust (Midtown East/
The East End, *I*)
Messis (Midtown West, *M*)
Opus (Midtown West, *E*)
Taro Grill (Downtown West, *M*)

MIDDLE EASTERN

Aïda's Falafel (Midtown West, *I*)
Jerusalem (Uptown, *I*)
Kensington Kitchen
(Midtown West, *I*)

PACIFIC RIM

Sequoia Grove (Downtown West, *E*)

PORTUGUESE

Chiado (Midtown West, *E*)

QUÉBÉCOIS

Montréal Bistro and Jazz Club
(Downtown East, *M*)

SEAFOOD

Filet of Sole (Downtown West, *M*)
Joso's (Midtown West, *M*)
The Lobster Trap (Uptown, *E*)
Whistling Oyster Seafood Cafe
   (Downtown West, *M*)

STEAK

Barberian's (Downtown West, *E*)
The Senator (Downtown East, *E*)

SWISS

Movenpick Bistretto (Midtown
   West, *M*)

THAI

Thai Magic (Uptown, *M*)
Vanipha (Downtown West, *I*)
Young Thailand (Downtown East, *I*)

VEGETARIAN

Annapurna Restaurant (Midtown
   West, *I*)
Free Times Café (Downtown
   West, *I*)

VIETNAMESE

Saigon Palace (Downtown
   West, *I*)

3 Downtown West

There's plenty of pleasurable dining to choose from in this area. One of the best streets on which to look for a selection of reasonably priced bistros frequented by artists and young professionals is Queen Street West. Dining in the theater district is, as in most other cities, fraught with pitfalls—high prices and poor quality—but I describe some exceptions below.

VERY EXPENSIVE

✪ **Lotus.** 96 Tecumseh St. ☎ **416/504-7620.** Reservations imperative—at least 2 weeks in advance. Main courses $28–$30. AE, MC, V. Tues–Sat 6–10pm. ASIAN/FUSION.

Currently the city's premier dining experience for original, market fresh, and dynamically flavored cuisine. Located off King, west of Bathurst, Lotus focuses on its menu—not its ambiance. The storefront's decor is plain, with a tiny bar, a blush of color on one wall, and some herbed vinegar for decorative accent. That's it. But the quality and inspiration that has gone into the food has won chef Susur Lee accolades—which means that this small restaurant is booked a long time in advance. Susur Lee, who hails from Hong Kong, creatively combines European and Asian styles and flavors to produce such thrilling dishes as rack of lamb with Thai green curry sauce with mango chutney and fresh mint chutney; or chicken breast filled with wild mushrooms and foie gras and served with vegetable blinis with apricot and mustard sauce.

The menu changes daily. The desserts, which currently cost $8 or $9, range from a classic baked raspberry tart in a light custard with white-chocolate ice cream to Peking-style fig fritters with caramel ice cream, mango puree, and hot chocolate sauce. Note that as we go to press, it's rumored that Mr. Lee is moving to New York City, so don't be surprised if things have changed by the time this guide is published.

EXPENSIVE

✪ **Avalon.** 270 Adelaide St. W. at John. ☎ **416/979-9918.** Main courses $16–$30. AE, DC, MC, V. Wed–Fri noon–2:30pm; Tues–Thurs 5:30–10pm, Fri–Sat 5:30–11pm. ECLECTIC.

The room is small, comfortable, and elegant and the cuisine is fresh and expertly prepared by one of the city's premier young chefs. Climb the short marble staircase past the dramatic floral centerpiece and you'll find yourself in an elegant room with handsome demi-lune stained-glass windows. You'll sit on floral fabric-covered banquettes at tables with beautiful place settings. The menu changes daily, but will likely

Downtown Toronto Dining

1-0337

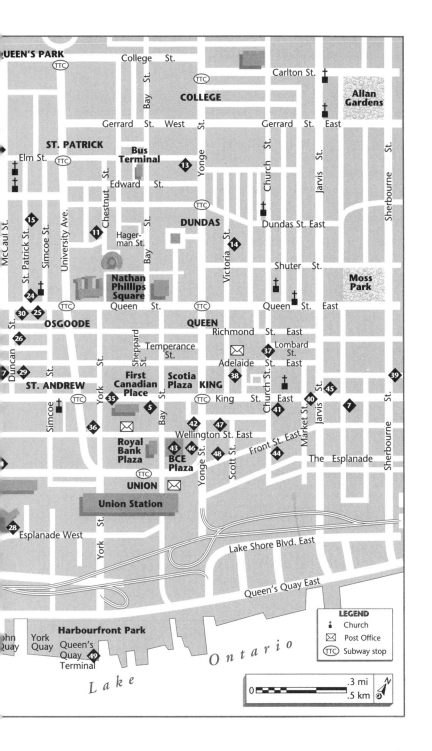

QUEEN'S PARK

College St.

Carlton St.

COLLEGE

Allan Gardens

Gerrard St. West

Gerrard St. East

ST. PATRICK

Bus Terminal

Elm St.

13

Edward St.

Church St.

Jarvis St.

Sherbourne St.

15

11

Hager-man St.

DUNDAS

Dundas St. East

Victoria St.

14

Shuter St.

Moss Park

Nathan Phillips Square

24

Queen St.

Queen St. East

30 25

OSGOODE

QUEEN

Richmond St. East

26

Temperance St.

Lombard St.

37

Adelaide St. East

7 29

ST. ANDREW

First Canadian Place

Scotia Plaza

KING

38

39

35

5

King St. East

45

40

7

Simcoe

36

41

42

47

Wellington St. East

Royal Bank Plaza

43 46

48

44

Front St. East

The Esplanade

Sherbourne St.

BCE Plaza

UNION

Union Station

York St.

28

Esplanade West

Lake Shore Blvd. East

Queen's Quay East

Harbourfront Park

John Quay

York Quay

Queen's Quay Terminal

49

O n t a r i o

L a k e

LEGEND
Church
Post Office
TTC Subway stop

.3 mi
.5 km
0

69

feature eight or so dishes prepared from the day's freshest seasonal ingredients. There might be a simple but tasty wood-roasted chicken with mashed potatoes and mushroom sauce, or perhaps, yellowfin tuna with fire-roasted pearl onions and preserved lemon salsa. Much of the produce is locally or organically raised. Appetizers are similarly inspired—on a recent visit, there were simple flavor-concentrated soups, and a particularly intriguing vegetable: asparagus with Vidalia onions and truffled walnut sauce. There's also a good, mixed wine list.

✪ **Barberian's.** 7 Elm St. ☎ **416/597-0225** or 416/597-0335. Reservations required. Main courses $19–$30. AE, DC, MC, V. Mon–Fri noon–2:30pm; daily 5pm–midnight. STEAK.

Steak houses, as far as I'm concerned, are usually rather dull establishments, but Barberian's is the best and brightest in town. The front half, both inside and out, remains essentially as built in 1860, and the three cozy interconnected rooms house a superb collection of Canadiana that includes several originals by the Group of Seven; a bust of Canada's first prime minister, Sir John A. Macdonald; one of the original grandfather clocks made in Canada; along with pre-Confederation money, coal-oil lamps, and firearms. Despite the traditional air, Barberian's exudes friendliness and lightness of touch.

Nonchalance does not extend to the food, however, which focuses on 10 or so steak and seafood dishes, all well worth the price. After 10pm, a fondue-and-dessert menu awaits the after-theater or late diner. The expensive wine list and decent martini selection suit the traditional crowd that dines here.

✪ **Canoe.** 54th floor Toronto Dominion Bank Tower, 66 Wellington St. W. ☎ **416/364-0054.** Main courses $18–$26. AE, DC, ER, MC, V. Mon–Fri 11:30am–2:30pm, 5–10:30pm. CANADIAN.

The foyer, with its framed autumn leaves, sets a natural tone for this restaurant, where the floors are fashioned from mushroom-stained walnut and the tables from cherry. On a clear day, the view is magnificent; when the clouds are low, and mist envelopes the tower, the setting is dramatic. The cuisine spotlights the very best Canadian ingredients (Digby scallops, Alberta beef, Grandview venison), and includes some spa-inspired dishes, such as grilled Northern walleye with a gratin of cauliflower and a horseradish vinaigrette. Full and expensive wine list. Great desserts, too.

✪ **Jump Cafe and Bar.** 1 Wellington St. W. ☎ **416/363-3400.** Reservations recommended for lunch and dinner. Main courses $17–$22. AE, DC, ER, MC, V. Mon–Fri 11:30am–4:30pm; Mon–Thurs 5–10pm, Fri–Sat 5–11pm. ECLECTIC.

A little hard to find, tucked away in Commerce Court, this is one of the city's power dining and drinking spots. It vibrates with energy. The streamlined atrium dining room has polished granite floors and warm maple tables; the grand space is broken up by palms and other strategically placed trees and shrubs. The bar area to the right of the entrance is presided over by a bust of Bacchus, and features a good selection of single malts and grappas. In summer, it's pleasant to sit out in Commerce Court.

In addition to the fresh daily specials, the menu features about nine dishes, such as grilled breast of chicken on hash-browned vegetables tossed with rosemary, honey and balsamic vinegar; grilled salmon on a Tuscan vegetable salad tossed with Geata olives, grilled tomato, and lemon; or roast rack of lamb on scallopped celeriac and sweet potato with roasted vegetables and stone-ground mustard sauce. There are also pizzas and pastas available. Among the desserts, I lust after the caramelized banana and chocolate bread pudding, but you may be seduced by the maple-glazed pecan pie with a Kentucky bourbon crème anglaise, or the dark chocolate fudge cake with white-chocolate ice cream and Bailey's Irish cream. The bar is so lively, it's sometimes hard to compete with the noise level of your fellow patrons.

✪ **La Fenice.** 319 King St. W. ☎ **416/585-2377.** Reservations recommended. Main courses $16–$26. AE, DC, MC, V. Mon–Fri noon–2:30pm; Mon–Sat 5:30–11pm. ITALIAN.

La Fenice's traditional northern Italian cuisine and understated decor draws a conservative business crowd. Really fresh ingredients and fine authentic olive oil are the hallmarks of its cuisine. There are 18 or so pasta dishes—*agnolotti al Gorgonzola e salvia* made with Gorgonzola, sage, and tomato, and also fettuccine salmonate with fresh salmon, dill, leeks, and cream are just a couple examples—plus a fine selection of Provimi veal, chicken, and fresh fish dishes. Dessert offerings include a refreshing raspberry sherbet, zabaglione, tiramisu, and fresh fruits in season. It can be noisy at La Fenice, and the service sometimes seems too precise and detached.

Lai Wah Heen. 110 Chestnut St. in the Metropolitan Hotel. ☎ **416/977-9899.** Main courses $10–$20 (with some dishes priced from $40 to $80). AE, DC, MC, V. Daily 11:30am–3pm; Sun–Thurs 5:30–10:30pm, Fri–Sat 5:30–11pm. CHINESE.

In Chinese, Lai Wah Heen means beautiful meeting place; and indeed, this restaurant is that, with two levels joined by broad black granite steps, and handsome, dramatically large pictograms decorating the walls. A specially equipped Cantonese kitchen delivers top quality Chinese food which has attracted many patrons from the local Chinese community. This is the place to try shark's-fin soup or abalone. There are six soups to choose from ranging from $12 to $60—the most expensive is a thickened chicken broth garnished with bean sprouts and Chinese cured ham. Similarly extravagant dishes can be found among the main courses—skillet-seared filet of garoupa nested on seaweed with crab bisque and topped with caviar, $55—along with more modest items, like the barbecued duckling in a coconut curry cream, or the oysters in a spiced Malaysian chili sauce. There's also a good selection of casseroles and rice and noodle dishes. At lunch, in addition to a short luncheon menu, there's a list of 44 dim sum to choose from. They're priced from $3.50 to $6.50.

Mercer Street Grill. 36 Mercer St. ☎ **416/599-3399.** Main courses $18–$27. AE, ER, MC, V. Mon–Fri noon–2:15pm; daily 5:15pm–closing (later on weekends than during the week). FUSION.

Great for pre- or posttheater dining, Mercer Street Grill has drawn rave reviews from local foodies for its inspired Asian fusion cuisine. Each finely prepared dish that emerges from the open kitchen in back is dramatically presented. Start with the handsome bucket of Prince Edward Island mussels steamed in a lemon-and-black-bean broth or the grilled Thai jumbo shrimp and scallops with a fresh mango roll and a sour orange vinaigrette. Each of the main dishes has a complex and enticing combination of flavors—from the roasted lemongrass chicken with wild mushroom rice, wok-fried greens and rosemary ginger jus to the pan-seared halibut with shrimp noodle cake, jade pesto, and ginger-glazed water chestnuts.

The dining room is sleek and modern with wood floors, and polished wooden tables set against olive drab walls with geometric mirrors as accents. The lighting is Milan modern, and the minimal decor is in keeping with the modern ambiance. Both lemon lovers and chocoholics are catered to with two spectacular desserts—the lemon treasure box, containing lemon cloud cake with a warm blueberry compote, lemon meringue tart, and shaved lemon ice, and the chocolate sushi, which are hand-rolled sheets of Belgian chocolate filled with raspberry, hazelnut, and white chocolate, and served with a raspberry nectar.

✪ **Sequoia Grove.** 14 Duncan St. ☎ **416/971-9708.** Main courses $12–$23. AE, ER, MC, V. Mon–Fri noon–3pm; daily 5–10:30pm. PACIFIC RIM.

An exhilarating place that is drawing rave reviews for its Pacific Rim–inspired cuisine as well as its dramatic high-ceilinged warehouse ambiance. A foyer featuring a cartographic mural plaster cast of Southeast Asia leads you into the airy, but somewhat noisy, main space. The decor within has a modern Italian feel, with laminated birch chairs set against exposed brick and ductwork, and halogen fixtures dressed in different-colored glass shades for light.

Out of the open kitchen come dishes charged with flavor. Among the highlights are the lobster taco served with Monterey Jack cheese, fresh coriander, grilled pineapple relish, and charred tomato salsa; and the tamarind-glazed half-smoked pork chops with green chili mole sauce. Dishes are either whipped up in the wok or else smoked or cooked slowly on the rotisserie. At the latter, the chef uses applewood, hickory, and mesquite to create such signature dishes as the spit-roasted ancho honey-glazed chicken cooked over applewood and served with jalapeno corn pudding and dried fruit compote. Don't stint on dessert either, for they are equally exciting, often juxtaposing idiosyncratic flavors, like the wonton Napoleon layered with coconut cream scented with Kaffir lime and served with a raspberry sauce. The wine list is predominantly Californian.

360 Revolving Restaurant. CN Tower, 301 Front St. W. ☎ **416/362-5411.** Main courses $18–$35. Daily lunch buffet $29.50 per person. Children's menu (ages 10 and under) $9.95. AE, DC, MC, V. Mon–Sun 10:30am–2:45pm and 4:30pm–10:15pm. CONTINENTAL.

Dining at such dizzy heights usually means that the view is terrific but the food is far from it. In this case, the food is almost equal to the view, even if some of the ingredients are a trifle rarefied, like the herb-seared steak of Canadian raised ostrich served with oyster mushroom and okra ratatouille. The menu certainly emphasizes Canadian ingredients—there's Angus beef, Aurora chicken, and New Brunswick salmon, the last served with a redolent smoked tomato vinaigrette.

The decor uses a lot of natural elements—stone, slate, wood, stainless steel, and glass, but it's not so inspiring that it distracts from the view. The art showcases on the interior walls are worth viewing, though. There's an excellent wine list with more than 275 wines.

✪ **Xango.** 106 John St. ☎ **416/593-4407.** Main courses $18–$24. AE, DC, MC, V. Tues–Fri noon–2:30pm; Mon–Sat 5–11pm. LATIN AMERICAN.

This restaurant is the major player in the latest trend toward authentic Latin cuisine. It's housed in an intimate, low-lit room furnished with wrought-iron chairs set on tile floors. There's a small outdoor balcony. Each dish is beautifully presented and so are the drinks—order a margarita and it will come in an extravagant art glass goblet. The cuisine is derived from several different Latin American countries. Among the specialty starters are the four or so ceviches. For me, the most flavorful is the Honduran version made with fresh tuna, chilies, ginger and fresh coconut. For a tasty vegetarian appetizer, select the *empanada cebolla*—an empanada filled with braised onions served with sliced pears, crumbled Spanish blue cheese, and walnut vinaigrette. Entrees range from the Peruvian *chupe*—fresh seafood in a spicy aji amarillo and lobster broth with roasted corn and potato—to the *vaca frita*, inspired more by Argentina, which consists of shredded and pan-seared skirt steak with pickled onions, *boniato* (similar to yams) puree, and a black-bean broth. These dishes are all well complemented by a wide selection of reasonably priced Spanish, South American, and Portuguese wines. Besides the daily selection of ice creams and sorbets, there are a few additional desserts like the chocolate flan with peanut brittle and whiskey cream and the coconut custard served with chocolate-dipped plantain chips.

MODERATE

Bayou Bistro. 275 Queen St. ☎ **416/977-7222.** Reservations recommended, especially at lunch. Main courses $7–$10 at lunch, $13–$17 at dinner. AE, DC, MC, V. Mon–Fri 11:30am–2:30pm; Mon–Thurs 5–10:30pm, Fri–Sat 5–11pm. CAJUN.

Bayou Bistro is a popular spot where the desserts are everyone's downfall—there's deep-fried ice cream with apple bourbon sauce, peanut-butter pie, and great sorbets, all freshly made. Start with crab cakes or a thick gumbo and follow with blackened salmon, shrimp Creole, or Jack Daniels pepper steak. There's always a pasta of the day, too. The atmosphere is light, modern, and informal—with bricks, poster art, and a maple bar.

Cities. 859 Queen St. W. ☎ **416/504-3762.** Main courses $12–$18. MC, V. Daily 5:30–10pm. ECLECTIC.

A small outpost, attracting a hip, young and not-so-young crowd, Cities offers great value. Tables are covered with butcher paper, chairs are basic black, and the art on the coral-colored walls is original. The cuisine is eclectic. Although the menu changes daily, you might find a tongue-tingling roasted red pepper soup or a three mushroom salad with warm walnut vinaigrette to start. Among the eight or so main dishes, there will always be a good balance between meat and seafood, such as a rack of lamb with rosemary infused glaze and, say, deep-sea scallops enhanced by a mango tarragon sauce. Their *tarte tatin* is as good as you'll find anywhere.

Filet of Sole. 11 Duncan St. ☎ **416/598-3256.** Reservations required 2 days in advance. Main courses $13–$40. AE, DC, MC, V. Mon–Fri noon–2:30pm; daily 5–11pm. SEAFOOD.

Conveniently located near the CN Tower and the theater district, this high-volume restaurant attracts theatergoers and conventioneers. Here, you'll find an oyster bar and an exhaustive seafood menu that also features daily specials. The restaurant serves everything from fish-and-chips to lobster with rice and a vegetable. Most of the dishes—bluefish, monkfish, red snapper, salmon, swordfish, tuna, mahi mahi, and many other varieties—are in the $13-to-$18 range. Daily specials have more zing to them, like the salmon steamed in a banana leaf with ginger, black-bean cilantro, and red curry sauce. For non–fish lovers, there's roasted chicken and several steak dishes. The dessert specialty is a frozen meringue basket filled with Grand Marnier, chocolate-pecan ice cream, fresh strawberries, and strawberry sauce—not to mention the chocolate truffle mousse and hot almond crepes. This is a bustling, busy, down-to-earth place.

Fred's Not Here Smokehouse and Grill. 321 King St. W. ☎ **416/971-9155.** Reservations recommended. Main courses $8–$11 at lunch, $13–$29 at dinner. AE, DC, MC, V. Mon–Fri noon–2pm; Mon–Sat 6–10pm. CANADIAN.

An extensive menu and lively bar scene attracts tourists and theatergoers to this down-stairs locale. The menu ranges from roasted rack of lamb in a Creole mustard crust with rosemary garlic jus, served with apple mint relish, to grilled salmon marinated in soya, rice vinegar, ginger, and thyme with mango pineapple salsa. The equally eclectic appetizers might include mixed dim sum along with New York State foie gras with burgundy poached pear and port vinaigrette. My favorites among the desserts are the pâté of white and dark chocolate with pistachio sauce and the banana fritters with caramel ice cream and chocolate sauce.

✪ Indulge. 676 Queen St. W. ☎ **416/504-5514.** Main courses $14–$20. MC, V. Tues–Thurs 5:30–10pm, Fri–Sat 5:30–11pm. FUSION.

An Important Note on Prices

Unless stated otherwise, **the prices cited in this guide are given in Canadian dollars,** which is good news for U.S. travelers because the Canadian dollar is worth 27% less than the American dollar, but buys nearly as much. As we go to press, $1 Canadian is worth 73¢ U.S., which means that your $100-a-night hotel room will cost only U.S. $73, and your $6 breakfast costs only U.S. $4.38.

Here's a quick table of equivalents:

Canadian $	U.S. $
$1	$0.73
$5	$3.65
$10	$7.30
$20	$14.60
$50	$36.50
$100	$73.00
$200	$146.00

In this small restaurant that seats roughly 40 people, George Betak creates his beguiling cuisine. He cooks in the open kitchen in the back; and on any given night, his eight richly flavored dishes might include beef tenderloin with smoked papaya guajillo pepper sauce, served with rosti potatoes and candied ginger; Caribbean-spiced baked grouper with plantain chips and nutty fruit coleslaw; or his signature dish, coconut-crusted rack of lamb served with wild mushroom purses. For an appetizer, order the southern spice king prawns flamed with tequila, and served with tropical fruit timbal and coriander oil, if they're on the menu. Original paintings by Toller Cranston line the deep purple walls.

KitKat Bar & Grill. 297 King St. W. ☎ **416/977-4461.** Main courses $14–$19. AE, DC, MC, V. Mon–Fri 11:30am–4pm; Mon–Thurs 4pm–11pm, Fri–Sat 4pm–midnight. ITALIAN.

Al Carbone presides over this restaurant at the heart of the theater district, making everyone who passes through the front door feel welcome and special. It's a favorite spot among American and Canadian on-camera personalities, journalists, TV and film producers and directors, and the occasional rock star or Hollywood actor. The room is long and narrow, the decor eclectic (old movie posters and cats); there's even a live tree rising up in the kitchen preparation area. You'll dine at tables spread with blue gingham tablecloths; the simple, comfort food includes such dishes as lemon chicken, honey garlic back ribs, steak, and several pasta choices. Eminently friendly and down-home. Singles are also made to feel very welcome. The Italian wine list is fairly priced.

La Bodega. 30 Baldwin St. ☎ **416/977-1287.** Reservations recommended for dinner. Main courses $13–$26; prix-fixe lunch $12.85, dinner $17.50. AE, DC, ER, MC, V. Mon–Fri noon–2:30pm; Mon–Sat 5–11pm. FRENCH.

Ensconced in an elegant town house, La Bodega, two blocks south of College and two blocks west of University Avenue, has been in business for more than 25 years. It's still a neighborhood favorite for its fine fresh food, moderate prices, and very comfortable atmosphere. The main menu features traditional French dishes—veal Calvados, steak au poivres—as well as a pasta of the day and usually a game dish.

Every day, the specials, usually inspired by the freshest produce at the market, are written on the blackboard menu. There's usually a dozen or so interesting choices, including several fresh fish dishes, such as horseradish encrusted monkfish. The best bet of all, though, is the prix fixe dinner for $17.50, offering a choice of two set menus—one meat, the other fish—with soup or salad and tea or coffee. At lunchtime, when the restaurant is especially popular, lighter fare is served, and a prix-fixe lunch is available for $12.85.

The dining rooms are quite fetching—the walls are graced with French tapestries, and the windows with swag curtains. French music adds a certain Gallic air. There's a definite glow about the place. In summer, the shaded floral-decorated patio, with umbrella-sheltered faux marble tables, is a popular dining spot.

✪ **Le Select.** 328 Queen St. W. ☎ **416/596-6405.** Reservations recommended. Main courses average $9 at lunch, $13–$18 at dinner; fixed-price meal $18. AE, DC, MC, V. Mon–Thurs 11:30am–11:30pm, Fri–Sat 11:30am–midnight, Sun noon–10:30pm. FRENCH.

One of Queen Street's longest-lasting bistros, Le Select still attracts a mixed crowd of well-heeled artists and professionals. They come for the Left Bank atmosphere, created by the authentic zinc bar, numerous French posters, French-style breakfronts, fringed fabric lampshades over the tables, and jazz music in the background.

Another draw is the moderately priced, French bistro food—from mussels steamed in white wine and shallots to *bavette aux echalottes* or confit de canard served with an orange sauce. Most dishes, such as the filet of salmon with basil, lemon, and ginger sauce, average under $15. The wine list is well rounded.

Left Bank. 567 Queen St. W., just east of Portland St. on the south side of the street. ☎ **416/504-1626.** Reservations recommended for dinner. Main courses $14–$24. AE, MC, V. Tues–Thurs 6–10pm, Fri–Sat 6–11pm. FRENCH.

The heavy tapestries and ornate carved French doors and bar give this restaurant a rich, renaissance feel that's more akin to the Loire Valley than to the Left Bank. The cuisine, however, is totally appropriate. The 10 or so main courses range from pommery pappardelle with rabbit ragout braised with red wine, pearl onions, smoky bacon and sage to rack of lamb with oven-dried tomatoes and a black olive, caper-scented jus. To start, try the nine-herb ricotta ravioli in a light tomato coulis with chanterelles, toasted pine nuts, and shaved Parmesan, or the wild mushroom flan. The wine list is predominantly French. The crowd is less Queen Street, and more conservative 20- or 30-somethings, with the occasional celebrity visitor in the brocade and satin VIP room. There's a billiards room downstairs.

Masa. 205 Richmond St. W. ☎ **416/977-9519.** Reservations recommended. Sushi $2.50 per piece; fixed-price dinners $14–$39. AE, DC, MC, V. Mon–Fri noon–2:30pm; Mon–Sat 5–11pm, Sun 5–10pm. JAPANESE.

Well known to Toronto aficionados of Japanese cuisine, Masa offers some of the most authentic Japanese food in the city. Seat yourself at the sushi bar and choose from a huge assortment, or dine Western- or tatami-style. Sake containers, Japanese prints, fans, and screens are scattered around the large room. There's a full range of appetizers—sliced fish cake, oysters in rice vinegar, and seaweed-pasted crab leg, to name just a few—or you can preface your dinner with one of the many fascinating soups—Tororo seaweed soup, for instance. The best deals, though, are the fixed-price dinners, which include clear soup, a small appetizer, rice, and such main courses as salmon teriyaki, raw tuna sashimi, or garlic beef yakiniku. Don't miss the *mitsu mame* dessert—seaweed jelly with black peas.

✪ **Mildred Pierce.** 99 Sudbury St. ☎ **416/588-5695.** Reservations not accepted. Main courses $13–$18. ER, MC, V. Mon–Fri noon–3pm, Sat–Sun 11am–3pm; Sun–Thurs 6–10pm, Fri–Sat 6–11pm. Take Queen W. to Dovercourt. Turn left, then right on Sudbury. The restaurant is located on the left at the back of a parking lot attached to Studio 99. FRENCH/CONTINENTAL/ECLECTIC.

This atmospheric, offbeat spot, which resembles a movie set, is frequented by in-the-know locals and is well worth seeking out. From the handful of tables outside, there's a great view of the CN Tower and the downtown skyline. The outdoor terrace is awaft in billowing cloth screens and climbing shrubs. Inside, the room has a theatrical flair with scrim curtains and vast murals of a large Roman feast featuring the apparent likenesses of the owner, the electrician, and other local foodies, including a critic or two. The glowing faux copper tables are set on a mosaic floor.

Out of the open kitchen comes a variety of fine daily specials, such as a loin of pork with a cabernet-cassis sauce and chutney. The menu features 10 or so main courses that range from fettuccine with roasted tomatoes, wilted greens, and a garlic chili oil garnished with black-olive pesto and shaved Parmesan reggiano to grilled salmon with steamed asparagus, lemon mayonnaise, and tomato-tarragon concasse. Start with the pan-fried sea scallops with a wasabi vinaigrette, fried wontons, and a cucumber and pickle salad or the deep-fried tiger shrimp dumplings, served with fresh mango, saffron-coconut milk sauce, and a hot chili-oil dip.

Depending on your passions, you'll want to save some room for dessert. I can recommend the rhubarb-meringue tartlet with strawberry-rhubarb sauce, but you might prefer the chocolate-pistachio pâté served with white and dark chocolate sauce or the profiteroles filled with vanilla ice cream and drizzled with chocolate sauce. The reasonably priced wine list is good; and an excellent brunch menu is also served.

N'Awlins. 299 King St. W. ☎ **416/595-1958.** Reservations recommended for dinner. Main courses $14–$22. AE, DC, MC, V. Daily noon–11pm. CAJUN/ITALIAN.

Jazz is played here every night, and the walls are studded, top to bottom, with photographs of historic and contemporary jazz greats. There's a long narrow bar in back and outdoor dining, too. The cuisine complements the ambience—just take the blackened chicken breast and grilled Cajun chicken, for example. Other dishes are more eclectic, such as tiger shrimp sautéed with garlic, leeks, and white wine on a bed of rice, or veal stuffed with spinach and mushrooms topped with a pesto cream sauce. There are pasta dishes, too. The dichotomy of the food that's served here—Cajun/Italian—is particularly apparent on the appetizer menu: Cajun calamari, anyone? This is a pre- and posttheater goer's favorite.

Peter Pan. 373 Queen St. W. ☎ **416/593-0917.** Reservations recommended for parties of six or more. Main courses $8–$17. AE, MC, V. Mon–Sat noon–4:30pm; Sun–Wed 6pm–midnight, Thurs–Sat 6pm–1am; brunch Sun noon–4pm. FUSION.

Another venerable survivor on Queen Street, Peter Pan still delivers exciting, moderately priced cuisine in a stylish 1930s ambiance complete with a tin ceiling and high-back booths lit by art deco sconces. The patrons are mostly bourgeois boomers. On the menu, you'll find pizzas, pastas, and a daily fish special, mostly flavored with Asian, Caribbean, and Mexican herbs and spices. You might start with mussels in a lime, cilantro, bourbon broth with fennel and gingered black beans, followed by a breast of chicken with apple chipotle marmalade. Desserts are always enticing, such as a pear tart with almond cream, or a Brazilian fig tart with kirsch sabayon.

Pink Pearl. 207 Queen's Quay W. ☎ **416/203-1233.** Reservations recommended. Main courses $10–$17. AE, DC, MC, V. Daily 11am–3pm and 5–11pm. CHINESE.

An attractive Chinese restaurant with views of Lake Ontario, Pink Pearl has been a local favorite for many years, because of the quality of its Cantonese-Szechuan food and the comfort of its decor. It caters more to Western palates than do the restaurants of Chinatown. To start, there are several hors d'oeuvres and eight soups to select from, including shark's-fin soup with chicken. The specialties of the house range from braised lobster with ginger and green onion, and sliced chicken sautéed with pineapple and green peppers, to shrimps Szechuan style. There's an intriguing dish called Rainbow Chopped in Crystal Fold, consisting of finely chopped pork, Chinese sausage, mushroom, bamboo shoots, water chestnuts, celery, and carrot sautéed and served in crisp lettuce. The wine list is French and Italian.

Another Pink Pearl can be found at 110 Bloor St. West (☎ **416/975-1155**).

Red Tomato. 321 King St. W. ☎ **416/971-6626.** Main courses $8–$11. AE, DC, MC, V. Mon–Fri 11:30am–12:30am, Sat noon–1am, Sun 4:30–10pm. CANADIAN.

At night, this popular downstairs bar/restaurant with a large central bar, video screens, wild murals, and exposed plumbing is virtually filled to capacity. The youngish crowd feasts on an array of pasta dishes, including farfelle with veal, capers, olive oil, and chili pesto; linguini with tomato, capers, anchovies, olives, and chilies; and gnocchi with four cheeses. About six pizzas are also offered.

St. Tropez. 315 King St. W. ☎ **416/591-3600.** Reservations recommended for dinner. Main courses $14.50–$20. AE, DC, ER, MC, V. Mon–Wed 11:30am–11pm, Thurs–Sat 11:30am–midnight. FRENCH.

Stucco, mock shutters, and pale washes of color effect a country French atmosphere at St. Tropez. In summer, the back courtyard, with its awning and vine-encrusted walls and statuary, is appealing to the mixture of tourists and local theatergoers who dine here. The bistro fare consists of such dishes as lamb with Dijon mustard sauce, salmon with a lime butter sauce, chicken marinated in tarragon and lemon, and, of course, steak frites and bouillabaisse. For dessert, try the classic crème brûlée or the *clafoutis.*

Taro Grill. 492 Queen St. W. (just west of Denison Ave. on the north side). ☎ **416/504-1320.** Reservations not accepted. Main courses $12–$17. AE, MC, V. Daily noon–4pm; Sun–Thurs 6–11pm, Fri–Sat 6pm–midnight. FRENCH/MEDITERRANEAN.

A small, distinctly hip spot with a mosaic floor, red walls, and a short menu. Head past the small bar and kitchen up front to the small dining area behind. Expect pastas, pizzas, and a daily fish special, but a breaded chicken breast stuffed with mushrooms and herbs and served in a Dijon cream sauce, or lamb chops served in a rosemary red wine glaze may also be offered. Appetizers are similarly straightforward—warm-goat-cheese-and-walnut salad, steamed mussels, and other salads.

Whistling Oyster Seafood Cafe. 11 Duncan St. ☎ **416/598-7707.** Reservations recommended for lunch only. Main courses $11–$25. AE, DC, ER, MC, V. Mon–Sat 11am–1am, Sun 4–11pm. SEAFOOD.

Families and middle-class Torontonians head to the Whistling Oyster for its happy oyster hour and a happy dim sum hour on Sundays from 4:30 to 10pm. At it, they enjoy 20 or so appetizers, including a variety of fresh clams and oysters, and such dishes as: steamed clams in wine, tomato, and garlic; blackened tiger shrimp with mangoes and Thai coleslaw; and conch fritters. Most items are under $3; everything is under $5. At other times, there's an extensive shellfish and fish menu that runs from $10 for *coquille maison* to $20 for Alaskan king crab legs. Be sure to check out the glittering mermaid suspended over the central bar; she's a conversation piece.

INEXPENSIVE

The Bagel. 285 College St. ☎ **416/966-7555.** Everything less than $9. V. Mon–Fri 7am–9pm, Sat 8am–6pm, Sun 8am–5pm. DELI.

You have to be a member of the "clean plate club" if you want to eat at the Bagel—otherwise the waitresses will scold you with "C'mon, eat already." Blintzes, bagels, lox, and cream cheese are the tops at this characterful spot. Sandwiches and dinner plates are also available.

The Eating Counter. 21–23 Baldwin St. ☎ **416/977-7028.** Reservations accepted for parties of 4–10 only. Main courses $7–$13. AE, DC, MC, V. Daily 11am–11pm. CHINESE.

Lines extend into the street from The Eating Counter, near McCaul and Dundas streets. Many of the eager patrons here are Chinese who relish the perfectly cooked Cantonese fare—crisp fresh vegetables; noodles; barbecue specialties; and, a particular favorite, fresh lobster with ginger and green onions. Ask the waiter to recommend the freshest items of the day. The decor is nonexistent, but the food is good.

Free Times Café. 320 College St. between Major and Robert. ☎ **416/967-1078.** Daily specials $7–$8. AE, MC, V. Mon–Sat 11:30am–12:45am, Sun 11:30am–10:45pm. VEGETARIAN.

The Free Times Café has a casual, avant-garde ambiance. Original art is on display, and folk and original acoustic music is featured nightly. It attracts a college-age and older crowd that appreciates the vegetarian fare. Everything is reasonably priced and includes such daily specials as chicken Dijonnaise, scallop and veggie stir-fry, and various pasta dishes. On Sundays, the place is filled with Jewish families drawn by the brunch spread called "Bella, did you eat?," a buffet spread of blintzes, potato latkes, salmon patties, lox and onions, beet salad, gefilte fish, and more—all for $12.99.

Hughie's Burgers. 22 Front St. W. ☎ **416/364-2242.** Everything less than $9.50. AE, DC, MC, V. Mon–Thurs 11:30am–11:30pm, Fri–Sat 11:30am–midnight. BURGERS.

Hughie's offers a variety of burgers, sandwiches, and salads. There's even a 10-ouncer for $9.50. A popular, pleasant hangout, especially in early evening.

Il Fornello. 214 King St. W. ☎ **416/977-2855.** Reservations recommended. Main courses $9–$13. MC, V. Mon–Fri noon–10pm, Sat 5–11pm. ITALIAN.

Il Fornello is famous for its 20 varieties of pizza, cooked in a wood-fired clay oven, and for a variety of popular Italian dishes—pasta, veal, and chicken. Also featured is an alternative menu with nondairy, nonyeast, and low-cholesterol items. Several other locations, too.

Kowloon Dim Sum. 5 Baldwin St. ☎ **416/977-3773.** Combination plates less than $6. AE, MC, V. Daily 10am–11pm. CHINESE.

Kowloon Dim Sum is a budget diner's delight for dim sum and barbecue specialties, but it's also known for its extensive seafood menu. Try the scallops with black beans and ginger, the salt baked shrimp, or the spectacular shark's-fin soup. The clientele is a nice mix of Chinese and Anglos who appreciate finer Chinese fare.

Lee Garden. 331 Spadina Ave. between St. Andrews and Nassau sts. ☎ **416/593-9524.** Reservations not accepted. Main courses $8–$13. MC, V. Daily 4pm–midnight. CHINESE.

Lee Garden is known for its seafood specialties— tiger shrimp with fresh pineapple; fresh oyster, clam, abalone, and crab cooked with green onion and ginger; shrimp with pepper and eggplant. The menu also features such pork, beef, and chicken dishes as honey-orange back ribs, chicken in black-bean sauce, and beef with chili peppers. But, it's the fish dishes that win acclaim from most Torontonians, and rightly so—they're sublime.

Palavrion. 270 Front St. W. ☎ **416/979-0060.** Reservations accepted. Most items $8–$12. AE, DC, ER, MC, V. Daily 7:30am–2am. CONTINENTAL.

This huge (380-seat) concept restaurant has to be one of the most expensive restaurant stage sets ever constructed, certainly the most expensive in Toronto. It cost $6.5 million to create, and the results are dramatic, to say the least. The concept mimics Movenpick Marche's stylish self-serve approach. Diners select their ingredients and watch them being cooked to order for lunch or dinner at several different stations—the rotisserie, the seafood counter, the pasta bar, and the dessert and gelateria bar. The ingredients are fresh, and although the flavoring tends to cater to a somewhat bland mass taste, people still flock here, attracted by the exciting, inspired decor and the fun of the experience. The brilliant wall colors—orange, yellow, and turquoise—are further illuminated with trompe l'oeil art. Huge light fixtures that look like old-style microphones loom over the bar area. In the area serving dessert and gelato, the floors are studded with individually crafted tiles. Even the bathrooms feature tiles in spectacularly different and inspiring hues. Upstairs, there's an Homage to Dali table designed by French tile artist Alain Vagh, which is reserved for special guests only.

Queen Mother Cafe. 208 Queen St. W. ☎ **416/598-4719.** Reservations not accepted. Most items $7–$10. AE, MC, V. Mon–Sat 11:30am–4:30pm; Sun–Thurs 5–11pm, Fri–Sat 5–midnight. INTERNATIONAL.

A simple restaurant with polished wood tables and bentwood chairs, this is another longtime favorite on Queen Street. Desserts are displayed in a glass case in the back. The menu offers such Laotian-Thai items as crispy chicken with garlic, coriander, and black peppercorn served with lime coriander sauce; jumbo black tiger shrimp with chili-garlic dipping sauce; and pad Thai; as well as burgers, sandwiches, and daily specials. Outdoor dining in summer.

Rivoli. 332 Queen St. W. ☎ **416/597-0794.** Reservations not accepted. Main courses $9–$14. AE, MC, V. Mon–Sat noon–4pm and 6pm–1am. CONTINENTAL.

Rivoli attracts a mixed, avant-garde artsy and boomer crowd. Its dinner menu features nine or so eclectic specialties such as pad Thai, Jamaican jerk chicken, prawns with jalapeno guava sauce, or the signature burger with caramelized onions served on challah. Three or so daily specials supplement the menu—usually one pasta, one meat, and one fish dish. The lunch menu features sandwiches such as grilled cheese made with challah or pita stuffed with falafel. In summer, the sidewalk patio is jammed. There's pool upstairs, and good nightly entertainment in the back room. The dining-room decor is appropriately surreal, and basic black. Seating is not designed for comfort, and noise can make easy conversation problematic.

Saigon Palace. 454 Spadina Ave. ☎ **416/968-1623.** Main courses less than $5. No credit cards. Sun–Thurs 9am–10pm, Fri–Sat 9am–11pm. CHINESE/VIETNAMESE.

A super-budget eatery—a Vietnamese-style cafe with minimal decor—Saigon Palace has hardly anything on the menu over $5. There's a fine beef with noodle soup for $4. The place is filled with Chinese and Vietnamese residents.

Tiger Lily's. 257 Queen St. W. ☎ **416/977-5499.** No reservations. Main courses $6–$11. AE, MC, V. Sun–Tues 11:30am–9pm, Wed 11:30am–10pm, Thurs 11:30am–11pm. ASIAN.

This casual noodle house attracts a youthful, health-conscious crowd that enjoys putting together its own Asian-style soup combinations and noodle dishes. At lunch, diners select cafeteria-style from the different-colored cardboard menus on the wall behind the counter. At dinner, there's table service and a menu featuring about a dozen noodle plates. Try the delicious noodle cake with barbecued pork or the

Vietnamese-style sweet-and-sour spicy rice noodles served with the fish of day. Beer and wine only.

Vanipha 193 Augusta Ave. ☎ **416/340-0491.** Most items $8–$13. V. Mon–Sat noon–11pm. LAOTIAN/THAI.

A Laotian/Thai restaurant in a plain but comfortable step-down storefront, Vanipha serves some tasty dishes. Try the pad Thai or grilled fish with tamarind sauce, accompanied by a special treat—sticky rice.

Wah Sing. 47 Baldwin St. ☎ **416/599-8822.** Reservations accepted for large parties only. Most items $7–$10. AE, MC, V. Sun–Thurs 11:30am–10pm, Fri–Sat 11:30am–11:30pm. CHINESE.

People come here to enjoy terrific seafood at reasonable prices—especially the lobster special, which is two lobsters for $15.95! There's plenty of other shellfish on the menu, like the mussels with black-bean sauce or the oysters with ginger sauce, along with traditional Chinese fare, too. The decor is minimal, but the food makes for crowds. Expect to wait.

Young Lok Gardens. 122 St. Patrick St. in Village by the Grange. ☎ **416/593-9819.** Reservations accepted for parties of six or more only. Main courses $6–$12; lunch special $7. AE, MC, V. Mon–Fri 11:30am–10pm, Sat–Sun 11am–10pm. CHINESE.

Sun Lok serves good Peking and Szechuan cuisine and tasty barbecue from a Mongolian grill. The atmosphere is casual and decorous at the same time, with bamboo lanterns and kites, fans, and umbrellas adding color to the scene. The latest addition is a fresh-fish market where you can select a fish and either have it steamed Chinese-style in black-bean sauce or ginger and scallion or have it grilled on the barbecue. Start with one of the clear soups, like seafood chowder or Chinese peasant soup, which is filled with tofu and chicken. Follow with Szechuan shrimp sautéed with cashew nuts; vegetables in a hot chili sauce; orange-spiced duck; or the Mongolian barbecued beef marinated in mustard, chili, wine, ginger, and plenty of garlic.

4 Downtown East

EXPENSIVE

Acqua. 10 Front St. W. ☎ **416/368-7171.** Reservations recommended. Main courses $16–$25. AE, DC, ER, MC, V. Mon–Fri 11:30am–11:30pm, Sat 5–11:30pm. ITALIAN.

One of the trendiest and most dramatic restaurants in Toronto, Acqua attracts the Bay Street crowd—investment bankers, traders and brokers—especially during happy hour, when the bar is filled with suits. Evoking the drama and color of Venice at carnival, the bar area (where you can dine) features curvaceous tables standing under sail-like flags. There's also a courtyard dining area that spills out into the BCE galleria; it's defined by striped poles, reminiscent of those that line Venetian canals. Starfish patterns decorate the floors and water cascades down a wall fashioned out of metal fish.

The cuisine is contemporary Italian. Grilled swordfish with Sicilian pepperonata and lemon-thyme caper butter, and a veal chop with grilled truffled polenta, Swiss chard, and pinot noir–porcini cream are just two of the menu's main attractions. In addition, there are a few pastas, plus a grand selection of appetizers, such as tequila marinated salmon with grilled corn and chipotle relish or peppered beef carpaccio on mesclun lettuce with aged Parmesan. For dessert, chocoholics won't be able to pass up the warm chocolate truffle soufflé with a bittersweet ganache center, marsala zabaglione, and peppered pineapple. There's a great selection of dessert wines, ports, and grappa as well as a top-of-the-line wine list.

Biagio. 157 King St. E. ☎ **416/366-4040.** Reservations recommended. Pasta and risotto $12–$16; main courses $16–$27.50. AE, DC, MC, V. Mon–Fri noon–2:30pm; Mon–Sat 6–10:30pm. ITALIAN.

This restaurant has one of the most beautiful, inviting courtyards in the whole city, as well as attractive high-ceilinged dining rooms with large, well-spaced tables that are perfect for carrying on deal-making conversations comfortably—a feature that endears it to the power crowd that frequents Biagio. The kitchen serves some of the best Italian food in the city, with a menu that features an array of extra-special pasta and risotto dishes. The lasagna arrives in a light-pink sauce studded with salmon, scallops, and shrimp, and the tagliolini comes with choice morsels of lobster. Risotto can be prepared with porcini, saffron, Gorgonzola and parsley, or shrimp and arugula. For the more robust appetite, there's *bistecca al barolo e funghi,* or a veal chop with wine, butter, and sage. To start, try the delicious carpaccio served with lemon, celery, arugula, and Parmesan cheese with a balsamic vinegar glaze; or the salmon with fennel, pink peppers, and orange.

Galileo. 193 King St. E. ☎ **416/363-6888.** Main courses $15–$24. AE, DC, MC, V. Mon–Fri noon–3pm; Mon–Sat 5:30–11pm. ITALIAN.

This handsome, modern Italian restaurant makes a statement with its curved-back chairs, impressive wine displays all set against lilac-colored walls, and dark-blue ceiling. The cuisine is innovative and inspirational, often using Asian spices and flavors combined with traditional Italian ingredients, such as rack of lamb in a grainy mustard herb crust and light green curry jus, served with crispy and spicy lentil rosti. Fish is also treated in exciting ways. Try the salmon with caponata sauce, slices of eggplant, peppers, capers, zucchini, red wine vinegar, olive oil, garlic, and fresh herbs. There's an expansive choice of appetizers—from grilled sea scallops on a skewer with artichokes in a light orange pepper coulis to carpaccio and a variety of tempting salads. For dessert, don't miss the tiramisu or the white chocolate tart. The wine list is very extensive.

La Maquette. 111 King St. E. ☎ **416/366-8191.** Reservations recommended. Main courses $15–$26. AE, MC, V. Mon–Fri noon–2:30pm; Mon–Sat 5:30–10:30pm. CONTINENTAL.

At La Maquette, the cuisine is either classic French or Northern Italian, with a modern twist. Start your meal with portobello mushroom and grilled eggplant, layered with goat cheese, and served on smoked tomato sauce; or baked Camembert, accompanied by pecan-orange chutney. Follow with one of the 10 or so entrees that might include grilled tuna loin on an arugula polenta cake, served in a sun-dried tomato and balsamic vinaigrette; or a grilled roast beef tenderloin served with a foie gras sauce and roast garlic mash. The menu also features pastas and risottos—including a delicious smoked pheasant-filled ravioli in roasted garlic Alfredo; and a Cajun risotto made with chicken, sausage, and shrimp with bell peppers, tomato and spice. The three-course pretheater menu is an excellent value at $19.95. The dining room, located at the top of a marble staircase, is light and elegant. Tables are amply spaced. In summer, the outdoor dining area that overlooks a small park with a waterfall is particularly pleasant.

Nami Japanese Seafood. 55 Adelaide St. E. ☎ **416/362-7373.** Reservations recommended Thurs–Sat. Sushi $4–$6; main courses $15–$29. AE, DC, MC, V. Mon–Fri noon–2:30pm; Mon–Sat 6–10:30pm. JAPANESE.

A Passion For Patios

By the time spring rolls around, the citizens of Toronto are desperate to lounge outside in the sunshine for as much of the day as possible. This may account for the city's profusion of patios, from tiny nooks tucked away in backyards to the vast expanse of patios that fill whole sidewalks, like those on John Street between Adelaide and Richmond. Here the patios stretch from **Zocalo** at the southern end to **Montana** at the northern end, with my favorite being the largest one at **Al Frisco's.** Perhaps the Torontonian passion for patios has something to do with the length and bitterness of Canadian winters.

To get you started on your own quest for the perfect patio, here are a few more of my favorites:

At the **St. Tropez** on King Street West, you step through an archway into a brick-floored courtyard covered with a striped tent-style awning. The vine-covered walls and sculpted figure serving as a planter make this a lovely romantic spot. In a similar vein, there's also **Biagio** across town, which has to possess one of the most fetching courtyards in the city, complete with a gurgling classical fountain.

For a flavor of South Beach or the tropics, there are several downtown patios worth seeking out. My favorite is at **Alice Fazooli's.** From Adelaide Street, walk down the passageway lined with hibiscus and you'll find a large bar and terrace sheltered by what looks like camouflage cloth. Here in the evenings you can be serenaded by a mariachi band while the fountain plays and, if need be, the flames of a fire flicker, lighting up the jungle mural.

Cabana-style bars, fountain and tropical plants, and a wonderful view are the lures at the **Oasis** atop Wayne Gretzky's; while a sparser wood-and-mesh–style patio with a cabana bar can be found at **Blu,** which has a distinctive South Beach flavor. The patios—rooftop and ground floor—at **Bamboo** are other downtown hot spots that are easy on the eye with their tropical murals, glass brick styling, and fountains.

In Yorkville, rooftop patios can be found at **Hemingways;** while the patio at the front and back of the **Bellair Cafe** is another crowd-pleaser.

Greektown and Little Italy are the neighborhoods where patios really take over. In Greektown along Danforth, they are large and lively and right out front, except at **Lolita's Lust.** In Little Italy, along College Street, they are equally large and lively and placed square out front, like the one at **Cafe Diplomatico,** but they can also be tucked away romantically in the back as at **Souz Dal** and **Wild Indigo.**

Wherever you find yourself in Toronto in summer, you'll find a patio. Even if you don't see one at first, always ask, because it's axiomatic that there will be one somewhere, even if it's only a few square feet. Patios come in all shapes, sizes, and styles; somehow or other, you can bet your life that the management of any dining or drinking establishment will have figured out how to carve out a patio somewhere on the premises. So go ahead, suss out your own secret patios throughout the city.

An upscale, expensive and ultrastylish restaurant, Nami attracts wealthy Japanese Torontonians and businesspeople. The prime attraction is the fresh sushi and sashimi. Up front, there's a sushi bar, and behind it, attractive booth seating or traditional tatami-style dining.

Start with *kaki, ebi* fry (oysters or shrimp), or beef sashimi—thinly sliced beef lightly coated and served with *ponzu* sauce. For a real treat, order the *tenshin* bento, which provides an assortment of sushi and sashimi; or the Love Boat, which includes salad, miso, tempura, sushi, sashimi, salmon teriyaki, beef katsu, deep-fried chicken, and fruits.

The Senator. 249 and 253 Victoria St. ☎ **416/364-7517.** Reservations recommended for dinner in the dining room. Main courses $8–$15 at lunch, $18–$33 at dinner. AE, DC, MC, V. Diner: Mon–Fri 7:30–8:30pm, Sat 8am–8:30pm, Sun 8am–3pm. Steak house: Tues–Fri 11:30am–2:30pm; Tues–Thurs 5–11:30pm, Fri 5pm–midnight, Sat 5pm–12:30am, Sun 5–10pm. STEAK.

In the diner, green leatherette booths, tiled floors, and down-home cuisine take you back to the 1940s. Here, you can still order a full breakfast of bacon and eggs, beans, home fries, and toast for $5. The luncheon menu features such comforting dishes as meat loaf, macaroni and cheese, fish-and-chips, liver and onions, burgers with fried onions and corn relish, and creamy rice pudding. Perhaps best of all, though, is the counter, where you can perch on a stool and order up a rich, old-fashioned milkshake.

The next-door dining room is decked out in mahogany, mirrors, and stained glass, with enclosed velvet booths. Theatergoers mingle with an artsy crowd waiting to attend the jazz-cabaret on the top floor. Some of the dishes served in the diner make an appearance here, but the prime attractions are steaks and chops, even though a few chicken and fish dishes, such as a chicken breast with rosemary lemon sauce and a grilled swordfish with a roasted red-pepper coulis have also found their way onto the menu. Find room for the desserts, which are good. The fine wine list is primarily Canadian-American.

MODERATE

Brasserie Les Artistes. 243 Carlton St. at Parliament. ☎ **416/963-9433.** Reservations recommended. Main courses $11–$15. AE, MC, V. Tues–Fri noon–2:30pm; Mon–Thurs 5–10:30pm, Fri–Sat 5:30–11pm. FRENCH.

For a modest bistro-style meal, try this neighborhood restaurant in Cabbagetown. The atmosphere is casual and friendly, the impressionist poster art evokes Paris at the turn of the century, and the tables are marble—a suitable setting for the traditional *moules marinière*, steak and frites, escalope of veal *aux fines herbes,* and rack of lamb with fresh mint—all palate pleasers to the local crowd.

Montréal Bistro and Jazz Club. 65 Sherbourne St. (at Adelaide). ☎ **416/363-0179.** Reservations recommended, especially on weekends. Lunch specials $9; main courses $12–$18. AE, MC, V. Mon–Fri 11:30am–3pm; Mon–Thurs 6–11pm, Fri–Sat 6pm–midnight. QUÉBECOIS.

Montréal, at Adelaide and Sherbourne, is the place to try Québécois specialties, such as the famous pea soup and the *tourtière,* a tasty meat pie. The food is good and reasonably priced. Lunch specials include soup or salad, and such main courses as veal roast with vegetables or linguine primavera. At night, the specialties include rack of lamb, Atlantic salmon with leeks and basil cream sauce, and vegetarian fusilli with asiago cheese and red-pepper sauce, with most items around $15. For dessert, try the special deep-fried ice cream with hot raspberry sauce. To the left of the entrance, you'll find one of Toronto's best jazz clubs.

Spiaggia. 2318 Queen St. E. ☎ **416/699-4656.** Reservations recommended. Main courses $11–$14. AE, DC, MC, V. Sun–Thurs 5–10pm, Fri–Sat 5–11pm. ITALIAN.

A small, casual Beaches bistro, Spiaggia is filled with tables covered in blue gingham and glass. It caters to a mostly local crowd, with a short menu that changes daily. The menu tends to feature pastas, such as a fusilli with sausage and spicy tomato sauce; or a linguine with clams, mussels, shrimp, and scallops in a tomato basil sauce. Desserts include tiramisu, chocolate-sambucca mousse, and a variety of gelati.

Takesushi. 22 Front St. ☎ **416/862-1891.** Reservations recommended. Sushi combinations $16–$30; tempura and teriyaki dishes $13–$15. AE, DC, MC, V. Mon–Fri noon–2:30pm and 5:30–10pm, Sat–Sun 5–10pm. JAPANESE.

This Japanese restaurant specializes in sushi and sashimi—which you can order individually, or in combinations of 8 or 10 pieces of nigiri, plus a makimono roll. For novices, there's even a beginner's sushi consisting of three pieces of nigiri, a California roll, and a smoked salmon roll. Other sushi thrills include *uni* (sea urchin gonads) and *kazunoko* (herring roe soaked in sake, soy, and broth), plus such daily specials as eel tempura and grilled salted quail. Traditional tempura and teriyaki dinners are also available. It attracts a young crowd, including Japanese ex-pats.

INEXPENSIVE

The Bombay Palace. 71 Jarvis St. (between King and Adelaide sts.). ☎ **416/368-8048.** Reservations recommended. Main courses $9–$16. AE, DC, MC, V. Daily noon–3pm and 6–10:30pm. INDIAN.

At Bombay Palace, you'll sit on comfortable banquettes, surrounded by exotic Indian statues and idols. There's a 28-dish daily lunch buffet that includes *bhuna gosht*, tandoori chicken, salads, vegetable curry, and more. At night, you can select from the à la carte menu, or opt for a dinner like the Palace, which includes chicken tandoor, chicken tikka, tandoori prawns, seekh kebab, beef pasanda, pulao, vegetable, naan, chutney, and pickles—all for $17.

Le Papillon. 16 Church St. (between Front St. and Esplanade). ☎ **416/363-0838.** Reservations recommended on weekends. Crepes $7–$10. AE, DC, MC, V. Tues–Fri noon–2:30pm; Tues–Wed 5–10pm, Thurs 5–11pm, Fri 5pm–midnight; Sat 11:30am–midnight; Sun noon–10pm. CREPES.

When you arrive, there'll probably be a line of eager young folks outside Le Papillon, located just east of Jarvis Street, as this is a popular place for a candlelit dinner and crepes of all kinds. Exposed brick, mirrors, greenery, blue gingham tablecloths, and modern lithographs set the tone. Before you taste the imaginative crepes, start with a vegetable cocktail, or a bowl of onion soup and a salad. There are 16 savory crepes, ranging from crepe Marie Claude (with sausages, apples, and Cheddar cheese) to crepe Continental (chicken, mushrooms, and peppers in béchamel). Then there are the dessert crepes, with sliced peaches, apples, and cinnamon.

Maccheroni. 32 Wellington St. E. ☎ **416/867-9067.** Reservations accepted for large parties only. Main courses $6–$9. AE, DC, ER, MC, V. Mon–Fri 11:30am–10pm, Sat 5–10pm. ITALIAN.

Swathes of brilliant color—mustard yellow, periwinkle, orange, and red—faux urns, and flowers will transport you to the Mediterranean at this low-priced stage set, which serves adequate, if not exciting food to the masses. Start with the bruschetta or the *crostini della casa* made with Gorgonzola. You can follow with a variety of pasta dishes—penne arrabiata, fettuccine Alfredo, lasagna, and fusilli primavera—or pizza. On Friday and Saturday nights, there's an all-you-can-eat buffet.

Movenpick Marche. On the galleria of BCE Place, Front St. E. ☎ **416/366-8986.** Reservations not accepted. Most items $5–$8. AE, DC, MC, V. Daily 9am–2am. CONTINENTAL.

This large restaurant, with a variety of seating areas, is a relatively recent innovation in food merchandising that attracts an eclectic crowd of office workers and professionals as well as tourists and other curiosity seekers. Pick up a tab at the entrance and stroll through the bustling market, where various stands, carts, and trolleys display fresh foods and ingredients. Stop at the rosticceria, and select a meat for the chef to cook. Pause at the seafood and raw bar, and pick out a fish for the grill, or peruse the pasta bar. Then wander over to the *bistro de vin,* and check out the cases of wine, or enjoy a *boccalino* of one of the open wines. A dependable place for breakfast, lunch, or dinner. If you hate standing and waiting in line for a meal, don't go at peak dining hours, when the place is mobbed, noisy, and frenetic.

Shopsy's. 33 Yonge St. ☎ **416/365-3333.** Sandwiches and main courses $6–$13. AE, DC, MC, V. Mon–Wed 7am–11pm, Thurs–Fri 7am–midnight, Sat 8am–midnight, Sun 8am–11pm. DELI.

Toronto's most famous deli was started in the garment district 72 years ago. Today, it's right across from the O'Keefe Centre, sporting a spiffy outdoor patio, arrayed with brilliant yellow umbrellas. They serve huge stuffed deli sandwiches, the most traditional being the corned beef and pastrami. It's a good breakfast spot, too.

Young Thailand. 81 Church St. (south of Lombard St.). ☎ **416/368-1368.** Reservations recommended. Main courses $9–$16. AE, DC, MC, V. Mon–Fri 11:30am–2:30pm; daily 5–11pm. THAI.

This large restaurant with minimal decor serves good Thai cuisine. Beef, pork, chicken, and seafood dishes fill the menu—sliced beef in hot spicy thick sauce; slices of chicken with shredded ginger, mushrooms, and onions; and pork with garlic, onions, chili pepper, and sweet basil leaves. Sweet-and-sour fish and spicy shrimp are among the close to 20 seafood dishes. Start with a stimulating *tom kha kai* soup made with coconut milk, lemongrass, chili, and chicken; or with one of the traditional salad or noodle dishes.

There's another branch at 111 Gerrard St. East between Jarvis and Church (☎ **416/599-9099**).

5 Midtown West

There's plenty of fine dining in this neighborhood, which includes Yorkville, but because of its many chic and expensive shopping areas, it's not always a pleasant experience. Rents are high, so consequently, prices are high, but the quality doesn't always match. That said, I have included in this section one or two selections that can be relied upon to deliver quality at a decent price.

EXPENSIVE

Bistro 990. 990 Bay St. (at St. Joseph). ☎ **416/921-9990.** Reservations required. Main courses $17–$27. AE, ER, MC, V. Mon–Fri noon–3pm; Mon–Sat 5–11pm. FRENCH.

A celebrity hot spot, Bistro 990 could have been air-lifted from the French provinces with its French doors, lace curtains, and outdoor cafe tables. The cuisine ranges from such traditional bistro dishes as roasted chicken with mashed potatoes, or steak and frites with Roquefort or bordelaise sauce, to seared shrimp with a smoked tomato-orange salsa. Among the appetizers, the steamed Prince Edward Island mussels in a red-tomato curry broth with ginger and fresh cilantro are extra-special, as are the escargots sautéed with garlic, bacon, onion and spinach in a white-wine cream sauce. Desserts change daily, but always include tarts and a selection of ice creams and sorbets.

✪ **Boba.** 90 Avenue Rd. ☎ **416/961-2622.** Main courses $20–$27. AE, DC, ER, MC, V. Mon–Thurs 5:30–10pm, Fri–Sat 5:30–10:30pm. FUSION.

Barbara Gordon and Bob Bermann were among the early Toronto restaurateurs to experiment with spicy, ethnic flavors at restaurants like Avocado Grill. They've returned to the city to provide food lovers with a sophisticated ethnic-inspired modern American cuisine that uses fresh local products. Start, for example, with the grilled

Midtown Toronto Dining

Aida's Falafel **12**
Annapurna **1**
Arlequin **3**
Azalea **22**
Bistro 990 **13**
Bloor St. Diner **10**
Boba **21**
Boulevard Café **19**
Il Posto **6**
Indian Rice Factory **2**
Jacques' Bistro du Parc **8**
Joso's **4**
Kensington Kitchen **16**
Lakes **5**
Le Paradis **20**
Le Rendez-Vous **14**
Messis **18**
Mori **9**
Movenpick Bistretto **7**
Opus **15**
Splendido **17**
Thai Magic **23**
Toby's Goodeats **11**

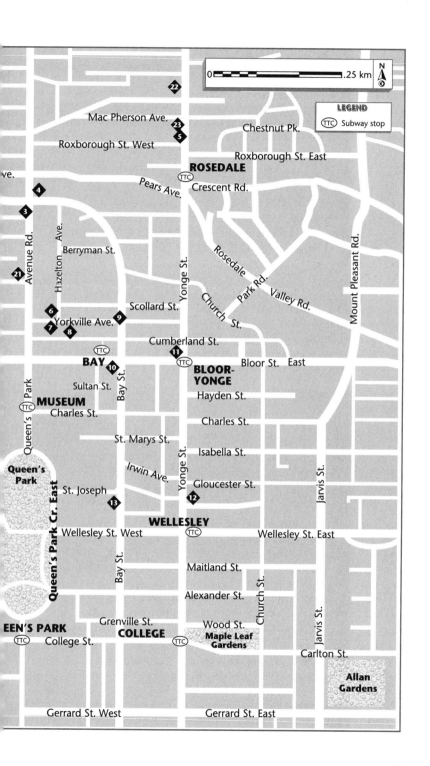

eggplant and smoked pepper salad with Woolwich chevre, or the Thai-flavored steak tartare served with shiitake mushroom salad and wonton crisps. Asian spices imbue the main dishes with delectable character—rice-paper–wrapped chicken breast on Thai black rice, with a spiced rice–wine vinegar sauce; or the grilled filet mignon with an Asian barbecue glaze, served with spicy cashew and roast pepper sauces are two good examples. Desserts are also extraordinary, especially the Valrhona chocolate triangle with crème fraîche ice cream, fresh raspberries, and raspberry sauce, or the lemon trio, a divine lemon tart in a cookie crust, with lemon buttermilk pudding, and lemon ice cream.

This finely prepared cuisine is served in a sunny garden ambiance, with large, spectacular floral arrangements. Mustard and lilac walls are adorned with paintings of flowers in profusion. It attracts a moneyed crowd—some in fine designer wear, others in jeans.

✪ **Chiado.** 864 College St. (at Concord Ave.). ☎ **416/538-1910.** Reservations recommended. Main courses $14–$20. AE, DC, MC, V. Mon–Sat noon–3pm and 5pm–11pm. PORTUGUESE.

Chiado refers to the district in Lisbon that's filled with small *bistrettos* like this one. It draws a professional, sophisticated crowd. Beyond the appetizing display at the front of the room, you'll discover a long, narrow, elegant dining room with marble floors, walls adorned with art, and tables set with specially painted fresh orchids. In summer, the storefront opens entirely onto the street, adding to the atmosphere. Among the appetizers, the *pinheta* of salted cod and the marinated sardines with lemon and parsley will appeal to the true Portuguese; others might prefer the grilled tiger shrimp served with sweet-pepper coulis. On the main menu, the poached filet of salted cod is pure Portuguese. Of the less traditionally Portuguese dishes, there are a few meat offerings, but I recommend the fish dishes. For a traditional Portuguese dessert, try the *natas do ceu,* a very rich cream dessert served over lady fingers and soaked with bitter almond liqueur. There's a good, reasonably priced wine list.

Opus. 37 Prince Arthur Ave. ☎ **416/921-3105.** Reservations recommended. Main courses $19–$24.50. AE, MC, V. Daily 5:30–11:30pm. FRENCH/MEDITERRANEAN.

A splashy place for the expense-account brigade. Beyond the small Erté-decorated bar, you'll enter a series of small, intimate rooms in a town house. The current chef hails from the Hotel Negresco, and has created a short menu that features healthful contemporary Mediterranean cuisine using many organically grown ingredients. Among the eight main courses, you might find grilled striped bass with potato galette and green onion sauce, or free-range pheasant with pistachio sausage and sun-dried cranberry jus. Whet the appetite with a fricassee of wild mushrooms with balsamic vinegar sauce, or the seared, marinated venison with smoked gruyere and roasted almonds in a balsamic vinaigrette. Opus has one of the most extensive and best wine lists in the city, featuring French, Californian, and Italian bottles.

✪ **Splendido Bar and Grill.** 88 Harbord St. ☎ **416/929-7788.** Reservations recommended well in advance. Main courses $13–$28. AE, DC, ER, MC, V. Daily 5–11pm. ITALIAN.

Splendido is one of the the city's scene-stealers—for its absolutely stunning dining room. It stretches on behind the black-gray granite bar up front, a riot of brilliant yellow lit by a host of tiny, fairylike track lights. The walls are hung with huge flower canvases by Helen Lucas.

The food is Italian with international inspirations, and the menu changes monthly. Start with the signature antipasto of poached shrimp wrapped in smoked salmon, prosciutto, and melon. Follow with either pasta, pizza, or a main course. For example, you might choose the white pizza made with roasted garlic, truffle paste, plum tomato, smoked chicken, and Pecorino cheese; or the penne with roasted shrimps, basil, arugula, garlic, and tomato sauce. Among the main courses, roast rack of veal with garlic mashed potatoes, asparagus, and sun-dried tomato aioli jus is a special treat; but so, too, is the sirloin steak with leek and potato strudel, mixed mushrooms, caramelized onions, and green peppercorn jus. If you're splurging, finish with a glass of one of the several ice wines, accompanied by a fragrant Tahitian vanilla bean crème brûlée, or the wafer-thin apple tart with caramelized orange sauce and caramel ice cream. It's a loud, lively place, so give it a pass if it's a romantic dinner you're seeking.

MODERATE

Arlequin. 134 Avenue Rd. (between Davenport and Bernard sts.). ☎ **416/928-9521.** Reservations recommended. Main courses $13–$18 at dinner. AE, DC, MC, V. Daily 11:30am–3pm; Mon–Sat 5:30–11pm. The front counter opens at 8am. CONTINENTAL.

Frequented by a well-heeled Rosedale and young professional crowd, Arlequin is a handsome, small restaurant with a counter display of fabulous pâtés, cheeses, salads, and baked goods up front. The menu is keyed to market-fresh ingredients, and might include grilled loin of lamb with plums and goat's cheese served with crisp polenta; or linguine with grilled fennel, garlic, marjoram, fresh tomatoes, and olive oil. The three-course prix-fixe dinners for $15.95 and $22.95 are excellent values. The first might offer soup or salad, and a main course selection such as mixed grill of lamb chops, capon sausage, and pomegranate beef kebab served with frites, followed by crème caramel or a marquise au chocolat. At brunch, similar dishes are supplemented by a variety of egg dishes.

Azalea. 1158 Yonge St. ☎ **416/968-0710.** Main courses $22–$29. AE, DC, MC, V. Mon–Fri noon–2:30pm; Mon–Sat 6–10pm. FRENCH.

Local Rosedale professionals flock to this minimally decorated, small, narrow dining room, especially on Friday and Saturday nights when live jazz combos play. The menu offers about five meat or fish dishes, many of which feature refreshingly new treatments of traditional ingredients, or items that appear infrequently elsewhere, like the braised skate with capers and julienne of red pepper, or the seared rack of lamb with curry sauce. To start, try the foie gras seared with port sauce, or the portobello mushroom risotto. There's a good French-American wine list.

Grappa. 797 College St. (1¹/₂ blocks west of Beatrice). ☎ **416/535-3337.** Reservations recommended at dinner. Main courses $11–$16. AE, ER, MC, V. Tues–Sun 5–11pm. ITALIAN.

Pass the small bar up front, and enter the low-lit romantically old-fashioned dining room, where the only decor is the oak curio cabinets filled with Barolos and other fine wines, and the mural on the back wall depicting the *vendange.* The meal will start with a dish of black olives, crusty fresh bread, and olive oil. The food is fresh and good, with such daily specials as a *zuppa di pesce* with shrimp, scallops, and mussels in a tomato-lemon broth. Other dishes you might find are salmon puttanesca with fresh and sun-dried tomatoes, black olives, chilies, and anchovies over spaghetti; or *pollo nuovo Genovese*—chicken breast topped with a salsa of mango and roasted red peppers in a pesto lemon sauce. The pizza with Gorgonzola, braised onions, wild mushrooms, and spinach is as piquant and appetizing as you can imagine. Raspberry *clafoutis,* dark chocolate mousse cake, and tiramisu are just a few of the dessert musts.

Il Posto. 148 Yorkville Ave. ☎ **416/968-0469.** Reservations recommended. Main courses $14–$25. AE, MC, V. Mon–Sat noon–2:30pm and 6–10:30pm. ITALIAN.

Right in the heart of high-rent Yorkville, where restaurants are constantly opening and closing, Il Posto, tucked away in York Square, has thrived for many years, and still offers a very attractive setting. You can dine inside or out on a brick terrace under a spreading maple tree. The menu features such Italian classics as *saltimbocca alla romana* (veal, prosciutto, and sage); as well as fresh fish dishes and flavorsome pastas, like the *penne alla puttanesca* made with tomatoes, olives, garlic, and anchovies. For dessert, besides some very special tartes, you might relish the oranges marinated in Grand Marnier, or the smooth, creamy zabaglione. The restaurant's beige walls, Italian prints, fresh flowers, and classical music create a serene dining atmosphere. The high-priced wine list doesn't intimidate the professional and moneyed clientele.

Jacques Bistro du Parc. 126A Cumberland St. ☎ **416/961-1893.** Omelets $10–$13; other main courses $16–$20; prix fixe $19. AE, MC, V. Mon–Sat 11:30am–3pm; daily 5–10:30pm. CONTINENTAL.

Ladies who lunch and French-speakers drop into this upstairs dining room in the heart of Yorkville for omelets and casual California-inspired fare. Everything about the small room is tasteful, from the fresh flowers on the bar and the French prints to the pictures of Paris. But the patrons come for the omelets—10 selections—and the half-dozen meat and fish dishes, such as coquilles St. Jacques in a California style with roasted green and red peppers, jalapeno, and tomato salsa; or rack of lamb with Dijon mustard. And, of course, there are salads, soups, and quiches, too.

Joso's. 202 Davenport (just east of Avenue Rd.). ☎ **416/925-1903.** Reservations recommended. Pasta $9–$14; main courses $14–$39. AE, MC, V. Mon–Sat 11:30am–3pm and 5:30–11pm. SEAFOOD.

Yugoslav Joseph Spralja—of Malka and Joso—has appeared on "The Tonight Show," and performed at Carnegie Hall, but since he gave up folk singing and guitar playing, he has taken to combing the fishmarkets for his restaurant, Joso's. Besides having a fascinating owner, this place has some interesting seafood, but also a rather idiosyncratic decor—erotic, ceramic sculptures of golf-ball–bosomed females— that might offend some.

If you don't care a fig about such indelicate matters, but you do care about fresh seafood prepared to retain its flavor, then stop by Joso's. At dinner, a selection of fresh fish will be presented to you; choose the one you like best, and it will be grilled, and served with a salad (such dishes are priced by the pound). Or, you can have octopus steamed in garlic-and-parsley sauce; deep-fried squid with salad; or spaghetti with an octopus, clam, and squid tomato sauce. A selection of exotic coffees is available, along with a special baklava, and Italian ice creams and sorbets. Bentwood cane chairs and pale-lemon tablecloths complete the decor of the tiny downstairs room. A larger room upstairs is similarly appointed.

Lakes. 1112 Yonge St. ☎ **416/966-0185.** Reservations recommended at dinner. Main courses $10–$18. AE, DC, MC, V. Mon–Fri noon–3pm; daily 6–11pm. CONTINENTAL.

This bar-and-grill, occupying a long, narrow room, is the essence of comfort and good taste, with its plush banquettes and art-covered walls.

The food reflects the same care and attention. There are only about seven main courses, supplemented by pasta dishes like Thai noodles with shrimp, chicken, and peanuts in a spicy siracha sauce; or more traditional angel-hair pasta in tomato sauce with sun-dried tomatoes, black olives, and garlic. The heartier dishes include a slow-roasted chicken with thyme jus and buttermilk mashed potatoes, Atlantic salmon with nage of mussels and tarragon, and beef tenderloin with Stilton and parsley sauce. To start, select the Woolwich goat's cheese on confit tomato salad with basil toast;

finish with the lemon tart served with a raspberry sauce, or the William pear with chocolate vacherin. There's a good selection of wines by the glass, as well as a number of single malts and martinis.

Le Rendez-Vous. 14 Prince Arthur Ave. ☎ **416/961-6111.** Reservations recommended. Main courses $17–$23. AE, CB, MC, V. Mon–Fri noon–2:30pm; daily 5:30–10pm. FRENCH.

At Le Rendez-Vous, you'll find a classic French decor and a variety of bistro-style dishes. In summer, the outdoor dining area is filled, along with the comfortable, plant-filled atrium inside. Rattan chairs, burgundy upholstery, and classical music complete the atmosphere.

Dishes range from fusilli with sun-dried tomato tapenade and Parmesan, to rack of lamb with fresh rosemary and garlic jus. For pre- or postdinner drinks, go downstairs to the wine cellar.

Messis. 97 Harbord St. ☎ **416/920-2186.** Main courses $10–$18. AE, DC, MC, V. Tues–Fri noon–2pm; Sun–Thurs 5:30–10pm, Fri–Sat 5:30–11pm. MEDITERRANEAN.

A favorite among local foodies, Messis offers good, reasonably priced northern Italian cuisine in warm and comfortable surroundings. The menu features a variety of pizzas, including one with oven-dried tomato tapenade, roasted onions, zucchini, mixed mushrooms, mozzarella and asiago cheeses; plus such pasta dishes as linguini with shrimp and calamari in a puttanesca sauce. In addition, there are about six fish and meat dishes: a pan-seared salmon glazed with mango-mustard and served with citrus vinaigrette and jasmine rice cake, or a rack of lamb with rosemary and chipotle-pepper smoked chicken glaze, served with jalapeno grit cake. The room is small, with a minimal decor. The walls are sponge-painted and stenciled in yellow; and the coral ceiling gives the dining area a warm glow. There's also an appealing awning-covered patio.

Movenpick Bistretto. 133 Yorkville Ave. ☎ **416/926-9545.** Reservations recommended at dinner, especially for small groups. Main courses $8–$18. AE, DC, ER, MC, V. Tues–Sat 7:30am–2am, Sun–Mon 7:30am–1am. CONTINENTAL/SWISS.

At this popular place, where people line up for dinner, you won't find fine dining, but you will find excellent value and gigantic desserts. Just ask for the Design Dessert menu, and you'll see what I mean. Although the menu features typical bistro fare like steak and frites, veal with mushroom cream sauce, and a croque-monsieur, my favorites are the Rösti dishes, like the one topped with fresh slices of Parmesan and prosciutto, mushrooms, peppers, and basil tomato sauce—all for $9.80, an amazing value. The fresh shellfish—on display at the entrance—is another very popular draw. This is one place in Yorkville where you'll receive value for your money, in a bright, lively atmosphere.

Southern Accent. 595 Markham St. ☎ **416/536-3211.** Reservations recommended. Main courses $14–$22. AE, ER, MC, V. Daily 5:30–10:30pm. In summer, lunch is served noon–3pm on the patio. CAJUN.

Southern Accent has a real down-home feel that draws Annex locals. The background music is cool, the art interesting, and the floral tablecloths somehow funky. There are three areas to dine in—upstairs in the dining room, downstairs on the bar level, or out on the tent-covered brick patio. The menu features gumbo, jambalaya, shrimp étouffée, and blackened fish with lemon. Don't miss the bread pudding with bourbon sauce.

✪ Trattoria Giancarlo. 41–43 Clinton St. (at College). ☎ **416/533-9619.** Reservations strongly recommended. Pasta and rice $11–$14; main courses $17–$20. AE, MC, V. Mon–Sat 5:30–11pm. ITALIAN.

This restaurant is one of my all-time favorite spots in Little Italy, if not in the city, and I find myself returning here time after time. It's small and cozy, and thoroughly Italian, with an outside dining area in summer. The tablecloths are covered with butcher paper, the floor is black-and-white tile, and the background music is opera or jazz.

For a real treat, start with the fresh wild mushrooms broiled with herbs, garlic, Parmesan and oil; or the carpaccio of beef lightly scented with white truffle-infused extra-virgin oil . Follow with any one of six pasta dishes—perhaps spaghettini with shrimp and *fra diavolo* sauce, or the risotto of the day. Good grilled fresh fish and meats are also part of the attraction, like the tender lamb marinated in grappa, lemon, and olive oil; or the swordfish grilled with fresh mint, garlic, and olive oil. For dessert, try the tiramisu, the crème caramel, or the delicious chocolate-raspberry tartufo. An evening here is always memorable, and the welcome real.

INEXPENSIVE

Aïda's Falafel. 553 Bloor St. W. ☎ **416/537-3700.** Main courses $3.50–$7. No credit cards. Sun–Thurs 11am–1:30am, Fri–Sat 11am–3am. MIDDLE EASTERN.

Aïda's Falafel, on Bloor Street at Bathurst, is a small, unassuming restaurant with a couple of tables out front. Tabbouleh, falafel, and shish kebab cost $2 to $6. There's also a branch in the Beaches on Queen Street East at Woodbine.

Annapurna Restaurant. 1085 Bathurst St. (just south of Dupont). ☎ **416/537-8513.** Most items less than $6.25. No credit cards. Mon–Tues and Thurs–Sat noon–9pm, Wed noon–6:30pm. VEGETARIAN.

About 2 decades ago, Shivaram Trichur opened the Annapurna Restaurant, just south of Dupont. Beyond the counter, where you can purchase various goodies, including a loaf of banana bread, books on yoga, and copies of *Meditation at the U.N.,* you'll find a room with no decor to speak of—but some fine, low-priced food. Enjoy the peaceful, smoke-free atmosphere, and the medieval background music, along with the young, intellectual, and interesting crowd that gathers here.

Nothing on the menu is over $6.25. My favorite choice is a *masala dosai,* a crepe filled with a spicy potato mixture and served with coconut chutney. Salads and vegetarian sandwiches supplement the south Indian dishes.

The Boulevard Café. 161 Harbord St. (between Spadina and Bathurst). ☎ **416/961-7676.** Reservations recommended for upstairs dining. Main courses $10–$18. AE, MC, V. Tues–Sun 11:30am–3:30pm and 5:30–10:30pm; daily in summer. LATIN AMERICAN.

A favorite gathering spot for young creative types as well as academics, The Boulevard Café is somehow reminiscent of Kathmandu in the 1960s, although the inspiration is Peruvian. Upstairs, there's a dining room furnished with wooden banquettes, softened by the addition of Peruvian cushions and South American wall hangings. The outside summer cafe is strung with colored lights and attracts an evening and late-night crowd. To start, the menu features empanadas (spicy chicken or beef pastry); tangy shrimp in a spiced garlic, pimiento, and wine sauce; and *tamal verde* (spicy corn, coriander, and chicken pâté). For the main course, the major choice is *anticuchos,* marinated and charbroiled brochettes of your own choosing: sea bass, shrimp, pork tenderloin, beef, or chicken. Burgers, lamb chops, and steamed mussels are some of the other selections.

Indian Rice Factory. 414 Dupont St. ☎ **416/961-3472.** Reservations recommended. Main courses $9–$15.25. AE, DC, MC, V. Mon–Sat noon–11pm, Sun 5–10pm. INDIAN.

A friend of mine raised in India swears by the Indian Rice Factory, operated by Mrs. Patel, who was born in the Punjab. It is an elegant place, with comfortable plush booths, a light-oak bar, and Indian artifacts. The food is decent and the prices are right. All the curries—chicken, beef, and shrimp—are under $11. The restaurant also serves a wide selection of Indian vegetarian dishes, including *aloo gobi* (a curried mixture of potato and cauliflower), *matar paneer* (peas and cheese cooked with spices), *aloo palak* (spinach with potatoes), and a complete thali for $13.25 with a meat or vegetable main course, a vegetable of the day, dal, rice, chapati, raita, pappadum, and kachumber. The wine list is better than expected.

✪ **Kensington Kitchen.** 124 Harbord St. ☎ **416/961-3404.** Reservations recommended. Main courses $8–$12. AE, CB, DC, ER, MC, V. Mon–Sat 11:30am–11pm, Sun 11:30am–10pm. MIDDLE EASTERN.

A comfortable, casual place filled with an academic crowd, the Kensington Kitchen has a minimal decor. A beaded-purse collection and a toy-airplane collection decorate the walls. There's a counter in the back for takeout. The menu is written bistro-style on a mirror and includes falafel, shish kebab, vegetarian chili, fish of the day, vegetable kebab on hummus, and daily seafood and pasta specials. There are two dining rooms—one upstairs, the other downstairs—but my favorite spot is on the deck out back under the spreading trees. There is a very well-selected wine list.

✪ **Mori.** 1280 Bay St. ☎ **416/961-1094.** Reservations recommended at dinner. Main courses $7.50–$12. AE, MC, V. Mon–Sat noon–4pm; Mon–Fri 4–10pm, Sat 4–11pm. JAPANESE.

Mori, a tiny Japanese cafe with wrought-iron tables and deep-blue tablecloths, is great for budget dining. The sushi and the salmon or chicken teriyaki, served with soup, oshitashi, and green tea, are the highlights. The variety of vegetarian sushi (spinach, carrot, and the like) is notable. So, too, is the vegetarian sukiyaki.

Toby's Goodeats. 93 Bloor St. W. ☎ **416/925-2171.** Burgers $5–$8. AE, MC, V. Tues–Sat 11:30am–1am, Sun–Mon 11:30am–midnight. BURGERS.

Capture those childhood dreams of milkshakes, Coke floats, and a good burger along with the rest of the crowd at Toby's Goodeats, a 1950s-style hamburger joint. The decor suits: a schizophrenic combination of Formica tables, cookie jars, funky posters, and the traditional brick-and-plants look. It's very crowded at lunchtime. A dozen burgers are priced from $5 to $6.50 for a 10-ouncer. In addition, there are salads, sandwiches, pizzas, and pastas.

Toby's Goodeats can also be found at 725 Yonge St. (☎ **416/925-9908**), the Eaton Centre (☎ **416/591-6994**), 542 Church St. (☎ **416/929-0411**), and First Canadian Place (☎ **416/366-3953**).

6 Midtown East/The East End

In the East End along Danforth Avenue, you'll find yourself in a veritable Little Greece. Streets are lined with tavernas; bouzouki music spills out onto the sidewalk, and restaurant after restaurant bears a Greek name. Most of these places are inexpensively priced.

INEXPENSIVE

Astoria. 390 Danforth Ave. ☎ **416/463-2838.** Main courses $9–$15. AE, MC, V. Mon–Wed and Fri–Sat 11am–1am, Sun and Thurs 11am–midnight. GREEK.

Astoria is a little fancier than most of the Greek restaurants in the neighborhood, with an outdoor patio complete with fountain. The offerings include shish kebab, quails over charcoal, a 12-ounce New York steak, and broiled seafood.

Bloor Street Diner. 55 Bloor St. W., Manulife Centre. ☎ **416/928-3105.** Most items $4–$18. Daily 7am–1am. LIGHT FARE.

The Bloor Street Diner is a convenient place for shoppers and late-nighters to stop for a wide selection of reasonably priced food. The handmade floor, wall tiles, and pottery evoke a Provençal atmosphere. The restaurant offers several dining experiences. The espresso bar serves a variety of coffees, plus salads, panini sandwiches, and crepes. La Rotisserie features roasted meats, poultry, and fish prepared in Provence style. Le Café/Terrasse serves light bistro-style meals and stays open until 1am daily. It's a great pleace to relax in summer on the stylish wicker-and-metal chairs. Live Sunday jazz brunch, too. Les Billiards is the latest pool hot spot.

Christina's/Byzas. 535 Danforth Ave. ☎ **416/778-1100.** Main courses $9–$17. AE, MC, V. Daily 11am–4:30am. GREEK.

This large restaurant is meant to be cool, and it succeeds. Crowds come for the festive atmosphere and the large selection of traditional appetizers—dolmades, marinated octopus, jalapenos stuffed with cream cheese, or chickpeas sautéed with onions, tomatoes, and spices. There are also plenty of traditional lamb dishes to choose from, along with moussaka and a variety of souvlaki. The bar area up front has stone floors and comfortable banquettes, while behind, the raised dining room has tables set on polished wood floors. The walls are decorated with large, fine-quality photographs of Greece. The sidewalk patio is usually jammed with all manner of people—families, young couples, and the occasional suit. On weekend evenings (Thurs-Sun), belly dancers entertain from 8:30 to 9:30pm, and the music goes on until 1:30 in the morning.

Lolita's Lust. 513 Danforth Ave. ☎ **416/465 6601.** Most items $9–$14. AE, MC, V. Tues–Sun 6pm–2am. GREEK/MEDITERRANEAN.

Lolita's is different from most of the other restaurants along Danforth in that it is small and low-lit, with only a handful of booths and tables, and its menu is more varied, with a broader range of Mediterranean, not just Greek, specialties. The traditional small plates, for example, go from roasted quail stuffed with onion, raisins, pine nuts, and dried cherry couscous to grilled calamari with anchovy, oven dried tomato, and black olives. Among the seven or so main dishes, try the stuffed pork tenderloin with feta, pine nuts, and honey-roasted onion au jus; or the roasted chicken with lemon and fried green onion. There's a small, convivial bar and tiny patio in the back.

Myth. 417 Danforth Ave. (between Logan and Chester). ☎ **416/461-8383.** Reservations not accepted. Main courses $9–$20. AE, DC, MC, V. Thurs–Sat 11:30am–4am, Sun–Wed 11:30am–2am. GREEK/ITALIAN.

This large restaurant evokes the atmosphere of classical Greece, when huge sailing vessels plied the Mediterranean. Giant shields adorn the walls, while banks of TVs play movies of Greek myths. Choose from among the long list of hot and cold appetizers, or the handful of pasta dishes and pizzas. The dramatic decor and five pool tables attract a huge, young crowd at night.

Omonia. 426 Danforth Ave. (at Chester). ☎ **416/465-2129.** Main courses $8–$16. AE, DC, ER, MC. Daily 11am–1am. GREEK.

Once one of the most popular local Greek tavernas, Omonia continues to offer a fun experience, complete with bouzouki sounds and jugs of wine to wash down the garlic-drenched food. Barbecued specialties, souvlaki, chicken, and pork selections are the main features. The Greek pictures, the patio, and the blue tablecloths provide an authentic ambiance.

ⓕ Family-Friendly Restaurants

Toby's Goodeats *(see p. 93)*   Enough kid-appealing items to satisfy even the fussiest child. Lots of locations.

Movenpick Bistretto *(see p.91)*   Caters to kids with a special menu, colored pencils, and drawing paper.

Jerusalem *(see p. 100)*   Features lots of finger-licking Middle Eastern foods that kids find very palatable, and fun to boot.

Kensington Kitchen *(see p. 93)*   There are pita sandwiches, brownies, and other kid-friendly fare. The airplanes and other toys that decorate the walls only add to its attraction.

✪ **Ouzeri.** 500A Danforth Ave. ☎ **416/778-0500.** Reservations not accepted. Main courses $7–$12. AE, DISC, ER, MC, V. Daily noon–3am; lunch served until 3pm; dips and appetizers only served 4–5pm. GREEK.

Ouzeri is one of the hottest places on Danforth—it's spirited, casual, and mobbed. People either jam into the few small, circular tables outside or occupy the tables inside, drinking one of the numerous international beers or wines by the glass. It's all très Athens, with tile floors, sun-drenched pastel hues, and eclectic art objects and art. The food is good and cheap. It runs the gamut from all kinds of seafood (prawns with feta and wine, sardines with mustard, calamari, broiled octopus) and all kinds of meat (pork, lamb, and beef kebabs, moussaka) to rice, pasta, and phyllo pie dishes. Various snacks, like hummus, *taramosalata,* mushrooms *à la grecque,* and *dolmades,* complete the menu,

At lunch, Ouzeri dishes out its version of dim sum, "meze sum"—hot and cold appetizers that are wheeled by on carts. Sunday brunch is a filling repast that begins with a buffet spread of appetizers and proceeds through cooked-to-order main courses. A frenetic, noisy scene, especially at night.

Pan on the Danforth. 516 Danforth Ave. ☎ **416/466-8158.** Reservations accepted for parties of six or more only. Main courses $11–$16. AE, MC, V. Sun–Thurs 5pm–midnight, Fri–Sat 5pm–1am. GREEK.

Pan is different from the other kebab houses on the street, thanks to its owner-chef, who produces imaginatively updated Greek cuisine. You can make a meal from the assortment of 20-odd hot and cold appetizers that are offered at this exciting, energetically charged hot spot. Among the more substantial dishes, try the grilled loin of lamb with a fig and orange glaze, and served with black olive mash and marinated artichokes.

7 Uptown

VERY EXPENSIVE

Chiaro's. In the King Edward Hotel, 37 King St. E. ☎ **416/863-9700.** Reservations recommended. Main courses $25–$38. AE, CB, DC, MC, V. Mon–Fri noon–2pm; Mon–Sat 6–10:30pm. FRENCH/CONTINENTAL.

For formal dining, Chiaro's, decorated in stunning gray lacquer with etched-glass panels and French-style chairs, specializes in fine French and continental cuisine. Start with smoked salmon carved from the trolley, or escargots and woodland mushrooms on a garlic essence. You might follow with a poached Dover sole tartare with shrimp, tomato, parsley, capers and cornichons; or a roast lamb with a lemon-thyme reduction, or a shelled lobster with lemon, orange, and honey sauce.

✪ **Truffles.** in The Four Seasons Hotel, 21 Avenue Rd. ☎ 416/964-0411. Reservations recommended. Main courses $26–$38. AE, DC, MC, V. Mon–Sat 6–11pm. CONTINENTAL.

Named one of the 10 best hotel restaurants in the world by *Hotel* magazine, and carrying a 5-diamond AAA rating, Truffles is certainly the premier hotel dining room in the city. The room provides a lavish setting for some exquisite cuisine. Fine materials have been used in the design of all the elements—from the marquetry floor that's fashioned from 11,000 pieces of oak, jojoba, and purpleheart wood to the curly maple walls and the custom-designed cabinets, mirrors, ceramics, and other art pieces. The cuisine is imaginative, fresh, and flavor-filled. For those who have to watch their diets, the alternative cuisine is a welcome feature on the menu, and not a hardship when you can enjoy wild mushroom risotto and baked sea bass with basil tarragon crumbs. Otherwise, you can start with the lobster salad with mustard chantilly sauce; the poached Hudson Valley foie gras in a wild mushroom broth; or the caramelized Provençal tomato tart with an anchovy vinaigrette and lamb lettuce. Follow with the baked salmon in a leek fondue sauce with black truffle mashed potatoes and salmon caviar; or the roasted venison with pear and red-wine sauce. At the conclusion, treat yourself to the spectacular pure Caraibe chocolate cake served with a raspberry cocoa sauce, or the equally inspired iced praline soufflé in chocolate netting with espresso cream.

EXPENSIVE

✪ **Centro.** 2472 Yonge St. ☎ 416/483-2211. Reservations recommended. Main courses $18–$30. AE, DC, MC, V. Mon–Sat 5–11:30pm. FRENCH/ITALIAN.

The limousine crowd treks here, three blocks north of Eglinton Avenue, to dine. Centro exhibits grand Italian style—it's a huge space with dramatic columns, a balcony, a wine bar, brilliant murals, and ultramodern Milan-style furnishings.

The cuisine is contemporary French-Italian. Among the dishes might be a filet of Canadian venison with a ragout of chestnuts, pearl onions, and mushrooms in a poivrade sauce; a grilled Provimi veal chop in a robust rosemary pinot-noir sauce; or sea scallops and red snapper in a ginger-tamari nage. There are also several pasta dishes. To start, try the terrine of Québec foie gras with Inniskillin ice-wine gelee, oven-dried pineapple, and warm brioche; or the local Woolwich goat cheese with yellow peppers, herb oil, and balsamic glaze. The international wine list is extraordinary.

The Lobster Trap. 1962 Avenue Rd. ☎ 416/787-3211. Reservations recommended. Complete dinners $23.95–$42.40. AE, DC, MC, V. Daily 5–11pm. SEAFOOD.

People wend their way north to The Lobster Trap, just north of Lawrence Avenue, for one reason only—it's the only place in the city where you can still pick out a 1- to 4-pound live lobster for an honest and fair price. You may even be sitting next to a celebrity in this dining room, where the tables have brown gingham tablecloths, and most are sheltered under a shingled construction to evoke a maritime atmosphere.

For a dinner with clam chowder or lobster bisque, a salad, rolls and butter, french fries or rice, a beverage, and a 1-pound lobster, steamed or broiled, and served with drawn butter, you'll pay $23.95. Prices rise gradually to $28 for a 1 1/2-pound crustacean. Other fish dinners are available, but stick to the lobster.

✪ **N 44.** 2537 Yonge St. ☎ **416/487-4897.** Reservations recommended. Main courses $20–$27. AE, DC, MC, V. Mon–Sat 5–11pm. INTERNATIONAL.

Those who really appreciate fine dining and have the money to indulge their habit, come north to this restaurant just south of Sherwood Avenue. A sleek art-deco beauty, it occupies a dramatic space with soaring ceilings. In the back, chefs work in the glassed-in kitchen, which is etched with the compass logo (North 44° is Toronto's latitude). The atmosphere is enhanced by mirrors, burnished stainless steel, and soft lighting that makes the room positively glow at night. The food is inspired by several international cuisines, although the emphasis is on Italian. On the dinner menu, you might find roasted rack of lamb with a pecan-mustard crust, served with a hearty Zinfandel sauce; soya-glazed red snapper with steamed clams in a saffron-scented broth; or strip steak with a salsa fresca. Pizzas and pastas are also featured. It's worth saving some room for the warm chocolate tower—a dramatic creation with a liquid center, accompanied by banana rum ice cream, and several different sauces. Besides an extensive (300-plus bottles) wine list, there are also 20 or so wines available by the glass. There's a very appealing mezzanine wine bar with piano entertainment Wednesday to Saturday.

✪ **Pronto.** 692 Mount Pleasant Rd. ☎ **416/486-1111.** Reservations required. Main courses $18–$26. AE, DC, MC, V. Daily 5–11:30pm. ITALIAN.

Behind its stucco facade, Pronto, just south of Eglinton Avenue, presents a striking and lovely low-ceilinged dining room that is vibrantly alive, and attracts a suitably well-heeled and well-dressed crowd. In the back, behind a tiled counter, you can see the chefs in their crisp white toques preparing the food. At the center of the room, there's always a lavish fresh-flower arrangement. A pianist adds to the atmosphere.

The cuisine matches the decor. The menu changes monthly, but among the appetizers you might find jerk jumbo quails served with a red bean, coconut chili in a callaloo nest; or seared deep-sea scallops on braised jicama leeks, with watercress and a carrot beet juice reduction. For a main course, try the pan-roasted breast of chicken stuffed with portobello mushrooms and sun-dried tomato, on a vegetable and potato rosti with black truffle jus; the grouper with a cilantro-and-orange glaze in a green mango butter sauce; or the rack of lamb encrusted in peppered pecans. Among the desserts, the dark-chocolate truffle tart with candied kumquats and orange zest is just the ticket.

✪ **Scaramouche.** 1 Benvenuto Place. ☎ **416/961-8011.** Reservations required. Main courses $20–$28; pasta dishes $13–$18. AE, DC, MC, V. Main room: Mon–Sat 6–10pm. Pasta bar: Mon–Fri 6–11pm, Sat 6pm–midnight. CONTINENTAL.

Scaramouche sustains its reputation as one of Toronto's top-class restaurants by drawing an "old money" crowd. A little difficult to find (it's located in the basement of an apartment building, four blocks south of St. Clair Avenue and Avenue Road), it's certainly worth seeking out. Try to secure a window seat, which grants a view of the downtown city skyline. The decor, the flower arrangements, and the careful presentation of the food make the experience special.

Although the menu changes frequently, it will feature a selection of hot and cold appetizers such as fresh calamari with grilled onion, leeks, and fennel in a cumin and saffron nage; or warm grilled lobster and roasted pepper terrine on an asparagus and sweet-onion salad with mango and vanilla vinaigrette. Among the eight or so entrees, you might enjoy the roasted rack of lamb with a red currant glaze, served in a sauté of caramelized onions, artichoke hearts, eggplant, leek, and roasted peppers; or the hickory-smoked and -grilled salmon with grilled vegetables wrapped in a buckwheat crepe with horseradish hollandaise. You can always select from the pasta-bar menu, which offers similar appetizers and excitingly prepared fettuccine, linguine, lasagna, and cannelloni. The desserts are equally celebrated—the warm, flourless chocolate cake on espresso shortbread with white-chocolate banana sauce and the Tahitian vanilla crème brûlée with fresh berries are particularly good. The wine list includes some great French and American selections.

Zachary's. In the Bristol Place Hotel, 950 Dixon Rd. ☎ **416/675-9444**. Reservations recommended. Main courses $25–$30. AE, DC, MC, V. Mon–Fri noon–2:30pm; Mon–Sat 6–10pm; brunch Sun 11am–3pm. ECLECTIC.

For years, Zachary's has been known as the one airport-area hotel restaurant serving consistently good food—an appropriate reputation for a restaurant named after Antoine Zachary Blanchard, chef to Napoléon, the Czars, and Queen Isabella II of Spain. House specialties include fresh Dover sole, rack of lamb crusted with grain mustard and served with a sweet garlic and shallot sauce, plus Asian- and Mediterranean-inspired dishes like the Thai shrimp and scallops in coconut ginger sauce, or the monkfish medallions in white wine tomato coulis. Traditional favorites— Caesar salad, lobster bisque—are found alongside such taste-tingling appetizers as the coconut dusted roasted black tiger shrimps, served with cilantro chutney, mustard fenugreek potato, and sweet yogurt, or the Cajun-spiced, seared alligator fillets served with ancho chili ketchup and mango relish. For dessert, I rated the toffee caramel cheesecake with butterscotch sauce at the top of the list. The hot-and cold- Sunday buffet bruch is also popular for distinguished dessert table and the chance to savor, among other things, a salmon-and-caviar omelet.

MODERATE

Brownes Bistro. 4 Woodlawn Ave. E. ☎ **416/924-8132**. Reservations recommended. Main courses $13–$20. AE, MC, V. Mon–Fri noon–2pm; daily 5:30–10:30pm. FRENCH/ LIGHT FARE.

Just south of St. Clair Avenue in the heart of Rosedale, Brownes Bistro attracts the mink-wrapped and suited crowd. The decor is low-key—mahogany combined with pale gray walls supporting black-and-white photographs of the French countryside. The bistro fare includes such comforting dishes as braised lamb shank with root vegetables, and New York strip loin with roasted garlic-shallot butter and frites. There are several fine pizzas and pasta dishes, too.

Coppi. 3363 Yonge St. ☎ **416/484-4464**. Reservations recommended at dinner. Main courses $15–$22. AE, ER, MC, V. Mon–Fri noon–2pm, Sat 5:30–10:30pm. ITALIAN.

Named after Fausto Coppi, the legendary Italian cyclist who died of malaria, this restaurant features poster-size photographs of Coppi at various stages of his career. It's a lively, modern, low-lit room, which attracts a knowing clientele that appreciates its not overpriced, but well-prepared cuisine. The kitchen turns out grilled dishes—calf's liver, chicken breast, salmon and red snapper—along with pasta and risottos. There's a well-priced, but predominantly Italian wine list.

Grano. 2035 Yonge St. ☎ **416/440-1986**. Reservations accepted for parties of six or more. Main courses $17–$19. AE, DC, MC, V. Mon–Fri 10am–10:30pm, Sat 10am–11pm. ITALIAN.

Grano is a wild Italian celebration—a celebration of down-to-earth food served in an atmosphere of washed Mediterranean pastels. It's casual and fun. The wine is served in tumblers; there's a courtyard out back; and the tables are painted in brilliant colors of mustard and cherry. The latest Italian art posters decorate the walls, large colorful majolica vessels abound, and arias waft over the whole scene. At the entrance, the display counters are filled with more than 50 different antipasti, and any three (piccolo) or seven (grande) of these can be ordered, ranging in price from $10 for a small all-vegetable plate to $24 for a large plate of salmon carpaccio. In addition, there are several pasta dishes, like the rigatoni siracusa with eggplant, peppers, olives, anchovies, and capers in a spicy tomato sauce; and the gnocchi in a pink sauce. The meat or fish entrees change daily. To finish, there's tiramisu, biscotti, and a variety of Italian custard-cream desserts.

Herbs. 3187 Yonge St. (north of Lawrence). ☎ **416/322-0487.** Reservations recommended. Main courses $12–$21. AE, DC, ER, MC, V. Mon–Fri 11:30am–2pm; Sun–Thurs 5:30–10pm, Fri–Sat 5:30–11pm. CONTINENTAL.

Brilliant colors and designs inspired by nature are the hallmarks of this appealing restaurant, which attracts a loyal, well-off Lawrence Park crowd. Walls of brilliant yellow, burnt orange, and crimson serve as backdrops for paintings, which are actually for sale. Tables sport floral-design tablecloths of brilliant pink, mauve, and turquoise topped with butcher paper.

The food is eclectically continental. Among the 12 or so main courses, you might find pan-roasted Atlantic salmon coated in freshly chopped herbs and served with a gazpacho sauce; a confit of duck on braised red cabbage, with potato galette and a cassis-and-blackberry glaze; or calf's liver with a blood-orange glaze. The desserts are sublime. You'll succumb to the lemon tart, served on a huge Villeroy & Boch china plate, and artistically presented with figs, strawberries, and an intense raspberry and crème sorbet.

La Grenouille. 2387 Yonge St. ☎ **416/481-3093.** Reservations recommended. Main courses $14–$20. AE, DC, MC, V. Mon–Fri noon–2:30pm and 5:30–10:30pm, Sat 6–11pm. FRENCH.

La Grenouille is a simple French bistro serving reasonably priced, well-prepared food to a largely local crowd. The atmosphere is provided by candlelight, French music, and a sage-green neon sign reflecting against the storefront window. Select from the nine or so entrees—orange roughy in a shallot-and-butter sauce; rabbit in white wine with mushrooms, tomatoes, and fresh herbs; and frog's legs, of course, sautéed in garlic butter, and sprinkled with fresh parsley and lemon juice. There is a selection of soups, including a Mediterranean fish soup served with Emmenthal, croutons, and rouille; or you can begin with various salads and appetizers, including deep-fried Brie on a coulis of fresh raspberries. Desserts are traditional French or Italian ice cream specialties, with the exception of the fresh pear ice flavored with pear eau-de-vie, set in Grand Marnier white-chocolate-chip ice cream and rolled in ground white chocolate. The wine list is strictly French.

Le Paradis. 166 Bedford Rd. (north of Davenport). ☎ **416/921-0995.** Reservations recommended. Main courses $8–$16.50; prix fixe $15.95. AE, MC, V. Tues–Fri noon–3pm; Tues–Sat 6–11pm, Sun, Mon 5:30–10pm. FRENCH.

At night when the French doors are flung open to the street and Le Paradis is filled with chattering diners being served by aproned waiters, you could swear that you're in a residential area of Paris. The room is long and narrow, with banquettes and tables stretching alongside one wall, facing the bar opposite. European posters and photographs only add to the atmosphere. The offerings are typical bistro fare—chicken roasted with tarragon; flank steak with fries—with some regional specialties, such as braised rabbit with onion, fennel, tomato, and garlic in white wine; or lamb and beef sausage, served on couscous. Many of the dishes, especially the seafood offerings, change daily and are listed on a blackboard. Desserts are traditionally French—

mousses, tartes, and ice cream concoctions. The best value is the three-course prix-fixe menu for only $17.50.

Thai Magic. 1118 Yonge St. ☎ **416/968-7366.** Reservations recommended. Main courses $10–$17. AE, MC, V. Mon–Fri 11:30am–2:30pm; Mon–Sat 5:30–11pm. THAI.

Magical, indeed, is this long, narrow restaurant filled with orchids, Thai statuary, and artifacts. Warm mauves and greens make it even more inviting—the perfect backdrop for the sophisticated cuisine. Start with a combination plate of appetizers, *tom yum kai* (a really spicy soup flavored with lemongrass and containing succulent shrimp), or the familiar noodle dish, pad Thai. For main courses, there are stir-frys and curries (like the flavorsome chicken green curry or shrimp red curry with okra) as well as such dishes as chicken with basil, tamarind fish, coriander lobster, or shrimp lemongrass—the last a specialty that uses a unique family recipe.

Trapper's. 3479 Yonge St. ☎ **416/482-6211.** Reservations recommended. Main courses $14–$23 at dinner. AE, MC, V. Mon–Fri 11:30am–2:30pm; Mon–Sat 5–10pm, Sun 5–9:30pm. CONTINENTAL.

Trapper's, between Lawrence Avenue and York Mills Road, draws moneyed suits. The seasonal menu features only the best Canadian ingredients. Start with the Prince Edward Island mussels steamed in Ontario Riesling, lemongrass, and a jalapeno tomato broth; or the baked almond-crusted local goat cheese with fresh pears and melon in a raspberry sauce. Follow with grilled Ontario pork tenderloin with a spiced orange-and-pecan glaze, or filet of Muskoka trout seared in Acadian spices with citrus fruit and toasted almonds or a cucumber, tomatillo, and dill salsa. Pasta dishes are also offered. The wine list is extensive.

INEXPENSIVE

Jerusalem. 955 Eglinton Ave. W. ☎ **416/783-6494.** Reservations not accepted. Main courses $9–$14. AE, MC, V. Mon–Thurs noon–11pm, Fri–Sat noon–midnight, Sun noon–10pm. MIDDLE EASTERN.

At Jerusalem, just west of Bathurst Street, it's the food and the prices that count. The decor is simple—just some hammered-brass tabletops on the walls—but the atmosphere is extremely warm, and the service friendly and unhurried. All the appetizers are less than $4—falafel, kibbeh (a cracked-wheat roll stuffed with ground meat, onions, and pine nuts), various styles of hummus, tahini, and tabbouleh (a delicious blend of cracked wheat with chopped tomatoes, onions, parsley, mint, lemon, and olive oil). You can follow them with liver fried in garlic and hot-pepper sauce, siniyeh (mixed ground lamb and beef with onions, parsley, and pine nuts, oven baked with tahini sauce), and lamb or beef shish kebab. Finish with a cup of thick, luxurious Turkish coffee.

8 Cafes & Java Joints

Diet books, Optifast, and Weight Watchers may still be fighting the battle of the bulge, but **Just Desserts,** 306 Davenport Rd. (☎ **416/922-6824**), is a worthy opponent, staying open practically around the clock on weekends, for those in need of a sugar fix. Around 30 desserts are available—as many as 8 different cheesecakes, 10 or so assorted pies, plus a whole array of gâteaux, tortes, and meringues (all around $5). I don't need to describe them—just go, order with a cappuccino or coffee, savor every bite, and feel bad afterward. At the Davenport branch, you can enjoy them in a nostalgic atmosphere created by oak swivel chairs, black-tiled tables, old-movie/Broadway melodies, and whimsical old-fashioned cookie jars. Open Monday through Wednesday 8am to 1am, Thursday and Friday 8am to 3am, Saturday 9:30am to 3am, and Sunday 9:30am to 1am. Also located at 139 John St. (☎ **416/ 599-0655**).

Dufflet Pastries, 787 Queen St. West (☎ **416/504-2870**), has extraordinarily beautiful and wonderful-tasting tarts and pastries that can be accompanied by a full range of coffees.

Demetre, 400 Danforth Ave. (☎ **416/778-6654**), is a great old-fashioned cafe, which is jammed on weekends with families enjoying Belgian waffles and outrageous sundaes as well as cakes, tortes, and baklava.

Many Torontonians swear that the best ice cream is found at the **Sicilian Ice Cream Company,** 710–712 College St. (☎ **416/531-7716**).

Long before Starbucks arrived on the North American scene, Torontonians were sipping fine coffees at a variety of small coffee chains as well as at many independent and characterful cafes. Today, even though Starbucks has opened in Toronto, many of the citizens remain loyal to their own coffee bars.

The two biggest chains are the **Second Cup** (about 30 branches) which offers a full range of different flavored coffees and espresso varieties plus cakes, muffins, croissants, and gift items, and **Timothy's** (about 20 branches), which invites you to pour your own selection from about 8 to 10 varieties. **The Croissant Tree,** with six or so branches, sells a variety of coffees plus a full range of pastry items. **Future Bakery & Cafes,** 739 Queen St. West (☎ **416/368-4235**), and 483 Bloor St. West (☎ **416/922-5875**), attracts an artsy, literate crowd. **Lettieri Espresso Bar-Cafe,** 94 Cumberland (☎ **416/515-8764**), and 441 Queen St. West (☎ **416/592-1360**), has all kinds of coffees—lattes, mochas, the works—plus focaccia sandwiches, and a full range of tarts, cookies, and pastries.

Some of the best authentic cafes are found in Little Italy along College Street West. Among the oldest (and one of the few that has not been "modernized"), is **Cafe Diplomatico,** 594 College St. (☎ **416/534-4637**), which has traditional mosaic marble floors, wrought-iron chairs, and an extra-large sidewalk patio. Old Italians, artists, and students all hang out here as they have done since the place opened in 1968. The young, beautiful, and hip gather at **Bar Italia,** 582 College St. (☎ **416/ 535-3621**), and also at the **College Street Bar,** 574 College St. (☎ **416/533-2417**), while an older and more sophisticated crowd comes together at **Sottovoce,** 595 College St. (☎ **416/536-4564**), the modern Italian cafe par excellence with ritzy Milan-style decor and music to match. Another small, intimate cafe-bar is **Wild Indigo,** 607 College St. (☎ **416/536-8797**), which has a tiny patio in the back.

In Yorkville, the **Cubita Cafe,** 848A Yonge St. (☎ **416/927-7905**), has plenty of atmosphere with its dark wood accents and fine Cuban coffee served with pastries and snacks. Lettieri has a branch here, too, on Cumberland.

On Queen Street, an artsy intellectual crowd enjoys the **Epicure Cafe,** 512 Queen St. (☎ **416/363-8942**), which also serves full lunch and dinner menus. Posters, marble tables, and jazz create a certain European ambiance. Farther west along Queen, the **Gypsy Coop,** at no. 815 (☎ **416/703-5069**), has a 1960s hippies air. Coffee is not the only king here. Instead, many different teas and infusions are available, which you can take with one of the super-rich and satisfying brownies.

Cafes also line Bloor Street in the Annex neighborhood. Among the more interesting is the **Daily Express Cafe,** 280 Bloor St. West (☎ **416/944-3225**), which produces its very own newspaper. It's atmospheric and draws mainly a student crowd.

6 What to See & Do in Toronto

It takes 5 or 6 days to really see Toronto's highlights. Although some of the major sights are centrally located, there are also several favorites outside the downtown core, and these take extra time and effort to reach. Ideally, you should spend 1 day each at Ontario Place, the Ontario Science Centre, Canada's Wonderland, and Harbourfront. In fact, that's what the kids will definitely want to do. Then there's also the zoo, which could take a whole day, complete with a picnic.

The Art Gallery of Ontario, Chinatown, and the Royal Ontario Museum (ROM), could be combined in a pinch, but the day might be too museum-oriented for some. Ontario Place could conceivably be combined with Fort York and Exhibition Place. En route to Canada's Wonderland, you could stop in at Black Creek Pioneer Village, but I don't recommend it since it will cut into your time at Canada's Wonderland, which really requires a full day.

As you can see, there are numerous major attractions in Toronto worthy of a whole day's visit. There are also many other downtown sights and neighborhoods—the CN Tower, the Eaton Centre, Yorkville, Queen Street, City Hall, and Casa Loma—that you may want to explore. Depending on your interests and whether you have children, there's enough to keep you going for several weeks in Toronto.

1 The Top Attractions

ON THE LAKEFRONT

Ontario Place. 955 Lakeshore Blvd. W. ☎ **416/314-9811,** or 416/314-9900 for a recording. Free admission, with some exceptions (like the CNE). IMAX movies $6 adults, $3 seniors and children 12 and under. All-day pass that admits you to the majority of attractions at CNE, and saves you more than $50 on admissions to individual attractions, is $18.95. Mid-May to Labor Day, daily 10:30am–midnight. Parking: $9. Take the subway to Bathurst or Dufferin, and buses south from there to Exhibition. Call TTC Information (☎ 416/393-4636) for special bus service details.

When this 96-acre recreation complex on Lake Ontario opened in 1971, it seemed futuristic—and 25 years later, it still does (the 1989 renovation no doubt helped). From a distance, you'll see five steel-and-glass pods suspended on columns 105 feet above the lake, three artificial islands, and, alongside, a huge geodesic dome. The five pods contain a multimedia theater, a live children's theater, a high-technology exhibit, and displays that tell the story of Ontario in vivid kaleidoscopic detail. The dome houses Cinesphere, where a 60- by 80-foot screen shows specially made IMAX movies.

Located under an enormous orange canopy, the Children's Village provides a well-supervised area where children aged 12 and under can scramble over rope bridges, bounce on an enormous trampoline, slide down a twisting chute, or, most popular of all, squirt water pistols and garden hoses, swim, and generally drench one another in the water-play section. Afterward, parents can use the convenient changing room and washroom facilities before moving on to three specialty children's theaters.

A stroll around the complex reveals two marinas full of yachts and other craft, the HMCS *Haida* (a destroyer, open for touring, that served in both World War II and the Korean War), a miniature 18-hole golf course, plenty of grassland for picnicking and general cavorting, and a wide variety of restaurants and snack bars serving everything from Chinese, Irish, German, and Canadian food to hot dogs and hamburgers. And don't miss the wildest rides in town—Rush River, which carries you along a lengthy flume in an inflatable raft; the Wilderness Adventure, another flume ride; Hydrofuge, a tube slide that allows you to reach speeds of 50 kilometers per hour (31 m.p.h.); and Sea Trek, a deep-sea simulator ride. There are also bumper and paddle boats, go-carts, and a game called Hoops that combines basketball, miniature golf, and billiards.

During the summer, the complex also offers a full range of entertainments at several theaters and stages, including the Molson amphitheater. For tickets, call TicketMaster at **416/870-8000.**

✪ **Harbourfront Centre.** Queen's Quay W. ☎ **416/973-3000** for information on special events, or 416/973-4000 for the box office. Take the LRT from Union Station, the no. 77B bus from Union Station or the Spadina subway station, or the no. 6 or 6A bus to the foot of Bay St. and walk west.

In 1972, the federal government took over a 96-acre strip of prime waterfront land to preserve the waterfront vista—and since then Torontonians have rediscovered their lakeshore. Abandoned warehouses, shabby depots, and crumbling factories have been refurbished, and a tremendous urban park now stretches on and around the old piers. The resulting Harbourfront has to be one of Toronto's most exciting happenings. It's a great place to spend the day.

Queen's Quay, at the foot of York Street, is the closest quay to town, and it's the first point you'll encounter as you approach from the Westin Harbour Castle. From here, boats depart for tours of the harbor and islands. An old renovated warehouse now houses a dance theater, plus two floors of shops, restaurants, and waterfront cafes.

After exploring Queen's Quay, walk west along the glorious waterfront promenade to York Quay. To get there, you'll pass the Power Plant, a contemporary gallery, and behind it, the Du Maurier Theatre Centre. At York Quay Centre you can secure a lot of information on programming as well as entertain yourself in several galleries, including The Craft Studio, where you can watch artisans blow glass, throw pots, and make silk-screen prints. On the other side of the center, you can attend a free Molson Dry Front Music outdoor concert, held all summer long at Molson Place. Also on the quay in the center is the Water's Edge Cafe, overlooking a small pond for electric model boats and a children's play area.

From here, take the footbridge to John Quay, crossing over the sailboats moored below, to the stores and restaurants on **Pier 4**—Wallymagoo's Marine Bar, and the Pier 4 Storehouse. Beyond on Maple Leaf Quay lies the Nautical Centre.

At the **Harbourside Boating Centre,** 283 Queen's Quay West (☎ **416/ 203-3000**), you can rent sail- and powerboats as well as sign up for sailing lessons.

A 4-hour rental costs from $45 to $395, depending on the boat's size. Week-long and weekend sailing courses are also offered.

The **Harbourfront Antiques Market,** at 390 Queen's Quay West, at the foot of Spadina Avenue (☎ **416/260-2626**), will keep antique-lovers busy browsing for hours. More than 150 antique dealers spread out their wares—jewelry, china, furniture, toys, and books. Indoor parking is adjacent to the market, and a cafeteria serves fresh salads, sandwiches, and desserts for rest stops. It's open May through October, Tuesday through Friday from 10am to 6pm, Saturday from 10am to 6pm, and Sunday from 8 to 6pm; November through April, Tuesday through Friday from 11am to 5pm, Saturday and Sunday from 10am to 6pm.

At the west end of the park stands **Bathurst Pier,** with a large sports field for romping around, plus two adventure playgrounds, one for older kids and the other (supervised) for 3- to 7-year-olds.

More than 4,000 events take place annually at Harbourfront, including a Harbourfront Reading Festival, held every Tuesday on York Quay, which attracts some very eminent writers. Other happenings include films, dance, theater, music, children's events, multicultural festivals and marine events. Two of the most important events are the annual Children's Festival and the International Festival of Authors. Most activities are free.

✪ **The Toronto Islands.** ☎ **416/392-8193,** for ferry schedules. Round-trip fare $3 adults, $1.50 seniors and ages 15–19, $1 for children 15 and under. Ferries operate all day, leaving from the docks at the bottom of Bay Street. To get there, take a subway to Union Station and the Bay St. bus south.

A little ferry will take you across to 612 acres of island park crisscrossed by shady paths and quiet waterways—a glorious spot to walk, play tennis, bike, feed the ducks, putter around in boats, picnic, or just sit. There are 14 islands in total, but the three major islands are Centre, Ward's, and Algonquin. The first is the busiest; the other two are home to about 600 people who live in modest cottages. Originally, the land was an archipelago, but in the mid-1800s a series of storms shattered the finger of land into islands.

On Centre Island, children enjoy **Centreville** (☎ **416/203-0405**), a 19-acre old-time amusement park, built and designed especially for them. But you won't find the usual neon signs, shrill hawkers, and the aroma of greasy hot-dog stands. Instead you'll find a turn-of-the-century village complete with a Main Street, tiny shops, a firehouse, and even a small working farm where the kids can pet lambs and chicks and enjoy pony rides. They'll also love trying out the miniature antique cars, fire engines, old-fashioned train, authentic 1890s carousel, flume ride, and the aerial cars. Admission is free, but there is a charge for the rides (84¢). Open daily from mid-May to Labor Day, 10:30am to 6pm.

DOWNTOWN

CN Tower. 301 Front St. W. ☎ **416/360-8500.** Admission $12 adults, $10 seniors, $8 children 5–12. Cosmic Pinball, Q-Zar, and Virtual World $8, $8, and $7, respectively. Any two combinations $17, $15, and $13; any four combinations $27, $25, and $23. Cosmic Pinball, Q-Zar, and Virtual World: summer, daily 10am–10pm; fall, Sun–Thurs 10am–8pm, Fri–Sat 10am–10pm; winter, Sun–Thurs 11am–8pm, Fri–Sat 11am–10pm. CN Tower: summer, daily 10am–midnight; fall, 9am–11pm; winter, 10am–10pm Subway: Union, then walk west along Front St.

As you approach the city, the first thing you'll notice is this slender needlelike structure. Tiny colored elevators glide to the top of its 1,815-foot-high tower—the tallest free-standing structure in the world.

As you enter the tower's base, look up through the atrium to the top—yes, that's where you're going. Glass-walled elevators on the outside walls of the tower whisk you to the 1,136-foot-high seven-level sky pod in just under a minute. From here, you can sometimes see all the way to Niagara Falls or even to Buffalo. One of the two observation levels is partially open to allow you to experience that dizzying sensation of height (vertigo sufferers beware).

Besides the view, the tower offers several futuristic attractions—the Cosmic Pinball, a simulator ride that duplicates the experience of a pinball, catapulting riders at a high velocity past flashing lights, flippers, bumpers, and other hazards; Q-Zar, an exhilarating, live-action laser tag game; and Virtual World, a virtual reality center, featuring two interactive games, Battletech and Red Planet. The games take place in spaces that are similar to the cockpit of a jet-fighter plane, and players are free to interact among themselves, not just with the computer, which makes the experience far more unpredictable. The pod also contains broadcasting facilities and **360,** a revolving restaurant (for lunch, dinner, or Sunday brunch reservations, call **416/362-5411**).

Atop the tower sits a 335-foot antenna mast that took 31 weeks to erect with the aid of a giant Sikorsky helicopter. It took 555 lifts to complete the operation. Above the sky pod is the world's highest public observation gallery, the Space Deck, 1,465 feet above the ground. The Outdoor Observation deck one floor below has a glass floor, which makes for a scary experience and a real bird's-eye view of the SkyDome. While you're up there, don't worry about the elements sweeping the tower into the lake: It's built of contoured reinforced concrete covered with thick glass-reinforced plastic, and designed to keep ice accumulation to a minimum. The structure can withstand high winds, snow, ice, lightning, and earth tremors.

SkyDome. 1 Blue Jays Way. ☎ **416/341-2770.** Tours $9.50 adults, $7 students 16 and under and seniors, $6 children 4–11, free for children under 3. Tour schedule depends on events/sports schedule. Subway: Union.

In 1989, the opening of the 53,000-seat SkyDome, home to the Toronto Blue Jays baseball team and the Toronto Argonauts football team, was a gala event. In 1992, SkyDome became the first Canadian stadium to host the World Series, with the Blue Jays grabbing the pennant that year and the following. The stadium itself represents an engineering feat, featuring the world's first fully retractable roof, which spans more than 8 acres, and a gigantic video scoreboard. So large is it that you could fit a 31-story building inside the complex when the roof is closed. Indeed, there's already a spectacular 11-story hotel with 70 rooms facing directly onto the field.

✪ Art Gallery of Ontario. 317 Dundas St. W., between McCaul and Beverley sts. ☎ **416/977-0414.** Admission $7.50 adults, $15 families (two adults plus children), $4 students and seniors, free for children under 12. Free on Wed 5–10pm, and for seniors on Fri. Thurs–Mon 10am–5:30pm; Wed 10am–10pm. Grange House: Thurs–Sun noon–4pm; Wed noon–9pm. Closed Mon–Tues in winter, Christmas Day, and New Year's Day. Subway: St. Patrick on the University line; or take the subway to Dundas and the streetcar west.

Impressions

A global psychiatrist, if asked to take a look at Toronto's rather unhealthy obsession with the CN Tower, would advise the city to take a cold shower and lie down on the couch for a spell.

—Allan Fotheringham, *Maclean's* (1975)

Downtown Toronto Attractions

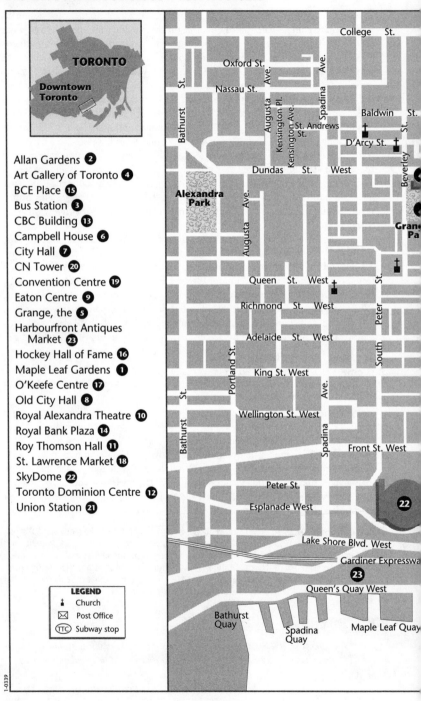

Allan Gardens ❷
Art Gallery of Toronto ❹
BCE Place ⓯
Bus Station ❸
CBC Building ⓭
Campbell House ❻
City Hall ❼
CN Tower ⓴
Convention Centre ⓳
Eaton Centre ❾
Grange, the ❺
Harbourfront Antiques
   Market ㉓
Hockey Hall of Fame ⓰
Maple Leaf Gardens ❶
O'Keefe Centre ⓱
Old City Hall ❽
Royal Alexandra Theatre ❿
Royal Bank Plaza ⓮
Roy Thomson Hall ⓫
St. Lawrence Market ⓲
SkyDome ㉒
Toronto Dominion Centre ⓬
Union Station ㉑

LEGEND
✝ Church
✉ Post Office
Ⓣ Subway stop

1-0339

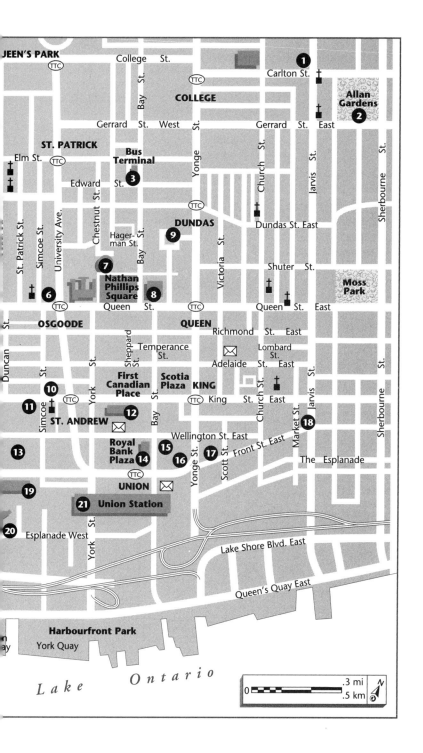

The exterior gives no hint of the light and openness inside this beautifully designed gallery. The newly refurbished and expanded gallery is dramatic and the paintings are imaginatively displayed. Throughout are audiovisual presentations and interactive computer presentations that provide information on particular paintings or schools of painters. Although the European collections are fine, I would concentrate on the Canadian galleries. The galleries displaying the Group of Seven—Tom Thomson, F. H. Varley, Lawren Harris, Emily Carr, and others—are extraordinary. In addition, other galleries show the genesis of Canadian art from earlier to more modern artists. Don't miss the galleries featuring Inuit art.

The Henry Moore Sculpture Centre, possessing more than 700 works on paper (woodcuts, lithographs, etchings, and drawings), and 143 sculptures (original plasters, bronzes, maquettes), is the largest public collection of his works. They were given to Toronto by the artist, supposedly because he was so moved by the citizens' enthusiasm for his work (remember, public donations bought the sculpture that decorates Nathan Phillips Square at City Hall). In one room, under a glass ceiling, 20 or so of his large works stand like silent prehistoric rock formations. Along the walls flanking a ramp are color photographs showing Moore's major sculptures in their natural locations, which fully reveal their magnificent dimensions.

The collection of European old masters ranges from the 14th century to the French impressionists and beyond. An octagonal room is filled with works by Pissarro, Monet, Boudin, Sisley, and Renoir. De Kooning's *Two Women on a Wharf* and Karel Appel's *Black Landscape* are just two of the more modern examples. Among the sculptures, you'll find Picasso's *Poupée* and Brancusi's *First Cry,* two beauties.

Behind the gallery and connected by an arcade stands The Grange (1817), Toronto's oldest surviving brick house, and the gallery's first permanent space. Originally the home of the Boulton family, it was a gathering place for many of the city's social and political leaders as well as for such eminent guests as Matthew Arnold, Prince Kropotkin, and Winston Churchill. Today it's a living museum of mid–19th-century Toronto life, having been meticulously restored and furnished to reflect the 1830s. Entrance is free with admission to the art gallery.

The gallery has an attractive restaurant/atrium bar open for lunch and dinner as well as a cafeteria, a gallery shop, plus a full program of films, concerts, and lectures.

MIDTOWN

✪ **Royal Ontario Museum.** 100 Queen's Park Crescent. ☎ 416/586-5549. Admission (including admission to the George R. Gardiner Museum of Ceramic Art) $8 adults, $4 seniors, students, and children 5–14, $16 families, free for children under 5; free for seniors all day on Tues, free for all Tues 4:30–8pm. Mon–Sat 10am–6pm (until 8pm on Tues), Sun 11am–6pm. Closed Christmas Day and New Year's Day. Subway: Museum or St. George.

The ROM, as it's affectionately called, is Canada's largest museum, with more than six million objects in its collections.

Among the many highlights is the world-renowned Chinese collection, to which a new suite of galleries was added in 1996. This space enabled the museum to supplement the already impressive collection with some 1200 additional Chinese artifacts. One of the collection's treasures is the impressive procession of 100 earthenware figures including ox-drawn carts, soldiers, musicians, officials and attendants dating from the early 6th to the late 7th century A.D. Visitors can also see outstanding examples of early weapons and tools, oracle bones, bronzes and jades, ceramic vessels, human and animal figures, and jewelry and fashion ornaments.

The Sigmund Samuel Canadiana Gallery displays a premiere collection of early Canadian decorative arts and historical paintings showcased in elaborate period room settings. Other highlights include the Roman Gallery (the most extensive collection in Canada), the world-class textile collection, nine life-science galleries (devoted to evolution, mammals, reptiles, and botany), and The Gallery of Indigenous Peoples, featuring changing exhibitions exploring the past and present cultures of Canada's indigenous peoples.

A favorite with kids is the Bat Cave Gallery, a miniature replica of the St. Clair bat cave in Jamaica, complete with more than 4,000 very lifelike bats roosting and flying through the air amid realistic spiders, crabs, a wild cat, and snakes. Kids also like the Dinosaur Gallery, featuring 13 dinosaur skeletons, and the Discovery Gallery, a minimuseum where kids and adults alike can touch authentic artifacts from Egyptian scarabs to English military helmets.

The ROM's light and airy cafeteria and dining lounge, with a small terrace for outdoor dining, is under the expert supervision of Jamie Kennedy, one of Canada's top chefs. It's well-worth stopping in for lunch or dinner.

✪ **George R. Gardiner Museum of Ceramic Art.** 111 Queen's Park. ☎ **416/586-8080.** Admission (including admission to the ROM) $8 adults; $4 seniors, students, and children; $16 families. Tues–Sat 10am–5pm, Sun 11am–5pm. From Victoria Day to Labor Day, it's open until 7:30pm on Tues. Closed Christmas Day and New Year's Day. Subway: Museum or St. George.

Across the street from the ROM, the George R. Gardiner Museum, North America's only specialized ceramics museum, houses a great collection of 15th- to 18th-century European ceramics in four galleries. The pre-Columbian gallery contains fantastic Olmec and Mayan figures, and objects from Ecuador, Colombia, and Peru. The majolica gallery displays spectacular 16th- and 17th-century pieces from Florence, Faenza, and Venice, and a Delftware collection of fine 17th-century chargers and other examples.

Upstairs, the galleries are given over to 18th-century continental and English porcelain—Meissen, Sèvres, Worcester, Chelsea, Derby, and other great names. All are spectacular. Among the highlights are pieces from the Swan Service—a 2,200-piece set that took 4 years (1737–41) to make—and an extraordinary collection of Commedia dell'Arte figures.

ON THE OUTSKIRTS

✪ **Ontario Science Centre.** 770 Don Mills Rd. (at Eglinton Ave. E.). ☎ **416/429-4100.** Admission $7.50 adults, $5.50 youths 11–17, $3 seniors and children 5–10, $17 families; children under 5 free. Summer, daily 10am–8pm; Sept 3 to Memorial Day, daily 10am–6pm. Closed Christmas Day. Parking $5. Take the Young St. subway to Eglinton; then the Eglinton bus going east; get off at Don Mills Rd. If you're driving from downtown, take the Don Valley Pkwy. and follow the signs from Don Mills Rd. north.

Described as everything from the world's most technical fun fair to a hands-on museum for the 21st century, the Science Centre really does hold a series of wonders for adult and child—with no fewer than 800 interactive exhibits. With more than a million people visiting every year, it's best to get here promptly at 10am—that way, you'll be able to get around without too much interference and negotiation.

Wherever you look, there are things to touch, push, pull, or crank. Test your reflexes, balance, heart rate, and grip strength; surf the Internet; walk through a tropical rain forest; watch frozen-solid liquid nitrogen shatter into thousands of icy shards; study slides of butterfly wings, bedbugs, fish scales, or feathers under the microscope; tease your brain with a variety of optical illusions; land a spaceship on the moon; watch bees making honey; see how many lights you can light or how high you can elevate a balloon with your own pedal power. The fun goes on and on in 10 separate, themed exhibit halls.

Midtown Toronto Attractions

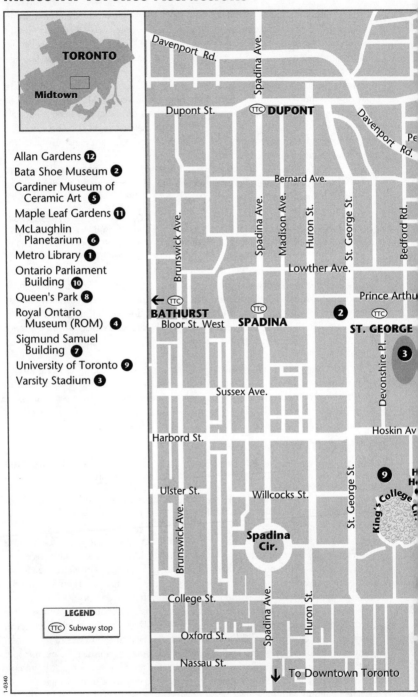

Midtown

TORONTO

Allan Gardens ⓬
Bata Shoe Museum ❷
Gardiner Museum of
 Ceramic Art ❺
Maple Leaf Gardens ⓫
McLaughlin
 Planetarium ❻
Metro Library ❶
Ontario Parliament
 Building ❿
Queen's Park ❽
Royal Ontario
 Museum (ROM) ❹
Sigmund Samuel
 Building ❼
University of Toronto ❾
Varsity Stadium ❸

Davenport Rd.
Spadina Ave.
Dupont St. ⓉⓉⒸ **DUPONT**
Davenport Rd.
Pe
Bernard Ave.
Brunswick Ave.
Spadina Ave.
Madison Ave.
Huron St.
St. George St.
Bedford Rd.
Lowther Ave.
Prince Arthu
← ⓉⓉⒸ
BATHURST
Bloor St. West
ⓉⓉⒸ
SPADINA
❷
ⓉⓉⒸ
ST. GEORGE
❸
Devonshire Pl.
Sussex Ave.
Hoskin Av
Harbord St.
❾
H
H
Ulster St.
Willcocks St.
St. George St.
King's College
**Spadina
Cir.**
College St.
Spadina Ave.
Huron St.
Oxford St.
Nassau St.
↓ To Downtown Toronto

LEGEND
ⓉⓉⒸ Subway stop

1-0340

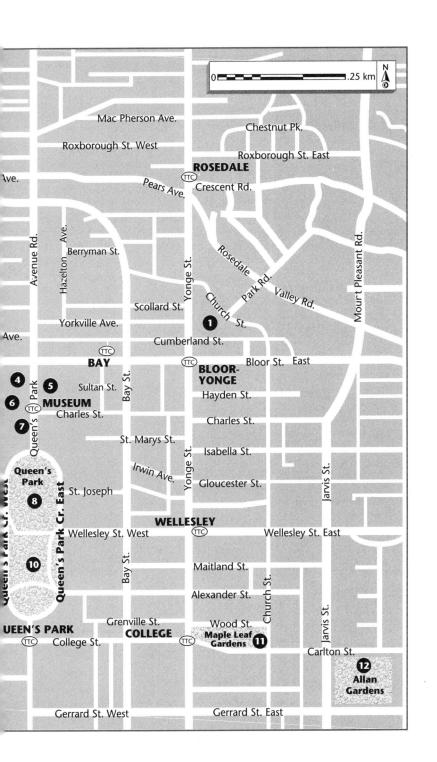

Mac Pherson Ave.

Roxborough St. West

Chestnut Pk.

Roxborough St. East

ROSEDALE

Pears Ave.

Crescent Rd.

Ave.

Rosedale

Avenue Rd.

Hazelton Ave.

Berryman St.

Yonge St.

Park Rd.

Valley Rd.

Mount Pleasant Rd.

Scollard St.

Church St.

Yorkville Ave.

1

Ave.

Cumberland St.

BAY

Bloor St. East

**BLOOR-
YONGE**

4 **5**

Sultan St.

Bay St.

Hayden St.

6

MUSEUM

Charles St.

Queen's Park

Charles St.

7

St. Marys St.

Isabella St.

Jarvis St.

Irwin Ave.

Yonge St.

Gloucester St.

**Queen's
Park**

St. Joseph

8

Queen's Park Cr. East

WELLESLEY

Wellesley St. West

Wellesley St. East

10

Maitland St.

Bay St.

Alexander St.

Church St.

Jarvis St.

Grenville St.

Wood St.

Carlton St.

UEEN'S PARK

College St.

COLLEGE

**Maple Leaf
Gardens** **11**

12

**Allan
Gardens**

Gerrard St. West

Gerrard St. East

0   .25 km

N

111

Throughout, there are small theaters showing film and slide shows, plus regular 20-minute presentations on lasers, metal casting, and high-voltage electricity (watch your friend's hair stand on end). At press time, an OMNIMAX theatre was scheduled to open shortly. Facilities include a licensed restaurant and lounge, cafeteria, and science shop.

✪ **The Metropolitan Zoo.** Meadowvale Rd. (north of Hwy. 401 and Sheppard Ave.), Scarborough. ☎ **416/392-5900.** Admission $10 adults, $7 seniors and children 12–17, $5 children 4–11, free for children under 3. Summer, daily 9am–7pm; winter, daily 9:30am– 4:30pm. Last admission is 1 hour before closing. Closed Christmas Day. Take the subway to Kennedy on the Bloor-Danforth line. Then take bus no. 86A north. Check with the TTC for schedules (☎ 416/393-4636). Driving from downtown, take the Don Valley Pkwy. to Hwy. 401 east and exit on Meadowvale Rd.

Covering 710 acres of woodland and meadow in Scarborough is a unique zoological garden containing some 5,000 animals, plus an extensive botanical collection. Many of the plants and animals are housed either in pavilions—including Africa, Indo-Malaya, Australasia, and the Americas—or in outdoor paddocks. It's a photographer's dream.

Six miles of walkways offer access to all areas of the zoo, or you can board the Zoomobile or monorail. Facilities include restaurants, a gift shop, first-aid, and a family center; strollers, wagons, and wheelchairs are also available. The zoo is equipped with ramps and washrooms for those with disabilities. The African pavilion is also equipped with an elevator for strollers and wheelchairs. There's ample parking, and plenty of picnic areas with tables.

✪ **The McMichael Collection.** Islington Ave., Kleinburg. ☎ **905/893-1121.** Admission $7 adults, $4 seniors and students, children under 5 free. Apr–Oct daily 10am–5pm; Nov–Mar Tues– Sun 10am–4pm.

Located in Kleinburg, 25 miles north of the city, the McMichael is worth a visit— for the setting as well as the art. The collection is displayed in a log-and-stone gallery that sits amid quiet stands of trees on 100 acres of conservation land. Specially designed for the landscape paintings it houses, the gallery is a work of art itself: the lobby has a pitched roof that soars to a height of 27 feet on massive rafters of Douglas fir; and throughout the gallery, panoramic windows look south over white pine, cedar, ash, and birch.

The work of Canada's famous group of landscape painters, the "Group of Seven," as well as Tom Thomson, David Milne, Emily Carr, and their contemporaries, is displayed here. These artists, inspired by the turn-of-the-century Canadian wilderness, particularly in Algonquin Park and northern Ontario, recorded its rugged landscape in highly individualistic styles. An impressive collection of Inuit and contemporary Native Canadian art and sculpture is also on display.

Founded by Robert and Signe McMichael, the gallery began in 1965 when they donated their property, home, and collection to the Province of Ontario. Since then, the collection has expanded to include more than 5,000 works. Amazingly, the gallery's unique atmosphere has been preserved—log-and-barnwood walls, fieldstone fireplaces, and homey decorative touches, such as hooked rugs and earthenware urns filled with flowers and dried leaves.

Paramount Canada's Wonderland. 9580 Jane St., Vaughan. ☎ **905/832-7000,** or 905/ 832-8131 for concert information at the Kingswood Music Theatre. Admission: Pay-One-Price Passport, including a day's unlimited rides and shows (excluding food, games, merchandise, and the music theater) $32.95 adults, $16.45 seniors and children 3–6, free for children under 3. Grounds admission only (no rides) $17.95. June to Labor Day daily 10am–10pm; Mid-May and

Sept–Oct Sat–Sun 10am–8pm. Closed early Oct to early May. Parking $6.50. Take subway to Yorkdale or York Mills, then GO Express Bus directly to Wonderland. If you're driving, take Yonge St. north to Hwy. 401 and travel west to Hwy. 400. Go north on Hwy. 400 to the Rutherford Rd. exit and follow the signs. Exit at Major MacKenzie, if you're coming south.

Nineteen miles (30 min.) north of Toronto lies Canada's answer to Disney World. The 300-acre park features more than 160 attractions, including 50 rides, a 20-acre water park called Splash Works, a participatory play area called Kid's Kingdom, and Top Gun Canada's only looping inverted jet coaster.

Among the most popular rides are Xtreme Skyflyer, which lets you experience a cross between hang gliding and skydiving, plunging you 15 stories in a spectacular free fall (additional fee required); Days of Thunder, which puts you in the driver's seat during a 200-mile-an-hour, high-stakes stock-car race; Jet Scream, a 360° looping starship; Vortex, Canada's only suspended roller coaster; The Bat, a backwards/forwards looping coaster; Skyrider, a stand-up looping coaster; and the Mighty Canadian Minebuster, the largest wooden roller coaster in the complex. Splash Works has 16 water rides, from speed slides and tube rides to special scaled-down slides and a kids pool. At Timberwolf Falls, riders plunge down a five-story waterfall. Top-name shows, ranging from the spectacular Paramount on Ice to a sea-lion show, appear at the Kingswood Theatre. To add to the thrills for kids and adults, Klingons, Vulcans, Romulans, and Bajorans (along with Hanna-Barbera characters) stroll around the park. Additional attractions include minigolf, batting cages, restaurants, and shops.

You'll probably need 8 hours to see everything. If you picnic on the grounds and forgo buying souvenirs, a family of four can do the park for about $130. Watch out, though, for the extra attractions not included in the admission pass, particularly the many "games of skill," which the kids love, but the purse hates.

2 More Attractions

ARCHITECTURAL HIGHLIGHTS

Casa Loma. 1 Austin Terrace. ☎ **416/923-1171.** Admission $8 adults, $5 seniors and youths, $4.50 children 6–16. Daily 9:30am–4pm. Subway: Dupont; then walk two blocks north.

Every city has its folly, and Toronto has a charming one—complete with Elizabethan-style chimneys, Rhineland turrets, secret passageways, an 800-foot underground tunnel, and a mellifluous-sounding name: Casa Loma.

Sir Henry Pellatt, who built it between 1911 and 1914 at a cost of $3.5 million (plus $1.5 million for furnishings), had a lifelong and incurably romantic fascination with medieval castles—so he decided to build his own. He studied European medieval castles and gathered materials and furnishings, bringing marble, glass, and paneling from Europe, teak from Asia, and oak and walnut from prime areas of North America. He imported Scottish stonemasons to build the massive walls that surround the 6-acre site.

It's a fascinating place to explore: the majestic Great Hall, with its 60-foot-high hammer-beam ceiling; the Oak Room, where three artisans took 3 years to fashion the paneling; the Conservatory, with its elegant bronze doors, stained-glass dome, and pink-and-green marble; the battlements and tower; Peacock Alley, designed after Windsor Castle; Sir Henry's suite, containing a shower with an 18-inch-diameter shower head; the 1,700-bottle wine cellar; and the 800-foot tunnel to the stables, where horses were quartered amid the luxury of Spanish tile and mahogany. The tour is self-guided; you'll be given an audio cassette on arrival. From May through October, the gardens are open, too.

City Hall. Queen St. W. ☎ **416/392-7341.** Free admission. Self-guided tours Mon–Fri 8:30am–4:30pm. Subway: Queen; then walk west to Bay or take the Queen St. streetcar west one stop.

An architectural spectacle, City Hall houses the mayor's office and the city's administrative offices. Daringly designed in the early 1960s by Finnish architect Viljo Revell, it consists of a low podium topped by the flying-saucer–shaped Council Chamber, enfolded between two curved towers. Its interior is as dramatic as its exterior. A cafeteria and dining room are located in the basement.

In front stretches **Nathan Phillips Square** (named after the mayor who initiated the project), where in summer you can sit and contemplate the flower gardens, fountains, and reflecting pool (which doubles as a skating rink in winter), as well as listen to concerts. Here also stands Henry Moore's Three-Way Piece No. 2, locally referred to as The Archer, purchased through a public subscription fund, and the Peace Garden, commemorating Toronto's sesquicentennial in 1984. In contrast, to the east stands the **Old City Hall,** a green-copper–roofed Victorian Romanesque-style building.

Eaton Centre. Dundas and Yonge sts. ☎ **416/598-8700.** Free admission. Mon–Fri 10am–9pm, Sat 9:30am–6pm, Sun noon–5pm. Subway: Dundas or Queen.

Buttressed at both ends by 30-story skyscrapers, this high-tech center, which cost over $250 million to build, stretches from Dundas Street and Yonge Street south to Queen Street, an area that encompasses six million square feet. **Eaton's Department Store** takes up one million square feet, and the rest is filled with more than 320 stores and restaurants and two garages. Some 20 million people shop here annually.

Inside, the structure opens into the impressive **Galleria,** an 866-foot-long glass-domed arcade dotted with benches, orchids, palm trees, and fountains; it's further adorned by Michael Snow's 60 soaring Canada geese, entitled Step Flight. The birds are made from black-and-white photos mounted on cast fiberglass frames. Three tiers rise above, reached by escalator and glass elevators, giving glorious views over this Crystal Palace and Milan-style masterpiece designed by Eb Zeidler (who also designed Ontario Place). Here, rain or shine, you can enjoy the sights, sounds, and aromas in comfort—don't be surprised by the twittering of the sparrows, some of whom have decided that this environment is as pleasant as the outdoors.

One more amazing fact about this construction: It was built around two of Toronto's oldest landmarks—**Trinity Church** (1847) and **Scadding House** (☎ **416/598-4521**), home of Trinity's rector, Dr. Scadding—because the public demanded that the developers allow the sun to continue to shine on the church's twin towers. It does!

Metropolitan Toronto Reference Library. 789 Yonge St. ☎ **416/393-7000.** Free admission. Summer: Mon–Thurs 9am–8pm, Fri 9am–6pm, Sat 9am–5pm; winter: Mon–Thurs 9am–9pm, Fri 9am–6pm, Sat 9am–5pm, Sun 1:30–5pm. Subway: Bloor.

If more libraries were built like this one, perhaps academia would be a more attractive profession. Step inside—a pool and a waterfall gently screen out the street

Impressions

It is impossible to give it anything but commendation. It is not squalid like Birmingham, or cramped like Canton, or hellish like New York, or tiresome like Nice. It is all right. . . .

—Rupert Brooke, *Letters from America* (1913)

noise—and the space opens dramatically to the sky. Every corner is flooded with light and air. I envy the citizens of Toronto for their architect Raymond Moriyama, who designed this incredible structure.

Ontario Legislature. 111 Wellesley St. W., at University Ave. ☎ **416/325-7500.** Free admission. Open Mon–Fri and weekends from Victoria Day to Labor Day. On weekends, tours are given every half-hour 9–11:30am and 1–4pm; call ahead at other times. Subway: Queen's Park.

East of the university, at the northern end of University Avenue, lies Queen's Park, surrounding the rose-tinted sandstone-and-granite Ontario Parliament Buildings, with stately domes, arches, and porte cocheres. At any time of year other than summer, drop in around 2pm, when the legislature is in session for some pithy comments during the question period, or take one of the regular tours. It's best to call ahead to check times.

Royal Bank Plaza. Front and Bay sts. Free admission. Year-round. Subway: Union.

Shimmering in the sun, Royal Bank Plaza looks like a pillar of gold—and in a way it is. More importantly, it's a masterpiece of architectural design. Two triangular towers of bronze mirror glass flank a 130-foot-high glass-walled banking hall. The external walls of the towers are built in a serrated configuration so that they reflect a phenomenal mosaic of color from the skies and surrounding buildings.

In the banking hall, hundreds of aluminum cylinders hang from the ceiling, the work of Venezuelan sculptor Jésus Raphael Soto. Two levels below, there's a waterfall and pine-tree setting that's naturally illuminated from the hall above.

CEMETERIES

Mount Pleasant Cemetery. 1643 Yonge St., or 375 Mount Pleasant Rd., north of St. Clair Ave. ☎ **416/485-9129.** Free admission. Daily 8am–dusk.

Home to one of the finest tree collections in North America, this cemetery is also the final resting place of many fascinating people. Of particular note are Glenn Gould, celebrated classical pianist; Drs. Banting and Best, codiscoverers of insulin; golfer George Knudson; and the Massey and Eaton families, whose mausoleums are impressive architectural monuments. Prime Minister William Lyon Mackenzie King; Canada's greatest war hero, Lt. Col. William Barker; and 52 victims of Air Canada Flight 621, which crashed en route to Los Angeles in 1970, were also laid to rest here.

Necropolis. 200 Winchester St., at Sumach St. ☎ **416/923-7911.** Free admission. Daily 8am–dusk.

This is one of the city's oldest cemeteries (1850). Many of the remains that are buried here, though, were originally buried in Potters Field, where Yorkville stands today.

Before strolling through the cemetery, pick up a History Tour at the office. You'll find the graves of William Lyon Mackenzie, leader of the 1837 rebellion; as well as those of his followers, Samuel Lount and Peter Matthews, who were hanged for their part in the rebellion. Anderson Abbot, the first Canadian-born black surgeon; Joseph Tyrrell, who discovered dinosaurs in Alberta; Ned Hanlan, world-champion oarsman; and many more notable Torontonians can be found in this 15-acre cemetery, beyond the porte cochere and Gothic Revival chapel, designed by Henry Langley, who is also buried in the cemetery.

HISTORIC BUILDINGS

Campbell House. 160 Queen St. W. ☎ **416/597-0227.** Admission $3.50 adults; $2.50 seniors, students, and children. Mon–Fri 9:30am–4:30pm; Sat–Sun noon–4:30pm (late May to mid-Oct). Subway: Osgoode.

Just across from Osgoode Hall, at the corner of University Avenue, sits the 1822 mansion of Loyalist and sixth chief justice of Upper Canada Sir William Campbell. In 1829, he retired to this mansion, where he resided until his death in 1834.

Colborne Lodge. High Park. ☎ **416/392-6916.** Admission $3.50 adults, $2.75 seniors and children 13–18, $2.50 children 12 and under. Tues–Sun noon–5pm. Call ahead; hours do change.

This charming, English-style Regency cottage with a three-sided veranda was built in 1836–37 to take advantage of the view of Lake Ontario and the Humber River. When it was built, it was considered to be way out in the country, and a bother to travel to during the harsh winters. In 1873, the owner, a Toronto surveyor and architect named John Howard, donated the house and surrounding land to the city in return for an annual salary, thus creating High Park—a great recreational area.

Fort York. Garrison Rd., off Fleet St. ☎ **416/392-6907.** Admission $5 adults, $3.25 teenagers 13–18 and seniors, $3 children 6–12. Summer (June–Oct): Mon–Wed and Fri 10am–5pm, Thurs 10am–7pm, Sat–Sun noon–5pm; winter: Tues–Fri 10am–5pm, Sat–Sun noon–5pm. Subway: Bathurst; then streetcar no. 511 south.

Established by Lieutenant Governor Simcoe in 1793 to defend "little muddy York," as Toronto was then known, Fort York, between Bathurst Street and Strachan Avenue, was sacked by Americans in 1813. You can tour the soldiers' and officers' quarters and clamber over the ramparts, as well as view demonstrations and exhibits. The fort is two blocks east of Exhibition Place.

Mackenzie House. 82 Bond St. ☎ **416/392-6915.** Admission $3.50 adults, $2.75 seniors and teenagers 13–18, $2.50 children 5–12. Sat–Sun noon–5pm. Subway: Dundas.

This typical mid–19th-century brick row house, two blocks east of Yonge and south of Dundas, gives some idea of what Toronto must have looked like then, when the streets were lined with similar buildings. It was purchased for William Lyon Mackenzie, leader of the 1837 rebellion, by concerned friends and fund-raisers, and he lived here from 1859 to 1861. It's furnished in 1850s style, and in the back there's a print shop designed after Mackenzie's own.

Osgoode Hall. 130 Queen St. W. ☎ **416/947-3300.** Free admission. Tours given Mon–Fri at 1 and 1:20pm July–Aug only. Subway: Osgoode.

To the west of City Hall extends an impressive, elegant wrought-iron fence in front of an equally gracious mansion, Osgoode Hall, currently the home of the Law Society of Upper Canada. The fence was originally built to keep cows from trampling the flower beds. Tours of the interior will show you the splendor of the grand staircase, the rotunda, the Great Library, and the fine portrait and sculpture collection. Building began in 1829 on this structure, troops were billeted here after the Rebellion of 1837, and the buildings now house the headquarters of Ontario's legal profession and several magnificent courtrooms—including one built with materials from London's Old Bailey. The courts are open to the public.

INDUSTRIAL TOURS

Canadian Broadcasting Centre. 250 Front St. W. Free tours of the facilities are given daily. ☎ **416/205-8605,** for times and reservations.

The headquarters for the English Networks of the CBC, this building was designed by Bregman and Hamann and Scott with John Burgee and Philip Johnson as consultants. It's one of the most modern broadcasting facilities in North America. From the minute visitors enter, they know they're in a studio facility because there's even a lobby viewing studio.

ChumCity. 299 Queen St. W. ☎ **416/591-5757,** to arrange a tour.

This innovative television station contrasts dramatically with the formality of the CBC. In the ChumCity building at the corner of John and Queen, visitors will discover a television factory where cameras are not hard-wired to studios or control rooms, but can be plugged into any one of 35 hydrants that allow them to go on-air in minutes. Instead of formal shows confined to studios, programs can virtually flow minute by minute from any working area in the building, including the hallways and rooftop. From this location, the cutting-edge company operates three channels—news, MuchMusic, which is similar to MTV, and Bravo, an arts channel. The staff is young and cutting-edge, with an impressive, fast-response news team. They have 100 permanently fixed remote-control cameras, 25 mobile news cruisers, plus remote terminals at key locations such as City Hall, Metro Hall, the TTC, and police headquarters. The results can be seen on CityPulse at noon, 6, and 11pm.

This futuristic, truly interactive TV station even invites casual visitors to air their opinions and grievances. Anyone can enter the video recording booths at the corner of John and Queen and record their views. The best are aired.

Toronto Stock Exchange. Exchange Tower, 2 First Canadian Place, at the northeast corner of King and York sts. ☎ **416/947-4670.** Free admission. Mon–Fri 9am–4:30pm; public presentations are given Tues–Thurs at 10am and 2pm, with an additional 2pm presentation Fri.

With $1 billion dollars of stock being traded every business day, this is Canada's premier marketplace, and the second-largest stock exchange in North America. Forty-five–minute public presentations, including video and computer demonstrations, are given twice a day Tuesday through Thursday, and once on Friday. The viewing gallery is open Monday through Friday from 9am to 4:30pm.

MARKETS

Kensington Market. Kensington and Augusta aves. and Baldwin St. Daily. Subway: College or Dundas; then take the streetcar west.

In the early 20th century, Kensington Market was a thriving market in the heart of what was then Toronto's Jewish community. Today, the area is part Portuguese, part Caribbean, part Jewish, and part Asian. There is no central market building, but rather a number of stalls and stores stretching along several streets—Augusta and Kensington avenues and Baldwin Street. Get here early on Saturday—the market's best day of the week.

St. Lawrence Market. 92 Front St. E. ☎ **416/392-7219.** Tues–Sat. Subway: King or Union.

This handsome food market is housed in a vast building constructed around the facade of the second city hall, built in 1850. Vendors sell fresh meat, fish, fruit, vegetables, and dairy products as well as other foodstuffs. The best time to visit is early Saturday morning, shortly after the farmers have brought their wares into town.

MUSEUMS

The Art Gallery of North York. 5040 Yonge St., Ford Centre for the Performing Arts, North York. ☎ **416/395-0067.** Free admission. Tues–Sun noon–5pm.

This two-year-old gallery is charged with collecting and exhibiting the best contemporary Canadian art created since 1985. Currently the collection includes works by Michael Krondl, Shelach Keeley, Lynn Donoghue, Stephen Cruise, and Mary Pratt.

The Bata Shoe Museum. 327 Bloor St. W., at the corner of St. George. ☎ **416/979-7799.** Admission $6 adults, $4 seniors/students, $2 children 5–14, $12 families. Tues–Wed and Fri–Sat 10am–5pm, Thurs 10am–8pm, Sun noon–5pm.

Anyone interested in shoes and fashion history will love this museum, housing the personal collection—10,000 items—of the Bata family. The building, which was designed by Raymond Moriyama, is spectacular. The main gallery, All About Shoes, is home to the plaster cast of the first human footprints discovered in Africa by anthropologist Mary Leakey, which date to 4 million B.C. It traces the development of shoemaking, featuring shoes of all types—including moon boots and deep-sea diving boots—as well as shoes of the rich and famous. In addition to the general historic exhibition, one display focuses on Canadian footwear fashioned by the Inuit, while another highlights 19th-century ladies' footwear. Another smaller gallery houses changing exhibits.

Design Exchange. 234 Bay St. ☎ **416/363-6121.** Admission $5 adults, $3.50 students and seniors, free for children 12 and under.

Located in the old Stock Exchange Building, this has become Toronto's design center. It showcases the work of design professionals, but the main purpose of the institution is to nurture designers of all types—graphic, industrial, interior, landscape, and urban—and serve as a clearing house and resource center for the design community. There's also a good bookstore.

Hockey Hall of Fame. 30 Yonge St. at Front in BCE Place. ☎ **416/360-7765.** Admission $8.75 adults, $5.75 seniors and children 3–13, children under 3 free. Summer: Mon–Sat 9:30am–6pm, Sun 10am–6pm; winter: Mon–Fri 10am–5pm, Sat 9:30am–6pm, Sun 10:30am–5pm.

Ice-hockey fans will be thrilled to see the original Stanley Cup (donated in 1893 by Lord Stanley of Preston), a replica of the Montréal Canadiens' locker room, Terry Sawchuck's goalie gear, Newsy Lalonde's skates, and the stick that Max Bentley used, along with photographs of the personalities and great moments in hockey history. Interactive displays and videos make it fun for all.

Black Creek Pioneer Village. 1000 Murray Ross Pkwy., Downsview, at Steeles Ave. and Jane St. ☎ **416/736-1733.** Admission $8 adults, $6 seniors, $4 children and students; children under 4 free. May–Aug daily 10am–5pm; Sept Wed–Sun 10am–5pm; Oct–Nov Wed–Sun 10am–4:30pm; Dec daily 10am–4:30pm; Mar–Apr Wed–Sun 10am–4:30pm. Closed Christmas Day and Jan to mid-Mar. Subway: Finch; then take bus no. 60 to Jane Street.

Life here moves at the gentler pace of mid–19th-century rural Ontario. You can watch the authentically dressed villagers going about their chores, spinning, sewing, rail splitting, sheepshearing, and threshing; enjoy their cooking; wander through the cozily furnished homesteads; visit the working mill; shop at the general store; or rumble past the farm animals in a horse-drawn wagon. There are more than 30 restored buildings to explore in this beautifully landscaped village. Special events are offered throughout the year, from a great Easter egg hunt to Christmas by lamplight.

For your convenience, there's a dining room serving lunch and afternoon tea (open May–Thanksgiving and December).

Canada Sports Hall of Fame. Exhibition Place. ☎ **416/260-6789.** Free admission. Mon–Fri 10am–4:30pm. Open most weekends, call ahead for hours. Subway: Bathurst; then take streetcar no. 511 south to the end of the line.

Located in the center of Exhibition Place, this three-floor sports hall is devoted to the country's greatest athletes in all major sports. It offers displays complemented by touch-screen computers that tell you everything you could want to know about particular sports personalities, famous race horses, and Canada's sport heritage.

Marine Museum. Exhibition Place. ☎ **416/392-1765.** Admission $3.50 adults, $2.75 teenagers 13–18 and seniors, $2.50 children under 12, free for children under 6. Tues–Fri

In case you want to see the world.

At American Express, we're here to make your journey a smooth one. So we have over 1,700 travel service locations in over 120 countries ready to help. What else would you expect from the world's largest travel agency?

do more

Travel

http://www.americanexpress.com/travel

In case you want to be welcomed there.

We're here to see that you're always welcomed at establishments everywhere. That's why millions of people carry the American Express® Card – for peace of mind, confidence, and security, around the world or just around the corner.

do more®

AMERICAN EXPRESS

Cards

In case you're running low.

We're here to help with more than 118,000 Express Cash

locations around the world. In order to enroll, just call

American Express before you start your vacation.

do more

Express Cash

And just in case.

We're here with American Express® Travelers Cheques and Cheques *for Two*.® They're the safest way to carry money on your vacation and the surest way to get a refund, practically anywhere, anytime.

Another way we help you...

do more

Travelers Cheques

10am–4pm, Sat–Sun noon–5pm. Subway: Bathurst; then take streetcar no. 511 south to the end of the line.

On the grounds of Exhibition Place, stands the Marine Museum, which interprets the history of Toronto Harbour and its relation to the Great Lakes. In summer, visitors can also board the fully restored 1932 *Ned Hanlan,* the last steam tugboat to sail on Lake Ontario.

The Museum for Textiles. 55 Centre Ave. ☎ **416/599-5321,** or 416/599-5515 for taped information. Admission $5 adults, $4 students and seniors, $14 family. Tues–Fri 11am–5pm (Wed until 8pm), Sat–Sun noon–5pm. Subway: St. Patrick.

This fascinating museum is internationally recognized for its collection of more than 7,000 historic and ethnographic textiles and related artifacts. Here you'll find fine Oriental rugs and cloth and tapestries from all over the world, including African storytelling cloth. A contemporary gallery also presents the work of contemporary artists.

NEIGHBORHOODS

The Beaches

This is one of the neighborhoods that makes Toronto a unique city. Here, near the terminus of the Queen Street East tram line, you can stroll or cycle along the lakefront boardwalk. Because of its natural assets, it has become a much sought-after residential neighborhood, and there are plenty of well-stocked and eminently browsable stores along Queen Street. Just beyond Waverley Road, you can turn down through Kew Gardens to the boardwalk and walk all the way past the Olympic Pool (jam-packed in summer) to Ashbridge's Bay Park.

✪ Chinatown. Dundas St. and Spadina Ave.

Stretching along Dundas Street west from Bay Street to Spadina Avenue and north and south along Spadina Avenue, Chinatown, home to some of Toronto's 350,000 Chinese citizens, is packed with fascinating shops and restaurants. Even the street signs are in Chinese here.

In **Dragon City,** a large shopping mall on Spadina that's staffed and patronized by Chinese, you'll find all kinds of stores, some selling exotic Chinese preserves like cuttlefish, lemon ginger, whole mango, ginseng, and antler, and others specializing in Asian books, tapes, and records, as well as fashions and foods. Downstairs, a fast-food court features Korean, Indonesian, Chinese, and Japanese cuisines.

As you stroll through Chinatown, stop at the **Kim Moon Bakery** on Dundas Street West (☎416/977-1933) for Chinese pastries and a pork bun or go to one of the tea stores. A walk through Chinatown at night is especially exciting—the sidewalks are filled with people and neon lights shimmer everywhere. You'll pass windows where ducks hang gleaming, noodle houses, record stores selling the Top 10 in Chinese, and trading companies filled with all kinds of Asian produce. Another stopping place might be the **New Asia Supermarket,** around the corner from Dundas Street at 299 Spadina Ave.

For details, see "Walking Tour 4" in chapter 7.

Greektown—The East End

This area stretching along the Danforth is hot, hot, hot and swings until the early hours when the restaurants and bars are still crowded and frenetic. During the day visitors can browse the traditional Greek stores—like **Akropol,** a Greek bakery that displays stunning multi-tiered wedding cakes in the window. It's an eclectic neighborhood. Along with the Greek food vendors and travel agents, you'll also find stores like the **Scandinavian Shoppe,** at no. 364, which sells great glass and ceramics; **Big Kids Hafta Play Too** (at no. 464), which has some really cool T-shirts; and some New Age and alternative stores.

Little Italy

This, along with Queen Street, is another hot spot in the city. The street hums at night as people crowd the coffee bars, pool bars, social clubs, and trattorias. It stretches along College Street between Euclid and Shaw.

Mirvish Village

One of the city's most famous characters is Honest Ed Mirvish, who started his career in the 1950s with his no-frills store at the corner of Markham and Bloor streets (one block west of Bathurst), where the signs screaming bargains hit you from every direction. Among other things, Ed Mirvish rose to save the Royal Alexandra Theatre on King Street from demolition, established a whole row of adjacent restaurants for theater patrons, and finally developed this block-long area with art galleries, restaurants, and bookstores. His latest triumph was, of course, the purchase and renovation of London's Old Vic.

Stop by and browse, and don't forget to step into Honest Ed's on the corner.

Queen Street West Village

This street has over the years been known as the heart of Toronto's funky, avant-garde scene. Along this street are several clubs—Bamboo and the Rivoli, in particular— where some major Canadian artists/singers have launched their careers. The street is lined with an eclectic mix of stores and businesses. Although recent trends have brought such mainstream stores as the Gap to the street, it still retains a raw, authentic neighborhood edge. There's a broad selection of good-value bistro-style restaurants, a number of fine secondhand antiquarian bookstores, and a lot of funky fashion stores as well as outright junk shops, nostalgic record emporiums, kitchen supply stores, and discount fabric houses. East of Bathurst the street is being slowly gentrified, but beyond Bathurst it still retains its rough-and-ready energy.

For details see "Walking Tour 3" in chapter 7.

Yorkville

This is the name given to the area that stretches north of Bloor Street, between Avenue Road and Bay Street. Since its founding in 1853 as a village outside the city proper, Yorkville has experienced many transformations. In the 1960s it became Toronto's Haight-Ashbury, the mecca for young suburban runaways otherwise known as hippies. In the 1980s it became the shopping ground of the chic, who dropped their money liberally at such designer-name boutiques as Hermès, Courrèges, Gianni Versace, Cartier, and Turnbull & Asser as well as at the neighborhood's many fine art galleries. In the early 1990s, the recession left its mark on the area—a fact that became glaringly obvious when Creeds, a Toronto institution, shut its doors. The restored town houses began to look a little forlorn, but today the energy is back and Bloor Street and Hazelton Lanes continue to attract high-style stores, including most recently a branch of Tiffany's.

Stroll around and browse—or sit out and have an iced coffee in the sun at one of the cafés on Yorkville Avenue, and watch the parade go by. Some good vantage points can be had at Hemingway's or at any one of many cafés along Yorkville Avenue. Most of these cafés have happy hours from 4 to 7 or 8pm.

Make sure you wander through the labyrinths of Hazelton Lanes between Avenue Road and Hazelton Avenue. There you'll find a maze of shops and offices clustered around an outdoor court in the center of a building that is topped with apartments—the most sought-after address in the city. In the summer, the courtyard is used for outdoor dining.

And while you're in the neighborhood (especially if you're an architecture buff), take a look at the redbrick building on Bloor Street at the end of Yorkville Avenue, which houses the Metro Library. If more libraries had been built like this one in the past, then perhaps study and learning would have come out of the dim and musty closets and into the world where they belong. Step inside—a pool and a waterfall gently screen out the street noise, and pine fencelike partitions undulate through the area like those you find along the sand dunes. Step farther inside and the space opens dramatically to the sky. Every corner is flooded with light and air.

PARKS & GARDENS

Allan Gardens. Stretching between Jarvis, Sherbourne, Dundas, and Gerrard sts. ☎ **416/392-7259.** Free admission. Daily. Subway: Dundas or Gerrard.

These gardens were given to the city by George William Allan, who was born in 1822 to wealthy merchant and banker William Allan. His father gave him a vast estate stretching from Carlton Street to Bloor Street between Jarvis and Sherbourne. George married into the Family Compact when he married John Beverley Robinson's daughter. A lawyer by training, he became a city councillor, mayor, senator, and philanthropist. The lovely old concert pavilion was demolished, but the glass-domed Palm House still stands in all its radiant Victorian glory.

Edwards Garden. Lawrence Ave. and Leslie St. ☎ **416/397-1340.** Free admission. Daily dawn to dusk. Subway: Eglinton; then take the Leslie or Lawrence bus.

This quiet, formal garden with a creek cutting through it is part of a series of parks. Gracious bridges arch over the creek, rock gardens abound, and rose and other seasonal flower beds add color and scent to the landscape. The garden is famous for its rhododendrons. The Civic Garden Centre operates a gift shop and gives walking tours on Tuesday and Thursday at 11am and 2pm.

High Park. In the West End, extending south of Bloor St. to the Gardiner Expressway. Free admission. Daily dawn to dusk. Subway: High Park.

This 400-acre park was John G. Howard's great gift to the city. He lived in Colborne Lodge, which still stands in the park. The park contains a large lake called Grenadier Pond, a small zoo, a swimming pool, tennis courts, sports fields, bowling greens, and vast expanses of green for baseball, jogging, picnicking, bicycling, and more.

3 Especially for Kids

Look under "The Top Attractions" and "More Attractions," above, for the following Toronto-area attractions that have major appeal for kids of all ages. I've summarized them here in what I think is the most logical order, at least from a kid's point of view (the first five, though, really belong in a dead heat).

Ontario Science Centre *(see p. 109)*   Kids race to be the first at this paradise of fun hands-on games, experiments, and push-button demonstrations—700 of 'em.

Paramount Canada's Wonderland *(see p. 112)*   The kids love the rides in the theme park. But watch out for those video games, which they also love—an unanticipated extra cost.

Harbourfront *(see p. 103)*　Kaleidoscope is an ongoing program of creative crafts, active games, and special events on weekends and holidays. There's also a summer pond, winter ice-skating, and a crafts studio.

Ontario Place *(see p. 102)*　Water slides, a huge Cinesphere, a futuristic pod, and other entertainments are the big hits at this recreational/cultural park on three artificial islands on the edge of Lake Ontario.

Metro Zoo *(see p. 112)*　One of the best in the world, modeled after San Diego's— the animals in this 710-acre park really do live in a natural environment.

Toronto Islands—Centreville *(see p. 104)*　Riding a ferry to this turn-of-the-century amusement park is part of the fun.

CN Tower *(see p. 104)*　Especially for the interactive simulator games.

Royal Ontario Museum *(see p. 108)*　The top hit is always the dinosaurs and the spooky bat cave.

Fort York *(see p. 116)*　For its reenactments of battle drills, musket and cannon firing, and musical marches with fife and drum.

The Hockey Hall of Fame *(see p. 118)*　Especially the interactive video displays and the memorabilia of those super heroes.

Black Creek Pioneer Village *(see p. 118)*　For craft and other demonstrations.

Casa Loma (see p. 113)　For the stables and the fantasy rooms.

Art Gallery of Ontario *(see p. 105)*　For its hands-on kids' exhibit.

4 Organized Tours

BUS TOURS　If you enjoy hop-on, hop-off bus tours, try the one offered by **Olde Town Toronto Tours Ltd.,** 900 Dixon Rd., Etobicoke, ON, M9W 1J7 (☎ **416/ 368-6877**). Tickets ($24 for adults, $11 for children) are valid for 24 hours, allowing you to disembark from the double-decker bus, whenever and wherever you wish. Tours operate year-round from 9am to 9pm in summer and from 9am to 4 pm in winter. **Grayline Tours,** 184 Front St. East (☎ **416/594-3310**), operates similar tours, going past such major sights as Eaton Centre, City Hall, the university, Yorkville, Casa Loma, Harbourfront, and the CN Tower. These tours are operated between early May and the end of October, and cost $25 adults, $22 seniors, and $16 for children under 12.

HARBOR & ISLAND TOURS　**Toronto Tours** (☎ **416/869-1372**) operates 1-hour tours of the port and the islands from May to September every hour on the hour between 10am and 5pm (until 8pm in July and Aug) for $14.75 adults, $11.75 seniors, and $8.75 for children 12 and under. Tours leave from 145 Queen's Quay West at the foot of York Street.

For a real thrill, board the three-masted, 96-foot schooner *The Challenge* for a 1- or 2-hour cruise weekdays at 2 and 4pm, and weekends at noon, 2, 4, and 5pm. Prices for the 1-hour cruise are $11.95 adults, $9.95 seniors and students, and $5.95 children 5 to 14; for 2 hours, it's $15.95, $12.95, and $9.95, respectively. For more information, call the **Great Lakes Schooner Company,** 249 Queens Quay West, Suite 111 (☎ **416/260-6355**).

HELICOPTER TOURS　For an aerial view of the city, contact **National Helicopters,** 11339 Albion Vaughan Rd., RR 1, Kleinburg (☎ **905/893-2727**), whose helicopters take off from the Island airport. The charge is $40 per person for 7 minutes.

WALKING/BIKING TOURS   Among the many available walking tours, some of the very best are led by the youthful, energetic, and enthusiastic Shirley Lum, a self-confessed foodie. Shirley was born in Toronto and loves her city. She is a graduate in politics, philosophy, and sociology and brings all of her expertise and enthusiasm to bear on the history and social life of whichever area she is exploring. She leads a wonderful tour through Old Chinatown that focuses on the history and personalities of the neighborhood and also includes stops at a variety of stores, including a tofu manufacturing store, an herbalist, a tea store, a bakery, and a Taoist temple. The highlight of the tour is a leisurely dim sum lunch at one of the best such emporiums in the community. It's great fun and you'll never look at Chinatown in quite the same way again. Shirley also offers tours of Rosedale and Yorkville, Kensington Market, the East End, and the St. Lawrence Market, as well as bike tours. Two-hour tours cost $12 adults, $10 seniors and students, $6 children under 12; 3-hour tours, including meals and tasting samples, cost $25, $20, and $12, respectively. Bike tours, which include a light lunch, afternoon snack, and T-shirt are $35, $30 and $25, respectively. For information and reservations, call **416/463-9233.**

During the summer, the Toronto Historical Board also offers free walking tours of several different neighborhoods, including Cabbagetown and Rosedale. Call **416/392-6827** for details.

5 Outdoor Activities

For additional information on golf courses, tennis, swimming pools, beaches, and picnic areas, call **Metro Parks** (☎ **416/392-1111**).

BIKING   *Bicycling* magazine recently named Toronto the number one cycling city in North America because of its large number of bike paths and local pedalers (7% of the population). And indeed the city is great for biking. Bikes can be rented from **Wheel Excitement,** 5 Rees St. (☎ **416/260-9000**) for $14 for the first 2 hours, plus $2 for each additional hour, or $26 a day. You can also rent bicycles from **McBride Cycle,** 180 Queens Quay West (☎ **416/203-5651**), on Harbourfront; **Toronto Island Bicycle Rental** (☎ **416/203-0009**) on Centre Island; and from **High Park Cycle and Sports,** 24 Ronson Dr. (☎ **416/614-6689**).

The Martin Goodman Trail, which runs from the Beaches to the Humber River along the waterfront, is ideal for biking. There's also a Lower Don Valley bike trail that starts in the east end of the city at Front Street and runs north to Riverdale Park. High Park is another good venue, along with the parks along the ravines. Official bike lanes are marked on College/Carlton streets, the Bloor Street Viaduct leading to the Danforth, Beverly/St. George, and Davenport Road. The Convention and Visitors Association has more detailed information on these bike lanes. **The Toronto Bicycling Network** (☎ **416/766-1985**) offers day and weekend trips.

BOATING   At the **Harbourside Boating Centre,** 283 Queen's Quay West (☎ **416/203-3000**), you can rent sail and power boats and take sailing lessons. For 4 hours, depending on the boat's size, sailboats cost from $45 to $395. Week-long and weekend sailing courses are also offered.

Impressions

Toronto is New York . . . run by the Swiss.

—Peter Ustinov

Harbourfront Canoe and Kayak School, 283A Queens Quay West (☎ 416/203-2277), rents kayaks for $30 a day or $15 an hour; canoes for $25 and $10, respectively.

Canoes, row- and pedal boats can also be rented on the Toronto Islands just south of Centreville.

CROSS-COUNTRY SKIING   Groomed trails are maintained in three or so of the parks, but the snowfall has been so poor recently that there's been virtually no skiing.

GOLF   Among the city's half dozen metro public golf courses, the following stand out:

Don Valley at Yonge St. south of Hwy. 401 (☎ 416/392-2465). Designed by Howard Watson, this is a scenic course with some challenging elevated tees and a par-5 12th hole. A good place to start your kids.

Humber Valley on Beattie Avenue, off Albion Road (☎ 416/392-2488). This par-70 links and valley-land course has three final holes that require major concentration.

Tam O'Shanter (☎ 416/392-2547) on Birchmount Avenue, north of Sheppard. This moderately difficult course has water hazards among its challenges.

In addition, there are several outstanding championship courses in the Toronto area. The most expensive ($125) is the **Glen Abbey Golf Club** course in Oakville (☎ 905/844-1800). Designed by Jack Nicklaus, it's where the Canadian Open is played. **The Lionhead Golf Club** in Brampton (☎ 905/455-4900) has two 18-hole par-72 courses, charging $125 for the longer course, and $110 for the slightly shorter course. In Markham, the **Angus Glen Golf Club** (☎ 905/887-5157) has a Doug Carrick–designed par-72 course and charges a $72 greens fee. **The Royal Woodbine** in Etobicoke (☎ 905/674-7773) has a challenging par-71 course, and charges $80.

FITNESS CENTERS   **Metro Central YMCA,** 20 Grosvenor St. (☎ 416/975-9622), has excellent facilities, including a 25-meter (27-yd.) swimming pool, all kinds of cardiovascular machines, Nautilus equipment, an indoor track, squash and racquetball courts, and aerobics classes. A reasonably priced day pass is available.

HORSEBACK RIDING   **Rouge Hill Stables,** just off Kingston Road (Hwy. 2) east of Sheppard Avenue (☎ 416/284-6176), offers 1-hour and 1½-hour trail rides through the Rouge Valley. Reserve ahead.

ICE-SKATING   Nathan Philips Square in front of City Hall becomes a free ice rink in winter, as does an area at Harbourfront Centre. Rentals are available. Artificial rinks are also found in more than 25 parks, including Grenadier Pond in High Park—a romantic spot with its bonfire and vendors selling roasted chestnuts. They're open from November to March.

IN-LINE SKATING   In-line skates can be rented from **Wheel Excitement** (see "Biking," above), and also from **Ready 2 Roll,** 2100 Bloor St. West (☎ 416/604-1900), near High Park.

JOGGING   Downtown sites might include Harbourfront and along the lakefront, or through Queen's Park and the University. The Martin Goodman Trail runs 20 kilometers (12.4 miles) along the waterfront from the Beaches in the east to the Humber River in the west, and it's ideal for jogging, walking, or cycling. It links to the Tommy Thompson Trail, which travels the parks stretching from the lakefront along the Humber River. Near the Ontario Science Centre in the Central Don Valley, Ernest Thompson Seton Park is also good for jogging. Parking is available at the Thorncliffe Drive and Wilket Creek entrances.

SWIMMING   **The University of Toronto Athletic Centre,** 55 Harbord St. at Spadina Avenue (☎ **416/978-4680**), opens its swimming pool free to the public on Sunday from 12:10 to 4pm. The **YMCA** at 20 Grosvenor St. also has a pool, which can be used on a day pass. There are a dozen or so outdoor pools (open June–Sept) in the municipal parks, including High and Rosedale Parks, and also indoor pools at several of the community recreation centers. For pool information, call **416/392-1111.**

There are public beaches on the Toronto Islands (off Hanlan's Point), as well as in the Beaches neighborhood (Woodbine Beach). Quite frankly, though, the waters of Lake Ontario are very polluted, and although people do swim in them, they do so at their own risk. Signs are posted when a beach is deemed unsafe, usually after a heavy rainfall.

TENNIS   There are tennis facilities in more than 30 municipal parks. The most convenient locations are the courts in High Park, Rosedale, and Jonathan Ashridge parks. They are open in summer only. At Eglinton Flats park, west of Keele street at Eglinton, six of the courts can be used in winter. Call Metro Parks for additional information (see above).

6 Spectator Sports

AUTO RACING   **The Molson Indy** is run at the Exhibition Place Street circuit, usually on the third weekend in July. For information, call **416/872-4639.**

BASEBALL   The **SkyDome,** on Front Street beside the CN Tower, is the home of the Toronto Blue Jays (World Series champs in 1992 and 1993). For information, contact the **Toronto Blue Jays,** P.O. Box 7777, Adelaide St., Toronto, ON, M5C 2K7 (☎ **416/341-1000**). For tickets, call **416/341-1234.**

BASKETBALL   Toronto's new basketball team, the Raptors, has generated an urban fever. Currently, the team is playing at SkyDome in a 45-game schedule from October to April. When a brand-new stadium is built, they'll move there. For information, contact the **Raptors Basketball Club,** 20 Bay St., Suite 1702, (☎ **416/214-2255**).

FOOTBALL   SkyDome is also home to the Argonauts football team, which plays in the Canadian Football League between June and November. For information, contact the club at SkyDome, Gate 9, P.O. Box 2005, Station B, Toronto (☎ **416/341-5151**).

GOLF TOURNAMENTS   Canada's national golf tournament, the **Bell Canadian Open,** is held at the **Glen Abbey Golf Club** in Oakville, about 40 minutes from the city. It's usually played over the Labor Day weekend.

HOCKEY   Some wag once said there's really only one religious place in Toronto, and that's Maple Leaf Gardens, 60 Carlton St. (☎ **416/977-1641**), where the city's ice-hockey team, the Maple Leafs, wield their sticks to the delight and screaming enthusiasm of fans. Tickets are nigh impossible to attain because many are sold by subscription; as soon as the remainder go on sale, there are lines around the block. The only way to secure tickets is to harass your concierge, pay a scalper, or call **Edwards and Edwards** at **416/363-1288.**

HORSE RACING   Horse racing takes place at **Woodbine Racetrack,** Rexdale Boulevard and Hwy. 427 in Etobicoke (☎ **416/675-6110**), famous for the Queen's Plate (contested in July); the Woodbine International, a world classic turf race (contested in Sept. or Oct.); the Breeders Crown; and the North America Cup. Woodbine also hosts harness racing in spring and fall.

About 100 miles outside Toronto, **Fort Erie Race Track** (☎ **905/871-3200**) is another beautiful racing venue. Harness racing takes place at **Mohawk Raceway,** 30 miles west of the city at Hwy. 410 and Guelph Line (☎ **416/675-7223**).

TENNIS TOURNAMENTS Canada's international tennis championship, the **Du Maurier Ltd. Open,** is an important stop on the pro-tennis tour, attracting stars like Becker, Agassi, and Sanchez Vicario. It's played in Toronto at the National Tennis Centre at York University, and in Montréal in late July, with the men's and women's championship alternating between the two cities. In 1997, women play in Toronto; men play in Montréal. In 1998, they alternate, and so on in subsequent years. For information, call **416/665-9777.**

City Strolls

Toronto is almost a distant cousin of Los Angeles: It's a huge, sprawling city, and it's difficult to imagine walking everywhere. Unlike Los Angeles, however, it is possible to explore parts of Toronto on foot, and the city is blessed with a super-efficient public transportation system.

The walking tours in this chapter aren't designed to give you an overview; instead, they'll introduce you to the most colorful, exciting neighborhoods in the city, as well as those areas that are packed with sights on almost every corner. We'll start with Harbourfront, which Torontonians have turned into a glorious playground opening onto the lake.

WALKING TOUR 1
Harbourfront

Start: Union Station.
Finish: Harbourfront Antiques Market.
Time: Anywhere from 3 to 8 hours, depending on how much time you spend shopping, eating, and daydreaming.
Best Time: Sunday, when the Harbourfront Antiques Market is bustling.

As you start your tour, pause to look at the beaux arts interior of Union Station. From here, either take the LRT to York Quay or walk down York Street to Queen's Quay West. Directly ahead, across the street, is the:

1. **Queen's Quay Terminal,** a large complex that houses more than 100 shops and restaurants and, on the third floor, a theater specially designed for dance. Built in 1927 when lake and railroad trade flourished, this eight-story concrete warehouse has been attractively renovated and turned into a light and airy two-story marketplace with garden courts, skylights, and waterfalls. The floors above are occupied by condominium apartments.

    Although you'll find few bargains here, some of my favorite stores on the street level are **Rainmakers,** selling zillions of whimsical umbrellas and parasol hats, plus terrific insulated rainwear, including rain slickers featuring cartoon characters; **Touch the Sky,** displaying colorful kites of all shapes and sizes; **Crabtree &**

Walking Tour—Harbourfront

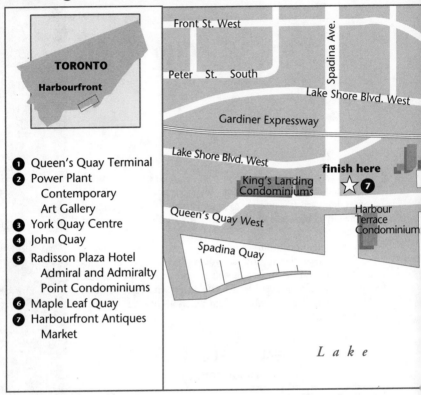

TORONTO
Harbourfront

Front St. West

Peter   St.   South

Spadina Ave.

Lake Shore Blvd. West

Gardiner Expressway

Lake Shore Blvd. West

King's Landing
Condominiums

finish here
⭐ ❼

Queen's Quay West

Harbour
Terrace
Condominium

Spadina Quay

Lake

❶ Queen's Quay Terminal
❷ Power Plant
   Contemporary
   Art Gallery
❸ York Quay Centre
❹ John Quay
❺ Radisson Plaza Hotel
   Admiral and Admiralty
   Point Condominiums
❻ Maple Leaf Quay
❼ Harbourfront Antiques
   Market

Evelyn, for soaps and other products to care for the body and appeal to the senses; and **Suitables,** for reasonably priced silk fashions.

On the upper level, there's also plenty to choose from: **SciTech** for science games, clocks, globes, and all kinds of fun items associated with all the sciences; the classic Canadian **Tilley Endurables,** founded by Torontonian Alex Tilley (who invented the world's most endurable and adaptable hat as well as multipocketed jackets); and **Table of Contents,** selling all kinds of kitchen gear, napkins, table-cloths, and utensils.

☕ **TAKE A BREAK**   If you want to sit out and watch the lakefront traffic—boat and human—go to **Spinnakers,** or the **Boathouse Cafe,** on the ground floor of Queen's Quay. Otherwise, go upstairs and dine at **Pink Pearl** (Chinese) or more casually at **La Bouchée.**

From Queen's Quay Terminal, walk along the water to:
2. **The Power Plant Contemporary Art Gallery,** a former power plant that has been converted to display modern art. The same building also houses the Du Maurier Theatre Centre, which presents works in French.

Behind this building, adjacent to Queen's Quay West, is the **Tent in the Park,** which shelters different events during the summer season. Walk west into the:
3. **York Quay Centre,** another interesting complex containing a number of restaurants and galleries which was converted from a 1940 trucking warehouse. Spend

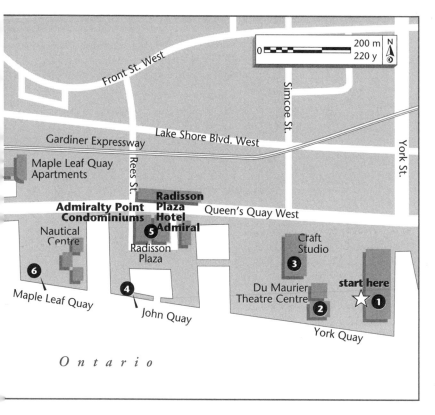

some time in the Craft Studio watching the glassblowers, potters, jewelry makers, and other artisans at work and browse in the store that sells their work.

On the waterfront side in front of York Quay, there's a pond where kids operate model boats in summer; in winter it turns into an ice-skating rink.

From York Quay, cross the Amsterdam Bridge above Marina 4, checking out the wealth that's bobbing down below. You'll arrive on:

4. John Quay. The first building you'll come to contains four restaurants, beyond which you'll see the towers of the:

5. Radisson Plaza Hotel Admiral and Admiralty Point Condominiums, and across Queen's Quay West, the HarbourPoint Condominiums. On the ground level of the Admiralty Point Condos are a few interesting stores: **The Nautical Mind,** which sells marine books, photographs, navigational charts, and boating videos; and the **Dock Shoppe,** filled with all kinds of sailing gear and fashions.

☕ **TAKE A BREAK** Pop into the **Radisson Plaza Hotel Admiral,** 249 Queen's Quay West, which has a couple of dining rooms, plus a pleasant poolside terrace if it's a sunny day. Or try something fresh from **Wallymagoo's** marine bar.

Continue west along Queen's Quay West past:

6. Maple Leaf Quay (unless you want to stop at the Nautical Centre to sign up for sailing classes and the like). Continue west and you'll see the Maple Leaf Quay Apartments on your right and the Harbour Terrace Condominiums farther along on your left on the waterfront. Next door to the westernmost tower of the Maple Leaf Quay Apartments is the:

7. **Harbourfront Antiques Market,** a terrific market in which more than 150 dealers sell fine furniture, jewelry, books, clocks, and art-deco items. On Sunday, there's also an outdoor market featuring less established dealers. Go on Sunday— few dealers are open during the week.

☕ **WINDOW DINING**   In the Harbourfront Antiques Market, **Sophie's** has great fresh salads, sandwiches, quiches, and desserts.

Board the LRT and head back to Union Station.

WALKING TOUR 2
The Financial District

Start: The CN Tower, near the corner of John and Front streets.
Finish: At one of Queen Street West's watering holes.
Time: 4 hours, depending on how long you take to browse.
Best Time: Anytime.

Start by going up the:

1. **CN Tower,** which is the tallest freestanding structure in the world. Back down at the base, exit at the corner of John and Front streets. From here, look east along Front Street to see the glistening golden Royal Bank towers. The CBC Center stretches along the north side of Front Street for a whole long block.

   Walk north on John Street, cross Wellington, and continue up to King Street. Turn right. On the northeast corner of King Street, sports fans will want to stop in at **Legends of the Game.** Doors with baseball-shaped handles open onto an emporium that features the Wall of Fame and every conceivable sports collectible.

   Continue walking along the north side of King Street to:

2. **The Princess of Wales Theatre,** which was opened in 1993 by the Princess herself, and was the brainchild of son and father David and Ed Mirvish. If you can, go inside and get a look at the 10,000-square-feet of murals created by Frank Stella. There's even one on the exterior back of the building worth walking around to see. Exit the theater and continue along King Street past a cluster of Ed Mirvish restaurant creations (drop into one just to check out the larger-than-life decor) and a wall of newspaper clippings about this gutsy, quintessential Torontonian who, with his great love and boostering of the city, seems a shyer version of New York's former mayor Ed Koch. Next you'll come to:

3. **The Royal Alex.** This beloved theater, named after the king's consort, was built in 1906 and 1907 by John M. Lyle in a magnificent beaux arts style and was saved and refurbished by Ed Mirvish in 1963. Named after Queen Alexandra, wife of Edward VII, it's Edwardian to a tee, loaded with gilt and velvet, and sporting an entrance foyer lined with green marble. Across the street from these two theaters stands the new Metro Hall designed by Brisbin Brook Beynon. Go in to see the interior art installations, especially the animal sculptures by Cynthia Short. Tours are given of the first three floors. Call **416/392-8000.**

   Also on the south side of the street, at the corner of King and Simcoe streets, is:

4. **Roy Thomson Hall,** named after newspaper magnate Lord Thomson of Fleet. Built between 1972 and 1982 and designed by Arthur Erickson, the building's

Walking Tour—The Financial District

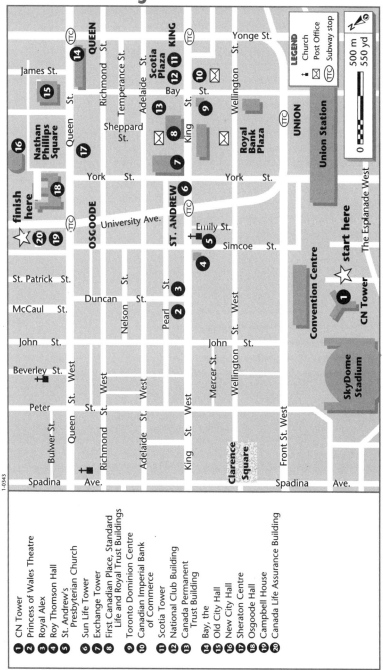

LEGEND
+ Church
⊠ Post Office
TTC Subway stop

0 — 500 m
0 — 550 yd

1. CN Tower
2. Princess of Wales Theatre
3. Royal Alex
4. Roy Thomson Hall
5. St. Andrew's
   Presbyterian Church
6. Sun Life Tower
7. Exchange Tower
8. First Canadian Place, Standard
   Life and Royal Trust Buildings
9. Toronto Dominion Centre
10. Canadian Imperial Bank
    of Commerce
11. Scotia Tower
12. National Club Building
13. Canada Permanent
    Trust Building
14. Bay, the
15. Old City Hall
16. New City Hall
17. Sheraton Centre
18. Osgoode Hall
19. Campbell House
20. Canada Life Assurance Building

exterior looks very space-age, and inside, the mirrored effects are dramatic. Tours are usually given of this fabulous concert hall at 12:30pm, but call ahead at **416/593-4828** to confirm this time, if you really do want to see behind the scenes. If you don't want to take a tour, at least go in for a look.

☕ **TAKE A BREAK** Your best bet for a leisurely lunch in this neighborhood is **Jump,** 1 Wellington St. West. For a quick and easy snack, seek out one of the casual dining spots in the concourse of **First Canadian Place.**

Continue walking east. You'll be walking through the heart of the financial district, surrounded by the many towers owned and operated by banks and brokerage, trust, and insurance companies. Cross Simcoe Street. On the northeast corner of King and Simcoe rises the first of the towers that makes up the Sun Life Centre; on the southeast corner stands:

5. **St. Andrew's Presbyterian Church,** a quietly inviting retreat from the city's pace and noise. Continue along the block to University Avenue. Opposite, on the northeast corner, is the:

6. **Sun Life Centre's** second tower, marked by a sculpture by Sorel Etrog. Farther along the block you'll find another sculpture, *Parent I* by Barbara Hepworth, in a courtyard setting complete with splashing fountain at the northwest corner of York Street. On the northeast corner stands the:

7. **Exchange Tower,** connected to the Toronto Stock Exchange at the corner of Adelaide and York streets.

Continue along King Street past:

8. **First Canadian Place** on the north side and the **Standard Life and Royal Trust Buildings** on the south, until you reach Bay Street. The first was designed by New York architect Edward Durell Stone with Bregman & Hamann and is faced with marble in contrast to the TD Centre, which is black. Again, there are views of the magnificent Royal Bank towers from here.

The intersection of Bay and King streets was once considered the precise geographical center of Toronto's financial power, and during the mining booms in the 1920s and 1950s, Bay Street was lined with offices that were filled with commission salesmen peddling stocks to the equivalent of the little ol' lady from Dubuque. This is the hub that gave Torontonians their reputation as a voracious band of money-grubbing folks that Hugh McLennan portrayed in his marvelous novel about Québec, *Two Solitudes.* Today it's called Mint corner because each corner is occupied by a major bank. Rising at King and Bay today is the:

9. **Toronto Dominion Centre,** built between 1963 and 1969 and designed by Mies van der Rohe in his sleek trademark style. The black steel and dark-bronze–tinted glass tower rises from its gray granite base launching pad. Here, tucked away by the Aetna Centre on the south side of Wellington Street, is one artist's reminder to the stockbrokers that Toronto's wealth is derived from other stock, too. Joe Fafard's *Pasture* is a whimsical sculpture featuring several bronze cows lazing on a small patch of grass.

Cross Bay Street. On the south side of King Street, architecture buffs will want to go into the:

10. **Canadian Imperial Bank of Commerce** (1929–31) just to see the massive banking hall—145 feet long, 85 feet wide, and 65 feet high—with its coffered ceiling, gilt moldings, and decorative sculpted friezes. The main entrance is decorated, for instance, with squirrels, roosters, bees, bears, and figures representing Industry, Commerce, and Mercury. For years, this 34-story building dominated the Toronto

skyline. It was designed by New Yorkers York and Sawyer, with Darling and Pearson. Note the carved heads on the top of the building depicting courage, observation, foresight, and enterprise. In the early 1970s I. M. Pei was asked to design a new complex while preserving the old building. He set the new stainless-steel bank tower that glistens (thanks to its mercury lamination) back from King Street, creating Commerce Court.

Opposite, on the north side of King Street, note:

11. **Scotia Tower,** the red-granite building, designed by Webb Zerafa Menkes Housden between 1985 and 1988.

Walk back to Bay Street and turn right going north. At no. 303 on the east side is the:

12. **National Club Building.** In 1874 the Canada First Movement, which had been started in Ottawa in 1868, became centered in Toronto. As its name suggests, the members were fervent nationalists. It established a weekly, *The Nation,* and entered politics as the Canadian National Association and founded the National Club. Eventually the movement's influence faded but its original ideas had lasting influence. The club moved to these premises in 1907. Today, it's a prestigious private club.

Across the street on the west side, at the corner of Bay and Adelaide streets, stands the:

13. **Canada Permanent Trust Building** (1928). Go in to view the beautifully worked art-deco brass and bronze, particularly the elevator doors, which are chased and engraved with foliage and flowers.

Cross Adelaide Street. As you walk up Bay Street, the magnificently solid Old City Hall is clearly in view, but first, on the east side of Bay between Richmond and Queen, look at or, if you like, stop into:

14. **The Bay,** one of Canada's venerable retailers. The Bay (formerly Simpson's), along with arch rival Eaton's, has influenced the development of the downtown areas of most major Canadian cities. If you like, go in and check out the art-deco bar in the SRO bar on the ground floor.

Ahead looms the:

15. **Old City Hall,** reflected dramatically to the right in the Cadillac Fairview Office Tower at the corner of James and Queen streets. This solid, impressive building, designed by Edward James Lennox, is built out of Credit River Valley sandstone in a magnificent Romanesque Revival style that is obviously influenced by H. H. Richardson. Begun in 1885, it was opened in 1899, and for years its clock tower was a familiar skyline landmark. Today, the building houses the provincial criminal courts. Go in to see the impressive staircase, columns with decorative capitals, mosaic floor, and stained-glass window (1898) by Robert McCausland depicting the union of Commerce and Industry watched over by Britannia. Note the carved heads on the exterior entrance pillars—supposedly portraits of the political figures and citizens of the period, including the architect himself. Pause on your way out to look down the canyon of Bay Street, the city's equivalent of New York's Wall Street. Bay Street curves around, and to your left there is suddenly the:

16. **New City Hall,** the city's fourth, built between 1958 and 1965; in modern sculptural style, it's the symbol of Toronto's post-war dynamism. Designed by Finnish architect Viljo Revell, who won the competition that was entered by 510 architects from 42 countries, including I. M. Pei, it has a great square in front with a fountain and pool to which office workers flock in summer to relax, and in winter to skate. The square is named after Nathan Phillips, Toronto's first Jewish mayor, who helped push the project through. The Council Chamber, supported on a

two-tier podium, looks like a flying saucer, but the glass walls make it seem open and accessible. Henry Moore's sculpture *The Archer* stands in front of the building—thanks to Mayor Phil Givens, who raised the money to buy it through public subscription after the city authorities refused to purchase it. This gesture encouraged Henry Moore to bestow a major collection of his works on the Art Gallery. The Council Chamber is flanked by two curved concrete towers that house the bureaucracy. From the air, the whole complex supposedly looks like an eye peering up at the heavens.

For the best view of City Hall, enter the:

17. Sheraton Centre, on the south side of Queen Street, and go up to the second-floor Long Bar, which overlooks the square.

☕ **TAKE A BREAK** For some light refreshment, stop in at one of several dining spots in the **Sheraton Centre,** 123 Queen St. West.

From City Hall, walk west along Queen Street. On your right behind an ornate wrought-iron fence that once kept out the cows you'll see:

18. Osgoode Hall, since the 1830s headquarters of the Law Society of Upper Canada, a kind of professional trade union. Named after the first chief justice of Upper Canada, the building was constructed in stages, starting with the East Wing in 1831 to 1832, the West Wing in 1844 to 1845, and the center block in 1856 to 1860. The last, with its Palladian portico, is the most impressive. Inside, the Great Library—112 feet long, 40 feet wide, and 40 feet high—with stucco decoration and coved domed ceiling is grand. The Ontario Supreme Court is across the street on the south side of Queen Street.

Keep walking west to University Avenue. On the northwest corner you can visit the:

19. Campbell House, the elegant Georgian residence of Sir William Campbell, a Scot who moved to York in 1811 and rose to become chief justice of Upper Canada. A handsome piece of Georgian architecture, it was moved to this location from a few miles farther east.

Behind Campbell House, on the northwest side of University Avenue, the:

20. Canada Life Assurance Building stretches northward. Atop the tower a neon sign provides weather reports—white flashes for snow, red flashes for rain, green beacon for clement weather, or red beacon for cloudy weather. If the flashes move upward, the temperature is headed that way, and vice versa.

At University Avenue and Queen Street, you can end the tour by boarding the subway at Osgoode to your next destination, or you can continue walking west along Queen Street to explore the many delights of this thoroughfare on our next tour.

WALKING TOUR 3
Queen Street West

Start: On the north side of Queen, just west of Simcoe.
Finish: At one of Queen Street West's watering holes.
Time: As long as it takes you to shop and browse the many stores.
Best Time: Weekdays or Saturdays, when all the stores are open.

This is one of the city's great alternative shopping and nightlife venues. The tour below includes a few stores you're most likely to enjoy browsing, but there are more along Queen Street West from University to Bathurst, and even beyond.

On the north side of the street, just west of Simcoe at no. 200, is:

1. **Dragon Lady Comics,** for collectors of old and new comic books.

On the south side, between Simcoe and John, you'll find:

2. **The Village Bookstore,** with a good selection of secondhand volumes, including some decent art books; **Cards & Presents,** which offers cool cards, paper products, and fiesta ware; and **Anji,** which has wonderful Afro-fashions created by Anji herself, as well as jewelry and crafts from local designers. Cross Duncan and pass **X-Rays,** a cafe-bar with the **Ultra Show Lounge** upstairs, one of the city's rock venues.

Farther along, you'll come to:

3. **Noise,** which sells the latest in sneakers (Etnies and Airwalk), Arnet sunglasses, and cool, colored cords, hats, and other fashion items for the Gen Xer. At the end of the block, at the corner of John and Queen, is:

4. **CityTV,** the voice and sound of the city. Here, if you have a gripe about something, you can go into the video recording box right at Speaker's Corner and complain to your heart's content. The best video clips are aired later. It's a fun, alternative TV station that also operates a music station similar to MTV and an arts channel, too.

Back on the North side is:

5. **The Queen Street Market.** Go in and you'll discover counters selling Chinese and barbecue food. There's also a juice bar and a Hillebrand wine outlet, as well as fresh fruit and vegetable stands. Also in this block are a couple of à la mode shoe stores— **John Fluevog** for the brightest, most colorful, and statement-making shoes, and **Scrubbies** for Doc Martens, police-, and combat boots and other motorcycle gear at reasonable prices. Cross John Street, and at no. 256 you'll find:

6. **Pages,** a large, well-stocked bookstore selling hardcovers and paperbacks and a very wide selection of magazines.

Still on the same side of the street, cross Beverley and you'll find:

7. **Angi Venni,** a young Canadian designer, at no. 274. **Robin Kay's** store emphasizes environmental concerns, stocking natural-fabric fashions, duvets, and bed linens, recycled paper products, and beeswax candles. **Du Verre** (no. 280), has a wide variety of glass vases, pitchers, and plates and proudly displays a sticker identifying it as an "alternative bridal registry." Next door, at no. 282, the **Bakka Science Fiction Book Shoppe** amasses a vast selection in the genre. **ION Fashion,** at no. 290, as its name would suggest, displays cool, hip clothing, including children's fashions and accessories. **Zephyr,** at no. 292, appeals to the natural world for inspiration, proffering polished rocks and minerals, pyramids, crystals, butterflies, and other natural collectibles. Soho Street cuts in here on the north.

On the south side, between John and Peter, are several fashion stores and some popular bistros and bars, such as:

8. **Black Market,** at no 323A, which features vintage clothing; **Pegabo,** which displays the latest shoes with attitude; and **Cotton Ginny,** which proffers simple, casual cotton wear.

🍽 **TAKE A BREAK** On both sides of the street, there are several favorite hangouts for the artsy crowd. **Le Select,** no. 328, offers a sheltered sidewalk patio and well-priced French bistro fare, whereas **Rivoli,** no. 332, is more avantgarde. On the south side, **Peter Pan,** no. 373, is an art-deco venue with an imaginative menu; **Chicago's,** at no. 335, and the **Bishop & the Belcher,** at no. 361, will answer any craving for typical bar/pub fare.

Back on the North side of the street, between Beverley and Spadina, you'll encounter some of the most venerable Queen Street clubs, such as:

9. **Bamboo,** which pioneered reggae and Caribbean sounds in the city, and **Rivoli,** where Holly Cole and others made their names. Also in this block are such stores as the quintessentially Canadian **Roots. David Mason** is upstairs at no. 342, and features a well-cataloged stock of antique, out-of-print, and secondhand books. **Grafix** has well-priced art supplies; **Le Chateau,** a Montréal original, offers engaging fashions. At no. 356, **Edwards Books and Art** has some of the best prices on art books in the city and regularly advertises discounted titles in the local newspapers. Although it stocks the latest fiction and nonfiction, the store specializes in fine illustrated books on gardening and art and architecture, as well as cookbooks.

Back on the south side, between Peter and Spadina, are several browsable stores. Among them are:

10. **Urban Mode,** at no. 387, for the latest Italian housewares; **Aldo,** for the latest foot fashions from Stone Ridge, Doc Martens, and others; and funky fashion stores like outrageous **Fashion Crimes,** at no. 395, for the most current funky and retro-style fashions. At no. 403, **Club Monaco** offers more tailored sports fashions; and at no. 415, you'll find **Steve's Music Store,** which features a vast array of musical instruments.

Continue on to Spadina Avenue and cross the street. On the south side, you'll find:

11. **Hype** (no. 459), offering the latest hip fashions, many of them fashioned from shimmering materials; as well as one of the street's old-time stores, **Buttons & Trims,** which is overflowing with fringes, buttons, and braids. **Siren,** at no. 463, has the latest PVC boots, leopard-pattern shirts, poet shirts fashioned from velvet, crop tops, and Danskin ankle pants for that hot club date. **Matmata** displays glorious ceramics from North Africa along with leather items, drums, and jewelry from the same region.

At no. 471, **The House of Ill Repute** features chainmail jewelry and some appropriate lacy and velvet bodices to go with it, as well as PVC skirts, pants, and more. The street is then taken over by a number of old-fashioned fabric and textile stores. Book lovers will want to climb up to **Robert Wright,** who specializes in literature and illustrated, film, and mystery books, and **James Fraser's** store, with a large collection of sci-fi, mystery, pulp, and horror titles. Farther along the street, **Steven Temple** offers fine literary first editions.

At no. 507 is the designer **Peach Berserk,** who makes her zany designs in the back room. Many of the garments carry written slogans. **Abelard** (no. 519) is one of my favorite antiquarian bookstores. Spacious, it has a broad selection of fine-quality stock, and offers comforts, too—lounge chairs and sofas that invite quiet, honest-to-goodness browsing.

Art on Beads (no. 523) provides the beads to create whatever anyone could imagine, along with buttons, jewelry, and some great buckles. **Niknak** has some cool stuff—sunglasses, fashion-conscious fun watches imported from New York, hair accessories, jewelry, and more.

Cross Augusta Avenue and you'll find:

12. **Browns',** at no. 545, selling Hugo Boss and other designer fashions for men 5 foot 8 and under, **Striders** for shoes, **Arka** for all kinds of Ukrainian newspapers, crafts, and books, and **Motuba** for every conceivable type of ribbon and trim. Cross Portland Street to:

13. **Preloved** (no. 611), a store that was opened by three models who now update secondhand clothing into hip, current fashions. You'll find great retro here in spades.

Walking Tour—Queen Street West

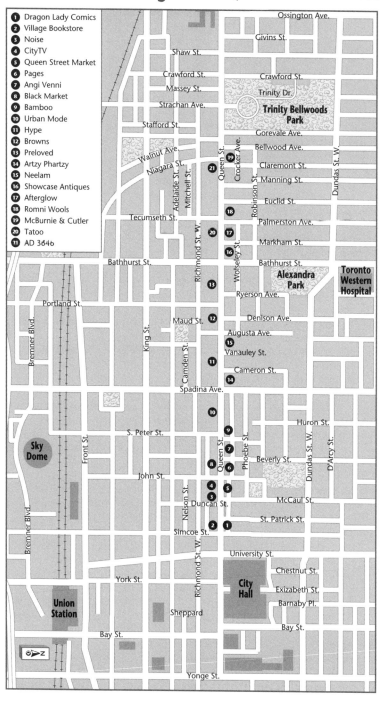

1. Dragon Lady Comics
2. Village Bookstore
3. Noise
4. CityTV
5. Queen Street Market
6. Pages
7. Angi Venni
8. Black Market
9. Bamboo
10. Urban Mode
11. Hype
12. Browns
13. Preloved
14. Artzy Phartzy
15. Neelam
16. Showcase Antiques
17. Afterglow
18. Romni Wools
19. McBurnie & Cutler
20. Tatoo
21. AD 3646

At **Nikolaou,** cooks will find some bargains on restaurant equipment and cooking utensils. The **Queens Trade Centre** at no. 635 is crammed with all kinds of junk. It's known for a great selection of musical instruments from banjos and mandolins guitars to trumpets, trombones, and accordions. **King's Outdoor Store** sells all kinds of outdoor camping gear, including terrific raingear and ranger vests. You will now be at Bathurst.

Back on the north side of Queen Street, between Spadina Avenue and Vanauley Street, you'll find:

14. **Artzy Phartzy** (no. 394), stocking an eclectic selection of 20th-century collectibles and jewelry; an assortment of fabrics, notions, and hardware stores. Cross Vanauley and you'll come to:

15. **Neelam Boutique,** selling Indian fashions, sarongs, sandals, incense burners, and jewelry, along with batik fashions. **Gebo Art Worx,** at no. 446, is a large collective featuring a variety of craft items and artworks by local artists—talismans, ceramics, candles, jewelry, tie-dyed T-shirts, and more. **Kimina** is great for tailored shirts and suits for women. **Maggies** (no. 450), specializes in dried flower arrangements, wreaths, and table decorations as well as fresh flowers. The **Day Before Yesterday** offers fine vintage clothing.

For those who still have some energy left, cross Bathurst and continue. Here, tucked in between some of the more seedy stores, are a few gems, notably on the north side of the street:

16. **Showcase Antiques** (at no. 610, between Bathurst and Markham), with 200 dealers on three floors selling furniture, jewelry, and decorative items from all periods and places.

17. **Afterglow** is a good hunting place for art-deco stuff, and **One Tree Hill** sells clothing accessories, handcrafts, and skirts and blouses mainly from Turkey. (Both are between Markham and Palmerston).

18. **Romni Wools** (no. 658), has a full range of yarns, plus sheepskin fashions and some fun sweaters; the **Tibet Shoppe** sells such sacred items as singing bowls as well as fashions and jewelry; **Algonquians** has fine quality art-deco furnishings, while **Cabaret** has some of the finest quality period clothing in the city. This is the place to purchase your retro fashions—velvet and sequined evening gowns, shoes, and that perfect smoking jacket.

Cross Euclid Avenue, and you'll encounter:

19. **McBurnie & Cutler,** another secondhand bookstore with a good selection of Canadian first editions, as well as books on travel, philosophy, and much more.

On the south side of the street, between Bathurst and Tecumseth, is:

20. **Tatoo,** a tatoo parlor, where you can pick a way-cool design and get it cut in right away. At no. 699, **Jalan** sells Indonesian and other furniture and crafts from Asia, including marble bowls from India, betel boxes from Burma, painted wood plates, and carved wooden friezes. Here, too, are another couple of retro fashion stars—**Metro** and **Morningstar.** If you're looking for some unique and bizarre decorative items to add some sparkle to your interiors, then stop in at **Lynn Robinson** for one of the planters with feet or an obelisk clock. Everything is handcrafted—ceramics, glass, and jewelry. Cross Tecumseth Street to:

21. **AD 3646,** to view its au courant furnishings, from chairs upholstered in cow skin to elaborate candleholders. At **Lost Horizons,** you can peel through the table runners, napkins, and Indian garments to find some fairly priced kids' clothes, or you can pore over the silver jewelry. **Alkatraz** has rack after rack of vintage clothing. At no 795, **Rangatan,** offers great Indonesian batik shirts, as well as pants, sarongs,

and jackets from the region, wooden animals, bags, and more. **World Art and Decor** has arts and crafts from Africa, including great batik fabrics, cushions, music, wood sculpture, drums, sandals, and T-shirts.

🎵 **WINDOW DINING**   There are plenty of places to stop for refreshment along these blocks. On the north side, between Augusta and Ryerson, is the **Epicure Cafe** at no. 512; or you can stop at the **Prague Deli**, no. 638, between Markham Street and Palmerston, and purchase take-out hot and cold sandwiches, danishes, or strudels. On the south side are several funky, fun cafes, most notably **Gypsy Coop,** east of Niagara at no. 815, with its candy in jars, assortment of teas, mismatched chairs and tables, couches, and pool table in back. There are great "skor" brownies. Between Niagara and Tecumseh, there's **La Calle,** a cafe-bar with a distinct salsa flavor. And at no. 787, there's **Dufflet,** for great ice cream floats, apricot squares, and luscious cakes and tortes.

WALKING TOUR 4
Chinatown & Kensington Market

Start: Osgoode subway station.
Finish: Toronto Public Reference Library.
Time: 6 to 8 hours, depending on whether or not you stop.
Best Time: Anytime except Monday (when the Art Gallery is closed).

From the Osgoode subway station, walk west on Queen Street. Turn right onto McCaul Street. On the west side of the street (left), if you're interested in crafts, you'll want to stop at:

1. Prime Gallery, at no. 52, which sells ceramics, jewelry, fabrics, and other art objects crafted by contemporary artisans.
    On the right is:

2. Village by the Grange, an apartment/shopping complex that's laid out in a series of courtyards (one even contains a small ice-skating rink). Go into the complex at the southern end and stroll through, emerging from the food market. En route you'll come across some small fashion boutiques and **18 Karat,** where the proprietors design and craft jewelry behind the counter (show them what you have in mind and they will craft it for you beautifully).

🎵 **TAKE A BREAK**   Also in Village by the Grange is one of the city's oldest and most popular Chinese restaurants—**Sun Lok.** The **Food Market** contains stalls selling everything—12 varieties of freshly brewed coffee, schnitzels, satay, Japanese noodles, salads, falafel, hot dogs, Chinese food, kebabs, pizza, and fried chicken.

Continue north along McCaul, passing the Ontario College of Art on the left side of the street, until you reach Dundas Street, where on the left you'll encounter a large Henry Moore sculpture entitled *Large Two Forms,* which is precisely what it is.
    Turn left. The entrance to the:

3. Art Gallery of Ontario is on the left. If you don't want to go in to see the collections, you can browse the gallery stores without paying admission.
    Cross to the north side of Dundas, opposite the Art Gallery. It's worth stopping in at the:

4. **Bau-Xi,** a gallery representing modern Canadian artists. From here, return to McCaul and turn left to Baldwin Street a short street containing so many ethnic restaurants that you can virtually dine around the world from China and Japan to France and Mexico. Farther along Baldwin on the corner of Beverley is:

5. **George Brown House,** at 50 Baldwin, the home of the founder of the reform newspaper, the *Globe* (1844) and a prominent politician. It was built in 1877 and even featured such a modern amenity as a shower. At the junction of Baldwin and Beverley, turn left and then right onto Dundas. Walk west into the heart of Chinatown, stopping in at the grocery stores, bakeries, bookstalls, and other emporiums selling foods, handcrafts, and other items from Asia.

   What follows are some of my favorite browsing stops along the stretch of Dundas Street between Beverley Street and Spadina Avenue. On the south or left side as you go west is:

6. **Tai Sun Co.,** at nos. 407–09, a supermarket displaying dozens of different mushrooms, all clearly labeled in English, as well as all kinds of fresh Chinese vegetables, meats, fish, and canned goods. **Melewa Bakery,** at no. 433, has a wide selection of pastries, like mung-bean and lotus-paste buns. Outside **Kiu Shun Trading,** at no. 441, dried fish are displayed, while inside you'll find numerous varieties of ginseng and such miracle remedies as "Stop Smoking Tea" and delicacies such as swallows' nests.

   On the north side of the street:

7. **J & S Arts and Crafts,** at no. 430, is a good place to pick up souvenirs, including kimonos and happy coats, kung-fu suits, address books, cushion covers, and all-cotton Chinatown T-shirts for only $6. **New World Book Store,** at no. 442, has a good selection of Chinese and other Asian-language dictionaries as well as Chinese cards.

   At the corner of Huron Street, on the north side of Dundas:

8. **Ten Ren Tea,** no. 454, sells all kinds of teas—black, oolong, and so forth—stored in large canisters in the back of the store, as well as charming small ceramic tea pots priced from $20 to $65. A large variety of gnarled ginseng root is also displayed for sale. Next door, **W Y Trading Co., Inc.,** has a great selection of records, CDs, and tapes—everything from Chinese folk songs and cantatas to current hit albums from Hong Kong and Taiwan. This is one place a non-Chinese-speaking visitor can read what the recording contains. **Furuya,** at no. 460, stocks Japanese specialties including some really fine sushi oke, lacquer trays, bowls, boxes, and sake sets, as well as food and other specialties. At no 482A, **Po Chi Tong** is a fun store to go into view the exotic remedies available, like deer-tail extract and liquid-gold ginseng or royal jelly. The best remedy of all time is the "slimming tea." Watch them weigh each item out and total the bill with a fast-clicking abacus.

   ☕ **TAKE A BREAK**   Right in Chinatown, **Champion House at 480 Dundas St. West,** is a good lunch stop that offers comfortable, elegant surroundings (in contrast to the strictly functional look that prevails in Chinatown) and good Chinese cuisine. The specialty is Peking duck, and a gong is sounded when it comes out of the kitchen. They have other dishes, too, like beef with ginger and green onions and also orange chicken, priced from $9 to $13.

   At Spadina, cross over to the southwest corner to:

9. **Dragon City,** an Asian-style shopping complex complete with a food court on the west side of Spadina at no. 280.

Walking Tour—Chinatown & Kensington Market

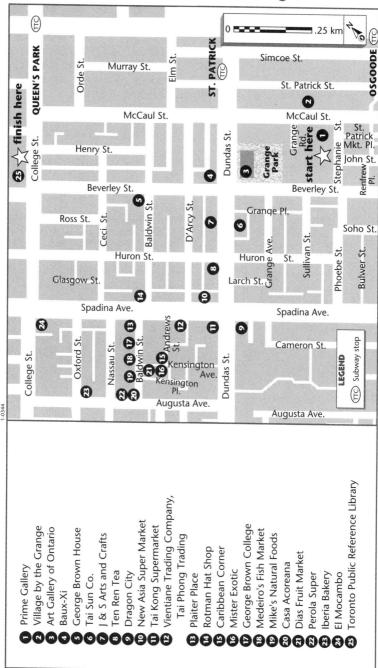

0 ──── .25 km

QUEEN'S PARK

ST. PATRICK

OSGOODE

Murray St.

Simcoe St.

Orde St.

Elm St.

St. Patrick St.

McCaul St.

McCaul St.

finish here

College St.

Henry St.

Dundas St.

Grange Rd.

St. Patrick Mkt. Pl.

John St.

Grange Park

start here

Stephanie St.

Renfrew Pl.

Beverley St.

Beverley St.

Ross St.

Ceci St.

Baldwin St.

D'Arcy St.

Grange Pl.

Soho St.

Huron St.

Grange Ave.

Sullivan St.

Phoebe St.

Bulwer St.

Glasgow St.

Huron St.

Larch St.

Spadina Ave.

Spadina Ave.

Oxford St.

Nassau St.

Andrews St.

Cameron St.

College St.

Baldwin St.

Kensington Ave.

Kensington Pl.

Dundas St.

LEGEND

TTC Subway stop

Augusta Ave.

Augusta Ave.

1-0344

1. Prime Gallery
2. Village by the Grange
3. Art Gallery of Ontario
4. Baux-Xi
5. George Brown House
6. Tai Sun Co.
7. J & S Arts and Crafts
8. Ten Ren Tea
9. Dragon City
10. New Asia Super Market
11. Tai Kong Supermarket
12. Vientiane Trading Company, Tai Phong Trading
13. Plaiter Place
14. Rotman Hat Shop
15. Caribbean Corner
16. Mister Exotic
17. George Brown College
18. Medeiro's Fish Market
19. Mike's Natural Foods
20. Casa Acoreana
21. Dias Fruit Market
22. Perola Super
23. Iberia Bakery
24. El Mocambo
25. Toronto Public Reference Library

141

Spadina Avenue is the widest street in the city because the wealthy Baldwin family had a 132-foot swath cut through the forest from Queen Street to Bloor Street so that they could view the lake from their new home on the top of Spadina Hill. Later, in the early 20th century, it became Toronto's garment center, the equivalent of New York's Seventh Avenue and the focal point of the city's Jewish community.

Although it's still the garment center, with wholesale and discount fashion houses, as well as the fur district (farther south around Adelaide), today Spadina Avenue is more Asian than Jewish.

If you enjoy strolling through supermarkets filled with exotic Asian delights, including such fruits as durian in season, then go into the:

10. New Asia Supermarket, at nos. 295–97, or cross the street and explore the:

11. Tai Kong Supermarket. Look at all the different provisions—chili and fish sauces, fresh meat and fish (including live tilapia in tanks), preserved plums, chrysanthemum tea and other kinds of infusions, moon cakes, and large sacks of rice.

☕ **TAKE A BREAK**　Join the Chinese at the food court serving all kinds of Asian cuisine downstairs at **Dragon City.** The stalls sell dim sum, noodles, curry, and all kinds of good Asian fare at low prices.

As the Asian community in Toronto has grown, other Chinatowns have been developed elsewhere, and much of the old original Chinatown now offers Thai, Vietnamese, and other Asian specialty stores. For example, there's the:

12. Vientiane Trading Company, at no. 334, where they label some vegetables in English, like lotus root, bamboo, and coriander.

Cross St. Andrews Street to no. 360, **Tap Phong Trading,** which has some terrific wicker baskets of all shapes and sizes: woks and ceramic cookware; heavy, attractive mortar and pestles; and other household items.

Cross Baldwin Street to:

13. Plaiter Place, at no. 384, which has a huge selection of finely crafted wicker baskets, birdcages, woven blinds, bamboo steamers, hats, and other fun items. Stop, too, at **Fortune Housewares,** no. 388, to shop for kitchen and household items—including all the good brand names—for at least 20% off prices elsewhere in the city.

Across the street is the:

14. Rotman Hat Shop, at no. 345, selling Panama hats that are as light as feathers and woven from the finest quality Ecuador plants. The store, which has been in business here for over 42 years, also stocks grouser hats and other fun headgear.

Now cross Spadina and double back to St. Andrews. Turn onto St. Andrews and note the synagogue on the north side of the street.

Walk along St. Andrews to Kensington Avenue and turn right. Here you'll be in the heart of the **Kensington Market** area, which has always reflected the current ethnic scene that exists in the city. Once it was primarily a Jewish market; later it became more Portuguese; today, it is a blend of Portuguese, Jewish, Caribbean, and Asian.

Walk north on Kensington Avenue. There are several West Indian grocery stores on this street, like:

15. Caribbean Corner, on the east side of the street, selling such items as plantains, yuca, sugarcane, papaya, mangoes, and other tropical products.

On the west side is:

16. Mister Exotic, at no. 70, which displays Caribbean specialties, while next door **Mendel's Creamery** sells smoked fish, herring, cheeses, and fine dill pickles. One more door down, **Global Cheese** offers an enormous selection at good prices.

Continue along Kensington Avenue to Baldwin Street. Turn right if you want to pop down and see:

17. the industrial factory-style buildings of **George Brown College,** named after the founder of the *Globe and Mail.* Turn back along Baldwin. On the north side of the street (the same side as George Brown College), you can check out the produce at:

18. **Medeiro's Fish Market.** Farther along you'll come to **Cheese Magic,** which sells all kinds of Middle Eastern specialties from olives to bhabaganoush. The comforting aromas wafting out of the **Baldwin Street Bakery** might lure you in to buy some bread. From here to the corner, the street is lined with stores like:

19. **Mike's Natural Foods, Reg,** and **Salamanca,** all selling an array of nuts, fruits and grains. Pick up some dried papaya, mango, pineapple, or apricots as a snack.

At the corner of Augusta Avenue is:

20. **Casa Acoreana,** an old-fashioned store stocking a full range of fresh coffees as well as some great pecans and filberts. On the south side of Baldwin, you'll pass:

21. **Dias Fruit Market,** selling all manner of fresh fruits and vegetables; **Abyssinia,** which specializes in African and West Indian products, several seafood stores displaying infinite varieties of fresh fish and salted cod piled up in boxes out on the sidewalk, and the **Royal Food Centre,** which sells a variety of Jamaican specialties, including goat meat.

At the end of Baldwin, turn right onto Augusta Avenue into the heart of the old Portuguese neighborhood. In addition to the discount and used clothing emporiums on the west side of the street, there are several Latino stores, such as:

22. **Perola Super at no. 247,** which displays cassava and strings of peppers hung up to dry as well as in bins—ancho, arbol, pasilla, plus more exotic fruits and herbs; and **Emporium Latino,** which sells cactus leaves and yuca, among many other Latin American items.

Cross Nassau Street to the:

23. **Iberica Bakery,** at no. 279, and the **Agniar Grocery,** both on the east side of the street. They represent the few remaining traces of the Portuguese presence in the Kensington Market area.

Turn right down Oxford Avenue and walk over to Spadina Avenue. Turn left to:

24. **El Mocambo,** the rock-and-roll landmark where the Rolling Stones played on March 4 and 5, 1977, in their heyday, and then hop on the trolley traveling east along College Street to the subway. Along the route, you'll pass on the left (north) side of the street what used to be the:

25. **Toronto Public Reference Library,** an attractive classical revival building now occupied by the University of Toronto bookstore and Koffler Student Centre. On the south corner of College Street and University Avenue, you'll see the weird-looking mirrored-glass **Hydro Place.**

WALKING TOUR 5
Queen's Park & the University

Start: Royal Ontario Museum.

Finish: Queen's Park.

Time: 3 to 4 hours (more if you stop in at the museum).

Best Times: Anytime except Monday (when the museum's closed).

Take the subway to Museum to the:

1. **Royal Ontario Museum (ROM),** which is, of course, the great repository of the city's collections.

Walk south to Queen's Park and follow its curve to the right past:

2. **Holwood,** the residence of wealthy meatpacker Sir Joseph Flavelle, which is now used by the university's School of Law. The elegant and richly decorated house was nicknamed Porker's Palace. Inside, the grand hall has decorative art-nouveau features and a ceiling painted in art-nouveau style by Gustav Hahn.

Walk around to Hoskin Avenue. On the south side of the street stands:

3. **Wycliffe College,** founded in 1877 as a Low Church Anglican college and built in red brick in Romanesque Revival style. It stands across from:

4. **Trinity College,** the Anglican High Church college, founded as an independent university in 1851 by first Anglican bishop Strachan after King's College (the original university foundation) was declared nonsectarian in 1849. Trinity became part of the university in 1904. The Gothic buildings, the chapel, and the gardens are attractive sights.

At Devonshire Place, turn right and walk north to:

5. **Massey College** (1960–63), enclosed behind modern, concertina-folded screenlike walls. It has a cloistered yet inviting air, with fountains playing in the quadrangle. Designed by Ron Thom, it has a traditional, serene yet modern quality with Frank Lloyd Wright and Japanese elements.

Farther up Devonshire Place you'll come to:

6. **St. Hilda's,** a classic Georgian-style building housing the women's college that is part of Trinity.

Turn around and come back to Hoskin. Turn right and walk over to St. George past St. Thomas Aquinas Chapel to see the dreadnought of a building, the:

7. **John P. Robarts Library,** the building everyone loves to hate. This huge concrete hulk houses the research library and the rare-book library.

From here, turn back along Hoskin to Tower Road and turn right, walking toward the:

8. **Soldier's Memorial Tower** (1924), inspired by Magdalen's Big Tom, which stands between Gothic Hart House on the left and Romanesque University College on the right. Go into:

9. **Hart House** (1910–19), named after Hart Massey. It's consciously Oxford-like in style and atmosphere. Today, every U of T student belongs to Hart House, once an exclusive male domain. View the small chapel containing a memorial window created by Rosemary Kilbourn for Alice and Vincent Massey. Drift past the common rooms, where you'll probably observe a few students sleeping or lolling on couches, and proceed to the East Wing, which contains the Great Hall with its hammerbeam ceiling, stained-glass windows, and impressive fireplace. From the High Table, a staircase leads to the Senior Common Room. Under the quadrangle, the Hart House Theatre is well known for its theatrical and other productions. The West Wing contains the Justina M. Barnicke Art Gallery, a fine collection of Canadian art.

Exit on the south side onto Hart House Circle. Proceed to your right around the circle. On the left is the:

10. **Stewart Observatory,** originally built in 1857 and reconstructed in 1908, and on the right stands:

11. **University College,** nicknamed the Godless College when it was founded in 1853 on nonsectarian lines. It was built from 1856 to 1859 by Cumberland and Storm in a fabulous Romanesque Revival style with fanciful towers and chimneys and

Walking Tour—Queen's Park & the University

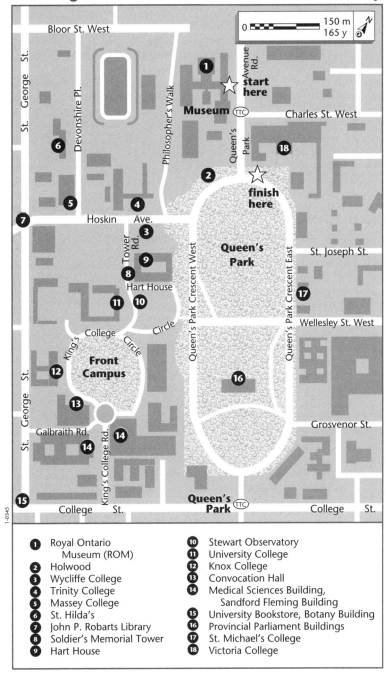

Key

1. Royal Ontario Museum (ROM)
2. Holwood
3. Wycliffe College
4. Trinity College
5. Massey College
6. St. Hilda's
7. John P. Robarts Library
8. Soldier's Memorial Tower
9. Hart House
10. Stewart Observatory
11. University College
12. Knox College
13. Convocation Hall
14. Medical Sciences Building, Sandford Fleming Building
15. University Bookstore, Botany Building
16. Provincial Parliament Buildings
17. St. Michael's College
18. Victoria College

intricately and heavily patterned round arches. Set around a quadrangle, the college has splendid East and West Halls in the south wing. The first women to enter the university were admitted to this college in 1884; there were nine at the end of that year. Go inside. The main staircase has a fantastic dragon newel post at the bottom.

Walk through into the quadrangle and around and out on the west side of the building. Turn left and walk south to King's College Circle. On your right will be:

12. Knox College. Go in to see the Gothic interior fan vaulting at the main entrance and the Caven Library with its hammerbeam ceiling.

Exit and continue around the circle to:

13. Convocation Hall, a monstrous Victorian bore. En route, you'll pass the far more elegant Simcoe Hall. Take some time to look back across the lawn at Hart House and the other university buildings across the circle.

Continue south to the:

14. Medical Sciences Building on the left, a concrete brutalist building, and the unimpressive classical revival **Sanford Fleming Building** on the right.

Exit onto College Avenue. If you want to, turn right to visit the:

15. University bookstore, at 214 College St., in the old city reference library, and then turn back and walk toward Queen's Park past the **Botany Building** and the lovely glass greenhouse that graces the rim of the park.

Walk into the park to the:

16. Provincial Parliament buildings (1886–92), an impressive example of Romanesque Revival created out of glorious pink sandstone. Beyond the entrance with its domed turrets is an impressive interior of carved wood, ornate cast and wrought iron, and a three-story legislative chamber with coved ceiling.

Exit at the northeastern rim of the circle to see:

17. St. Michael's College, which began in 1852 as a Roman Catholic boys' school, became affiliated with the university in 1881, and formally became a college in 1910. Nearby:

18. Victoria College, which was established in 1836 in Cobourg, Ontario, and moved here in 1892 when it became part of the University of Toronto. Originally a Methodist institution, it has been related to the United Church of Canada since 1925.

Note: Free tours of the university sponsored by the Alumni Association are given Monday through Friday at 10:30am and 1 and 2:30pm through the summer only. Call **416/978-5000.**

WALKING TOUR 6
St. Lawrence & Downtown East

Start: Union Station.
Finish: King subway station.
Time: 2 to 3 hours, allowing for browsing time.
Best Time: Saturday (when the St. Lawrence Market is in full swing).
Worst Time: Sunday (when it's closed).

Begin at:

1. Union Station. Check out the interior of this classical revival beauty which opened in 1927. Note the soaring vitrified tile ceiling.

Across the street, at the corner of York and Front streets, stands the:

2. **Royal York Hotel,** a venerable railroad hotel, longtime gathering place for Torontonians, and home of the famous Imperial Room cabaret/nightclub, which used to be one of Eartha Kitt's favorite venues (it's still there, but for dining and dancing only). The hotel was once the tallest building in Toronto and the largest hotel in the British Commonwealth. Check out the lobby with its coffered ceiling and opulent furnishings.

Walk east on Front Street and, at the corner of Bay and Front, look up at the:

3. **Royal Bank Plaza,** two triangular gold-sheathed towers, one 41 floors, the other 26, joined by a 130-foot-high atrium. The mirrored glass is enhanced by 150 pounds of gold. It was designed by Webb Zerafa Menkes Housden and built between 1973 and 1977.

Cross Bay and continue east on Front Street. On the south side of the street is the impressive sweep of **One Front Street,** the main post office building, which for some reason reminds me of Buckingham Palace. On the north side of the street is the city's latest financial palace, Bell Canada Enterprises's:

4. **BCE Place,** Go inside. It's impressive and you can also enjoy the Movenpick Marche and the other stores in the concourse. It was designed by Skidmore, Owings, and Merrill with Bregman & Hamann in 1993. The twin office towers are connected by a huge glass-covered galleria five stories high, spanning the block between Bay and Yonge. It connects the old Midland Bank building to the twin towers and was designed by artist-architect Santiago Calatrava with Bregman & Hamann. Here, too, is the state-of-the-art **Hockey Hall of Fame.**

⏺ **TAKE A BREAK** For a unique dining experience, stop in at **BCE Place's Marche,** which simulates a market dining experience. Across the courtyard, for fine dining, try the dramatically designed **Acqua.** Downstairs, there's also a food court with a variety of fast-food and casual dining choices.

Back out on Front Street, continue to the northwest corner of Yonge and stop to admire the:

5. **Bank of Montréal** (1885–86), a suitably ornate building for the most powerful Canadian bank in the 19th century, banker to the colonial and federal governments. Inside, the banking hall rises to a beamed coffered ceiling with domed skylights of stained glass. The exterior, embellished with carvings, porthole windows, and a balustrade, is a sight in itself. From here, you can look along Front Street and see the weird mural by Derek M. Besant that adorns the famous and highly photogenic Flatiron or Gooderham Building (1892).

6. **The Gooderham Building** was built as the headquarters of George Gooderham, who had built upon his distilling business expanding into railroads, insurance, and philanthropy. At one time his liquor business was the biggest in the British Empire. The building occupies a triangular site and the western tip of the five-story structure is beautifully curved—the windows as well—and topped with a semicircular tower.

Continue along Front Street, crossing Yonge to stop in at the:

7. **O'Keefe Centre** and across Scott Street the neighboring **St. Lawrence Centre.** In the former, the National Ballet of Canada and the Canadian Opera Company perform.

Continue along Front Street to:

8. **The Beardmore Building** (1872), at 35–39 Front St. East. This and the many other cast-iron buildings that line the street were the heart of the warehouse district in the late 19th century, close to the lakefront and rail heads. Now they're

occupied by stores like **Frida Crafts,** which sells imports from Guatemala, India, and Bangladesh, as well as jewelry, bags, candles, and other knickknacks; and **Mountain Equipment Co-op,** stocked with everything an outdoor adventurer needs. At nos. 41–43, note the Perkins Building, and at 45–49, the only building with a totally cast-iron facade. Continue to Church Street, browsing in the stores.

Cross Church Street. More stores in which to browse follow. At no. 83, **Wonderful Whites** features everything that is indeed white and wonderful—Victorian linens, lace, pillows—as well as china and glass.

☕ **TAKE A BREAK**   The obvious and most fun place to stop is in the St. Lawrence Market at one of the stands offering fresh produce. Other choices, though, are **Le Papillon,** around the corner on Church Street, which features a raft of savory and dessert crepes, or **Pizzeria Uno** on Front Street.

Cross Market Street to the:

9. St. Lawrence Market, in the old market building on the right. Enter this great market hall, which was constructed around the city's second city hall (1844–45). The elegant pedimented facade that you see as you stand in the center of the hall was originally the center block of the city hall. Today the market is filled with all kinds of vendors selling fresh eggs, Mennonite sausage, seafood, meats, cheeses, and baked goods. On Thursday through Saturday the north building across the street hosts a farmers' market exhibiting fresh produce starting at 5am.

Exit where you came in. Cross the street and cut through Market Lane Park and the shops at Market Square past the north market building. Turn right onto King Street to the:

10. St. Lawrence Hall (1850–51), the focal point of the community in the mid-19th century. This hall was the site of grand city occasions, political rallies, balls, and entertainment. Frederick Douglass delivered an antislavery lecture here; Jenny Lind and Adelina Patti sang here in 1851 and 1860, respectively; Gen. Tom Thumb appeared here in 1862; and George Brown campaigned for Confederation here in this most elegant Palladian-style building with its domed cupola.

Cross the street and enter the 19th-century garden with a cast-iron drinking fountain for people, horses, and dogs, and neatly trimmed flower beds that are filled with seasonal flowers. If you like, you can sit on a bench and rest while you admire the handsome proportions of St. Lawrence Hall and listen to the chimes of:

11. St. James Cathedral, which is adjacent to the garden on the north side of King Street. York's first church and first Anglican church was built here from 1803 to 1807. Originally a frame building, it was enlarged in 1818 and 1819 and replaced in 1831. The first incumbent was the Rev. George O'Kill Stuart, followed by John Strachan (pronounced Strawn), later the first bishop of Toronto, who conducted himself with great pomp from his mansion on Jarvis Street and wielded great temporal as well as spiritual power in the city. The second church was burned in 1839 and the first cathedral was erected, but this, too, was destroyed by fire, in the great fire of 1849. The present building was begun in 1850 and finished in 1874. Inside, there's a Tiffany window in memory of William Jarvis at the northern end of the east aisle. It also boasts the tallest steeple in Canada.

From here, you can also view one of the early retail store buildings that were built when King Street was the main commercial street. Nos. 129–35 were originally built as an Army and Navy Store, using cast iron, plate glass, and arched

Walking Tour—St. Lawrence & Downtown East

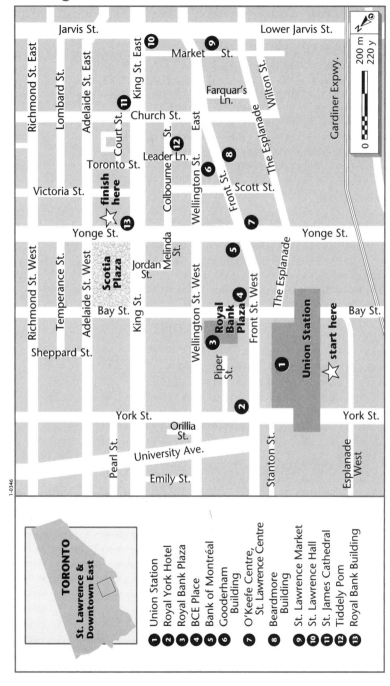

windows so that the shopper could see what was available in the store. Sandwiched between the Toronto Sculpture Garden, note, too, nos. 111 and 125.

☕ **WINDING DOWN** From St. James, the venerable **King Edward Hotel** is only a block away if you need refreshment. Afternoon tea is served or you can stop for light fare or lunch in the **Café Victoria.** Both **La Maquette,** 111 King St. East, and **Biagio,** 157 King St. East, have very appealing outdoor dining courtyards.

From St. James, go south on Church Street and turn right into Colbourne Street. If you have kids, you might enjoy browsing at:

12. Tiddely Pom, which is devoted exclusively to children's books. Wine enthusiasts might want to check out **Wine Not,** an establishment that sells everything you need to make beer and wine—from corks and labels to glucose and vats.

From Colbourne, turn left down Leader Lane to Wellington, where you can enjoy a fine view of the mural on the Flatiron building and also of the rhythmic flow of mansard rooflines along the south side of Front Street.

Turn right and proceed to Yonge, then turn right and walk to King Street. Note the building on the northeast corner of Yonge and King before catching the subway. It's the:

13. Royal Bank Building (1913–15), designed by Carrere & Hastings.

WALKING TOUR 7
Bloor/Yorkville

Start: At the corner of Bloor and Yonge streets.
Finish: At the corner of Bloor and Yonge streets.
Time: As long as you want to make it—depends on how serious a shopper or collector you are. Just walking it will take an hour.
Best Times: Tuesday through Saturday (when everything is functioning).
Worst Time: Monday (when many of the galleries are closed).

Walk west along Bloor Street from Yonge Street on the north side of the street. The first complex you'll come to is the:

1. Holt Renfrew Centre, not to be confused with the Holt Renfrew store itself, which is the ultimate high-class Toronto emporium (the equivalent of Bloomingdale's or Bergdorf in New York).

Downstairs in the center, you'll find several restaurants, including **Timothy's** for coffee. Also down here is one of my favorite fun stores, **Science City,** which is filled with books, games, puzzles, and models, all relating to the sciences— life, chemistry, physics, and astronomy—as well as serious stuff like telescopes, trilobites, and hologram watches.

At street level you'll pass Marks & Spencer, the famous British department store, known for its well-priced cottons and other fashions, and **Eddie Bauer,** great for casual, good-looking sportswear.

☕ **TAKE A BREAK** On Holt Renfrew Centre's upper level, the **Bloor Street Diner** stays open from 11am to 3am daily and offers a broad menu featuring everything from hot entrees to sandwiches.

Walking Tour—Bloor/Yorkville

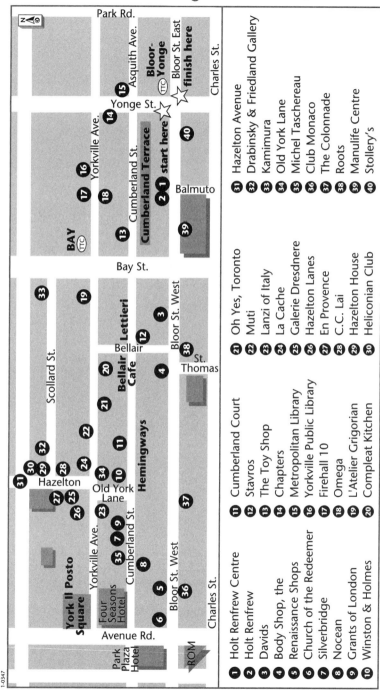

Park Rd.

Bloor-Yonge TTC

Bloor St. East finish here

Yonge St. start here

Cumberland Terrace

Cumberland St.

Balmuto

BAY TTC

Bay St.

Scollard St.

Lettieri

Bellair

Bellair Cafe

Bloor St. West

St. Thomas

Hemingways

Hazelton

Old York Lane

York II Posto Square

Yorkville Ave.

Cumberland St.

Four Seasons Hotel

Bloor St. West

Charles St.

Avenue Rd.

ROM

Park Plaza Hotel

1. Holt Renfrew Centre
2. Holt Renfrew
3. Davids
4. Body Shop, the
5. Renaissance Shops
6. Church of the Redeemer
7. Silverbridge
8. Nocean
9. Grants of London
10. Winston & Holmes

11. Cumberland Court
12. Stavros
13. The Toy Shop
14. Chapters
15. Metropolitan Library
16. Yorkville Public Library
17. Firehall 10
18. Omega
19. L'Atelier Grigorian
20. Compleat Kitchen

21. Oh Yes, Toronto
22. Muti
23. Lanzi of Italy
24. La Cache
25. Galerie Dresdnere
26. Hazelton Lanes
27. En Provence
28. C.C. Lai
29. Hazelton House
30. Heliconian Club

31. Hazelton Avenue
32. Drabinsky & Friedland Gallery
33. Kamimura
34. Old York Lane
35. Michel Taschereau
36. Club Monaco
37. The Colonnade
38. Roots
39. Manulife Centre
40. Stollery's

151

2. **Holt Renfrew** itself is a delight to shop. It's filled with designer boutiques—Yves St. Laurent, Calvin Klein, Donna Karan, Anne Klein, Moschino, Ralph Lauren, and Victor Costa.

Continue west along Bloor to Bay Street and you'll pass Emporio Armani and then a branch of the Gap. Cross Bay Street, eyeing:

3. **David's,** at no. 66, for shoes; **Capezio** for shoes and leotards; Bally's for more shoes; Banana Republic for fine quality casual wear; and **Harry Rosen** (no. 82), one of Toronto's foremost men's designers.

Cross Bellair Street and continue past:

4. **The Body Shop** and **Speedo** to **Brendan Bedding & Bath,** for gorgeous linens and bath accessories. Continue along, and you'll pass **Louis Vuitton; Bocci,** for shoes; and the **French Connection,** for the latest in young fashions.

At Avenue Road you'll come to:

5. **The Renaissance Shops,** where you'll find **Secrett,** a jewel-box–like jewelry store; **Groucho & Co,** which sells everything a man desires—cigars, lighters, Mont Blanc and Carain d'Ache pens, among other gift items; and the **Irish Shop,** which offers fetching fashions, accessories, housewares, and books.

This modern retail development is the backdrop to the:

6. **Church of the Redeemer** (1879), a quiet enclave on Bloor Street with inviting outdoor benches set against the stone building with its slate roof and stolid belfry.

Cut through Renaissance Shops to Cumberland, browsing as you go. Turn right onto Cumberland.

☕ **TAKE A BREAK**   **Il Posto,** 148 Yorkville Ave., is an attractive Yorkville restaurant tucked away in a courtyard. In summer, it's pleasant to lunch outside. Fine Italian cuisine and desserts.

Start on the north side at:

7. **Silverbridge,** at no. 162, which sells beautifully crafted modern jewelry. Move on to **Taschen** for fine leathers and **Featherdown Quilts** for bedroom comforts.

Backtrack slightly across the street to:

8. **Nocean,** at no. 161, featuring fun games and useful gadgets, all sleekly designed, many from New York's Museum of Modern Art.

Back on the north side, move on to:

9. **Grants of London** for brilliantly colored avant-garde ties, ultraluxurious robes, and spiffy suspenders.

Continue on the north side to the corner of Old York Lane to:

10. **Winston & Holmes** (no. 138), a tobacco shop selling Dunhill Havana and La Gloria de Cubana, among many other cigars, plus shaving gear and Mont Blanc writing implements. They will mail order. Farther along there's a traditional Toronto fashion favorite, **Marilyn Brooks,** which stocks this veteran Canadian designer's own designs and those of today's up-and-coming designers. Continue on to no. 124, the **Papery,** which stocks stationery, photo albums, illustrated shopping bags, and cards.

At no. 140, you'll want to visit the **Guild Shop,** the **Ontario Crafts Council Store,** which sells very striking ceramics, glass, baskets, jewelry, fabrics, and other craft items. Upstairs, Inuit art is on display—sculpture and paintings. You'll pay $1,500 for a soapstone bear, but it's worth coming here to see the work that is scouted and brought from the northern regions.

Turn left down a passageway to:

11. Cumberland Court, which shelters a number of shops, including the store/ studio where jeweler **Peter Cullman** works. Retrace your steps back out of Cumberland Court and as you turn left to cross Bellair, note the park across the street. Financed by taxpayers' money, it's proved controversial. It was designed by Oleson Worland Architects with Martha Schwartz/Ken Smith/David Meyer Landscape Architects. It's meant to show the various natural terrains of Canada from upper pine forests to wetlands. The focal point of the park is a huge granite outcropping that is a billion years old, weighs 650 tonnes, and was transported from Northern Ontario.

☕ **TAKE A BREAK**   The **Bellair Café** is still the place to see and be seen for the boomer generation, either in the back courtyard or out front. A glass of wine will cost $6.50; main courses range from $11 to $15. Go for a drink and a snack and to watch the street scene. The terrace out back is especially pleasant. On the opposite corner of Bellair, **Letticri** at 94 Cumberland is another good stopping place for whatever kind of coffee you fancy, accompanied by pastries or focaccia sandwiches.

Stay on the south side of the street once you cross Bellair and you'll encounter:

12. Stavros, a tailor and shirtmaker, and **Kidding Awound,** stocking hundreds of music boxes, clockwork toys, and miniatures.

Cross Bay to:

13. The Toy Shop, on the north side—two floors filled with kids' games, toys, and books. On to **Dinah's Cupboard,** which has great salads and pâtés to go, gourmet teas, coffees, and vinegars, plus frozen items like vegetarian pasta to take home and pop in the oven. Before turning left on Yonge, book lovers will want to drop into **Britnells** across the street on Yonge, a little to the south of Cumberland.

Turn left onto Yonge. You'll pass:

14. Chapters for secondhand books; the **Kitchen and Glass Place,** which stocks a full range of kitchenware and masses of glasses; **Cubita,** an inviting cafe/store selling Cuban coffee and some pastries; and the **Cookbook Store,** an adventurous cook's dream come true.

Across Yonge Street stands:

15. The Metropolitan Library (1973–77), designed by Raymond Moriyama. It doesn't look that terrific from the outside, but go in and experience the interior. It'll make reading and studying seem a natural and wonderful part of life. Not everyone agrees, of course.

Turn left onto Yorkville Avenue and walk west. On the right stands:

16. The Yorkville Public Library (1906–07), at no. 22, which was built with an endowment from Andrew Carnegie. With its porticoed entrance, it looks important.

Just down the street on the same side stands:

17. Firehall 10 (1876), at no. 34, an endearing Yorkville landmark that was rebuilt, except for the tower, from 1889 to 1890. The tower where the hoses are stored bears the coat of arms of the Town of Yorkville, saved from the town hall when it was demolished. The images—a beer barrel, jack plane, brick mold, anvil, and bull's head—represent the vocations of the town's early councillors.

Across from the Firehall is:

18. Omega Centre Bookstore, filled with New Age titles. Whole sections are devoted to such subjects as shamanism, Zen, graphology, Jung, and more.

Cross Bay Street to:

19. L'Atelier Grigorian, on the right, stocking a fantastic selection of classical and jazz CDs.

Walk west and cross Bellair. On the left (south) side of the street you'll find:

20. The Compleat Kitchen at no. 87. Upstairs also at no. 87, **Primitives** has objects from Bali and Indonesia. **Paper Things** raises funds for the National Ballet by selling personalized stationery, while the **Candle Emporium** offers a full range of imaginative candles.

Farther down the street:

21. Oh Yes, Toronto has suitable gifts to bring home, including attractive, good-quality T-shirts. **Ulysses Bookshop,** at no. 101, has a terrific selection of travel books.

Across the street:

22. Muti, at no. 88, has stunning modern Italian majolica ceramic pottery. **Namaste** (no. 112) features Himalayan imports, including some fine quality Tibetan jewelry. **Herat Carpets,** at the corner of Hazelton Avenue, offers a visual treat.

☕ **TAKE A BREAK** There are several possibilities for stops in this neighborhood. Good ethnic choices on Yorkville Avenue are **Zero** (no. 69) for Japanese, **Little Tibet** (no. 81) for Tibetan food, and **Mandaloon** (no. 113) for Lebanese. A good popular cafe/bar is **Hemingway's** at 142 Cumberland. In Hazelton Lanes (55 Avenue Rd.), the best option is **Hazelton Gourmet,** where you can also enjoy the outdoor courtyard at the center of the complex. **Movenpick Bistretto,** 133 Yorkville Ave., is another good choice for great desserts or a good-value lunch.

Back on the south side, pass by Old York Lane to:

23. Lanzi of Italy (no. 123), which has stylish items for the desk and an assortment of fine leather goods. At **Arctic,** no. 125, there's an assortment of Inuit sculpture, jewelry, clothes, fur hats, and so on. You'll need to know how to sift out the quality items here.

Across the street:

24. La Cache displays a handsome mix of tablecloths, napkins, jewelry, and fashions. **L'Elegante** (no. 122) is a discount designer fashion house, while next door at no. 124, **Maison de la Presse** offers foreign newspapers and magazines, including all of the major U.S. papers.

Turn back from the Maison and go down Hazelton Avenue. First on the left you'll come to:

25. Galerie Dresdnere, and then **Kinsman Robinson, Nancy Poole's Studio,** and **Miriam Shiell**—all well-known galleries.

Beyond Laura Ashley, turn left into:

26. Hazelton Lanes. Hazelton Lanes is a difficult-to-negotiate collection of stylish boutiques and stores that is laid out on two levels around a central courtyard. It was designed by Webb Zerafa Menkes Housden in 1976 and contains luxury apartments as well as the shopping floors. The signs are poor and it's easy to get disoriented in this circular maze, where you'll find the *sine qua non* names of fashion and design. On the lower concourse there's **Chez Catherine,** a boutique that has dressed wealthy fashionable Toronto women for many years; **Gianni Versace, Krizia,** and **Valentino; Fogal** for fashionable hose and underwear in rainbow colors; the **General Store** at several locations, featuring kitchen/housewares in one location and gifts for the person who has everything (calculators, something called a fishing mate, Newtonian puzzles, and Filofax) at another; **Classical Record**

Shop; Turnbull & Asser for custom-made shirts; **Barts Leather and Suede** for men's leather fashions; **Brown's Shoes,** which besides its own label sells such well-known designers as Bruno Magli; **Timothy's Coffees of the World; Gianfranco Ferré** for dramatic feminine tailoring; and **Aquascutum** for the traditional look.

TAKE A BREAK Both **Lox, Stock & Bagel** and **Hazelton Gourmet** have access to the outdoor courtyard. In my opinion, Hazelton Gourmet is the best choice for luncheon or snacks.

On the upper level, the shopping feast continues with more great names, like **Rodier** and **Marci Lipman,** whose fun and artistic designs for kids' fashions include original T-shirts and many very appealing creations. **Mark McClaine** has good-looking Asian and Western antiques; **Joan & David**—names that need no description; plus, there are **Teuscher Chocolate of Switzerland** and **Roots,** a Canadian specialty store selling leather bags as well as T-shirts, sweaters, and shorts. **Alfred Sung** is another fashion name, and so are **Ralph Lauren** and **Giorgio Emporio.** Farther on near the entrance to Avenue Road is **Giorgio Femme.**

You could spend the whole day shopping at Hazelton Lanes. Here I ask that you do a circular browse through and exit where you entered, returning in timely fashion to Hazelton Lane.

Back outside, turn left to:

27. **En Provence,** featuring fabulous country French tablecloths, napkins, and place mats; Limoges china, featuring brilliantly colored designs and glazes by Laure Jady; and other decorative household items. Expensive and luxurious. Art lovers will want to stop into **Mira Godard,** a well-known city gallery that represents such famous Americans as Robert Motherwell, Larry Rivers, Frank Stella, Jacques Lipchitz, David Hockney, and Jasper Johns, plus many Canadians, such as Lawren Harris and Clark McDougall.

Backtrack a little and cross the street to relish the offerings at:

28. **C.C. Lai,** selling exquisite Asian art—furniture inlaid with mother-of-pearl, wonderful Oriental screens, Buddhas, jewelry, and more. Also check out the **Glass Art Gallery** at no. 21. **Acca Kappa** has top-notch bath oils, soaps, and other bath accessories like shaving brushes, robes, and towels. Next door **Tarantino** displays exquisite mens' fashions including Stefano Ricci shirts and other accessories. **Budd Sugarman** specializes in super fine antiques.

Continue north along Hazelton. On the right side you'll come to:

29. **Hazelton House,** at no. 33, originally part of the Olivet Congregational Church (1890), which now houses several galleries including **Sable-Castelli, Gallery 7,** and the ultracommercial **Circle Gallery.**

Next door, look at the facade of the church housing:

30. **The Heliconian Club,** which was founded in 1909 as a forum for women in the arts by Mary Smart, a teacher at the Toronto Conservatory of Music. Since 1921 the club has occupied this Carpenter Gothic Revival church built in 1876 as the Olivet Congregational. Note the triangular wooden lancet windows and filigree decoration. Next door in two town houses are **English Picture Framers** (at no. 37), which exhibits fine prints and also sells Isle of Wight Glass, beautifully crafted English contemporary art glass, and **Escada,** selling top-of-the line women's fashions.

Continue along:

31. **Hazelton Avenue,** observing the handsome Victorian homes on either side. Nos. 49–51 and 53–55 are particularly worth noting. No. 74 has an especially

attractive fan window above the entrance and decorative window bays. No. 68 has a highly decorated gable.

Continue to Berryman; retrace your steps, turn left down Scollard, and stop at the:

32. Drabinsky & Friedland Gallery, at no. 122. (Gallery One is across the street.)

Continuing along Scollard Street, you reach the corner of Bay Street and:

33. Kamimura, exhibiting Japanese art.

From Scollard, cut through Village Stream, which connects to Yorkville Avenue. Turn right and walk along the south side to:

34. Old York Lane. Take it through to Cumberland. Turn right along Cumberland. On the north side, tucked downstairs, are stores that we missed earlier, like:

35. Michel Taschereau and **Ronald Windebanks,** both fine antiques dealers.

☕ **TAKE A BREAK**   For an elegant stop, head into the **Four Seasons Studio Cafe** or stop in for the afternoon tea served in the lobby. In the Renaissance Plaza, you could also stop for a luncheon at **Enoteca.** The plaza has more casual dining spots, too.

Go through Renaissance Plaza back to Bloor Street. Cross the street and "do" the south side of Bloor, walking east, from:

36. Club Monaco, the casual fashion store, which is housed in an elegant classical revival building that once served as a bank, past **Marc Laurent** for avant-garde designer clothes, **Mont Blanc,** and **Benetton** to **Betty Hemmings,** which has exquisite leather goods. This will bring you to:

37. The Colonnade, at no. 131. Built between 1961 and 1964, it was one of the first buildings to combine residence, office, and retail space. It still does so, with restaurants like Dynasty taking full advantage of the overhanging forecourt. Several stores are found at this address—their storefronts stretching along the street— **Marina Rinaldi** for fashions, **Florsheim** for shoes, **Lalique** for exquisite glass, and **Max Mara, Jaeger, Hermès, Town Shoes,** and **Chanel.** Continue walking along in front of the concourse, past such famous names as **Giorgio Couture** (no. 111), **Royal de Versailles, Cartier,** and **Cole Haan,** all at no. 101.

Cross St. Thomas Street to:

38. Roots, a quintessential Canadian store, and just down the street the first Canadian outpost of New York's very own **Tiffany & Co.** at no. 85.

Cross Bay Street to:

39. The Manulife Centre (no. 55), where you'll find **Birks,** a very traditional Canadian store that offers well-priced silver, crystal, and china, including Royal Doulton. **Ashley China** is another premier place to buy fine china, glass, and silver.

☕ **WINDING DOWN**   There are several possibilities here—**Toby's Goodeats** for burgers and sandwiches; and the **Bloor Street Diner** in the Holt Renfrew Center for a more elegant atmosphere and dining.

Cross Balmuto Street and walk to Yonge Street for a look at the merchandise at:

40. Stollery's, located in a 1929 building at the corner of Bloor and Yonge streets. A traditional Canadian store, it has good stocks of Daks, Aquascutum, Burberry, and other British-inspired fashions for men and women.

Shopping 8

Toronto's major shopping areas are the Bloor/Yorkville area, for designer boutiques and top-name galleries; Queen Street West, for a more funky mixture of fashion, antiques, and bookstores; and a number of shopping malls/centers, such as Queen's Quay on the waterfront, the two-block-long Eaton Centre, and other smaller complexes like College Park, Royal Bank Plaza, and Village by the Grange.

1 The Shopping Scene

The two great names in Toronto retailing are Eaton's and the Hudson's Bay Company (formerly Simpson's), both founded in the mid-19th century. They're still here and thriving. Canadian fashion names to look for are Alfred Sung, Cy Mann, and Norma.

The two major markets are Kensington Market and the St. Lawrence Market.

Best buys are mainly Canadian arts and crafts, which can be imported into the United States duty-free.

Store hours are generally Monday to Wednesday from 9:30 or 10am to 6pm and Saturday and Sunday from 10am to 5pm, with extended hours (8–9:30pm) on Thursday and usually Friday.

Provincial sales tax is 8%, but out-of-province visitors can reclaim it. Nonresidents can also reclaim the 7% goods-and-services tax (GST). See "Fast Facts: Toronto," chapter 3.

2 Shopping A to Z

ANTIQUES

You'll find the greatest concentration of good-quality antiques at the Harbourfront Antiques Market, best visited Sunday when all the dealers are in residence (during the week many are at their stores). The finest antiques can be found in the Bloor/Yorkville area, with many shops a short walk from the Four Seasons Hotel, and in the Mount Pleasant/St. Clair area along the 500-, 600-, and 700-block of Mount Pleasant Road. The more funky and often more recent collectibles can be found at various stores along Queen Street West. Markham Village also has several antiques stores.

Abacus Antiques. 6 Ripley Ave. ☎ **416/760-9358.**

This store specializes in handmade furniture fashioned from Canadian oak, pine, maple, and cherry—custom-made rolltop desks, cabinets, tables, and chairs—and reproduction Country, Mission, and Shaker designs.

There's another one at Harbourfront Antiques Market.

Bernardi Antiques. 707 Mount Pleasant Rd., south of Eglinton Ave. ☎ **416/483-6471.**

Look here for discontinued Doulton figurines, glass art, paintings, carpets, silver, and furniture.

C. C. Lai. 9 Hazelton Ave. ☎ **416/928-0662.**

This cluttered store has fine Chinese antiques—exquisite inlaid furniture and screens, Buddhas, and jewelry—really beautiful pieces, both large and small.

Circa Antiques. 166 Davenport Rd. ☎ **416/961-3744.**

Circa is one of the best places to find formal and country French furniture, from Louis XIV and XV through Louis XVI and Second Empire. Buffets, tables, armoires, chairs, and desks are the main stock, along with sconces and chandeliers.

Fifty One Antiques Ltd. 21 Avenue Rd. ☎ **416/968-2416.**

A specialist in 17th- and 18th-century furniture, as well as Empire, Biedermeier, and other later styles, Fifty One Antiques also has lots of accessories, like lamps made from old vases, carvings, European paintings, and more.

✪ **Harbourfront Antiques Market.** 390 Queen's Quay W. ☎ **416/260-2626.**

The 100-plus dealers here sell fine-quality antiques. On summer Sundays there's also a market outside featuring less-established dealers. Although it's relatively quiet during the week, it's hopping on weekends, when more than 150 dealers open up; you'll have to get there early. Hours are Tuesday through Friday from 11am to 6pm, Saturday from 10am to 6pm, and Sunday from 8am to 6pm.

Journeys End. 612 Markham St. ☎ **416/536-2226.**

This is an appropriate name for the miscellaneous assortment of estate china, jewelry, silver, and furniture that winds up here in an amorphous display. The store is eminently browsable.

Mark McLaine. Hazelton Lanes. ☎ **416/927-7972.**

This marvelously eclectic store has unique items, like a pair of never-worn 1929 leather shoes, as well as pine furniture, French sconces, costume jewelry (especially deco), carved wood and stone pieces, silver frames, perfume bottles, and blue-and-white Oriental ware. You'll find reproductions, too. It's a great place to browse. Prices range from $16 to $6,000.

✪ **Michel Taschereau.** 176 Cumberland St. ☎ **416/923-3020.**

In this fine store you'll have to thread your way through the dense collection very carefully. You'll find 18th- and 19th-century English and French furniture, including large armoires, and French and English china, like Coalport, Derby, and Worcester. There's Lalique glass and Canadian folk art also.

Mostly Movables. 785 Queen St. W., west of Bathurst St. ☎ **416/504-4455.**

A large selection of furniture, mostly purchased at estate sales, is featured here, including wardrobes, dressers, couches, and dining-room sets (for as little as $950).

An Important Note on Prices

Unless stated otherwise, **the prices cited in this guide are given in Canadian dollars,** which is good news for U.S. travelers because the Canadian dollar is worth 27% less than the American dollar, but buys nearly as much. As we go to press, $1 Canadian is worth 73¢ U.S., which means that your $100-a-night hotel room will cost only U.S. $73, and your $6 breakfast costs only U.S. $4.38.

Here's a quick table of equivalents:

Canadian $	U.S. $
$1	$0.73
$5	$3.65
$10	$7.30
$20	$14.60
$50	$36.50
$100	$73.00
$200	$146.00

Most of the pieces date from the 1920s on and cost $150 and up. Turn-of-the-century Canadian pine plus British oak furniture from the 1920s and 1930s is also available.

The Paisley Shop Limited. 889 Yonge St. ☎ **416/923-5830.**

A specialist in 18th- and 19th-century English furniture—dining tables, chairs, sideboards, mirrors, and desks—the Paisley Shop Limited also offers such accessories as porcelain, glass, and chandeliers. Upstairs is a selection of floral and other patterned cushions and lamps.

R. A. O'Neill Antiques. 100 Avenue Rd. ☎ **416/968-2806.**

This is the place for country furniture—pine and butternut from around the world—French, German, English, American, Dutch, and Irish. Along with tables, chairs, chests, and cupboards, the stock includes samplers, baskets, lamps, decoys, and brass and tin objects.

Red Indian and Empire Antiques. 536 Queen St. W. ☎ **416/504-7706.**

The eclectic mixture of objects here spans the 1930s to the 1950s—fountain pens, Coke memorabilia, neon clocks, Bakelite jewelry, torchère lamps, wall sconces, mirrors, figurines, and other nostalgia. It's open Monday through Saturday from 11:30am to 6pm.

✪ **Ronald Windebanks.** 21 Avenue Rd. ☎ **416/962-2862.**

This store is filled with treasures found by Mr. Windebank, who has a good eye for the unique object with character and whimsy. There's an eclectic array of furniture, porcelain, crystal, glass, botanical and ornithological prints, antique garden furniture, and grand urns, plus some charming carved animal folk art.

Showcase Antique Mall. 610 Queen St. W. ☎ **416/703-6255.**

Three hundred dealers display their wares on the four floors of this complex. There's every conceivable collectible from clocks, art deco, coins, and jewelry to jukeboxes,

Elvis and Beatle memorabilia and lunch boxes. This is a good place to start or add to any collection.

Stanley Wagman Antiques. 111 Avenue Rd. ☎ **416/964-1047.**

A major purveyor of French furniture, both country and formal, as well as art deco, Stanley Wagman also features marble fireplaces, chandeliers, and wall sconces.

Whim Antiques. 561 Mount Pleasant Rd. ☎ **416/481-4474.**

In this interesting shop, you will find antique and estate jewelry, rare Belleek pieces, silver, and other objets d'art.

ART

Most of these galleries are open Tuesday to Saturday from 10:30am to 5:30pm, so don't come around on Sunday or Monday. Note that one place to see the latest works by contemporary artists is 80 Spadina Ave. at King Street, which contains four floors of art galleries.

Albert White. 80 Spadina Ave., at King St. ☎ **416/703-1021.**

This gallery for oils, sculpture, and prints has been open since 1966 and is one of the few places specializing in international art, representing such great names as Picasso, Henry Moore, Botero, Francis Bacon, and many others.

Bau-Xi. 340 Dundas St. W. ☎ **416/977-0600.**

This bilevel gallery exhibits paintings, sculpture, drawings, and prints by contemporary Canadian artists—Ted Godwin, Jack Shadbolt, Joseph Plaskett, Claude Breeze, Brian Kipping, Roly Fenwick, Robert Marchessault, and Hugh Mackenzie.

Bay of Spirits Gallery. 156 Front St. W. ☎ **416/971-5190.**

This gallery features the artwork of the Pacific Coast Indians—totem poles, masks, prints, and jewelry.

Circle Gallery. 33 Hazelton Ave. ☎ **416/961-5806.**

This is the place for the commercial and popular names in prints and lithography—Erté, Lebadang, Vasarely, and others.

Del Bello. 788 King St. W. ☎ **416/504-2422.**

This gallery specializes in showing international contemporary artists—European, Canadian, and American. It's well known for its annual miniature art show, held in December and January, which features works of 1,500 artists from 40 or more countries.

Drabinsky and Friedland Gallery. 122 Scollard St. ☎ **416/324-5766.**

Originally called the Marianne Friedland Gallery, this gallery has shown contemporary Canadian and American artists for decades, representing such figures as Alex Colville, Harold Town, Milton Avery, Philip Pearlstein, Al Held, Hans Hofmann, Margaret Priest, Karen Kulyk, Wolf Kahn, Ronald Boaks, Rafael Goldchain, and Suzanne Olivier.

Du Verre Glass. 280 Queen St. W. ☎ **416/593-0182.**

This store displays the works of some of Canada's finest glass blowers plus a beautiful selection of ceramics and handcrafted wood furniture and Murano glass.

✪ **Eskimo Art Gallery.** 12 Queen's Quay W. (opposite Westin Harbour Castle). ☎ **416/366-3000.**

This gallery carries about 500 small and large high-quality Inuit sculptures, most from Cape Dorset or Baffin Island. Prices range from $30 to $14,000. It's certainly one of the largest collections in the city.

✪ **Feheley Fine Arts.** 45 Avenue Rd. (2nd floor). ☎ **416/323-1373.**

Inuit art is the specialty of this prestigious gallery. The Feheleys have collected, exhibited, and sold Inuit sculpture, prints, and drawings for over 30 years, and they personally select each artist and work of art. The gallery, therefore, offers a wide selection of the finest-quality sculpture and graphics from the Canadian Arctic; they range from small and primitive bone and ivory carvings to contemporary pieces.

Galerie Dresdnere. 12 Hazelton Ave. ☎ **416/923-4662.**

This is another major gallery featuring contemporary Canadian artists, such as Peter Krausz (Montréal) and Stephen Lack (Montréal and New York), maritime realist Tom Forrestall, Bob Boyer (Regina), and Richard Overfield (Vancouver). Galerie Dresdnere has long been associated with artists from Montréal's Automatist School, such as Jean-Paul Riopelle and Borduas, and other important contemporary Canadian art movements.

Gallery Moos. 622 Richmond St. W. ☎ **416/504-5445.**

Another longtime Toronto gallery, in business for more than 30 years, this establishment represents international and Canadian contemporary artists, including Jean-Paul Riopelle.

Gallery One. 121 Scollard St. ☎ **416/929-3103.**

A fixture on the Toronto art scene for 20 years, this gallery is associated with the abstract painters Jack Bush, Kenneth Lochhead, Joseph Drapell, Harold Feist, and Douglas Haynes, as well as with other Canadian artists like Anne Meredith Barry, David Blackwood, Christopher Broadhurst, Brian Burnett, William Goodrige Roberts, and sculptor Alan Reynolds. It also represents American artists Helen Frankenthaler, Kenneth Noland, and Stanley Boxer.

The Gallery Shop. In the Art Gallery of Toronto, 317 Dundas St. W. ☎ **416/979-6610.**

Adjacent to the bookstore, this shop carries a great selection of reproductions of international and Canadian art, as well as posters and juvenile prints. Framing and laminating services are available.

Glass Art Gallery. 21 Hazelton Ave. ☎ **416/968-1823.**

This gallery features the work of contemporary glass artists from all over the world. When I visited, the show featured the sculptural art of nine French artists. The exhibition changes every month, and the gallery also keeps on hand samples from artists they represent.

✪ **Isaacs/Inuit Gallery of Eskimo Art.** 9 Prince Arthur Ave. ☎ **416/921-9985.**

Inuit sculpture, prints, drawings, wall hangings, and antiquities from across the Arctic are featured here, in association with the Isaacs Gallery, the oldest contemporary gallery in the city. The pieces are museum quality. The gallery also specializes in early Native Canadian art and artifacts.

✪ **Jane Corkin.** 179 John St. ☎ **416/979-1980.**

This gallery specializes in historical and contemporary photographs by international and Canadian photographers. It represents 20 contemporary artists, many of whom are Canadians, and also carries the works of such masters as André Kertesz, Irving Penn, and Horst.

Kamimura. 1300 Bay St., at Scollard. ☎ **416/923-7850.**

This long, narrow downstairs gallery specializes in Japanese prints. It's open Tuesday through Saturday from 11am to 5pm.

Kaspar Gallery. 27 Prince Arthur Ave. ☎ **416/968-2536.**

Specializing in Canadian art from the 19th century to the Group of Seven, the Kaspar Gallery features watercolors and contemporary artists, too.

Kinsman Robinson. 14 Hazelton Ave. ☎ **416/964-2374.**

This bilevel gallery exhibits such contemporary Canadian artists as the color-drunk Norval Morrisseau, Henri Masson, Robert Katz, John Newman, and Stanley Cosgrove, plus sculptors Esther Wertheimer, Maryon Kantaroff, and Robert Davidson.

Mira Godard. 22 Hazelton Ave. ☎ **416/964-8197.**

Another major international player in Toronto, Mira Godard represents, among many others, such famous names as Botero, Robert Motherwell, Frank Stella, Larry Rivers, Jacques Lipchitz, David Hockney, and Jasper Johns, as well as Canadian greats Lawren Harris and Jean-Paul Riopelle.

Nancy Poole's Studio. 16 Hazelton Ave. ☎ **416/964-9050.**

For over 20 years this gallery has been exhibiting painting, sculpture, and ceramics of a roster of about 25 contemporary artists. It also specializes in Canadian impressionist works. Every 2 weeks the gallery mounts one-artist shows, except during the summer, when group shows take over.

Sable-Castelli. 33 Hazelton Ave. ☎ **416/961-0011.**

This gallery specializes in contemporary Canadian art, with names like David Craven, and others.

Sandra Ainsley. 2 First Canadian Place at the corner of Adelaide and York. ☎ **416/362-4480.**

If you want to view the most beautiful and up-to-the-minute glass being crafted today then this is the place to come. The gallery also displays sculpture and jewelry.

BOOKS

✪ **Abelard Books.** 519 Queen St. W. ☎ **416/504-2665.**

This is one of my favorite rare-book stores in the city. It has a fabulous collection of early editions and other rare books, with every subject clearly cataloged. Armchairs invite leisurely browsing. It's a real book-lover's haven.

About Books. 83 Harbord St. ☎ **416/975-2668.**

At this used-book store, the titles are all well cataloged and the selection is extensive—particularly strong in literature. Out-of-print and antiquarian volumes are available.

✪ **Albert Britnell Book Shop.** 765 Yonge St., north of Bloor St. ☎ **416/924-3321.**

A Toronto tradition, this wonderful store has a great selection of hard- and softcover books displayed handsomely on wooden shelves. The staff is very knowledgeable and helpful.

Another Man's Poison. 29 McCaul St. ☎ **416/593-6451.**

This store is heaven for any aspiring architect, interior designer, or graphic artist because it's filled with a large worldwide stock of books on graphics, architecture, 20th-century design, antiques, and collectibles—all aspects of design.

Atticus Books. 84 Harbord St. ☎ **416/922-6045.**

The preeminent Toronto dealer in scholarly used books, it also stocks antiquarian books and illuminated manuscripts and has an art room in the back.

Bakka Science Fiction Book Shoppe. 282 Queen St. W. ☎ **416/596-8161.**

This store is the answer to a science-fiction buff's dreams. It stocks paperback and hardcover versions of both new and used science fiction and fantasy.

Bob Miller Book Room. 180 Bloor St. W. (Lower Concourse). ☎ **416/922-3557.**

This academic bookstore carries a wide selection of titles in the humanities and social sciences. Look for the fiction titles listed under "Recommended Reading" in chapter 1—you're likely to find them here.

Book Cellar Yorkville. 142 Yorkville Ave. ☎ **416/925-9955.**

This store is well stocked with art, travel, history, and fiction and also has a large selection of domestic and foreign magazines in the back room. It also stays open late—until 11pm during the week and until midnight on weekends.

Book City. 501 Bloor St. W. ☎ **416/961-4496.**

This store offers good discounts (10%) on new books as well as a large selection of remainders. It's a well-stocked general bookstore with large philosophy and religion sections. It's open late daily.

There are other branches at 348 Danforth Ave. and 2350 Bloor St. West.

Children's Book Store. 2532 Yonge St., north of Eglinton. ☎ **416/480-0233.**

Here you'll find books, cassettes, and videos for kids from birth to age 14. A staff of librarians and teachers assist selection. It's the ultimate choice of book-loving kids. There are special events, too, on Sunday afternoons in the fall.

Coles The World's Biggest Bookstore. 20 Edward St. ☎ **416/977-7009.**

With 17 miles of bookshelves and more than a million books categorized into more than 50 specialty departments, Coles boasts that if you can't get it here, it doesn't exist. The store also stocks software, videos, magazines, and cassettes. Coles also has locations in Commerce Court Concourse (☎ **416/868-1782**); in the Eaton Centre (☎ **416/979-9348**); and at various other locations in the city and in the suburbs. It's open late.

The Cookbook Store. 850 Yonge St., at Yorkville Ave. ☎ **416/920-2665.**

Everything's here for the cook and food lover, including international cookbooks organized by cuisine, wine books, professional books for restaurateurs, dessert books, health books, and cooking and wine magazines.

✪ **David Mason.** 342 Queen St. W. ☎ **416/598-1015.**

Another fine used-book store with plenty of first and collector's editions, the store has a huge selection on all subjects. There's a great bookish atmosphere.

✪ **David Mirvish Books and Books on Art.** 596 Markham St. ☎ **416/531-9975.**

This is a fabulous, large store specializing in current books on the visual arts— ceramics, sculpture, photography, art history, architecture, and other related subjects. Some out-of-print and rare titles are here, too. Good discounts are offered. Open Thursday and Friday until 7pm.

Dragon Lady Comic Shop. 200 Queen St, W., at University. ☎ **416/596-1602.**

Comic aficionados will find old and new comics here from 1950 to the present, as well as books related to comics. There are also posters and such collectibles as *Life* magazines (from 1915 on).

Edwards Books and Art. 356 Queen St. W. ☎ **416/593-0126.**

Edwards has a large selection of art, design and general books, limited editions, autographed firsts and out-of print titles. It's also known for its bargain books. The best bargains of the week are listed in the Saturday *Globe and Mail.*

Also at 170 Bloor St. West at the Park Plaza (☎ **416/961-2428**), 2200 Yonge St. at Eglinton (☎ **416/487-5431**), and 2179 Queen St. East in the Beaches.

Gulliver's Travel Bookshop. 609 Bloor St. W., two blocks west of Bathurst St. ☎ **416/537-7700.**

The store carries a full range of travel guidebooks, as well as travel accessories like phrase books, maps, and background destination reading.

New Ballenford Books. 600 Markham St. ☎ **416/588-0800.**

For interior designers and others interested in architecture, landscaping, urban planning, and design of any sort, this store is a treasure trove.

Old Favourites Book Shop. Hwy. 7, east of Markham. ☎ **905/294-3865.**

This is possibly the largest collection of used books in the country—about 300,000 to 400,000 paperbacks and hardbacks. Among the rare-book specialties are equestrian titles focusing on carriages, coaches, and horses.

Open Air Books & Maps. 25 Toronto St. ☎ **416/363-0719.**

This is the place to go for travel guidebooks, maps, and other books relating to the outdoors and ecology.

Pages. 256 Queen St. W. ☎ **416/598-1447.**

This large store is a fine, well-stocked general bookstore, with an extensive selection of foreign, literary, and other magazines.

Seekers Books. 509 Bloor St. W., at Borden. ☎ **416/925-1982.**

This store offers an eclectic assortment of new and used books, with an emphasis on Eastern religions, the occult, meditation, and other New Age titles, as well as literature and general books.

Smithbooks. Toronto Dominion Centre. ☎ **416/362-5967.**

This member of the famous Canadian chain is a well-stocked general bookstore, with plenty of titles on Toronto, along with best-sellers and a good selection of newspapers and magazines.

There are many locations in the metro area, including the Eaton Centre (☎ **416/979-9376**); Hudson's Bay Centre (☎ **416/967-7177**); Scotia Plaza (☎ **416/366-7536**); the Royal Bank Plaza (☎ **416/865-0090**); Queen's Quay (☎ **416/868-0928**); and most of the airport terminals.

Steven Temple Books. 489 Queen St. W., 2nd floor. ☎ **416/703-9908.**

This rare-book store specializes in 19th- and 20th-century literary first editions, with a large stock of Canadian literature. There's also a broad selection of good-condition used volumes in various fields.

Theatrebooks. 11 St. Thomas St. ☎ **416/922-7175.**

The ultimate performing-arts bookstore carries books and magazines on all aspects of theater, film, opera, and dance, including plays, film scripts, critcism, history, and cultural studies.

Toronto Women's Bookstore. 73 Harbord St. ☎ **416/922-8744.**

This feminist bookstore has sections for lesbians, books by and about women of color, literary criticism, fiction, and titles that deal with violence against women and children.

Ulysses. 101 Yorkville Ave., between Bay St. and Avenue Rd. ☎ **416/323-3609.**

A travel-book specialist, the store is well stocked with travel guidebooks, maps, travel literature, and other travel accessories.

The University of Toronto Bookstore. 214 College St. ☎ **416/978-7907.**

With much more than just textbooks, this academic and general bookstore also features medical, computer, and children's books, plus U of T–crested gifts and clothes.

Writers & Co. 2005 Yonge St., 2^1/$_2$ blocks north of Davisville. ☎ **416/481-8432.**

This store carries a broad selection of fiction and poetry titles as well as children's books, travel narratives, and books on jazz.

CHINA, SILVER & GLASS

✪ **Ashley China.** 55 Bloor St. W. ☎ **416/964-2900.**

The ultimate store for china, silver, and glass, this beautiful establishment has elegant table displays of very expensive china, crystal, and flatware—all the top names at decent prices from Baccarat and Kosta Boda to Portmeirion and Waterford.

✪ **Birks.** Manulife Centre. 55 Bloor St. W. ☎ **416/922-2266.**

A quintessential, reliable Canadian store known for its jewelry, Birks also carries the top names in china, glass, silver, and other table accessories, like handsome cork table-mats. Prices are pretty good.

There are more stores at the Eaton Centre (☎ **416/979-9311**), First Canadian Place (☎ **416/363-5663**), and other in-town and suburban locations.

CRAFTS

✪ **The Algonquians Sweet Grass Gallery.** 668 Queen St. W., near Bathurst St. ☎ **416/703-1336.**

This store, owned by an Ojibwa, has been in business for 20 years or so, specializing in Native Canadian arts and crafts—Iroquois masks, porcupine quill boxes, sculpture, antler carvings, prints, tamarack decoys, as well as moccasins and famous Cowichan hand-knits from British Columbia.

The Arctic Bear. 125 Yorkville Ave. ☎ **416/967-7885.**

This store has an eclectic assortment of Inuit soapstone sculpture, fur and beaver hats, and some Native Canadian clothes and jewelry. You'll need to know precisely what you're looking for.

Arts on King. 169 King St. E. ☎ **416/777-9617.**

This is a very large complex in a landmark building housing crafts and fine art galleries.

Art Zone. 592 Markham St., at Bloor and Bathurst sts. ☎ **416/534-1892.**

Here you'll find a variety of glass art—stained glass, slumped glass (bent into marvelous shapes), and fused glass, in which the colors have been melted together. Some glass jewelry sells for $10 to $15, but prices can rise into the thousands for custom work. The studio is adjacent.

✪ **The Craft Gallery/Ontario Crafts Council.** 35 McCaul St. ☎ **416/977-3551.**

At this showcase for fine contemporary crafts from across Canada, shows change every 6 to 8 weeks and will feature everything from stained glass to ceramics and weaving. There's a library upstairs.

Five Potters Studio. 131A Pears Ave., between Avenue and Bedford rds. ☎ **416/924-6992.**

Located upstairs, this studio displays and sells the work of five women ceramists who have worked together for many years. Their work varies: Some pieces are functional, others sculptural; some are hand-worked, other pieces fashioned on the wheel. Feel free to observe the potters at work but call ahead for an appointment.

Frida Craft Stores. 39 Front St. E. ☎ **416/366-3169.**

Canadian crafts plus items and artifacts from Africa, Asia, and Latin America are aesthetically displayed in a handsome high-ceilinged space. Everything from rugs, fabrics, and bags to costume jewelry, clothes, candles, and knickknacks is here. Open daily.

✪ **Guild Shop.** 118 Cumberland St. ☎ **416/921-1721.**

Famous for Native Canadian crafts. This store has a wonderful selection of the best contemporary Canadian ceramics, glass, woodwork, jewelry, textiles, and more. The store also sells Inuit and Native Canadian art.

Lynn Robinson. 709 Queen St. W. ☎ **416/703-2467.**

The raku and bronze items are by Lynn Robinson, but the store also features glass, clay, wood, and leather items crafted by Canadians as well as furniture and jewelry.

Prime Gallery. 52 McCaul St. ☎ **416/593-5750.**

This gallery displays contemporary crafts in all materials—ceramics, clay, fabric, and metal (jewelry). Prices range anywhere from $50 for a ceramic teapot to $8,000 for a brilliantly colored ceramic sculpture by Montréaler Paul Mathieu.

Snow Lion. 575 Mount Pleasant Rd. ☎ **416/484-8859.**

If you're looking for craft items imported from the Orient then head north to this store, which stocks screens, porcelains, howdahs, lamps, Tibetan paintings, and hand-knotted carpets. Silver jewelry and Buddhist texts and accessories are also available.

DEPARTMENT STORES

Eaton's. Eaton Centre. 290 Yonge St. ☎ **416/343-2111.**

There are numerous Eaton's in metro Toronto. The flagship store is in the four-level Eaton Centre, which stretches two blocks from Dundas Street to Queen Street.

The Hudson's Bay Company. Queen and Yonge sts. ☎ **416/861-9111.**

Arch rival to Eaton's, this downtown store (formerly Simpson's) still has a venerable feel.

Marks & Spencer. Manulife Centre, 55 Bloor St. W. ☎ **416/967-7772.**

This is a branch of the famous British store that's known for quality goods and clothes at reasonable prices.

DISCOUNT

Honest Ed's. 581 Bloor St. W. ☎ **416/537-2111.**

The original store that launched Ed Mirvish to fame and fortune has perhaps the biggest, most frenetic electric sign in Toronto. Check it out—as Ed says, it can't be beat, as long as you know what you're looking for. A Toronto experience.

Marilyn's. 130 Spadina Ave. ☎ **416/504-6777.**

In the heart of the garment center, Marilyn has been in business for more than 20 years, specializing in good-value discounted Canadian fashions. Each rack here carries 200 garments organized by color. The staff is trained to sift through the vast stock and create whole looks for women, dressing them from head to toe, including accessories. In this warehouse atmosphere you'll find discounts of 20% to 80%.

FASHIONS

CHILDREN'S

Marci Lipman Graphics. Hazelton Lanes. ☎ **416/921-1998.**

This store stocks original, fun, art T-shirts and other kids' clothes with neat, unique designs.

MEN'S

In addition to the listings below, Holt Renfrew carries men's clothing. See "Women's," below.

Alan Cherry. 33 Avenue Rd. ☎ **416/967-1115.**

Alan Cherry carries designer wear as well as his own private-label clothes made in Italy. At the clearance center in the back of the store the old inventory winds up at discount—it's worth a look. There's some women's clothing, too.

Bulloch Tailors. 65 Front St. E., at Church St. ☎ **416/367-1084.**

A Toronto institution for more than 50 years, Bulloch has a reputation for out-fitting the city's doctors, professionals, military men, and politicos. The emphasis is still on custom tailoring, with suits beginning at $900, but there's also a selection of ready-to-wear, most of which is made by Bulloch.

George Bouridis. 193 Church St., between Dundas and Shuter sts. ☎ **416/363-4868.**

For almost 30 years this gentleman has been fashioning custom-made shirts and blouses as well as dressing gowns. He has 400 to 500 fabrics on hand from which to choose, from Switzerland, England, France, and Germany. Women's silk blouses cost $250 and up; men's 100%-cotton shirts, from $125. They'd retail for much more.

Harry Rosen. 82 Bloor St. W. ☎ **416/972-0556.**

Torontonians have been coming to this handsome traditional English-style store for years. On three floors it features the best from Armani, Valentino, Isaia, Corneliani, Calvin Klein, Brioni, Hugo Boss, and many other big names. The latest showstopper is the new Ermenegildo Zegna shop. Good shoe selection, too. Don't miss the "Great Wall of Shirts."

Irish Shop for Men. 150 Bloor St. W. (in Renaissance Plaza). ☎ **416/922-9400.**

Best known for its jackets and linen shirts, the Irish Shop carries great sports jackets, including Donegal tweeds, plus shirts, trousers, caps, hats, and picnic blankets.

Mr. Mann Clothiers. 41 Avenue Rd., ☎ **416/968-2022.**

A Canadian name for custom-made suits and shirts, Cy Mann has been in business for more than 40 years. Among the famous names he has dressed are Raymond Burr, Dick Cavett, Bill Cosby, and Paul Anka, as well as many CEOs. Prices are high, reflecting the quality of the workmanship, but they're still lower than you'd find in the United States. Suits are priced from $700, and they'll even custom-make one in 3 days.

Stollery's. 1 Bloor St. W. ☎ **416/922-6173.**

This venerable store has been at this corner since 1901; it was originally a men's store, especially well known for its vast selection of shirts (with different sleeve lengths). Today it also stocks women's wear, with such English fashion names as Burberry, Aquascutum, DAKS, and Austin Reed.

Thomas K. T. Chui. 754 Broadview Ave. ☎ **416/465-8538.**

For more than 20 years Mr. Chui has been dressing the wealthy and the famous. The custom suits cost from $900; there are custom-made shirts, also.

WOMEN'S

Asylum. 42 Kensington Ave. ☎ **416/595-7199.**

Scour the racks for new and vintage clothing at this Kensington Market outlet. Dresses, reworked vintage jeans with patchwork and tattoos, men's Hawaiian shirts, belts, shoes, and skull-and-crossbone–design items—they're all here.

Benetton. 102 Bloor St. W. ☎ **416/968-1611.**

Stylish, colorful, well-fashioned clothes at bearable prices are available for everyone. There's another outlet in the Eaton Centre.

Chanel. 131 Bloor St. W. ☎ **416/925-2577.**

The name says it all—classic all the way. This boutique, one of two in Canada, carries the designer's full line, including ready-to-wear and accessories—shoes, handbags, belts, and more.

Chez Catherine. 55 Avenue Rd. ☎ **416/967-5666.**

A long-established doyenne of the Canadian fashion scene, this store consists of four designer boutiques—Valentino, Versace, Gianfranco Ferré, and Krizia—plus a showcase of other European designers. It's known for its personalized service. There's a full line of accessories, including shoes.

✪ **Club Monaco.** 403 Queen St. W. ☎ **416/979-5633.**

If you're looking for casual wear and sportswear, this is a very pleasant shopping experience. There are other locations at the Eaton Centre; Hazelton Lanes; 1950 Queen St. East, in the Beaches; and the Yorkdale Shopping Centre.

F/X. 391 Queen St. W. ☎ **416/585-9568.**

This ultrahip store features the latest from outrageous designer Vivienne Westwood and also Betsey Johnson, among others. They sell one hundred fifty shades of nail polish, plus other accessories to go with the garb.

Gianni Versace. 55 Avenue Rd. (in Hazelton Lanes). ☎ **416/922-1900.**

Fine Italian design is the hallmark of Gianni Versace's clothing and accessories.

✪ **Holt Renfrew.** 50 Bloor St. W. ☎ **416/922-2333.**

This beautiful, well–laid-out store has several boutiques, including Giorgio Armani, Donna Karan, Anne Klein, Yves St. Laurent, and more. Of course, you'll find top-quality fashions and accessories.

✪ **Irish Shop.** 150 Bloor St. W. (in Renaissance Plaza). ☎ **416/922-9400.**

This is a lovely store, well-stocked with Irish fashions, lace, shawls, and accessories, as well as books.

Jaeger. 131 Bloor St. W. (in the Colonnade). ☎ **416/966-3544.**

The classic British name for fashions, Jaeger requires no explanation. If you like the look, it's here.

Krizia Boutique. 55 Avenue Rd. (in Hazelton Lanes). ☎ **416/929-0222.**

Upbeat and creative as ever, this boutique stocks the full line from Milan—jackets, pants, sweaters, and dresses, as well as belts and jewelry.

Lola Leman's. Hazelton Lanes, 55 Avenue Rd. ☎ **416/921-6228.**

For truly individual hand-knits and crocheted garments fashioned from marvelous imported yarns, you can't beat this boutique. In fact, so enticing are they that some customers claim they're addicted to Lola's designs.

Marilyn Brooks. 132 Cumberland St. ☎ **416/961-5050.**

This is the place to come to check out Canadian designers' women's fashions. Marilyn herself has been a designer for more than 30 years but she still supports young up-and-coming designers.

Roots. Hazelton Lanes, 55 Avenue Rd. ☎ **416/961-8479.**

This Canadian store proves that Canada has style. The quality of the casual clothes is good. People appreciate the hooded sweats, the Robbie Robertson jackets, and the many leather accessories including the sturdy Tuff boots. There is great children's clothing too.

Also at Eaton Centre and 312 Queen St. West.

Suitables. Queen's Quay, 207 Queen's Quay W. ☎ **416/203-0655.**

The emphasis here is on silk—silk blouses, skirts, and suits fashioned from a full range of different quality silks with prices starting as low as $40. Needless to say, some folks come from far and wide every year to pick up a supply. The store also stocks some great Canadian cotton vests and other unique items.

FOOD

Arlequin Restaurant. 134 Avenue Rd. ☎ **416/928-9521.**

The display up front is mouthwatering—salads, pâtés, melt-in-the-mouth croissants, pastries, and more.

Daniel et Daniel. 248 Carlton St. ☎ **416/968-9275.**

You'll find a full display of all kinds of foods and gourmet items—breakfast pastries, hot and cold hors d'oeuvres, salads, sandwiches, quiches, minipizzas, and desserts.

Dinah's Cupboard. 50 Cumberland St. ☎ **416/921-8112.**

This small, cluttered store has a fine selection of gourmet items to go, as well as frozen dishes to take home and microwave. Great salads, pâtés, vegetarian pasta, and croissants, as well as teas, coffees, vinegars, oils, and herbs.

✪ Dufflet Pastries. 787 Queen St. W., near Bathurst St. ☎ **416/504-2870.**

This specialty baker supplies many restaurants with their pastries and desserts. The special Dufflet cakes include a white-and-dark–chocolate mousse, toasted almond meringue, and many other singular creations. Fine coffees and teas and light lunches are served, too.

Global Cheese Shoppe. 76 Kensington Ave. ☎ **416/593-9251.**

More than 150 varieties of cheese are discounted here. It's worth the trip to Kensington Market.

Sweet Temptations. 207 Queen's Quay Terminal. ☎ **416/203-0512.**

This store is famous for offering every kind of candy available—chocolate-covered almonds and peanuts, gummy bears, and a broad selection of Canadian and imported chocolates, including handmade Belgian chocolates that sell for $1.50 or $1.75 a piece. Frozen yogurt and ice cream are also available.

✪ Ten Ren Tea. 454 Dundas St. W., at Huron St. ☎ **416/598-7872.**

At this fascinating Chinatown store, you can pick up some fine Chinese tea, which is stored in large canisters at the back of the store. The tiny ceramic teapots also make nice gifts in the $20-to-$30 price range. Many people are beginning to collect them.

Teuscher of Switzerland. 55 Avenue Rd. (in Hazelton Lanes). ☎ **416/961-1303.**

Some consider this Swiss chocolatier among the finest in the world. Teuscher produces 100-plus confections including about 20-plus kinds of truffles. The best natural ingredients—fruits, nuts, marzipan, and nougat are used and blended together using no chemicals or additives. All are handmade in Zurich and flown in once a week.

FURS

Fur sales take place twice a year—in summer when business is slow (the best time to negotiate a deal) and every January right after Christmas when the dealers are anxious to get rid of their inventory.

The wholesale fur warehouse is the **Balfour Building,** at 119 Spadina Ave.; it's worth starting here and shopping all the showrooms you can find in the building.

A la Mode Furs. 686 Bathurst St. ☎ **416/539-9999.**

This name includes several long-time local fur wholesalers—Sable Bay Furs, Leader Furs (established 1873), Stanley Walker, S. Kuretzky (an original), and Norcan Furs. On the premises you'll find 13,000 square feet of space divided into several showrooms. Mink is the number-one item, followed by beaver, raccoon, fox, sable, and lynx. The prices are wholesale, but in summer, when business is slow, they're even better.

Imperial Fur Company. 80 Bldg. D, Nashdene Rd., Unit 90–91, Scarborough. ☎ **416/292-1179.**

Check out the factory showroom for mink, fox, raccoon, and coyote. If you don't find a design you like, they'll custom-make a coat for you.

Norman Rogul Fur Company. 480 Adelaide St. W. ☎ **416/504-7577.**

This is the reputed furrier to Her Majesty the Queen and other royals and celebrities.

GIFTS & MORE

E. K. R. Zephyr. 292 Queen St. W. ☎ **416/593-0795.**

Wind chimes, jewelry, and wooden toys and rocking animals are the stock-in-trade of this appealing cooperative for Canadian crafts.

The Gallery Shop. In the Art Gallery of Toronto, 317 Dundas St. W. ☎ **416/979-6610.**

Books, gifts, jewelry, reproductions, and rental art are all offered in this large gallery off the museum's lobby.

✪ **General Store.** 55 Avenue Rd. (in Hazelton Lanes). ☎ **416/323-1527.**

An amazing collection of gifts for the person who has everything—from ultradesigned calculators and Newtonian puzzles to Filofaxes and the best carrot peeler on the market. There's a large collection of Swatch watches, too.

✪ **Geomania.** 1 First Canadian Place. ☎ **416/364-1500.**

Geomania is filled with highly polished, brilliantly colored pieces of minerals and stones, some fashioned into elegant jewelry, others crafted into vases, bookends, and other decorative pieces.

J & S Arts & Crafts. 430 Dundas St. W. ☎ **416/977-2562.**

In the heart of Chinatown, this store has a variety of good reasonably priced gifts and souvenirs—kimonos and happy coats, kung-fu suits, cushion covers, address books and diaries with handsome silk-embroidered covers, and all-cotton Chinatown T-shirts for only $6.

Legends of the Game. 322A King St. W. ☎ **416/971-8848.**

Anyone looking for a gift for a sports lover ought to find something at this temple to sports, complete with a Wall of Fame and baseball-handled entrance doors. Memorabilia of all sports are on sale, including autographed photos, old and new baseball and hockey cards, old and new comics, and jerseys that have been worn by players.

Oh Yes, Toronto. 101 Yorkville Ave. ☎ **416/924-7198.**

This is the ultimate souvenir store—everything in it features the Toronto name. Sweats, T-shirts, oven mitts, bags, buttons, and mugs range in price from $2 to $30.
    There are also branches at Queen's Quay West (☎ **416/203-0607**), Eaton Centre (☎ **416/593-6749**), Terminal 3 (☎ **905/672-8594**), and Terminal 2 (☎ **905/612-0175**).

Rotman Hat Shop. 345 Spadina Ave. ☎ **416/977-2806.**

This store has been in business here for over 40 years, and it retains the flavor of yesterday, when the area was more Jewish than it is today. Here you'll find the finest, light-as-a-feather Panama hats, as well as other fun headgear, like grouser hats.

✪ **Science City.** 50 Bloor St. W., in the Holt Renfrew Centre. ☎ **416/968-2627.**

A favorite of kids and adults alike, this store has an assortment of games, models, kits, and books relating to science—physics, chemistry, and biology—as well as very expensive telescopes and optics, hologram watches, trilobites, and other fossil specimens. All kinds of fun, mind-expanding stuff.

Touch the Sky. 207 Queen's Quay W. ☎ **416/203-0578.**

Kites and windsocks are the specialty here, plus wind chimes, mobiles, Frisbees, and balloons—great inexpensive gifts.

HOUSEWARES & KITCHENWARE

✪ **En Provence.** 20 Hazelton Ave. ☎ **416/975-9400.**

This store has a beautiful selection of French decorative items for the home—ceramics, table accessories, wrought-iron and wood furniture, and, on the second floor, the most luxurious fabrics by Souleiado for household use. This is French country style at its best.

Fortune Housewares. 388 Spadina Ave. ☎ **416/593-6999.**

This well-stocked store has a great selection of utensils and other household/kitchen items—chopping boards, aprons, Copco pots, and other brand-name items—at 20% or more off the regular prices around town.

Plaiter Place. 384 Spadina Ave. ☎ **416/593-9734.**

This must be the city's premier wicker emporium, bar none. Every conceivable use is made of wicker: You'll find all kinds of objects made from wicker and bamboo here—birdcages, blinds, steamers, hats, and baskets galore in all shapes, sizes, and styles.

Tap Phong Trading Co. 360 Spadina Ave. ☎ **416/977-6364.**

All kinds of utensils, woks, bamboo steamers, ceramic and stainless-steel cookware, mortar and pestles, and terrific baskets are jammed into this small space. It's fun shopping.

JEWELRY

Birks Jewelers. 220 Yonge St., in the Eaton Centre. ☎ **416/979-9311.**

A well-known Canadian retailer with stores in towns across Canada, Birks stocks fine silver and jewelry at fair prices. Also at the Manulife Centre (☎ **416/922-2266**), First Canadian Place (☎ **416/363-5663**), and at other in-town and suburban locations.

✪ **18 Karat.** 71 McCaul St. ☎ **416/593-1648.**

The owners of this store will craft jewelry on the premises according to your design. They will also do repairs and redesigns of antique settings. Show them what you have in mind and they will execute it.

First Toronto Jewellery Exchange. 215 Yonge St. ☎ **416/340-0008.**

Thirty stores are under one roof across the street from Eaton Centre. As you can imagine, there's a huge variety of diamonds, pearls, gold and silver rings, chains, and earrings on display.

Peter Cullman. Cumberland Court, 99 Yorkville Ave. ☎ **416/964-2196.**

You can watch Cullman here in his studio crafting his beautiful pieces that are inspired by nature and organic forms. He apprenticed in Germany. All of his pieces—rings, bracelets, and necklaces—are beautifully and meticulously handcrafted.

Silverbridge. 162 Cumberland St. ☎ **416/923-2591.**

The sterling-silver jewelry here is designed and handcrafted by Costin Lazar and manufactured in Toronto. It's modern and reflects the talents of Mr. Lazar, who is also a sculptor. Necklaces, bracelets, rings, and earrings, as well as cuff links, money clips, and key holders are priced from $60 to $1,400.

Yonge Dundas Jewellery Exchange. 295 Yonge St. ☎ **416/340-0008.**

This complex contains more than 20 stores.

MAGAZINES, INTERNATIONAL NEWSPAPERS & BOOKS

Great Canadian News Company. BCE Place. ☎ **416/363-2242.**

More than 2,000 magazines and 60 newspapers all displayed under one roof—a print-media buff's dream.

Lichtman's News & Books. 144 Yonge St. at Richmond. ☎ **416/368-7390.**

Local and international newspapers and magazines, as well as hard- and softcover books, are sold here and also at the Atrium on Bay, at Yonge and Bloor streets, and at Yonge and Eglinton.

Maison de la Presse Internationale. 124 Yorkville Ave. ☎ **416/928-2328.**

This large store has foreign magazines and newspapers galore. It's a convenient place to pick up the *New York Times, Wall Street Journal, Financial Times,* and the like.

MALLS & SHOPPING CENTERS

Atrium on Bay. Bay and Dundas sts. ☎ **416/980-2801.**

Sixty stores on two floors sell fashions, shoes, jewelry, and more.

College Park Shops. 444 Yonge St. ☎ **416/597-1221.**

More than 100 stores spread out on two floors, this is a more intimate and less harried version of the Eaton Centre.

✪ **Eaton Centre.** 220 Yonge St. ☎ **416/598-2322** or 416/595-1691.

This glass-domed galleria has more than 360 shops and restaurants on four levels, with plenty of places to rest and eat lunch, too. This is where the real people shop.

✪ **Hazelton Lanes.** 55 Avenue Rd. ☎ **416/968-0853.**

An elegant shopping complex featuring all the great designer fashion names along with specialty shops. About 85 stores in all on two levels. It has some pleasant dining stops too.

Holt Renfrew Centre. Bloor St. W. No phone.

Not to be confused with the store of the same name, which is far more upscale, the center is much more down to earth. You wouldn't find Teas 'n' Tarts in Holt Renfrew. My favorite store on the downstairs level is Science City.

✪ **Queen's Quay Terminal.** 207 Queen's Quay. ☎ **416/203-0510.**

More than 60 shops and restaurants, including fashion and gift boutiques, are housed here in a converted waterfront warehouse. Remember, the rents are high. Open daily from 10am to 9pm.

Royal Bank Plaza. Bay and Front sts. ☎ **416/974-2880.**

More than 60 shops are directly accessible from Union Station and the subway. Don't miss the building above.

Village by the Grange. 122 St. Patrick St., between Queen and Dundas sts. ☎ **416/598-1414.**

More than 40 shops are complemented by several major restaurants. The International Food Market is good for budget dining.

MARKETS

✪ **Kensington Market.** Along Baldwin, Kensington, and Augusta aves. No phone.

Originally a Jewish market, then a Portuguese market area, today it offers all kinds of ethnic foods from Middle Eastern to West Indian. It's a Toronto experience.

⚫ **St. Lawrence Market.** 92 Front St. E. ☎ **416/392-7219.**

This historic market is still favored by Torontonians for its fresh produce—from figs to fish. The best day is Saturday when the farmers come into town and the market opens at 5am. Hours are Tuesday through Thursday from 8am to 6pm, Friday from 8am to 7pm, and Saturday from 5am to 5pm.

MUSIC

Classical Record Shop. 55 Avenue Rd. (in Hazelton Lanes). ☎ **416/961-8999.**

Listen to the melodies emanating from this store. It stocks a large selection of CDs, audio tapes, and videos for the classical-music lover.

HMV. 333 Yonge St. ☎ **416/596-0333.**

One of the city's largest music emporiums, HMV also offers an added bonus: the opportunity to listen before you buy. There are also several other locations.

L'Atelier Grigorian. 70 Yorkville Ave. ☎ **416/922-6477.**

This store has a fantastic selection of CDs—jazz and classical only.

Record Peddler. 619 Queen St. W. ☎ **416/504-3828.**

This specialty store stocks British imports, LPs, and CDs in rock, blues, jazz, and reggae—no classical or country.

Sam the Record Man. 347 Yonge St.

This famous Toronto record outlet is so vast and busy that the telephone number is unlisted. It has the largest laser-disc selection in the city. The interactive department on the mezzanine features software and video games.

TOBACCO

Winston & Holmes. 138 Cumberland St. ☎ **416/968-1290.**

Although it's not old, this store has all the appearance of tradition and age. A large selection of well-made pipes is on display behind glass; there's a broad selection of Cuban and other cigars, and all the other smoking requisites. Fine fountain pens are stocked, too, along with men's shaving accoutrements and toiletries. Mail order is available. Also at Queen's Quay (☎ **416/203-0344**) and 2 First Canadian Place (☎ **416/363-7575**).

TOYS

Carriage Trade Dolls. 584 Mount Pleasant Rd. ☎ **416/481-1639.**

At this real specialty doll store, there's a good selection of antique collectibles as well as some serious modern collector pieces such as Ann of Green Gables. Although the emphasis is on collectible dolls, Carriage Trade also stocks modern vinyl and porcelain dolls, including some that are anatomically correct, dolls that you can wash, and so on.

Kidding Awound. 91 Cumberland St. ☎ **416/926-8996.**

Windup toys—music boxes and clockwork toys—antique toys, and other amusing items dating from the 1950s to the 1990s are found here. It's great therapy for adults.

Kidstuff. 738 Bathurst St., one block south of Bloor St. ☎ **416/535-2212.**

This store does not stock video and computer games, but concentrates instead on cooperative games, Lego, Playmobile, puppets, art supplies, and other imported and educational toys.

Little Dollhouse Company. 617 Mount Pleasant Rd. ☎ **416/489-7180.**

This charming store makes all-wood handcrafted dollhouse kits in about 12 different styles, many Victorian, complete with shingles, siding, doors, and windows. They also sell dollhouse furniture, lighting, wallpaper, and building supplies—wood, metal, and plastic—and display 100 room settings. Dollhouse kits range from $50 to $500, while finished dollhouses are about twice the price.

Science City Jr. 50 Bloor St. W. ☎ **416/968-2627.**

This is a great store, full of games, puzzles, models, and books about science, and serious stuff like telescopes, trilobites, and hologram watches.

Top Banana. 639 Mount Pleasant Rd. ☎ **416/440-0111.**

This traditional toy store features educational, Canadian and imported toys, like Brio wooden trains from Sweden, Ravensburger puzzles and games, Eduframe toys, art supplies, and plenty of products from Playmobil, Lego, Playskool, and Little Tikes. There are audio cassettes and books, too.

The Toy Shop. 62 Cumberland St., at Bay St. ☎ **416/961-4870.**

The two floors of creative toys, books, and games here include videos from around the world.

WINES

You'll have to shop the LCBO outlets. Look them up in the *Yellow Pages* under "Liquor Control Board of Ontario," or call the info line at **416/365-5900.** The most convenient downtown locations are 20 Bloor St. East (☎ **416/925-1434**); 87 Front St. East (☎ **416/368-0521**); Manulife Centre, 55 Bloor St. West (☎ **416/925-5266**); the Eaton Centre (☎ **416/979-9978**); and Union Station (☎ **416/368-9644**). More extensive selections are found at the **Vintages** stores, like the one in Hazelton Lanes on the concourse.

9

Toronto After Dark

Toronto's performing-arts scene is terrific. On the music and dance end of things, the city's must-see companies are the National Ballet of Canada, the Canadian Opera Company, the Toronto Symphony, the Toronto Dance Theatre, Tafelmusik, and the Mendelssohn Choir. For comedy, it's hard to beat Second City, still the cradle for so many of America's great comedy artists.

Toronto's reputation for theater is second only to New York's. Visitors can enjoy major Broadway shows at landmark theaters or explore the repertory of smaller resident companies. For additional entertainment, there are enough bars (cigar, martini, and pool bars currently being the trendiest), clubs, and cabarets to keep anyone spinning virtually all night long.

For local performances and events, check out *Where Toronto* and *Toronto Life*, as well as the *Globe and Mail*, the *Toronto Star*, and the *Toronto Sun*. For the hipper scene, get hold of a copy of *Eye* or *Now*, both free and available at Maison de la Presse and many other bookstores and stores around the city.

DISCOUNT TICKETS   For day-of-performance half-price tickets, go to the **Five Star Ticket Booths** at Yonge and Dundas streets outside the Eaton Centre on the southwest corner. Cash and credit cards are taken. It's open Tuesday through Saturday from noon to 7:30pm and Sunday from 11am to 3pm. For information, call **416/596-8211.**

1 The Performing Arts

Toronto's major performing-arts venues include **Massey Hall,** 178 Victoria St. (☎ **416/593-4828**), a Canadian musical landmark, which hosts a variety of musical programming from classical to rock; **The O'Keefe Centre,** 1 Front St. East (☎ **416/872-2262**), home to the Canadian Opera Company and the National Ballet of Canada, which also presents headline entertainers like Celine Dion and international performing-arts companies; and the **St. Lawrence Centre for the Arts,** 27 Front St. East (☎ **416/366-7723**), which is home to the Canadian Stage Company in the Bluma Appel Theatre, and to a variety of other ensembles and acts in the Jane Mallet Theatre. **Roy Thomson Hall,** 60 Simcoe St. (☎ **416/593-4828**), is Toronto's premier concert hall and home to the Mendelssohn

Choir and the Toronto Symphony Orchestra, which performs here from September to June. It also features an array of international musical artists. The hall was designed to give the audience a feeling of extraordinary intimacy with every performer—none of the 2,812 seats is more than 107 feet from the stage. The exterior of the building itself is spectacular—dove-colored, petal-shaped, and enveloped in a huge glass canopy that's reflective by day and transparent by night. The **Glenn Gould Studio,** 250 Front St. West (☎ 416/205-5555), is a small radio-performance hall for chamber and other recitals, and a memorial to the great, eccentric, reclusive Toronto pianist whose career was cut short when he died at age 50. **The Ford Centre for the Performing Arts,** 5040 Yonge St. (☎ 416/872-2222), is home to the North York Symphony and also hosts a variety of musical events and recitals in its George Weston Recital Hall, as well as such major musicals as *Sunset Boulevard* and *Ragtime* in the Apotex Theatre. **The Premiere Dance Theatre,** Queen's Quay Terminal, 207 Queen's Quay West (☎ 416/973-4000), was specifically designed for dance and Toronto's leading contemporary dance companies—Toronto Dance Theatre, Dance Makers, and the Danny Grossman Dance Company—perform their seasons here.

OPERA & CLASSICAL MUSIC

In addition to the many major musical venues mentioned above, visitors should also check to see what's being performed at such churches as **Trinity-St. Paul's,** 427 Bloor St. West (☎ 416/964-6337), and **St. Patrick's,** Dundas and McCaul sts. (☎ 416/483-0559).

Canadian Opera Company. 227 Front St. E. ☎ 416/872-2262. Tickets $30–$95.

The Canadian Opera Company began its life in 1950 with 10 performances of 3 operas. It now stages 8 different operas at the O'Keefe Centre, spread over the 8 months from September to April.

Tafelmusik Baroque Orchestra. 427 Bloor St. W. ☎ 416/964-6337. Tickets $20–$38.

This group plays baroque music on authentic period instruments, giving a series of concerts at Trinity/St. Paul's United Church at 47 Bloor St. West. Other performances are given in Massey Hall.

Toronto Mendelssohn Choir. 60 Simcoe St. ☎ 416/598-0422. Tickets $8–$45.

A world-renowned choir, this group first performed in Massey Hall in 1895. Its repertoire ranges from Verdi's *Requiem,* Bach's *St. Matthew Passion,* and Handel's *Messiah* to the soundtrack of *Schindler's List.*

Toronto Symphony Orchestra. 60 Simcoe St. ☎ 416/593–4828.

The symphony performs at Roy Thomson Hall from September through June. The repertoire ranges from classics to pop and new Canadian works. In June and July concerts are given at outdoor venues throughout the city.

DANCE

Dance Makers. 927 Dupont. ☎ 416/535-8880. Tickets $20–$32.

Artistic director Serge Bennathan has helped his company secure international recognition for its provocative mix of stylized physical movement and theater. Among its repertoire, the most recent and most exciting work is the Sable/Sand trilogy performed to music by Toronto composer Ahmed Hassan, which *Dance* magazine described as evoking images "at once earthy, smoldering, vulnerable, and proud."

Danny Grossman Dance Company. 511 Bloor St. W. ☎ 416/531-8350 or 416/531-5268. Tickets $20–$32.

A local dance favorite whose choreography is noted for its athleticism, theatricality, humor, and passionate social vision. The company performs both new works and revivals of modern-dance classics. Refreshing, fun, and exuberant.

✪ National Ballet of Canada. 157 King St. E. ☎ **416/366-4846.** Tickets $15–$75.

Most famous of all Toronto's cultural contributions is perhaps the National Ballet of Canada. It was launched at Eaton Auditorium in Toronto on November 12, 1951, by English ballerina Celia Franca, who served initially as director, principal dancer, choreographer, and teacher. Over the years, the company and such stars as Karen Kain have achieved great renown. Among the highlights of its history have been its 1973 New York debut (which featured Nureyev's full-length *Sleeping Beauty*); and Baryshnikov's appearance with the company soon after his defection in 1974. Since 1989, the company has been led by Canadian Reid Anderson.

Besides its tours of Canada, the United States, and overseas, the company performs its regular seasons in Toronto at the O'Keefe Centre in the fall, winter, and spring, as well as making summer appearances in smaller communities throughout Ontario. The repertory includes the classics, as well as works by Glen Tetley *(Alice)*, Sir Frederick Ashton, Jerome Robbins, and William Forsythe *(the second detail)*. James Kudelka, who has created *The Miraculous Mandarin, The Actress,* and *Spring Awakening,* was appointed artist-in-residence in 1991.

Toronto Dance Theatre. 80 Winchester St. ☎ **416/973-4000** (the Premiere Dance Theatre). Tickets $21–$35.

The leading contemporary dance company in Toronto burst onto the scene 26 years ago, bringing an inventive spirit and original Canadian dance to the stage. Today, Christopher House directs the company; he joined it in 1979 and has contributed more than 30 new works to the repertoire. Exhilarating, powerful, and energetic—don't miss their Handel Variations, Artemis Madrigals, Sacra Conversazione, or the Cactus Rosary. The company performs two seasonal programs per year at the Premiere Dance Theatre.

THEATER

The best time to capture the flavor of Toronto's theater life is during the Fringe Festival. Many of the city's smaller companies have no permanent performance space, and only perform erratically wherever they can secure temporary space. What you choose to see will depend on what's scheduled while you're in town, so to do your own talent-scouting check the local newspaper for listings of the myriad productions offered. Only those companies that have permanent homes are listed here.

In addition, don't forget that two major theater festivals—the Shaw Festival in Niagara-on-the-Lake and the Stratford Festival in Stratford—are only a day trip away.

LANDMARK THEATERS

In addition to **O'Keefe Centre** and the **St. Lawrence Centre for the Arts** (see "The Performing Arts," above), the city's other big theaters include:

The Elgin and Winter Garden Theatres. 189–191 Yonge St. ☎ **416/872-5555.** Tickets $25–$80.

After an extensive renovation in the 1980s, these two theater gems, which originally opened as a double-stacked vaudeville theater in 1913, have been dusted off for the 1990s. The 1,500-seat Elgin has a domed ceiling; the upstairs Winter Garden seats 1,000, and has a wonderful bosky atmosphere. Suspended from its ceiling and lit with lanterns are more than 5,000 branches of beech leaves which were harvested, preserved, painted, and fire-proofed. Both theaters offer everything from Broadway musicals and dramas to concerts and opera performances.

Guided tours are given at 5pm Thursday and 11am Saturday (Sunday, too, during July and August). The tour costs $4 for adults, $3 for students and seniors. Call **416/363-5353.**

Pantages Theatre. 244 Victoria St. ☎ **416/872-2222.** Tickets $56–$95; discount seats available 2 hours before the performance.

This magnificent old theater has been restored to host splashy Broadway shows like *The Phantom of the Opera,* which reopened the theater. It originally opened in 1920, showing silent films and hosting vaudeville performances.

Princess of Wales Theatre. 300 King St. W. ☎ **416/872-1212.** Tickets $27–$95.

This spectacular theater was opened by the Princess of Wales herself. It was built for the production of *Miss Saigon* and has a stage that is large enough to accommodate the landing of a full-size helicopter. The interior has been dramatically decorated by hundreds of feet of colorful murals by Frank Stella. He also designed the lighting.

Royal Alexandra Theatre. 260 King St. W. ☎ **416/872-1212**. Tickets $25–$95.

Shows from Broadway migrate north to the Royal Alex. Tickets are often snapped up by subscription buyers, so your best bet is to write ahead to the theater (260 King St. W., Toronto, ON, M5V 1H9).

The theater itself is quite a spectacle. Constructed in 1907, it owes its current lease on life to owner Ed Mirvish, who refurbished it (as well as the surrounding area) in the 1960s. Inside it's a riot of plush reds, gold brocade, and baroque ornamentation, with a seating capacity of 1,493. Apparently, you're wise to avoid the second balcony, as well as the seats under the circle.

THEATER COMPANIES & SMALLER THEATERS

Buddies in Bad Times. 12 Alexander St. ☎ **416/975-8555.** Tickets $10–$15.

This gay, or queer (as the company prefers to be called), theater company produces radical new Canadian works that celebrate difference and blur as well as reinvent the boundaries between gay and straight, gay and lesbian, male and female. The repertoire includes cabaret and comics in two spaces. Often wild and wacky, always raw and cutting edge.

Canadian Stage Company. 26 Berkeley St. ☎ **416/368-3110.** Tickets $40–$60; discount tickets for seniors and students sometimes available 30 min. before the performance.

The Canadian Stage Company performs comedy, drama, and musicals in the St. Lawrence Centre and also presents free summer Shakespeare performances in High Park. Call for dates and programs.

Factory Theatre. 125 Bathurst St. ☎ **416/504-9971.** Tickets $10–$23.

Since 1970, the Factory Theatre has been presenting new Canadian plays on its two stages. Here, promising new authors get the chance to develop and showcase their works. In the past, productions have toured successfully in London and New York. The Bathurst streetcar runs nearby.

Native Earth Performing Arts Theatre. 720 Bathurst St. ☎ **416/531-1402.** Tickets $10–$18.

This small company is dedicated to performing works that express and dramatize the Native Canadian experience.

Canada—The Funny Country

If Americans ever think about Canada, and this is rare enough, the last thing they think of is humor. For the most part, they think of Canada and Canadians as a rather boring bunch of people, who live through harsh winters, migrate south in the form of snowbirds, and tack an "eh" onto the end of every sentence. But how many of those same Americans know that much of what they laugh at on TV, in the movies, and on stage is either written or performed by Canadians? Without them, there would have been no "Saturday Night Live," no "SCTV," and no *Spy* magazine, and Ed Sullivan and David Letterman would have had to look elsewhere for their sidekicks.

For many years, Canada has exported a great number of acting talents—from Mary Pickford, the sweetheart of the silent screen, to Hollywood's most highly paid comedic actor, Jim Carrey. Famous Canadians on TV have included Lorne Greene, of "Bonanza" fame, "Star Trek's" William Shatner, and Jason Priestley of "Beverly Hills 90210." Even Superman was invented by a Canadian, Joe Shuster.

The Canadian comedy invasion really began with Lorne Michaels, the creator of "Saturday Night Live." Before that career-catapulting move, he honed his comedic talents by writing for Woody Allen and "Laugh In," and helped to bring fellow Canadian humorists, like Earl Pomerantz, who wrote for "Mary Tyler Moore" and "The Cosby Show" before creating "Major Dad," south as well. After the creation of "SNL," Michaels continued to encourage more Canadians to pursue comedy careers in the States, most notably Dan Aykroyd, whom he asked to join the cast of "Saturday Night Live." And, most recently, it was Michaels who brought "Kids in the Hall" to American TV.

The early pioneers who influenced many of these comics were two stalwarts on the "Ed Sullivan Show," Johnny Wayne and Frank Shuster, but it was Second City

Tarragon Theatre. 30 Bridgman Ave. ☎ **416/531-1827.** Tickets $14.50–$23.50; on Sun, pay what you can afford.

The Tarragon Theatre, near Dupont and Bathurst, opened in the early 1970s and continues to produce original works by Canadian playwrights—Michel Tremblay, Michael Ondaatje, John Murrell, Joan MacLeod, and Judith Thompson, for example—and an occasional classic or off-Broadway play. It's a small, intimate theater where you can get beer, wine, coffee, and apple juice in the foyer.

Theatre Passe Muraille. 16 Ryerson Ave. ☎ **416/504-7529.** Tickets $8–$24.

One of Canada's leading alternative theaters, Theatre Passe Muraille delivers innovative and provocative theater by such contemporary Canadian playwrights as John Mighton, Daniel David Moses, and Wajdi Mouawad. It was started back in the late 1960s by a group of actors who performed original Canadian material. There are two stages, the Mainspace seating 220, and the more intimate Backspace seating 70.

Toronto Truck Theatre. 94 Belmont St. ☎ **416/922-0084.** Tickets $20.

The Toronto Truck Theatre is the home of Agatha Christie's *The Mousetrap*, now in its 19th year. It's Canada's longest-running show.

✪ **Young People's Theatre.** 165 Front St. E. ☎ **416/862-2222.** Tickets $12–$22.

that became the great breeding ground for comedy actors. It launched the careers of Dan Aykroyd, Bill Murray, Mike Myers, Andrea Martin, and Eugene Levy. It was such a successful breeding ground that Second City's producer started his own TV show, "SCTV," mainly to protect his acting talent from being stolen. In so doing, he launched another generation of comedians—John Candy, Martin Short, Rick Moranis, and Catherine O'Hara—who went on to Hollywood film careers. Second City also helped spawn a sketch comedy industry that produced "Kids in the Hall" and "Royal Canadian Air Farce," among other TV shows. Many of these great comedic talents—Jim Carrey, Howie Mandel, and Harland Williams, for example—cut their teeth in Toronto's comedy clubs, such as Yuk Yuk's, which continues to groom young Canadian comics today.

Indeed, the list of Canadian funny men and women could go on and on—from director Ivan Reitman (*Meatballs, Dave*) to a good many of the *National Lampoon* team (Ted Mann and Sean Kelly). Still other Canadians are on the writing teams for such successful American sitcoms as "Roseanne," "Seinfeld," and "Home Improvement."

There's no real explanation for this phenomenon, except perhaps that Canadians think of themselves as outsiders, and are intense observers of the American scene, particularly American pop culture and TV. It seems as well that they've inherited some of their British forebears' appreciation and talent for irony and satire. In fact, this satiric tradition can be traced back to such humorists as Stephen Leacock and seen among the long line of talented Canadian fiction writers, from Mordecai Richler to W. P. Kinsella. While America was born in rebellion and has always celebrated rebellion, Canadians emphasize conformity and obedience to authority—a combination that seems to produce an irrepressible satirical nature in the young and quick-witted.

In Toronto, you'll have no problem finding kids' entertainment, for the city takes its children's theater very seriously, as evidenced by the Young People's Theatre. Here, in a theater seating 468, such whimsical, fun productions as *Jacob Two-Two Meets the Hooded Fang*, a musical by Mordecai Richler, as well as such classics as *The Diary of Anne Frank* are mounted. There might be one problem: Kids have been known to weep when the show ends.

DINNER THEATER & COMEDY SHOWS

The Laugh Resort. 26 Lombard St. ☎ **416/364-5233.** Cover charges Tues–Wed $5, Thurs $7, Fri $12, Sat $15.

If you want to share some laughter with the likes of Gilbert Gottfried, Paula Poundstone, and up-and-coming comics, this is the place.

Limelight Supper Club. 2026 Yonge St. ☎ **416/482-5200.** Dinner and show, $45; Show only, Sat $35.

Musical revues and comedy are the specialty at the Limelight, where you can have dinner while enjoying the entertainment.

✪ **Second City.** 110 Lombard St. ☎ **416/863-1111.** Show only, Mon–Thurs $13.50, Fri $16.50, Sat $20.50, Sun $11. Dinner and show costs $32.95, $35.95, and $39.95, respectively. Reservations required.

One of Toronto's wittiest theater groups, Second City specializes in improvisational comedy. This is the company that nurtured the late John Candy, Dan Aykroyd, Bill Murray, Martin Short, Mike Myers, Andrea Martin, and Eugene Levy and continues to turn out talented young actors. The skits are always funny and topical. Its home is an old fire hall that now houses a theater seating 200, and a restaurant.

Second City has had a marked impact on North American entertainment with its various workshops, touring company, seasoned resident company, and internationally syndicated TV series.

Ukrainian Caravan. 5245 Dundas St. W. ☎ **416/231-7447.** Dinner and show, $22–$35 per person.

For an evening of Cossack dance, song, and comic repartee, head for the Ukrainian Caravan at Kipling Street. There are shows on Saturdays only; dinner begins at 7:30pm, the show at 9pm.

Yuk-Yuk's Superclub. 2335 Yonge St. ☎ **416/967-6425.** Tickets, Sun–Thurs $7, Fri $10, Sat $14. Dinner/show packages from $23.20.

Situated in the heart of Yorkville, Yuk-Yuk's is Canada's original home of stand-up comedy. Comic Mark Breslin founded the place in 1976, inspired by New York's Catch a Rising Star and Los Angeles's the Comedy Store. Some of the more famous homegrown alumni who performed here include Jim Carrey, Harland Williams, Howie Mandel, and Norm MacDonald, all of whom started at Yuk Yuk's in Toronto. Other guests have included Jerry Seinfeld, Robin Williams, and Sandra Bernhard. Also out near the airport at 5165 Dixie Rd. (☎ **416/967-6425**).

2 The Club & Music Scene

COUNTRY, FOLK, ROCK & REGGAE

✪ **Bamboo.** 312 Queen St. W. ☎ **416/593-5771.** Call 10am–5pm. Cover Mon–Wed $5, Thurs $5–$7, Fri–Sat $10.

Bamboo is a Queen Street institution that introduced reggae to the city many years ago. Still decked out in Caribbean style and colors, it offers an exciting assortment of cutting-edge reggae, calypso, salsa, hip-hop, soul, and R&B. The club (with a tiny dance floor) takes up one side of the space, while a small restaurant decorated with masks from New Guinea occupies the other.

The menu mixes Caribbean, Indonesian, and Thai specialties. Thai spicy noodles are really popular, blending shrimp, chicken, tofu, and egg. Lamb and potato roti and Caribbean curry chicken served with gado gado, banana, and steamed rice are other examples. Music starts at 10pm. Drinks average $5.

Birchmount Tavern. 462 Birchmount. ☎ **416/698-4115.** Cover Fri–Sat $5.

This is the city's longtime country-music venue, attracting a broad range of Canadian and American artists, including Lynn Anderson, Johnny Paycheck, and many more. Wednesday to Sunday from 9pm to 1am.

El Mocambo. 464 Spadina Ave. ☎ **416/968-2001.** Cover varies.

A rock-and-roll landmark—it's where the Stones chose to take their gig in the 1970s, and today it hosts the likes of Liz Phair in the upstairs area. Monday night is when local cutting-edge bands perform. Sunday and Wednesday are popular DJ dance-mix nights.

Free Times Cafe. 320 College St. between Major and Robert sts. ☎ **416/967-1078.** Cover $4–$6.

The back room is one of the city's regular folk and acoustic music venues. Monday night is open house.

Horseshoe Tavern. 370 Queen St. W. ☎ **416/598-4753.** Cover Thurs–Sat $4–$10.

An old, traditional Toronto venue. Its back room is mythologized as the place where the Police, the Band, Blue Rodeo, and Barenaked Ladies played when they were young and hungry. The Horseshoe attracts a cross-section of people from age 20 to 60. Live music on Thursday to Saturday attracts a hard-driving crowd; Monday through Wednesday are country nights. Bands go on at 10pm.

Lee's Palace. 529 Bloor St. W. ☎ **416/532-1598.** Cover varies.

Definitely grungy, Lee's Palace is a home to local alternative bands, but it also served as the venue that introduced Oasis, Sloan, and Nirvana to Toronto. The downstairs room rocks every night. There's a DJ dance bar upstairs that spins alternative rock 7 nights a week.

✪ **The Rivoli.** 332 Queen St. W. ☎ **416/597-0794.** Cover $5–$8.

Currently this is the club for an eclectic mix of performances, including grunge, blues, rock, jazz, and poetry reading. Holly Cole launched her career here, and Tori Amos made her Toronto debut in the back room, too. Shows begin at 9:30pm and continue to 1am. People dance if so inspired. Upstairs, there's a billiards room and espresso bar.

JAZZ, RHYTHM & BLUES

Toronto is a big jazz town—especially on Saturday afternoon, when many a hotel lounge or restaurant lays on an afternoon of rip-roaring rhythm. The best time to be in the city for jazz is during the 11-day **Du Maurier Downtown Jazz Festival** in late June, when legendary international artists perform traditional and fusion jazz, blues, and gospel at 50 different venues around town.

In addition to the clubs listed below, **Bamboo,** listed under "Country, Folk, Rock & Reggae," above, also offered some of the hottest jazz in town when I last visited.

Ben Wick's. 424 Parliament St. ☎ **416/961-9425.** No cover.

There's jazz, usually on Saturday night only, at this comfortable English-style pub named after local cartoonist Ben Wick. The music begins at 8:30pm.

The Black Swan. 154 Danforth Ave. ☎ **416/469-0537.** Cover varies.

A friendly laid-back locale for both local and visiting blues performers is casual and reasonably priced. There's pool, too.

The Chelsea Bun. At the Chelsea Inn, 33 Gerrard St. ☎ **416/595-1975.** No cover.

The Chelsea Bun is another of my favorite Saturday-afternoon jazz spots, where the crowd gathers at 3pm and listens until 7pm. Six days a week there's also a piano player and a live band playing Top 40 tunes from 9pm to 1am.

Judy Jazz. Holiday Inn on King, 370 King St. W. ☎ **416/593-7788.** Cover varies; $8 Fri–Sat.

Currently this is where the artists come to jam until 4am during the du Maurier Jazz Festival. At other times, this lower level sophisticated club-restaurant features jazz Monday to Saturday from 9pm to 1am.

✪ **Montréal Bistro Jazz Club.** 65 Sherbourne St. ☎ **416/363-0179.** Cover varies.

This is a cool atmosphere for an array of jazz artists—the Carol Welsman Quartet, the Memo Acevedo Quintet, and Marion McPartland. It's great, too, because the bistro is next door.

✪ **Top O' the Senator.** 249 Victoria St. ☎ **416/364-7517.** Cover $5–$20.

Toronto's most atmospheric jazz club is a long, narrow room with a bar down one side and a distinct 1930s look. It's a great place to hear fine jazz by international artists like Ray Brown and Terence Blanchard. The atmosphere is only added to by the funky movie theater seats set around tables, the couches alongside the performance area, and portraits of band leaders and musicians on the walls. Open Tuesday to Sunday. On the third floor a quiet, comfortable lounge is a great spot for an intimate after theater drink.

DANCE CLUBS

Dance clubs come and go with tremendous alacrity—the hottest spot can either close or turn into one of the most decidedly unhip places almost overnight—so bear with me if some of those listed below have disappeared or changed by the time you visit. Meanwhile, here are some of the currently crowded spots on the Toronto scene.

First, let me remind you about **Horizons,** in the CN Tower, which changes from a cocktail bar into a dance club at 9 or 10pm. See "The Bar Scene," later in this chapter.

Berlin. 2335 Yonge St. ☎ **416/489-7777.** Cover Tues $8, Thurs $3, Fri–Sat $10.

This is one of the more sophisticated clubs, attracting a well-heeled crowd ranging in age from 25 to 55. Currently it's indulging in a Latin craze, with salsa on Tuesday night. Wednesday is Greek night and on Thursday there's dancing to a DJ; weekends there's more dancing to the house band and a DJ, too. Berlin is open Tuesday and Thursday until 2am, Friday and Saturday until 3am; it's closed other days.

Cha Cha Cha. 11 Duncan St. ☎ **416/598-3538.**

Above the Filet of Sole and Whistling Oyster, this supper club attracts an older crowd with its Latin rhythms (salsa, merengue), deco accents, and fireplace.

Chick 'n' Deli. 744 Mount Pleasant Rd. ☎ **416/489-3363.** No cover.

At Chick 'n' Deli, south of Eglinton Avenue, Tiffany-style lamps and oak set the background for Top 40 or R&B tunes every night. The dance floor is always packed.

Chicken wings and barbecue are the specialties, along with nachos, salads, and a selection of sandwiches—club, smoked meats, and so on. On Saturday afternoon the sounds are Dixieland. Entertainment begins at 9pm Monday to Friday (from 5pm on Sunday and from 3:45 pm on Saturday with the sounds of Dixieland).

Crocodile Rock. 240 Adelaide St. W. ☎ **416/599-9751.**

Casual and laid back, without any trace of attitude, this place spins 70s and 80s dance sounds for the 25- to 40-year-old crowd, which includes a good many suits from Bay Street. Eclectic sounds and scene. There's pool, too.

Cutty's Hideaway. 538 Danforth Ave. ☎ **416/463-5380.** Cover $10–$15.

This has been a Caribbean hot spot in Greektown for a decade. Calypso and reggae bands entertain on weekends, easily luring the many island regulars out onto the dance floor. It's popular with young and old alike.

Deluge at Atlantis. Ontario Place. ☎ **416/260-8000.** Cover $6–$10.

House dancers get the crowd going at this waterfront venue where well-dressed yuppies come to party and check each other out. Open Thursday through Saturday year-round.

Fluid Lounge. 217 Richmond St. W. ☎ **416/593-6116.** Cover $5–$10.

Only the dressed-to-kill gain entry to this haven for the beautiful and hip, with moody lighting and a simulated underwater decor. Sports celebrities sometimes drop by to groove to the neo-funk, industrial, and mainstream dance sounds. No running shoes or sportswear permitted.

Hangar. 100 St. George St. ☎ **416/978-4701.** Cover depends on event, generally $2–$3.

This student venue is operated by the Students Administrative Council. Live bands, pool tables, pub grub, and plenty of beer.

Hard Rock Cafe. 1 Blue Jays Way (enter by Skydome's Gate 1). ☎ **416/341-2388.** No cover.

Neither of Toronto's Hard Rocks is affiliated with the U.S. chain. In fact, North America's original Hard Rock Cafe is at 282 Yonge St. (☎ **416/362-3636**), still operating after 18 years. Both of these spots feature rock 'n'roll memorabilia collections, and a musical background to burger and sandwich dining.

Ivory. 69 Yorkville. ☎ **416/927 9929.** Cover $5–$10.

This club is frequented by an upscale, well-heeled older crowd. If you want to fit in, it helps to look like an anorexic blond model at this exotic Middle Eastern oasis decked out in golden hues and beaded fabrics. Wednesday is Latin night when the dance floor throbs to merengue, salsa, and tango.

The Joker. 318 Richmond St. W. ☎ **416/598-1313.** Cover $5–10.

A huge Euro-style multilevel entertainment palace. The first floor features pool tables and Internet-surfing hardware. The second and third floors are where the dance action heats up, especially on the top floor where ravers take over.

Limelight. 250 Adelaide St. W. ☎ **416/593-6126.** Cover $5–$7.

Occupying three floors, the limelights first floor is for dancing, the second for pool, and the third for lounging in the so-called "Greek Room." A young crowd comes Thursday nights. Alternative and retro sounds play on weekends.

Loose Moose. 220 Adelaide St. W. (between Simcoe and Duncan sts.). ☎ **416/971-5252.** No cover.

This is a crowd-pleaser for the younger set, who like the multilevel dance floors, DJ, billiard tables, booze, and schmooze. Check out the moose art. Pizza, chicken, and ribs are the dinner favorites, washed down with more than 60 different brews. Starts every night at 9pm.

Misty's. At the Toronto Airport Hilton International, 5875 Airport Rd. ☎ **416/677-9900.** Wed–Thurs no cover; Fri $3; Sat $5.

A successful club for more than 20 years, Misty's is still popular thanks to its theme nights—1950s and 1960s on Wednesday, with a variety of sounds served up from Thursday to Sunday starting at 8pm.

Orchid. 117 Peter St. ☎ **416/598-4990.** Cover $5–$10.

With its up-to-the-minute design, this glam club attracts an over-25 crowd who dances to disco sounds on Wednesday, and alternative music on Thursday and weekends.

Phoenix Concert Theatre. 10 Sherbourne St. ☎ **416/323-1251.** Cover varies; Fri–Sat $5–$8.

This rock venue showcases such artists as Screaming Headless Torsos, Patti Smith, and the Smashing Pumpkins, and gets the crowds dancing on weekends to a mixture of sounds—retro, Latin, alternative, and funk. The milieu might make you think you've returned to ancient Egypt or Greece.

Power. 230 Adelaide St. W. ☎ **416/977-1731.** Cover $5–$10.

This 20-something powerhouse rocks to acid house and acid jazz. The fashion-conscious crowd is attracted by the additional amusements staged on the multiple TVs and at the pool tables. No jeans on Saturday.

Rockit. 120 Church St. (south of Richmond). ☎ **416/947-9555.** Cover Fri–Sat $5–$10.

In this pizzeria, bar, and dance club, different nights feature different sounds and attract different crowds. On Friday and Saturday, a DJ spins the dance tunes—mixing R&B, hip-hop, reggae, salsa, and merengue.

Sneaky Dees. 431 College St. ☎ **416/603-3090.** No cover.

The pool tables and Mexican food complement the alternative rock spun by the DJ in the club upstairs until 1:30am. Downstairs, the bar is open weekdays until 3am, 5am on weekends.

Studebakers. 150 Pearl St. ☎ **416/591-7287.** No cover.

Drop in here if you want to hear the old sounds from the 1950s, 1960s, and 1970s. It's nostalgia time.

Whiskey Saigon. 250 Richmond St. W. ☎ **416/593-4646.** Cover varies.

In two large rooms—one black, one white—the crowds frolic to their heart's content in Euro-disco style. Thursday is cheap night. Weekends it's retro. Open Wednesday to Sunday.

3 The Bar Scene

The current night scene has spawned a flock of attractive bistros with billiard tables. You can enjoy cocktails, a reasonably priced bistro meal, and a game of billiards in a comfortable, aesthetically pleasing decor.

Note: Bars and pubs that serve drinks only are open Monday through Saturday from 11am to 1am. Establishments that also serve food are open Sunday, too.

PUBS & BARS

First, let me list some of my favorite hotel bars. For a comfortable bar where you can really settle into some conversation, go to the rooftop bar atop the ✪ **Park Plaza** at 4 Avenue Rd. (☎ **416/924-5471**). An old literary haunt, it's comfortable and the view and outdoor terrace are splendid. Another favorite in Yorkville is **La Serre** at the Four Seasons, 21 Avenue Rd. (☎ **416/964-0411**), which offers a full range of single malts and martinis and welcomes cigar aficionados. It was actually named by *Newsweek* as one of the world's best bars. The fairly formal **Chartroom,** at the Westin Harbour Castle, 1 Harbour Sq. (☎ **416/869-1600**), has a good view of the lake and the island ferry. The **Consort Bar** at the King Edward Hotel, 37 King St. East (☎ **416/863-9700**), is also comfortable. The Library Bar at the Royal York is renowned for the quality of its martinis while the **Chelsea Bun,** at the Chelsea Inn, 33 Gerrard St. West (☎ **416/595-1975**), has a fine selection of single-malt whiskeys and good musical entertainment. If you prefer a pubby atmosphere, there's the **Good Queen Bess,** in the Sheraton Centre, 123 Queen St. West (☎ **416/361-1000**). At the airport, check out the **Banyan Tree** at the Regal Constellation, 900 Dixon Rd. (☎ **416/675-1500**), a comfortable piano bar.

And now for the independents.

Al Frisco's. 133 John St. ☎ **416/595-8201.**

Upstairs, people crowd around the pool tables or jam the dance floor moving to retro sounds. Downstairs cozy fireplaces enhance the atmosphere of this gathering spot featuring Mediterranean fare—pizzas, pastas, and such entrees as veal chop with artichokes in balsamic jus, or grilled sea bass in a sweet pepper sauce, for example. The extra-large outdoor patio is jammed in summer with a mix of tourists, suits, and casual professionals in their late 20s.

Alice Fazooli's. 294 Adelaide St. W. ☎ **416/979-1910.**

Baseball art and memorabilia, including a full-scale model of an outfielder making a wall catch, fills this large bar and dining room. It's always jam-packed with an older business crowd either quaffing in the bar or feasting in the back on crabs cooked in many different styles, pizza, pasta, and raw-bar specialties. The garden patio with a fountain is great in the summer. There are more than 50 wines by the glass.

Allen's. 143 Danforth Ave. ☎ **416/463-3086.**

Allen's sports a great bar for more than 80 beer selections and 40-plus single malts. Guinness is the drink of choice on Tuesday and Saturday night when folks reel and jig in fine abandon to the Celtic-Irish entertainment.

Atlas. 129 Peter St. ☎ **416/977-7544.**

Fashion-conscious singles in their 30s gather here, filling the sidewalk patio, jamming themselves into the downstairs bar area, or hanging out upstairs, where there's a small dance area for rocking to the sounds of funk and rock. Also upstairs, tucked away in the corner, is a dining room that offers Cal-Italian cuisine with dishes priced from $17 to $24.

Bar Italia & Billiards. 582 College St. ☎ **416/535-3621.**

Downstairs, a young, trendy, and good-looking crowd quaffs drinks or coffee and snacks on Italian sandwiches. Upstairs, guys (mostly) gather around six pool tables. If you're seeking quiet, go early in the evening before the scene changes to a veritable fiesta.

Bellair Café. 100 Cumberland St. ☎ **416/964-2222.**

The midtown Bellair Café has a sleek, suede ambiance that still attracts successful, now middle-aged boomers. It gets really jammed every night and on weekends, both inside at the square bar and outside on the terrace. Drinks cost from $6 to $8.

The Bishop Belcher. 361 Queen St. W. ☎ **416/591-2352.**

This British style pub that offers 14 drafts on tap and a decent selection of single malts. Their classic pub fare includes bangers and mash, shepherd's pie, and a ploughman's lunch.

Blu. 340 Adelaide St. W. ☎ **416/506-9366.**

This sleek, cool spot attracts a 20-something, multiethnic crowd who comes for the rotis, the spare retro maple and chrome ambience, and the background Caribbean and big-band music. In summer, the unique back deck with its cabana style bar affects a tropical South Beach air.

Bovine Sex Club. 542 Queen St. W. ☎ **416/504-4239.**

This alternative rock venue is not for the faint of heart. Intimidating metal sculptures and other shock-value art contribute to the funky atmosphere. Strictly for the nose-ring and body-pierced set.

The Brunswick House. 481 Bloor St. W. ☎ **416/964-2242.**

For a truly unique experience, go to the Brunswick House, a cross between a German beer hall and an English north-country workingmen's club. Waiters move between the Formica tables in this cavernous room, carrying high trays of frothy suds to a largely student clientele. Impromptu dancing to background music, and pool- and shuffleboard playing drowns out the sound of at least two of the large-screen TVs, if not the other 18. This is an inexpensive place to down some beer. Upstairs, there's live-broadcast thoroughbred and harness racing from international tracks, including Hong Kong.

Cameron Public House. 408 Queen St. W. ☎ **416/703-0811.**

Old and new hippies still hang here in the front room, with its festooned bar. Local bands try out in the back room.

Centro. 2472 Yonge St. ☎ **416/483-2211.**

Downstairs at the restaurant, this comfortable, well-patronized bar is a relaxing place to listen to the pianist and get to know the sophisticated mid-30s-and-up crowd. Closed Sunday.

C'Est What? 67 Front St. E. ☎ **416/867-9499.**

This brewery and wine bar is located downstairs in one of the city's historic ware-house buildings. The rough-hewn walls and cellarlike atmosphere are reminiscent of a Paris *cave.* On one side, it's casual and comfortable, attracting a young, politically conscious crowd (board games are available), drawn by the "ethnoclectic" menu (noodles, pasta, tortillas), and extensive beer and single malt selections. On the other, live melodic folk-acoustic groups entertain. There's a cover charge, depending on the group. A daily menu is served from 11:30am; brunch on weekends 11:30am to 3pm.

Club Lucky Cafe & Bar. 117 John St. ☎ **416/977-8890.**

This sophisticated cigar/piano bar only opens on weekends and draws an older crowd.

The Duke of Westminster. First Canadian Place. ☎ **416/368-1555.**

Designed in England and shipped and assembled here, this pub offers 16 beers and ales on tap (usually about $4 a half pint, $6 a pint, for imported premium beers). The Duke of Westminster offers a classy English atmosphere that seems to attract those very English types for a good frothy English pint, and a game of darts or pool. Closed weekends.

The Gem. 1159 Davenport Rd. ☎ **416/654-1182.**

A small, down-to-earth, retro-style spot, the Gem attracts an artist/musician crowd. The music is 1950s and 1960s, and the decor nostalgic kitsch—black, red, and vinyl in a tacky-trendy style.

Hemingway's. 142 Cumberland St. ☎ **416/968-2828.**

This Yorkville watering hole with a fun, large, summer rooftop patio features piano or other entertainment Thursday to Saturday. A pint of beer is $4.95.

Jack Russell Pub. 27 Wellesley St. E. ☎ **416/967-9442.**

This comfortable local pub attracts a mixed crowd—families, professionals, and students—and is located in an old heritage house. The main pub, complete with dart board, is warmed in winter by a fire, and offers a patio in summer. Upstairs on the third floor, there's a large tavern with a game room. In between, there's the Henley room, decked out with rowing regalia. A friendly place to go and chat, the Jack Russell Pub sells 12 types of draft.

Madison. 14 Madison Ave. ☎ **416/927-1722.**

Madison has to be one of the city's most popular gathering places, with people (many students) jamming every floor and terrace of this town house. The newest development is the billard room with 10 tables. Everyone seems to know everyone else.

Milano. 325 King St. W. ☎ **416/599-9909.**

Up front, there's a bar and beyond it lie several billiard tables. The dining area is off to the side. In summer, French doors open to the street, making for a pleasant Parisian atmosphere. The bistro-style food consists of burgers, sandwiches, and such items as tiger shrimp.

Montana. 145 John St. ☎ **416/595-5949.**

This is a kicky Western saloon with an upstairs log-cabin–style nook with a fireplace and a bison trophy. Live bands playing mostly nostalgic music entertain. There's billiards, too. The relaxed, casual crowd hangs out inside as well as on the sidewalk patio outside.

Orbit Room. 580A College St. ☎ **416/535-0613.**

With the sleekest decor on College, Orbit attracts a sophisticated, older crowd. Up front, there's a glitzy, chrome bar with semicircular banquettes and glitzy etched glass. House bands play R&B and soul in the back.

✪ **The Real Jerk.** 709 Queen St. E. ☎ **416/463-6055.**

The original Real Jerk was out east and small. It became so popular, it moved to this larger space. Here, as before, the hip crowd digs the moderately priced, super-spiced Caribbean food—jerk chicken, curries, shrimp Creole, rotis, and patties—the lively ambiance, and the hot background music. Reservations aren't accepted. Open Tuesday through Saturday from 4:30pm to 1am and Sunday from 2 to 11pm.

✪ **Rotterdam.** 600 King St. W. (at Portland St.). ☎ **416/504-6882.**

This brew pub is a beer-drinker's heaven, serving more than 200 different labels as well as 30 different types on draft. It's not an after-work crowd that gathers here, but by 8pm the tables in the back are filled, and the long bar is jammed. In summer the patio is fun, too.

Shag Club. 923 Dundas St. W. ☎ **416/603-2702.**

This is Aladdin's cave for the young, hip set where they can trip on the projected images of the given moment, without taking any acid. It's intimate and comfy casual.

Souz Dal. 636 College St. ☎ **416/537-1883.**

This is my favorite boîte on College Street. It's dark and intimate, painted in deep-purple and mustard shades, and decorated in an exotic Moroccan fashion. Kilims adorn the walls; the bar is fashioned out of copper. The small patio protected by a trellis is lit by candles. Great martinis and margaritas as well as tropical drinks, like the Havana made with rum, guava juice, and lime.

Ted's Collision and Body Repair. 573 College St. ☎ **416/533-6425.**

This raw autoshop-inspired bar with a rough-and-ready, scratched up look has a small patio in the back furnished with tables and market-style umbrellas. It attracts a young drinking crowd thanks to live folk-rock entertainment.

Wayne Gretzky's. 99 Blue Jays Way. ☎ **416/979-7825.**

Hockey fans will want to visit this shrine to the blond-haired hockey genius from nearby Brantford. It's filled with memorabilia—photos, uniforms, and equipment are displayed in several cases—charting Gretzky's rise from the junior leagues in Sault Ste. Marie through his professional debut with the Indiana Raptors to his career with the Edmonton Oilers. Don't eat here, unless you simply have to say that you dined at *his* place. Better to have a drink at the long bar or in the rooftop Oasis. There, you can sit at the cabana-style bar, which is scented with hibiscus and affords a fine view of the CN Tower.

Wheatsheaf Tavern. 667 King St. W. ☎ **416/504-9912.**

Designated a historic landmark, this is the city's oldest tavern, having been in operation since 1841. Classy it ain't, but for sports mavens, it's home, with five screens showing great moments in sports. The jukebox features 1,200 choices, and there's also a pool table and an outdoor patio.

WINE BARS

In addition to the bar listed here, there's also **Enoteca** at 150 Bloor St. West in Yorkville, and the very comfortable wine bar at **N 44,** 2537 Yonge St., uptown.

✪ **Vines.** 38 Wellington St. E. ☎ **416/869-0744.** Subway: King.

Vines provides a pleasant atmosphere in which to sample a glass of champagne or any one of 30 wines, priced between $4 and $7 for a 4-ounce glass. Salads, cheeses, and light meals, served with fresh French sticks, are available.

COCKTAILS WITH A VIEW

Horizons. 301 Front St. W. ☎ **416/360-8500.** $12 charge for the elevator.

For obvious reasons, Horizons, perched on the CN Tower, can be difficult to get into because of the crowds. But it's worth the wait—just to gaze at the panoply of Toronto's lights down below. It's open from 10am to 10pm Sunday through Thursday and from 10am to 1am Friday and Saturday. No jeans are allowed on Friday and Saturday nights. At 9 or 10pm, it converts from a cocktail bar to a dance club.

Panorama. 55 Bloor St. W. ☎ **416/967-0000.**

From this 51st floor perch above Bloor and Bay, visitors can see north and south for 150 miles (at least on a clear day). Go for the lit skyline and the Latin ambience (Rio carnival mural) and music. The seating is comfortable; more than a dozen types of cigars are available. Go early if you want a window seat.

4 The Gay & Lesbian Scene

Toronto's large, active gay and lesbian community has created a great, varied nightlife scene. Heavy leather bars include **Boots/Kurbash,** 592 Sherbourne St. (☎ **416/921-0665**) and the **Black Eagle,** 459 Church St. (☎ **416/413-1219**). Less raunchy venues follow.

Aztec. 2 Gloucester St. ☎ **416/975-8612.** No cover.

Friday and Saturday are line-dancing nights at this mixed gay male and lesbian spot. There are two stories for dancing in a light and spacious venue that's known for its brunch.

The Barn/The Stables. 418 Church St. ☎ **416/977-4702.**

This is one of the city's oldest gay bars. The second floor dance floor is jammed; the third floor is for "back room" liasons. There are afternoon underwear parties on Sundays, and sex videos, too. Don't expect to talk.

Colby's. 9 St. Joseph St. ☎ **416/961-0777.**

The music is retro and current for the young dance crowd. There's pool, too.

The Rose Cafe. 547 Parliament St. ☎ **416/928-1495.**

This is the city's most popular lesbian bar, with a pool table and game room downstairs that's furnished with old, cozy couches, and a restaurant and dance area upstairs. In summer, the fenced-in patio is the place to cool off.

Sailor. 465 Church St. ☎ **416/975-8899.**

This bar-restaurant is attached at the hip to Woody's. There are two bars with video screens, and a good crowd, especially on weekends for brunch from 11am to 4pm.

Woody's. 467 Church St. (south of Wellesley). ☎ **416/972-0887.**

A friendly and popular local bar, Woody's is frequented mainly by men, but welcomes women. It's considered a good meeting place.

5 Cinemas & Movie Houses

Cineplex. In the Eaton Centre. ☎ **416/593-4535.** Tickets $8.50 (less before 6pm and all-day Tues).

Although it's easy enough to find movie-theater listings in the daily newspapers, you should know about Toronto's exceptional film buffs' heaven, Cineplex. Always wary of describing anything as the biggest, let me just say that the film complex houses 17 theaters with seating capacities ranging from 57 to 137.

Exterior screens over the Cineplex entrance in the Eaton Centre display ongoing slide presentations, and a board in the lobby lists all movies and starting times. Recent releases are the staples.

There's also a Cineplex Market Square at 80 Front St. East (☎ **416/364-2300**).

Cinematheque Ontario. 70 Carlton. ☎ **416/967-7371,** or 416/923-3456 (box office). Tickets $7.50 adults, $3.75 seniors.

This organization shows the best in contemporary cinema. The programs include directors' retrospectives, plus new films not available for commercial release from France, Germany, Japan, Bulgaria, and other countries. The films are shown at the Art Gallery of Ontario.

Within two hours of Toronto by car, there are several places that make an enjoyable day trip. My favorites—Niagara-on-the-Lake, Niagara Falls, and Stratford—are described in this chapter.

For visitor information about the area surrounding Toronto, contact the **Ontario Ministry of Tourism and Recreation,** 77 Bloor St. West, Toronto, ON, M7A 2R9 (☎ **800/Ontario,** or 416/314-0944). The offices are open Monday through Friday from 8:30am to 5pm (daily from mid-May to mid-Sept). You can also write to **Ontario Travel,** Queen's Park, Toronto, ON, M7A 2E5.

1 Niagara-on-the-Lake

Only 1¹/₂ hours from Toronto, Niagara-on-the-Lake is one of the best-preserved and prettiest 19th-century villages in North America, with its lakeside location and tree-lined streets bordered by handsome clapboard and brick period houses. Such is the setting for one of Canada's most famous events, the Shaw Festival.

ESSENTIALS

VISITOR INFORMATION The **Niagara-on-the-Lake Chamber of Commerce,** 153 King St. (P.O. Box 1043), Niagara-on-the-Lake, ON, L0S 1J0 (☎ **905/468-4263**), will provide information and help you find accommodations at one of 90 local bed-and-breakfasts. It's open Monday to Friday from 9am to 5pm, Saturday and Sunday from 10am to 5pm.

GETTING THERE Driving from Toronto, take the QEW Niagara via Hamilton and St. Catharines and exit at Highway 55.

Amtrak and **VIA** operate trains between Toronto (☎ 416/366-8411) and New York that stop in St. Catharines and Niagara Falls. Call **800/361-1235** in Canada or **800/USA-RAIL** in the United States.

THE SHAW FESTIVAL

Devoted to the works of George Bernard Shaw and his contemporaries, the festival, which opens in mid-April and runs to the end of October, performs 10 or 11 plays in three theaters: the historic Court House, the exquisite Festival Theatre, and the Royal George Theatre.

Some recent performances have included Shaw's *The Devil's Disciple, Pygmalion,* and *The Doctor's Dilemma,* and *An Ideal Husband* by Oscar Wilde.

Side Trips from Toronto

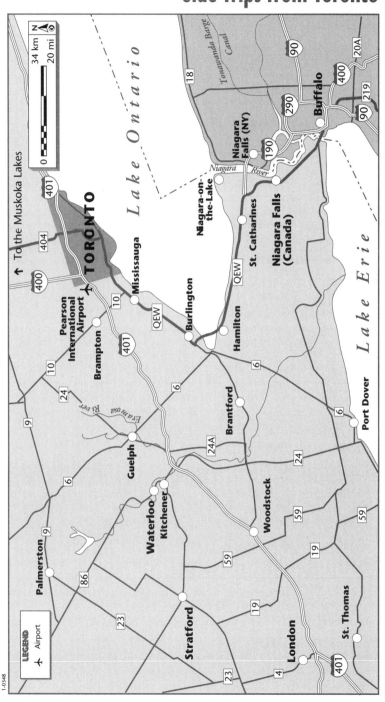

An added attraction are the free lunchtime conversations (on Saturdays at 11:30am in July and August), the Friday chats that introduce performances on Friday evenings in July and August, and the Tuesday evening question-and-answer sessions that follow performances.

Ticket prices range from $12 (for lunchtime performances) to $60 on weekends. For more information, contact the Shaw Festival, P.O. Box 774, Niagara-on-the-Lake, ON, L0S 1J0 (☎ **800/511-7429,** or 905/468-2172).

EXPLORING THE TOWN

Niagara Historical Society Museum. 43 Castlereagh St., at Davy. ☎ **905/468-3912.** Admission $2.50 adults, $1.50 seniors and youths 12–18, 50¢ children. Jan–Feb weekends 1–5pm; Mar, Apr, Nov, Dec daily 1–5pm; May–Oct daily 10am–5pm.

The Niagara Historical Museum houses over 20,000 artifacts pertaining to local history, including many possessions of United Empire Loyalists who first settled the area at the end of the American Revolution. The museum also offers guided walking tours of the area , but they must be booked 2 weeks in advance and are only given to groups of 15 or more.

✪ **Fort George National Historic Park.** Niagara Pkwy. ☎ **905/468-6614.** Admission $4 adults, $2 ages 6–16; free for seniors and children 5 and under; family rate, $12. Mid-May to June daily 9:30am–4:30pm; July to Labor Day daily 10am–5pm; Labor Day to Oct daily 9:30am–4:30pm; Nov to mid-May Mon–Fri by appointment only.

South along the Niagara Parkway at the Fort George National Historic Park, it's easy to imagine taking shelter behind the stockade fence and watching for the enemy from across the river, even though today there are only condominiums on the opposite riverbank. The fort played a key role in the War of 1812, when the Americans invaded and destroyed it in May 1813. Although rebuilt by 1815, it was abandoned in 1828 and not reconstructed until the 1930s. View the guard room with its hard plank beds, the officers' quarters, the enlisted men's quarters, and the sentry posts. The self-guided tour includes interpretive films and, occasionally, performances by the Fort George Fife and Drum Corps.

A NOSTALGIC SHOPPING STROLL

A stroll along Queen Street will take you by some entertaining shops. At the 1866 **Niagara Apothecary Shop,** 5 Queen St.(☎ **905/468-3845**), with its original black-walnut counters and the contents of the drawers marked in gold-leaf script, the original glass and ceramic apothecary ware is on display. **Maple Leaf Fudge,** 14 Queen St. (☎ **905/468-2211**), offers more than 20 varieties that you can watch being made on marble slabs. **Greaves Jam** is run by fourth-generation jam makers. **Loyalist Village,** at no. 12 (☎ **905/468-7331**), has distinctively Canadian clothes and crafts, including Inuit art, Native Canadian decoys, and sheepskins. The **Shaw Shop,** next to the Royal George, has GBS memorabilia and more. There's also a Dansk outlet and several galleries selling contemporary Canadian and other ethnic crafts, and a charming toy store, the **Owl and the Pussy Cat,** at 16 Queen St. (☎ **905/ 468-3081**).

JET BOATING THRILLS

Don a rain suit, poncho, and life jacket and climb aboard a jet boat at the dock across from 61 Melville St. at the King George III Inn. The boat will take you out onto the river for a trip along the stone-walled canyon to the whirlpool downriver closer to the falls. Trips which operate from May through October last an hour. Reservations are needed. Call **905/468-4800.**

Niagara-on-the-Lake

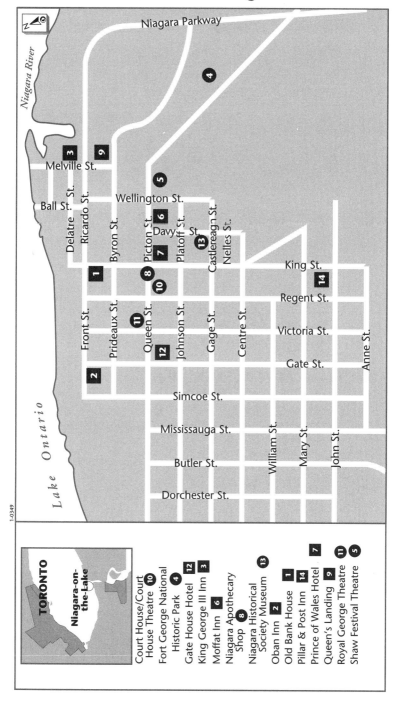

Niagara Parkway

Niagara River

Melville St.

Ball St.

Delatre St.

Ricardo St.

Wellington St.

Byron St.

Picton St.

Davy St.

Platoff St.

Castlereagh St.

Nelles St.

King St.

Regent St.

Victoria St.

Gate St.

Anne St.

Front St.

Prideaux St.

Queen St.

Johnson St.

Gage St.

Centre St.

Simcoe St.

Mississauga St.

William St.

Mary St.

John St.

Butler St.

Dorchester St.

Lake Ontario

TORONTO

Niagara-on-the-Lake

Court House/Court House Theatre **10**

Fort George National Historic Park **4**

Gate House Hotel **12**

King George III Inn **3**

Moffat Inn **6**

Niagara Apothecary Shop **8**

Niagara Historical Society Museum **13**

Oban Inn **2**

Old Bank House **1**

Pillar & Post Inn **14**

Prince of Wales Hotel **7**

Queen's Landing **9**

Royal George Theatre **11**

Shaw Festival Theatre **5**

1-0349

From Vinegar to Vintage—Ontario Wines Come of Age

Not so long ago (in the early 1980s, in fact) Canadians were embarrassed about their local wines, and restaurateurs were loath to feature them on their menus, even though the government and the tax structure encouraged them to do so. Today, only 15 years later, Ontario wines are bursting out all over and are prominently and proudly featured on the wine lists of top-class Canadian restaurants. In short, they have come of age, thanks very largely to the establishment of the VQA appellation in 1988.

There are three designated Ontario viticultural areas—Niagara Peninsula, Pelee Island, and Lake Erie North Shore. In order to carry each designation, wines must contain 85% grapes from the viticultural area, and must be made 85% from the variety named on the label—in order to carry a varietal name. The Ontario wine area is parallel to Provence and Languedoc-Rousillon in France, Chianti in Italy, the Rioja region in Spain, and the Mendocino Valley in California. All three Ontario regions benefit from the climatic effects of the Great Lakes, which temper the heat and cold of the seasons, and the wind buffer provided by the Niagara Escarpment. The Niagara wine growing region runs along the south shore of Lake Ontario from Stoney Creek to Niagara Falls. It produces good quality wines which are winning medals in international competitions, but the region has also won worldwide acclaim for the consistent production and quality of one wine in particular—ice wine—so much so that Canada is now the number-one producer of this elixir that enhances desserts of every kind, except chocolate. Ice wine is made from frozen

TOURING NIAGARA-ON-THE-LAKE WINERIES

If you take Hwy. 55 (Niagara Stone Road) out of Niagara-on-the-Lake, you'll come to **Hillebrand Estates Winery** (☎ **905/468-7123**), just outside Virgil. It's open year-round; tours are given daily at 11am and 1, 3, and 4pm; the wine shop is open 10am to 6pm daily.

If you turn off Hwy. 55 and go down York Road, you'll reach **Château des Charmes,** west of St. Davids (☎ **905/262-5202**). One-hour tours are given daily. Open 10am to 6pm.

The **Konzelmann Winery,** Lakeshore Road (☎ **905/935-2866**), can be reached by driving out through Mary Street. Tours are given June to late August Wednesday to Saturday at 2pm; in winter, on Saturday only.

If you prefer to take a tour, you can board the trolley operated by Niagara-on-the-Lake Trolley Tours, which tour several wineries. Price range from $32 and up. For information call **905/468-2123.** For other wineries in the region, see the box titled "From Vinegar to Vintage: Ontario Wines Come of Age," above, or "Winery Tours," in the Niagara Falls section of this chapter.

WHERE TO STAY

In summer, don't despair if you're having trouble nailing down a room somewhere. Contact the chamber of commerce, which provides an accommodations-reservations service. Your best bets are bed-and-breakfast accommodations.

EXPENSIVE

Gate House Hotel. 142 Queen St. (P.O. Box 1364), Niagara-on-the-Lake, ON, L0S 1J0. ☎ **905/468-3263.** 10 rms. A/C TV TEL. $160–$180 double. AE, DC, MC, V. Closed Jan–mid-Mar.

grapes, usually Riesling or Vidal, which are then pressed, producing a juice that is intensely sweet and highly acidic. Temperature is critical to the process. The frozen grapes must not melt; if they do, the concentration of the juice is diluted. Here on the Niagara escarpment, the climate is ideal for its production. First, the grapes are left to freeze. If they survive the birds and other predators, they are harvested under unusually bitter cold conditions, then pressed while still frozen, and left to ferment. One of the reasons ice wine is so expensive is that it takes about 5 kilos of grapes to produce enough juice to make 1 bottle of wine (compared to 1 kilo normally). In addition to ice wine, the region also produces some fine chardonnays, Rieslings, gewürtztraminers, cabernet sauvignons, merlots, pinot noirs, and gamays.

Among the major estate wineries which were the first to produce good varietal wines are: **Inniskillin,** RR #1 (Line 3 at the Niagara Parkway), Niagara-on-the-Lake (☎ 905/468-3554); **Chateau des Charmes,** 1025 York Rd., St. David's (☎ 905/262-4219); and **Hillebrand,** Hwy. 55, Niagara-on-the-Lake (☎ 905/468-7123). In addition, there are many smaller companies, which are pushing the larger estates to produce better and better wines, such as: **Cave Spring,** 3836 Main St., Jordan (☎ 905/562-3581); **Vineland Estates,** RR #1, 3620 Moyer Rd., Vineland (☎ 905/562-7088); Reif, RR #1, Niagara Parkway (☎ 905/468-7738); **Henry of Pelham,** 1469 Pelham Rd., St. Catharines (☎ 905/684-8423); **Konzelmann,** RR #3, 1096 Lakeshore Rd., Niagara-on-the-Lake (☎ 905/935-2866); and **Stoney Ridge,** 1468 Hwy. 8, Winona (☎ 905/643-4508).

Instead of being done in country-Canadian, the rooms here are decorated in cool, up-to-the-minute Milan style. Guest rooms have a turquoise marbleized look accented with ultramodern basic black lamps, block marble tables, leatherette couches, and bathrooms with sleek Italian fixtures.

✪ **Oban Inn.** 160 Front St. (at Gate St.), Niagara-on-the-Lake, ON, L0S 1J0. ☎ 905/468-2165. 22 rms. A/C TV TEL. $140–$165 standard double, $185–$210 double with lake view. Winter midweek and weekend packages available. AE, DC, ER, MC, V.

With a prime location overlooking the lake, the Oban Inn is the place to stay. It's located in a charming white Victorian house with a green dormer-style roof and windows, plus a large veranda. The gardens are a joy to behold and are the source of the bouquets on each table in the dining room and throughout the house.

Each of the comfortable rooms is unique. They are furnished with comfortable antique reproductions—corn-husk four-poster beds with candlewick spreads, ginger-jar lamps, and club-style sofas. Old prints might adorn the walls—it's all very homey and comfortably old-fashioned.

Bar snacks and light lunches and dinners are available downstairs in the pubby piano bar, with its leather Windsor-style chairs and hunting prints over the blazing fireplace. The dining room's dinner menu is priced from $19 to $23.

Pillar & Post Inn. 48 John St. (at King St.), Niagara-on-the-Lake, ON, L0S 1J0. ☎ 905/468-2123. 122 rms and suites. A/C MINIBAR TV TEL. $160–$210 double; $175 fireplace room; $205–$375 suites. Extra person $20. AE, DISC, ER, MC, V.

Rustic to every last inch of barn board, the Pillar & Post has 48 rooms with wood-burning fireplaces. Although all are slightly different, each room will certainly contain early Canadian-style furniture, Windsor-style chairs, a color TV tucked into a pine cabinet, and historical engravings, plus modern conveniences. In the back there's a secluded pool (some rooms facing the pool on the ground level have bay windows and window boxes).

Carriages and the Cannery dining rooms, the latter occupying a former canning factory and basket-manufacturing plant, offer the same menus with main courses priced from $18 to $24. The menu features continental cuisine—rack of lamb with caramelized onion butter There's also a comfortable lounge.

Indoor and outdoor pools, a fitness room, a health spa with a variety of treatments, an outdoor whirlpool, and bike rentals round out the facilities.

Prince of Wales Hotel. 6 Picton St., Niagara-on-the-Lake, ON, L0S 1J0. ☎ **905/468-3246.** Fax 905/468-1310. 105 rms. A/C TV TEL. May–Oct, $130–$160 double; from $250 suite; Nov–Apr, $120 double. Extra person $12. Special packages available. AE, DC, MC, V.

For a lively atmosphere that retains the elegance and charm of a Victorian inn, the Prince of Wales has it all: full recreational facilities; lounges, bars, and restaurants; and 105 rooms, some with colonial-style furniture and others with brass beds—all tastefully decorated with antique Federal reproductions and color-coordinated carpeting, drapes, and spreads. Most rooms have minibars.

The original section of the hotel was built in 1864. In the Prince of Wales Court, rooms are larger, huge wardrobes house TVs, and botanical prints on the walls set the tone. The newer wing has been well designed to match the original redbrick and cream exterior with its slate dormer roof.

An impressive old oak bar from Pennsylvania dominates the quiet bar off the lobby. Royals, the elegant main dining room, serves breakfast, lunch, and dinner, offering a dozen dinner entrees, from roasted rack of lamb served with a shallot-and-mint sauce to grilled Atlantic salmon served with red-pepper cream. Prices range from $19 to $24. At lunch, light dishes are featured, such a span-seared ginger scallops with tomato, shallots, and coriander or cheese ravioli with garlic, pine nuts, sweet basil, and roasted tomatoes. ($9–$12). Three Feathers Café is light and airy for breakfast, lunch, or tea. The Queen's Royal lounge is a pleasant drinking spot.

There's also an indoor pool, whirlpool, exercise room, and a platform tennis court. Aerobics classes and massage therapy are offered, and bicycles are available for rent.

Queen's Landing. P.O. Box 1180, at the corner of Byron and Melville sts., Niagara-on-the-Lake, ON, L0S 1J0. ☎ **905/468-2195.** 137 rms. A/C MINIBAR TV TEL. $180 room without fireplace; $190 room with fireplace; $225 room with fireplace and Jacuzzi. AE, DC, ER, MC, V.

Overlooking the river but also within walking distance of the theater, the Queen's Landing is a fine establishment where 70 rooms have fireplaces and some 32 have Jacuzzis. Each room is spacious and comfortably furnished with pine furnishings, a half-canopied or brass bed, wingback chairs, and a large desk; each is also equipped with a push-button phone, a color cable TV, and a clock radio.

The lounge, with its fieldstone fireplace, is cozy; and in summer the dining room looks out over the yacht-filled dock. At dinner, about a dozen or so fish and meat dishes are offered, priced from $19 to $26. Breakfast, lunch, and Sunday brunch are served here, too.

There's an indoor pool, whirlpool, sauna, exercise room, and lap pool, and bicycle rentals can be arranged.

A Sports Enthusiast's Paradise

White Oaks Inn and Racquet Club. Taylor Rd., Niagara-on-the-Lake, ON, L0S 1J0. ☎ **905/688-2550.** 90 rms, 17 suites. A/C TV TEL. $130–$140 double; $160 Executive Suite. AE, DC, ER, MC, V.

Not far from Niagara-on-the-Lake, the White Oaks is a fantastic facility for the fitness freak. Anyone can come here, spend the whole weekend, and not stir outside the resort. Take a break and enjoy the lounge area, the outdoor terrace cafe, a formal restaurant, and a pleasantly furnished cafe/coffee shop, or schedule a massage.

The rooms are as good as the facilities, each featuring oak furniture, gray-blue or blue-rose decor, vanity sinks, and additional niceties like a phone in the bathroom and complimentary shampoo, cologne, and toothbrush. The Executive Suites also have brick fireplaces, marble-top desks, Jacuzzis (some heart-shaped), and bidets. Deluxe suites also have sitting rooms and the ultimate in furnishings.

Four outdoor tennis courts, eight air-conditioned indoor tennis courts, six squash courts, two racquetball courts, a Nautilus room, jogging trails, a sauna, suntanning beds, and a day-care center with a fully qualified staff round out the facilities.

MODERATE

The King George III Inn. 61 Melville St., Niagara-on-the-Lake, ON, L0S 1J0. ☎ **905/ 468-4800.** Fax 905/468-7004. 8 rms. A/C TV. $109–$119 standard double; $132 double with balcony. All rates include continental breakfast. MC, V.

Down by the harbor, the George III offers attractive rooms with pretty wallpaper and quilts and flounce pillows on the beds. Amenities include clock radios, TVs, hair dryers, and coffeemakers. A continental breakfast is delivered to your door. Room 8 has a large balcony.

Moffat Inn. 60 Picton St., Niagara-on-the-Lake, ON, L0S 1J0. ☎ **905/468-4116.** 22 rms. A/C TV TEL. May to mid-Oct and Christmas/New Year's holidays, $85–$120 double; mid-Oct to late Apr, $65–$120 double. AE, MC, V.

Niagara-on-the-Lake has another fine accommodation at the Moffat. There are 22 comfortable rooms available (7 with fireplaces). Most are furnished with brass beds and wicker and bamboo pieces, TVs, and hair dryers. A nice touch is the tea kettle and appropriate supplies in every room. Free coffee is available in the lobby. Restaurant and bar on premises. Note all rooms are nonsmoking.

✪ **The Old Bank House.** 10 Front St. (P.O. Box 1708), Niagara-on-the-Lake, ON, L0S 1J0. ☎ **905/468-7136.** 2 rms (without bath), 4 rms (with bath), 2 suites (with bath). A/C. $95 double without bath, $120–$125 double with bath; $150 one-bedroom suite; $250 Rose Suite. All rates include breakfast. AE, MC, V.

The Georgian Old Bank House, beautifully situated by the river, was built in 1817 as the first branch of the Bank of Canada. The inn is operated by Marjorie Ironmonger. In the main house on the second floor there are two rooms sharing a bath, two rooms with private baths, and a two-bedroom suite. On the ground floor, there are two charming rooms and another suite—all with private entrances. The Garden room with its trellised deck is particularly appealing. All rooms are tastefully decorated and have air-conditioning; all but one have a refrigerator and coffee or tea supplies. The sitting room, with a fireplace, is very comfortable and furnished with Sheraton and Hepplewhite pieces.

WHERE TO DINE

In addition to the restaurants profiled below, the **Niagara Home Bakery,** 66 Queen St. (☎ **905/468-3431**), is the place to stop for chocolate-date squares, cherry squares, croissants, cookies, and individual quiches. For a down-home breakfast or lunch, go to the **Stagecoach Family Restaurant,** 45 Queen St. (☎ **905/468-3133**). Do note that credit cards are not accepted, however.

MODERATE

The Buttery. 19 Queen St. ☎ **905/468-2564.** Reservations recommended (required for Henry VIII feast). Henry VIII feast $45; tavern menu main courses $7–$15; dinner main courses $14–$19. MC, V. Summer, daily 11am–10pm; other months daily noon–8pm. Henry VIII feast, Fri at 9pm and Sat at 9:30pm; tea, daily 2–5pm. CANADIAN/ENGLISH/CONTINENTAL.

The Buttery has been a main-street dining landmark for years, known for its weekend Henry VIII feasts, when "serving wenches" will "cosset" you with food and wine while jongleurs and musickers entertain you. You'll get broth, chicken, roast lamb, roast pig, sherry trifle, syllabub, and cheese to be washed down with a goodly amount of wine, ale, and mead.

A full tavern menu is served from 11am to 5:30pm, featuring spareribs, filet mignon, shrimp in garlic sauce, and English specialties. The dinner menu lists breast of chicken with chardonnay sauce and leg of lamb served with a real garden-mint sauce. Finish with key lime pie or mud pie. Take home some of the fresh baked goods—pies, strudels, dumplings, cream puffs, or scones.

Fans. 135 Queen St. ☎ **905/468-4511.** Main courses $8–$18 at dinner, $5–$8 at lunch. AE, MC, V. Daily noon–10pm. Closed Mon in off-season. CHINESE.

Some of the best food in town can be found in this comfortable Chinese spot, decorated with fans, cushioned bamboo chairs, and round tables spread with golden tablecloths. In summer, the courtyard also has tables for outdoor dining. The cuisine ranges from Cantonese to Szechuan. Singapore beef, moo shu pork, Szechuan scallops, and lemon chicken are just a few of the dishes available. If you wish, you can order Peking duck with 24 hours advance notice.

Ristorante Giardino. 142 Queen St. ☎ **905/468-3263.** Main courses $20–$30 at dinner. AE, MC, V. Summer, daily noon–2pm and 5:30–9pm. Winter, daily 5:30–9pm. ITALIAN.

On the ground floor of the Gate House Hotel is this sleek, ultramodern Italian restaurant with gleaming marble-top bar and brass accents throughout. The food is northern Italian with Asian and other accents, with a dozen or so main courses— filet of Chilean sea bass with tarragon, tomato and black olives; crisp breast of Muscovy duck with orange ginger sauce; or roasted rack of lamb in Dijon and sesame-seed crust in a Barolo-and-shallot reduction. Desserts include amaretto tiramisu—lady fingers soaked in amaretto and espresso, buried in sweet cream cheese, and topped with cocoa.

INEXPENSIVE

The Harbourfront Grill. 61 Melville St. ☎ **905/468-0451.** Main courses $8–$18. MC, V. Daily 11:30am–9pm. Closed mid-Nov to Apr 15. CANADIAN.

Down by the harbor, the George III is a good budget dining choice for chicken wings, burgers, sandwiches, and stir-frys, plus steaks and grilled seafood. There's a publike atmosphere and a pleasant outdoor patio.

2 Niagara Falls

Niagara Falls, with its gimmicks, amusement parks, wax museums, daredevil feats, and million motels (each with a honeymoon suite complete with a heart-shaped bed), may seem rather tacky and commercial, but somehow the falls still steal the show; and on the Canadian side, along the Niagara Parkway with its parks and gardens, nature manages to survive in all its glory.

The biggest news for the region at press time is the planned opening of Casino Niagara in December 1996. The three-story casino is being developed on the old

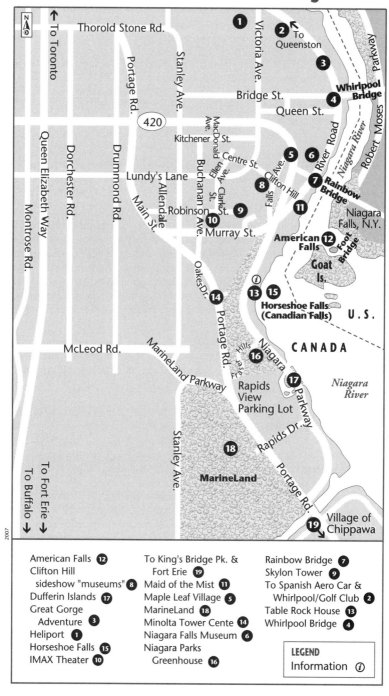

Niagara Falls

To Toronto

Thorold Stone Rd.

N

1

2 To Queenston

3

Victoria Ave.

Portage Rd.

Stanley Ave.

Whirlpool Bridge

4

Bridge St.

Queen St.

420

Kitchener St.

MacDonald Ave.

Centre St.

Ellen Ave.

River Road

Niagara River

Robert Moses Parkway

5 **6**

7 Rainbow Bridge

Lundy's Lane

Buchanan Ave.

Allendale Ave.

Clark St.

Falls Ave.

Clifton Hill

8

Niagara Falls, N.Y.

11

Robinson St.

Main St.

9

10

Murray St.

American Falls

12

Foot Bridge

Goat Is.

Dorchester Rd.

Queen Elizabeth Way

Montrose Rd.

Drummond Rd.

Oakes Dr.

14

13 **15**

Horseshoe Falls (Canadian Falls)

U.S.

McLeod Rd.

MarineLand Parkway

Portage Rd.

Hills Fras

Niagara

16

CANADA

17

Niagara River

Rapids View Parking Lot

Parkway

Rapids Dr.

Stanley Ave.

18

MarineLand

Portage Rd.

To Fort Erie

To Buffalo

19 Village of Chippawa

2007

American Falls **12**
Clifton Hill
  sideshow "museums" **8**
Dufferin Islands **17**
Great Gorge
  Adventure **3**
Heliport **1**
Horseshoe Falls **15**
IMAX Theater **10**

To King's Bridge Pk. &
  Fort Erie **19**
Maid of the Mist **11**
Maple Leaf Village **5**
MarineLand **18**
Minolta Tower Cente **14**
Niagara Falls Museum **6**
Niagara Parks
  Greenhouse **16**

Rainbow Bridge **7**
Skylon Tower **9**
To Spanish Aero Car &
  Whirlpool/Golf Club **2**
Table Rock House **13**
Whirlpool Bridge **4**

LEGEND
Information *i*

Maple Street Village property, at the foot of Rainbow Bridge. It will provide a 96,000-square-foot gaming space, plus several restaurants and entertainment lounges.

ESSENTIALS

VISITOR INFORMATION   Contact the **Niagara Falls Canada Visitor and Convention Bureau,** 5433 Victoria Ave., Niagara Falls, ON, L2G 3L1 (☎ **800/ 563-2557,** or 905/356-6061), or the **Niagara Parks Commission,** Box 150, 7400 Portage Rd. South, Niagara Falls, ON, L2E 6T2 (☎ **905/356-2241**).

Summer information centers are open at Table Rock House, Maid of the Mist Plaza, Rapids View parking lot, and at the Visitor and Convention Bureau on Victoria Avenue.

GETTING THERE   If you're driving from Toronto, take the QEW Niagara.

Amtrak and **VIA Rail** operate trains between Toronto (☎ **416/366-8411**) and New York, stopping in St. Catharines and Niagara Falls. Call **800/361-1235** in Canada or **800/USA-Rail** in the United States.

GETTING AROUND   One used to be able to park along the main street/parkway in Niagara Falls, but that is now forbidden; instead the way to get around is to travel aboard the **People Movers** (☎ **905/357-9340**). Park at Rapid View ($11), several kilometers from the falls, or in Preferred Parking (overlooking the falls—it costs more), and then take the People Mover, an attraction in itself. It makes nine stops from Rapid View to the Spanish Aero Car. Shuttles to the falls also operate from downtown and Lundy's Lane; an all-day pass (only good in season) costs $4 for adults, $2 for children 6 to 12.

A MONEY-SAVING PASS   To save money, buy an Explorer's Passport, which secures admission to Table Rock Scenic Tunnels, Great Gorge Adventure, and the Niagara Spanish Aero Car. It costs $16.85 for adults, and $8.45 for children 6 to 12.

SEEING THE FALLS

The most exciting way to see the falls is from the decks of the ✪ *Maid of the Mist,* 5920 River Rd. (☎ **905/358-5781**). This sturdy boat takes you right in—through the turbulent waters around the American Falls, past the Rock of Ages, and to the foot of the Horseshoe Falls, where 34.5 million gallons fall per minute over the 176-foot-high cataract. You'll get wet, and your glasses will mist, but that won't detract from the thrill of the experience.

Boats leave from the dock on the parkway just down from the Rainbow Bridge. Trips operate daily from mid-May through October 24. Fares are $9.55 for adults and $5.90 for children 6 to 12; it's free for children 5 and under.

You can go beneath the falls via the elevator at Table Rock House, which drops you 125 feet through solid rock to the **Journey Behind the Falls** (☎ **905/ 354-1551**) and viewing portals. Open year-round. Admission is $5.50 for adults and $2.75 for children 6 to 12; children under 6 free.

To view the falls from above most spectacularly, take a 9-minute spin ($140 for two people!) in a chopper over the whole Niagara area. Helicopters leave from the heliport, adjacent to the whirlpool at the junction of Victoria Avenue and Niagara Parkway, daily from 9am to dusk, weather permitting, except in January. Contact **Niagara Helicopters,** 3731 Victoria Ave. (☎ **905/357-5672**).

Or you can ride up in the external glass-fronted elevators 520 feet to the top of the **Skylon Tower Observation Deck** at 5200 Robinson St. (☎ **905/356-2651**). At the tower's base are 40 boutiques and stores in which to browse, and an indoor amusement park and typical vending outlets. The observation deck is open daily from

The Power and Pace of Niagara Falls

Seeing the falls for the first time is always a thrill. But did you know that if you were to revisit the Falls 10 years from now, you would find that they had shifted from their current location?

In fact, about 12,000 years ago Niagara Falls was 7 miles downstream from its present position. Why and how is this, you ask? Because of erosion. The tumbling waters cut away the shale and sandstone layers that are underneath the dolomite on top. Until the 1950s, the falls eroded at an average rate of 3 feet per year. Today, the rate has slowed to 1 foot every 10 years.

The approximately 35-mile-long river that tumbles over the falls is one of the world's greatest sources of hydroelectric power. It flows from Lake Erie to Lake Ontario, dropping its short course about 326 feet between the two lakes. At the Horseshoe Falls, the drop is about 170 feet; and at the American Falls, it's anywhere from 70 to 110 feet. More than 6 million cubic feet of water go over the crest line of the falls every minute at peak daytime hours. This churning river provides the driving force for almost 2 million kilowatts of electricity from a number of power plants on the Canadian side, while another 2.4 million kilowatts—enough to light 24 million 100-watt bulbs—are generated by the Robert Moses and the Lewiston plants on the American side. It's a remarkable feat, considering that the first electricity was generated in 1893 by a tiny 2,200-kilowatt plant built just above the Horseshoe Falls, in order to power an electric railway between Queenston and Chippawa. Now the river supplies power to entire cities and regions.

No tours are offered of plants on the Canadian side, but the Robert Moses Niagara Power Plant on the American side has a visitor center and tours. Call **716/ 285-3211** for information.

10am to 9pm (from 8am to 1am June through Labor Day). Adults pay $6.95, seniors $5.95, and children 12 and under, $3.95.

A similar perspective can be gained from the observation floors atop the 325-foot **Minolta Tower Centre**, 6732 Oakes Dr. (☎ **905/356-1501**). On-site attractions include the *Waltzing Waters* (a computerized music, light, and water show, shown nightly from May to October for free) and a family entertainment center featuring a simulator ride and other games. The tower is open daily year-round from 9am to 11pm (closed Dec. 24–25). The Entertainment Centre is open April to November daily from 9am to 9pm. Admission to the tower is $5.95 for adults, $4.95 for students and seniors, children under 10 are admitted free.

If you want to experience what it must be like going over the falls without risking your life, then head for **Ride Niagara** located directly under the Rainbow Bridge at 5755 River Rd. (☎ **905/374-RIDE**). Before you experience going over the falls in this computerized motion simulator, you'll see a short video showing some of the weirder contraptions folks have devised for going over the falls. Then you take an elevator down to the shuttle, which takes you over the falls. Admission is $7.95 adults, $6.95 seniors, $3.95 children 5 to 12, free for children under 5. Open May 10:30am to 7:30pm; June through Labor Day 9am to 10:30pm; September through October 10:30am to 6pm; and winter noon to 5pm.

For a thrilling introduction to Niagara Falls, stop by the IMAX Theater and view the raging, swirling waters in *Niagara: Miracles, Myths, and Magic,* shown on a six-story–high screen. It's at 6170 Buchanan Ave. (☎ **905/374-IMAX**). Admission is $6.50 adults, $5.50 seniors and children 12 to 18, $4.75 children 6 to 11, free for children under 6.

THE FALLS BY NIGHT   Don't miss seeing the falls lit by 22 xenon gas spotlights (each producing 250 million candlepower of light), in shades of rose pink, red magenta, amber, blue, and green. Call **800/563-2557** in the U.S., or **905/356-6061** for schedules. The show starts around 5pm in winter, 8:30pm in spring and fall, and 9pm in summer.

Also from mid-May to the end of August, don't miss the fireworks displays over the falls every Friday evening at 10pm. Additional fireworks displays are given on major U.S. and Canadian summer holidays.

✪ EXPLORING ALONG THE NIAGARA PARKWAY

The Niagara Parkway makes the Canadian side of the falls much more appealing than the American side. This 35-mile stretch of unspoiled parkland and gardens is a refreshing respite from the honky-tonk.

From Niagara Falls, you can drive all the way to Niagara-on-the-Lake, taking in attractions en route. About half a mile north of Niagara Falls, you'll reach the **Spanish Aero Car** (☎ **905/354-5711**), a cable car that will whisk you on a 3,600-foot jaunt between two points in Canada. It takes you high above the whirlpool, providing excellent views of the surrounding landscape. Admission is $4.75 for adults, $2.40 for children 6 to 12, free for children under 6. Open daily May 1 to the third Sunday in October: from 9am to 6pm in May, until 8pm in June, until 9pm in July and August, from 10am to 7:30pm in September, and 9am to 5pm in October.

From here you'll pass the **Whirlpool Golf Club** (☎ **905/356-1140**), an outstanding public course. Greens fees are $34 for 18 holes; $22 for 9 holes.

After passing the Whirlpool Golf Club, the next stop is the **School of Horticulture**, and its **botanical gardens.** Stop for a free view of the vast gardens before going on to look at the **Floral Clock,** containing 25,000 plants in its 40-foot-diameter face.

At press time, the biggest planned event here was the late 1996 opening of the **Niagara Parks Butterfly Conservatory** (☎ **905/356-8554**). Here, in the botanical gardens, visitors can expect to view more than 2,000 butterfies (50 different international species) free-flying in a lush tropical setting, floating among such nectar-producing flowers as lantanas and pentas. The large bright-blue luminescent Morpho butterflies from Central and South America should be particularly gorgeous. Interpretive and other programs will be given in the auditorium and two smaller theaters. There'll also be a native butterfly garden outside, attracting the more familiar swallowtails, fritillaries, and painted ladies. The conservatory will be open daily (hours had not been established at press time). Admission, however, will be $6 adults, $3 children 6 to 12, free for children under 6.

From here you can drive to **Queenston Heights Park,** site of a major battle during the War of 1812. On October 13, 1812, an American force invaded Canada here. Although the British forces won the Battle of Queenston Heights, General Brock was killed. You can take a walking tour of the battlefield.

Picnic or play tennis (for $5 an hour) in this shaded arbor before visiting the **Laura Secord Homestead,** on Partition Street in Queenston (☎ **905/262-4851**). The home of this redoubtable woman contains a fine collection of Upper Canadian furniture from the 1812 period, as well as artifacts recovered from an archaeological dig. It's open from Victoria Day weekend (late May) to Labor Day, daily 10am to 6pm. Tours are given every half hour, and admission is $1. Note that on overcast days the house is closed because it's too dark inside to see anything.

Next stop is the Georgian-style **McFarland House** (☎ **905/468-3322,** or 905/356-2241), built in 1800 and home to John McFarland, "His Majesty's [George III] Boat Builder." It's open daily: Victoria Day to June 30 from 1 to 4pm; July until Labor Day from 11am to 5pm. Admission is $1.50 for adults and $1 for children. The last tour is at 4:30pm.

From here the parkway continues toward Niagara-on-the-Lake, lined with fruit farms and wineries, notably the **Inniskillin Winery,** Line 3, Service Rd. 56 (☎ **905/468-3554,** or 905/468-2187), **Reif Winery,** 15608 Niagara Pkwy. (☎ **905/468-7738**), and **Kurtz Orchards,** at the corner of East-West line and the parkway (☎ **905/468-2937**). The first is especially famous for its ice wine. It's open May to October, Monday through Saturday from 10am to 6pm; and November to April, Monday through Saturday 10am to 5pm. The self-guided tour is detailed and informative and features such sidebars as the history of the cork, as well as the wine-making process. They are given daily at 10:30am and 2:30pm from June to October (Saturdays only from November to May). At Reif Winery, tours are given on Saturdays only.

A trip along the parkway will take you by the Table Rock complex to the **Park Greenhouse,** a year-round free attraction (open daily from 9:30am to 7pm during July and August, until 4:15pm in other months).

Farther along, you can visit the **Dufferin Islands,** where the children can swim, rent a paddle boat, and explore the surrounding woodland areas, while you play a round of golf on the illuminated nine-hole par-three course. Open from the second Sunday in April to the last Sunday in October.

A little farther on, stop for a picnic in **King's Bridge Park,** and stroll along the beaches before driving on to **Fort Erie** (☎ **905/871-0540**), a reconstruction of the fort that was seized by the Americans in July 1814, besieged later by the British, and finally blown up as the Americans retreated across the river to Buffalo. Guards in period costume stand sentry duty, fire the cannons, and demonstrate drill and musket practice. Open from the first Saturday in May to Canadian Thanksgiving (U.S. Columbus Day) from 10am to 6pm daily. Admission is $4 for adults, $2.50 for children 6 to 16, free for kids under 6.

MORE TO SEE & DO

Everyone loves **Typhoon Lagoon,** 7430 Lundy's Lane (☎ **905/357-3380**), a family theme park with five water slides, a wave pool, and a hot tub. Take a picnic and spend the day (there's also a snack bar). It's open spring through fall, daily from 10am to 6pm. Admission is $14.95 per day ($9.95 for children aged 3 to 10), which entitles you to come back at night (or anytime) when the lights go on. The kids can also ride three small slides designed especially for them.

At **MarineLand,** 7657 Portage Rd. (☎ **905/356-8250**), King Waldorf, Marine-Land's sea-lion mascot, presides over the performances of killer whales, dolphins, and sea lions. The indoor aquarium features a display of freshwater fish and a marine multispecies show with harbor seals as the main attraction. Visit the animal display areas where you can pet and feed the deer and see buffalo, elk, rhea, and more. There are three restaurants or you can spread your picnic lunch on one of the many tables provided.

MarineLand also has theme-park rides: The big thriller is Dragon Mountain®, a roller coaster that loops, double-loops, and spirals its way through 1,000 feet of tunnels.

Open July and August daily 9am to 6pm; other months, 10am to 4pm. The park closes at dusk and is closed from October to late May. Admission in summer is $20.95 adults, $17.95 children 5 to 9; $17.95 and $14.95, respectively, at other times; children under 4 enter free anytime. For taped information, call **905/ 356-9565.** To get there, drive south on Stanley Street and follow the signs. From QEW, take the McLeod Road exit and follow the signs.

The **Niagara Falls Museum,** 5651 River Rd. (☎ **905/356-2151**), displays everything from Egyptian mummies to shells, fossils, and minerals, and the "Freaks of Nature" display. Open daily in summer from 8:30am to 11pm; in winter hours are irregular, usually weekends only, from 10am to 5pm. Admission is $6.75 for adults, $4.95 for students 12 to 18, $6.25 for seniors, and $3.95 for children under 11, free for children under 5.

There's a whole slew of sideshows on **Clifton Hill**—Ripley's Believe It or Not, Castle Dracula, the Houdini Museum, Movieland Wax Museum, and Louis Tussaud's Wax Museum—all of them charging about $6 for adults and $3 for children.

WINERY TOURS

Niagara is nestled into the fruit- and wine-producing area of the Niagara escarpment. The Niagara peninsula has over 25,000 acres of select vineyards cultivating some 45 varieties of wine grapes. There are a number of wineries in the region: Inniskillin, Andrés, and Vincor. At **Vincor,** 4887 Dorchester Rd. (☎ **905/357-2400**), the largest winery in Canada, you can see champagne processed in the European way by fermenting the wine in the bottle, and at any of the wineries you can view the winemaking process from the moment the grapes enter the crush house to the fermentation, bottling, and packaging stages. And then comes the fun part—the wine tasting.

Probably the best time to visit is during vendange or harvest season, from the first week in September to the end of October. At Vincor, 1-hour tours are offered year-round for $2, Monday through Friday at 10:30am and 2 and 3:30pm and 2 and 3:30pm Saturday and Sunday. Call **905/357-2400,** or write: Vincor Winery Tours, 4887 Dorchester Rd., P. O. Box 510, Niagara Falls, ON, L2E 6V4. For other winery tours and tastings, write to: Andrés Wines, P.O. Box 10550, Winona, ON, L8E 5S4 (☎ **800/263-2170** or 905/643-TOUR).

WHERE TO STAY

In Niagara Falls, it seems as though every other sign advertises a motel. In summer, rates fluctuate according to what the market will bear—some proprietors won't even quote rates ahead of time. You can secure a reasonably priced room if you're lucky enough to arrive on a "down night." For example, at a very fine hotel, I was offered a room for $55 when the official rates were $89 and up. So push a little. Keep requesting a lower rate. Don't take no for an answer.

VERY EXPENSIVE

Renaissance Fallsview Hotel. 6455 Buchanan Ave., Niagara Falls, ON, L2G 3V9. ☎ **905/ 357-5200.** 262 rms. A/C MINIBAR TV TEL. $99–$299 double; $159–$199 whirlpool rooms. AE, DC, DISC, ER, MC, V. Free parking.

The Renaissance features tastefully furnished rooms with oak furniture and TVs tucked away in cabinets. Bathrooms have double sinks and all the modern accoutrements. There's a restaurant and a rooftop cafe on the 18th floor. Facilities include an indoor pool; whirlpool; health club with saunas, squash and racquetball courts, and a fitness and weight room.

Skyline Brock. 5685 Falls Ave., Niagara Falls, ON, L2E 6W7. ☎ **800/263-7135** or 905/ 374-4444. 233 rms. A/C TV TEL. Mid-June to Sept, $129–$219 double; Oct–Dec and Apr to mid-June, $99–$140 double; winter, $80–$109 double. Children under 18 stay free in parents' room. Extra person $10. Special packages available. AE, DC, DISC, ER, MC, V. Parking $4.25.

For an unmarred view of the falls, try the Skyline Brock or the Skyline Foxhead. The Brock has been hosting honeymooners and falls visitors since 1929. It still has a certain air of splendor, with a huge chandelier and marble walls in the lobby. About 150 of the rooms face the falls. City-view rooms are slightly smaller and less expensive.

The 10th-floor Rainbow Room, with a lovely view, serves a popular continental menu that includes half a roast chicken with cranberry sauce, salmon hollandaise, and prime rib, priced from $16 to $25. Isaac's Bar is available for drinks and there's also the Lobby Cafe.

Skyline Foxhead. 5875 Falls Ave., Niagara Falls, ON, L2E 6W7. ☎ **800/263-7135** or 905/ 374-4444. 399 rms. A/C TV TEL. Mid-June to Sept, $169–$279 double; Oct–Dec and Apr to mid-June, $125–$175 double; winter, $90–$120 double. Extra person $10. Children under 18 stay free in parents' room. Special packages available. AE, DC, DISC, ER, MC, V. Valet parking $10.

Built over 20 years ago, the Foxhead has 399 rooms (about half with balconies) spread over 14 floors, and it has recently undergone an extensive renovation. Each room has a private bath or shower, a color TV with in-room movies, and climate control.

The 14th-floor penthouse dining room takes fair advantage of the view with its large glass windows and serves a daily buffet for breakfast, lunch, and dinner, with nightly dancing to a live band (in season). Or there's the Steak and Burger for reasonably priced fare. An outdoor rooftop pool rounds out the facilities.

EXPENSIVE

Holiday Inn by the Falls. 5339 Murray St. (at Buchanan), Niagara Falls, ON, L2G 2J3. ☎ **905/356-1333.** 122 rms. A/C TV TEL. Late-June to Labor Day, $100–$170 double; late April to late June, $60–$125 double; Labor Day to mid-Oct, $75–$125 double; mid-Oct to late April, 60–$90. Extra person $5–$10; rollaway bed $10; crib $5. AE, DC, DISC, ER, MC, V.

The Holiday Inn by the Falls has a prime location right behind the Skylon Tower, only minutes from the falls. It's not part of the international hotel chain (the owner had the name first and still refuses to sell it). Each room is large, with ample closet space, an additional vanity sink, color-coordinated modern furnishings, a telephone, and a color TV. Most of the rooms have balconies. Dining facilities, a gift shop, indoor and outdoor heated pools, and a patio are available.

The Village Inn. 5685 Falls Ave., Niagara Falls, ON, L2E 6W7. ☎ **800/648-7200** or 905/ 374-4444. 205 rms. A/C TV TEL. Mid-June to Oct, $160 double; Apr to mid-June, $90 double. Special packages available. Closed Jan–Mar. Parking $4. AE, DC, DISC, MC, V.

Behind the two Skylines, the Village Inn is ideal for families—all its rooms are large. Some family suites have 700 square feet, which includes a bedroom with two double beds and a living room. There is an outdoor heated swimming pool and a restaurant.

MODERATE

The Americana. 8444 Lundy's Lane, Niagara Falls, ON, L2H 1H4. ☎ **800/263-3508** or 905/ 356-8444. 82 rms, 29 suites. A/C TV TEL. Late June to late Aug, $80–$135 double; Sept–June, $50–$90 double. Extra person $10. AE, DISC, ER, MC, V. Free parking.

The Americana is one of the nicer moderately priced motels on this strip, set in 25 acres of grounds with a pleasant shady picnic area, one tennis court, indoor and outdoor swimming pools, a whirlpool, sauna, and squash court. The large rooms are fully equipped with telephones, color TVs, vanity sinks, and full bathrooms. Some suites have whirlpool tubs and fireplaces. A dining room, lounge, and coffee shop are on the premises.

Honeymoon City Motel. 4943 Clifton Hill, Niagara Falls, ON, L2G 3N5. ☎ **905/357-4330.** 77 rms, 6 suites. A/C TV TEL. Mid-May to June, $76.50 double; July–Sept, $96.50 double; Oct–Dec, $68.50 double; Jan to mid-May, $54.50 double. Rates go up substantially on weekends in the summer to as high as $150. Jacuzzi rooms are $150 and anywhere from $189 to $230 on weekends. AE, DISC, MC, V. Free parking.

Just up Clifton Hill, around the corner from the Foxhead, window boxes with ge-raniums draw the eye to the Honeymoon City Motel. Two floors of rooms sit around a courtyard with an outdoor heated pool; the honeymoon suites have heart-shaped Jacuzzis and extra-plush decor, while the other rooms have standard furniture, clock radios, full bathrooms, and color TVs. Rooms 54 through 58 have a direct view of the falls; 12 rooms have private balconies. Convenient facilities include a washer-dryer, a gift shop, two restaurants, and a beer garden.

Michael's Inn. 5599 River Rd., Niagara Falls, ON, L2E 3H3. ☎ **800/263-9390** or 905/ 354-2727. 130 rms. A/C TV TEL. June 1–Sept 15, $100–$250 double; $275–$500 bridal suite. Oct–May, $80–$200 double; $200–$400 bridal suite. AE, CB, DC, ER, MC, V. Free parking.

At this four-story white building overlooking the Niagara River gorge, the large rooms are nicely decorated with modern conveniences. Many are whirlpool-theme rooms like the Oriental or Safari. The first features lacquer chests and wallpaper patterned with peonies and plum trees, while the second sports leopard-pattern linen on the waterbed, wicker furnishings, and palms and tropical plants in the double Jacuzzi. There's a solarium pool out back. The Ember's Open Hearth Dining Room is just that: The charcoal pit is enclosed behind glass so you can see all the cooking action. There's a lounge, too.

INEXPENSIVE

Nelson Motel. 10655 Niagara River Pkwy., Niagara Falls, ON, L2E 6S6. ☎ **905/295-4754.** 25 rms. A/C TV TEL. June 16–Sept 12, $60–$90 double; Sept 13 to mid-Nov and mid-Mar to June 15, $40–$55 double. Closed mid-Nov to mid-Mar. Rollaways and cribs extra. MC, V. Free parking.

For budget accommodations, try the Nelson Motel, run by John and Dawn Pavlakovich, who live in the large house adjacent to the motel units. The units have character, especially the family units with a double bedroom adjoined by a twin-bedded room for the kids. Regular units have modern furniture, some with color TVs, others with black-and-white. All units face the fenced-in pool and neatly trimmed lawn with umbrellaed tables and shrubs (none has a telephone). The Nelson Motel is located a short drive from the falls overlooking the Niagara River, away from the hustle and bustle of Niagara itself.

A NEARBY PLACE TO STAY IN QUEENSTON

✪ **South Landing Inn.** At the corner of Kent and Front sts. (P.O. Box 269), Queenston, ON, L0S 1L0. ☎ **905/262-4634.** 23 rms. A/C TV. Mid-Apr to end of Oct, $90–$110 double; Nov to mid-Apr, $60–$70 double. AE, MC, V. Free parking.

In the nearby village of Queenston, the South Landing Inn has rooms with baths and color TVs. Five units are in the old original inn built in the early 1800s and their early-Canadian furnishings, including poster beds, reflect this era. The rest are in the modern annex. There's a distant view of the river from the inn's balcony. In the origi-nal inn you'll also find a cozy dining room with red-gingham covered tables, where breakfast is served for $4.

CAMPING

There's a **Niagara Falls KOA** at 8625 Lundy's Lane, Niagara Falls, ON, L2H 1H5 (☎ **905/354-6472**), which has 365 sites (some with electricity, water, and sewage) plus three dumping stations. Facilities include water, flush toilets, showers, fireplaces, store, ice, three pools (one indoor), sauna, and game room. Fees are $23 minimum for two; each additional adult, $5; each additional child 4 to 17, $3; hookups range from $3 for electricity, $4 for water and electricity, and $6 for water, electricity, and sewage. Open April 1 to November 1.

WHERE TO DINE

In addition to the places below, the **Pinnacle**, 6732 Oakes Dr. (☎**905/356-1501**), offers a Canadian and continental menu and a remarkable view, since it's located atop the Minolta tower. There's also a vista from atop the 520-foot tower at the **Skylon Tower Restaurants**, 5200 Robinson St. (☎ **905/356-2651,** ext. 259), where you can enjoy reasonably priced breakfast, lunch, or dinner buffets in the Summit Suite dining room, or pricier continental fare for lunch and dinner in the Revolving Restaurant.

EXPENSIVE

Casa D'Oro. 5875 Victoria Ave. ☎ **905/356-5646.** Reservations recommended. Main courses $12–$22. AE, DC, DISC, ER, MC, V. Mon–Fri noon–3pm and 4–11pm, Sat 4pm–1am, Sun 4–10pm. ITALIAN.

For fine Italian dining amid opulent surroundings (gilt busts of Caesar, Venetian-style lamps, statues of Roman gladiators, and murals of Roman and Venetian scenes), go to Casa d'Oro. Start with clams casino, or the brodetto Antonio (a giant crouton topped with poached eggs, floating on a savory broth garnished with parsley, and accompanied by grated cheese). Follow with specialties like saltimbocca alla romana, pollo cacciatore, or sole basilica (flavored with lime juice, paprika, and basil). Then, if you can bear it, choose from the dessert wagon or really spoil yourself with cherries jubilee or bananas flambé and an espresso.

At the back of the Casa d'Oro, stroll over the Bridge of Sighs and onto the disco floor of the Rialto Room, where you can dance from 9pm to the wee hours to Top 40 music, except on Sunday, Monday, and Tuesday. Wednesday is karaoke night; on other nights there's a DJ.

Happy Wanderer. 6405 Stanley Ave. ☎ **905/354-9825.** Reservations not accepted. Main courses $10–$26. AE, MC, V. Daily 8am–11pm. GERMAN.

Real gemütlichkeit greets you at the chalet-style Happy Wanderer, where you can lay your knapsack down and tuck into a host of schnitzels, wursts, and other German specialties. Transport yourself back to the Black Forest among the beer steins and the game trophies on the walls. The several rooms include the Black Forest Room, with a huge, intricately carved sideboard and cuckoo clock, and the Jage Stube, with solid wood benches and woven tablecloths. At lunch there are omelets, cold platters, sandwiches, and burgers. Dinner might start with goulash soup, proceed with bratwurst, knockwurst, rauchwurst (served with sauerkraut and potato salad) or a schnitzelwiener, Holstein, or jaeger. All entrees include potatoes, salad, and rye bread. Desserts include, naturally, Black Forest cake and apple strudel (under $5).

INEXPENSIVE

Betty's Restaurant & Tavern. 8921 Sodom Rd. ☎ **905/295-4436.** Main courses $8–$16. AE, MC, V. Mon–Sat 7am–10pm, Sun 9am–9pm. CANADIAN.

Betty's is a local favorite for honest food at fair prices. It's a family dining room where the art and generosity surface in the food—massive platters of fish-and-chips, roast beef, and seafood platters, all including soup or juice, vegetable, and potato. There are burgers and sandwiches, too, all under $7. If you can, save room for enormous portions of home-baked pies. Breakfast and lunch also offer good low-budget eating.

Niagara Parkway Commission Restaurants

Queenston Heights. 14276 Niagara Pkwy. ☎ **905/262-4274.** Main courses $19–$26. AE, DC, MC, V. Mon–Sat 11:30am–3pm, Sun 11am–3pm; Sun–Fri 5–9pm, Sat 5–10pm. Closed Jan–Mar. CANADIAN/CONTINENTAL.

The star of the Niagara Parkway Commission's eateries stands dramatically atop Queenston Heights. Set in the park among fir, cypress, silver birch, and maple, the open-air balcony affords a magnificent view of the lower Niagara River and the rich fruitland through which it flows. Or you can sit under the cathedral ceiling with its heavy crossbeams where the flue of the stone fireplace reaches to the roof. At lunchtime, light entrees, seafood, pizza, pasta, salads, and lamb burgers (from $9 to $13) are offered. At dinner, among the selections might be poached filet of Atlantic salmon with Riesling chive hollandaise, grilled pork with apples and cider dijon mustard sauce, or prime rib. Afternoon tea is also served from 3 to 5pm in summer season.

Go for a drink on the deck. There's a terrific view.

Table Rock Restaurant. Niagara Pkwy. ☎ **905/354-3631.** Reservations recommended. Main courses $13–$20. AE, DISC, MC, V. Summer, Sun–Thurs 9am–10pm, Fri–Sat 9am–11pm; winter, lunch and dinner only. CANADIAN/INTERNATIONAL.

Located only a few yards from the Canadian Horseshoe Falls, the Table Rock Restaurant offers such dinner choices as prime rib; grilled tiger shrimp marinated with tomato, onion, garlic, olive oil, and rum; barbecued salmon or roast prime rib. Pizza, pasta, ribs, and light entrees are the luncheon choices. Breakfast is also a good bet here.

Victoria Park Restaurant. 6345 Niagara Pkwy. ☎ **905/356-2217.** Main courses $13–$21. AE, MC, V. Early May to mid-Oct, daily 11:30am–10pm. Closed late Oct to early May. CANADIAN/CONTINENTAL.

Within a stone's throw of both the Canadian and the American falls, the Victoria Park offers a terrace for outdoor dining, a comfortable inside dining room warmed by its globe lights, a cafeteria, and a fast-food outlet pushing hot dogs and ice cream. In the dining room and terrace, you'll find an elaborate menu with a whole range of appetizers (bruschetta and tiger shrimp with spicy salsa and Dijon mayonnaise) and main courses that include prime rib, lemon chicken breast, and fettuccine with shrimp and okra. The main-dish prices include vegetable, potato, and fresh-baked rolls. There's a children's menu featuring burgers and lasagna.

WHERE TO STAY & DINE NEARBY

Jordan is a small village of shops and also the location for one of the area's finer wineries, Cave Springs. Here, in this quiet enclave, visitors can find elegant lodgings and one of the best dining experiences in the region.

The Vintners Inn. 3845 Main St., Jordan, ON, L0R 1S0. ☎ **905/562-5336.** 9 suites. A/C TEL. $205–$235 double. AE, ER, MC, V.

Right in the village, this modern accommodation has handsome suites with an elegantly furnished living room, fireplace, and whirlpool tub. Seven of the suites are duplexes—one of them, the deluxe loft, has two double beds on its second level—and two are garden-level suites with high ceilings. The inn's restaurant, On the Twenty, is across the street (see review below).

On the Twenty Restaurant & Wine Bar. 3836 Main St., Jordan. ☎ **905/562-7313.** Main courses $16–$24. AE, DC, MC, V. Daily 11:30am–3pm, 5–10pm. Closed Mon in winter. CANADIAN.

Sophisticated food lovers head for this delightful gardenlike haven overlooking Twenty Mile Creek. Chef Michael Olson has built a fine reputation and this is one of the best places to dine in the Niagara Falls area. It's located in an old winery, and the dining rooms, which look out over pretty gardens, are extremely appealing. The cuisine celebrates local ingredients and wines. For example, there might be spit-roasted Spring Creek pork loin in Niagara Falls maple wheat beer glaze with red on-ion relish, or High River beef medallions on gewürztraminer horseradish hollandaise, as well as seafood dishes. To start, select the Prince Edward Island mussels steamed in Niagara Falls Old Jack ale, garlic, and scallion. Naturally, there's an extensive selection of Ontario wines, including ice wines, to go with the lemon tart, fruit cobbler, and other items on the dessert list.

3 Stratford

Home of the world-famous Stratford Festival, this town manages to capture the prime elements of the Bard's birthplace, from the swans on the Avon River to the grass banks that sweep down to it. Picnic under a weeping willow before attending a Shakespearean play.

ESSENTIALS

VISITOR INFORMATION   For first-rate visitor information, go to the **Informa-tion centre** by the river on York Street at Erie. It's open from May to early Novem-ber, Sunday and Monday from 10am to 5pm, and Tuesday through Saturday from 9am to 8pm. At other times, contact **Tourism Stratford,** 88 Wellington St., Stratford, ON, N5A 6W1 (☎ **800/561-SWAN,** or 519/271-5140).

GETTING THERE   Driving from Toronto, take Highway 401 west to Inter-change 278 at Kitchener. Follow Highway 8 west onto Highway 7/8 to Stratford.

   Amtrak and **VIA Rail** operate several trains daily along the Toronto-Kitchener-Stratford route.

✪ THE STRATFORD FESTIVAL

Since its modest beginnings on July 13, 1953, when *Richard III,* starring Sir Alec Guinness, was staged in a huge tent, Stratford's artistic directors have all built on the radical, but faithfully classic base originally provided by Tyrone Guthrie to create a repertory theater with a glowing international reputation.

   Stratford has three theaters: the **Festival Theatre,** 55 Queen St. in Queen's Park, with its dynamic thrust stage; the **Avon Theatre,** 99 Downie St., with a classic proscenium; and the **Tom Patterson Theatre,** an intimate 500-seat theater on Lakeside Drive.

   World-famous for its Shakespearean productions, the festival also offers both classic and modern theatrical masterpieces. Recent productions have included *The Merchant of Venice, King Lear, As You Like It,* Meredith Willson's *The Music Man, Amadeus* by Peter Shaffer, and Tennessee Williams's *Sweet Bird of Youth.* Among the com-pany's alumnae are such famous names as Dame Maggie Smith, Sir Alec Guinness, Sir Peter Ustinov, Alan Bates, Christopher Plummer, Irene Worth, Julie Harris, and Gordon Thompson. Present company members include Brian Bedford, William Hutt, Martha Henry, and Barbara Byrne.

   In addition to attending plays, visitors may enjoy a variety of fringe activities: "Meet the Festival," a series of informal discussions with members of the acting company, production, or administrative staff; "Post Performance Discussions" that follow Thursday evening performances; and backstage or warehouse tours, offered every Wednesday, Saturday, and Sunday morning from mid-June to the end of October. The last cost $5 for adults, $2.50 for seniors and students (advance reser-vations recommended).

The season usually begins early in May and continues until mid-November. For tickets, call **519/273-1600;** or write to the Stratford Festival, P.O. Box 520, Stratford, ON, N5A 6V2. Tickets are also available in the United States and Canada at Ticketron outlets. Telephone orders are taken beginning in late February.

EXPLORING THE TOWN

Are there summer pleasures in Stratford besides the theater? Within sight of the Festival Theatre, **Queen's Park** has picnic spots beneath tall shade trees or down by the water's edge where the swans and ducks gather. To the east and west of the theater, footpaths follow the Avon River and Lake Victoria.

Past the Orr Dam and the 90-year-old stone bridge, through a rustic gate, lies a very special park, the **Shakespearean Garden.**

If you turn right onto Romeo Street North from Highways 7 and 8 as you come into Stratford, you'll find the **Gallery/Stratford,** 54 Romeo St. (☎ **519/271-5271**), which mounts varied shows. September through June it's open Sunday and Tuesday through Saturday noon to 5pm; July through the first week of September it's open Monday noon to 5pm, and Tuesday through Sunday 10am to 7pm. Admission is $3.50 for adults, $2.50 for students 12 and up and seniors.

Stratford is a historic town, and 1¹/₂-hour **guided tours of early Stratford** are given Monday through Saturday July to Labor Day, leaving at 9:30am from the visitors booth by the river.

Paddleboat and canoe rentals are available at the Boathouse, located behind and below the information booth. Open daily from 9am until dark in summer. Contact **Avon Boat Rentals,** 40 York St. (☎ **519/271-7739**).

WHERE TO STAY

When you book your theater tickets, you can also, at no extra charge, book your accommodations. The festival can book you into the type of accommodation and price category you prefer, from guest homes with $35 rates to first-class hotels charging over $125. Call or write the **Festival Theatre Box Office,** P.O. Box 520, Stratford, ON, N5A 6V2 (☎ **800/567-1600** or 519/273-1600).

HOTELS/MOTELS

Expensive

Bentleys. 107 Ontario St., Stratford, ON, N5A 3H1. ☎ **519/271-1121.** 13 suites. A/C TV TEL. July–Oct $150 double (50% off Sun and Mon); Nov–June $100 double. Extra person $20. AE, DC, ER, MC, V.

The soundproof rooms here are in fact luxurious duplex suites, each with a bathroom, telephone, air-conditioning, a color TV, and an efficiency kitchen. Period English furnishings and attractive drawings, paintings, and costume designs on the walls make for a pleasant ambiance. Five of the suites have skylights.

Festival Motor Inn. 1144 Ontario St. (P.O. Box 811), Stratford, ON, N5A 6W1. ☎ **519/ 273-1150.** Fax 519/273-2111. 183 rms. A/C TV TEL. Main building, $95 double, $105 twin. Outside units (with no inside access and no refrigerator), $90 double. New deluxe rooms $120–$160 double. Extra person $10; cot $8. Winter rates about 30% lower. AE, DC, MC, V.

With its black-and-white motel-style units, the Festival Motor Inn is set back off Highways 7 and 8 in 10 acres of nicely kept, landscaped grounds. The place has an old English air with its stucco walls, Tudor-style beams, and high-back red settees in the lobby. The Tudor style is maintained throughout the large modern rooms, all with wall-to-wall carpeting, matching bedspreads and floor-to-ceiling drapes, reproductions of old masters on the walls, and full bathrooms. Some of the bedrooms have

Stratford

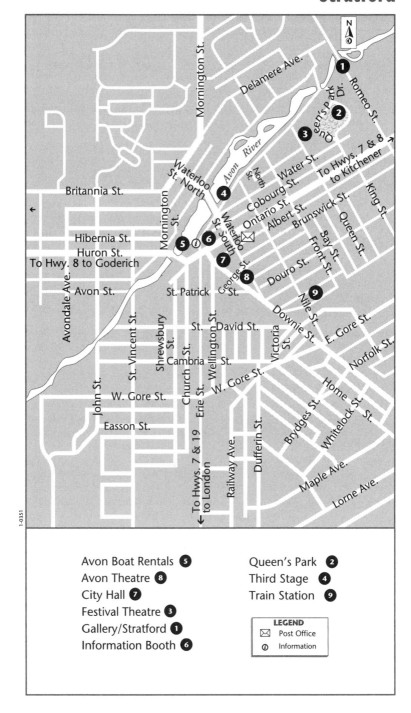

Avon Boat Rentals ❺
Avon Theatre ❽
City Hall ❼
Festival Theatre ❸
Gallery/Stratford ❶
Information Booth ❻

Queen's Park ❷
Third Stage ❹
Train Station ❾

LEGEND
⊠ Post Office
ⓘ Information

charming bay windows with sheer curtains, and all rooms in the main building have refrigerators. Other facilities include a dining room, coffee shop, and an indoor pool with outdoor patio.

The Queen's Inn. 161 Ontario St., Stratford, ON, N5A 3H3. ☎ **519/271-1400.** 32 rms. A/C TV TEL. May–Oct, $100 small double, $130 queen, $150–$200 suite. Nov 1–May 1, $60 small double or queen, from $75 suite. AE, MC, V.

Conveniently located in the town center, the Queen's Inn has rooms pleasantly decorated in pastels and pine. Facilities include the Boar's Head Pub and the Soltar Restaurant, specializing in southwestern cuisine.

Moderate

23 Albert Place. 23 Albert St., Stratford, ON, N5A 3K2. ☎ **519/273-5800.** 34 rms. A/C TV TEL. $80–$90 double; $110 minisuite; from $130 suite. MC, V.

Right around the corner from the Avon Theatre, the Albert Place sports large rooms with high ceilings. Furnishings are simple and modern. Some rooms have separate sitting rooms. Complimentary coffee, tea, and donuts are available in the lobby for guests in the early morning.

A PICK OF THE BED-AND-BREAKFASTS

For more information on the Stratford bed-and-breakfast scene, write to **Tourism Stratford,** 88 Wellington St., Stratford, ON, N5A 6W1 (☎ **519/271-5140**). It's open 8:30am to 5pm Monday to Friday.

Acrylic Dreams. 66 Bay St., Stratford, ON, N5A 4K6. ☎ **519/271-7874.** 4 rms (3 with bath). A/C. $75–$95 double; $110–$130 suite. Rates include breakfast. Two-night minimum on weekends. No credit cards.

Acrylic Dreams has a fun, modern, artsy atmosphere thanks to its artist-owners. The house is furnished with cottage-style antiques, except for the living room, which is furnished in a New Wave–style with transparent acrylic furniture. Upstairs, there's a suite decorated in Provençal colors with a private bath and living room. On the ground floor, there are two doubles with baths. The largest is decorated with angel-patterned wallpaper and contains an antique white iron-and-brass bed. The smaller room is decorated in buttery yellow with cherubs and has an antique double bed. The final room, which shares a bath, features an antique four-poster bed. The full breakfast varies from day to day, but might include orange juice and coffee, peaches and peach yogurt, scrambled eggs, and bagels; there's never any meat, though (the owners are vegetarians). There's a phone for guests' use, and the suite has a TV.

Ambercroft. 129 Brunswick St., Stratford, ON, N5A 3L9. ☎ **519/271-5644.** 4 rms (all with bath). A/C. $80 double. All rates include continental breakfast. MC, V.

At this inviting 1878 Gothic Revival–style home, there's a comfy front parlor with plenty of slipcovered chairs and sofas, a small TV room, and a patio out back. An extended continental breakfast is served—fresh fruit, cereal, muffins, and croissants. No smoking.

Avonview Manor. 63 Avon St., Stratford, ON, N5A 5N5. ☎ **519/273-4603.** 4 rms (two with bath). A/C. $75–$85 double. All rates include breakfast. No credit cards.

Located on a quiet street in an Edwardian house, Avonview Manor has four rooms with fans, all attractively and individually furnished. One room has a brass bed covered with a floral-pattern quilt and flouncy pillows, and is large enough for a chaise lounge and chair. Another room has a cherry acorn bed, a cherry dresser, and a love seat. Two of the rooms share a bath.

A full breakfast is served in a bright dining room overlooking the garden, and a kitchen equipped with an ironing board is available on the first floor. The living room is very comfortable, particularly in winter, when guests can cozy up in front of the stone fireplace. Smoking is allowed only on the porch. There's also an in-ground pool and hot tub.

Brunswick House. 109 Brunswick St., Stratford, ON, N5A 3L9. ☎ **519/271-4546.** 6 rms (none with bath). $60 and up. All rates include breakfast. No credit cards.

If you stay here you'll enjoy the very literate surroundings created by owners Geoff Hancock and Gay Allison—portraits of Canadian authors and poetry on the walls, books everywhere, and the chance to run into a literary personality. There are six rooms sharing two baths, all nicely decorated, and with ceiling fans. One is a family room with a double and two single beds. Each room has a personal decorative touch—a Mennonite quilt, posters by an artist friend, or a parasol atop a wardrobe. A full breakfast is served. Smoking is restricted to the veranda. Very conveniently located within walking distance of the center of town and theaters.

۞ Deacon House. 101 Brunswick St., Stratford, ON, N5A 3L9. ☎ **519/273-2052.** 6 rms. A/C. $90–$105 double. Extra person $20. All rates include continental breakfast. Off-season packages available. V.

Deacon House, a shingle-style structure built in 1907, has been restored by Dianna Hrysko and Mary Allen. They have six rooms, all with baths, that are decorated in a country style, with iron-and-brass beds, quilts, pine hutches, oak rockers, and rope-style rugs. My favorite rooms are on the top floor. The living room, with a fireplace, TV, wingback chairs, and a sofa, is comfortable. The guest kitchen is a welcome convenience; so too is the second-floor sitting/reading room. A continental breakfast is served. This is a great location, within walking distance of everything.

Flint's Inn. 220 Mornington St., Stratford, ON, N5A 5G5. ☎ **519/271-9579.** 2 rms (with shared bath), 1 suite (with bath). A/C. $65 double; $85 suite. All rates include breakfast. No credit cards.

This steep-mansard–roofed house, built in 1862, has three air-conditioned units. One is a large suite with a sun porch, a balcony, a private bath, and a refrigerator. The iron-and-brass bed sports an old quilt, and among the decorative features are an old butter churn and a bottle collection. The other two rooms share a bathroom. The living room, with its marble fireplace and pine furnishings, is inviting. At breakfast, homemade muffins, juice, and coffee are accompanied by eggs Benedict or something similar. The garden is well kept and filled with the wonderful scent of lilac in season.

The Maples. 220 Church St., Stratford, ON, N5A 2R6. ☎ **519/273-0810.** 5 rms (1 with bath). A/C. $55–$100 single or double. All rates include continental breakfast. V.

The Maples is owned and run by Michelle Bergsma, who keeps five nice rooms—four doubles and one single—and serves juice, fruit, and homemade breads and muffins at breakfast. The house is a redbrick Victorian with a balcony. It's within walking distance of the theaters.

Woods Villa. 62 John St. N., Stratford, ON, N5A 6K7. ☎ **519/271-4576.** 6 rms (1 with bath). A/C TV. $105–$120 double. All rates include breakfast. DISC, MC, V.

This late 18th-century house is home to Ken Vinen, who has a passion for collecting and restoring Wurlitzers, Victrolas, and player pianos, which are found throughout the house. There are six rooms (five sharing two bathrooms). Five have fireplaces, and all have color TVs, refrigerators, and air-conditioning. Rooms are large and an excellent value. Guests are welcome to use the attractively landscaped outdoor pool, the lounges, and the TV in the living room.

Ken has other talents—at breakfast he may choose to make some doughnuts or muffins, served along with a full meal consisting of whatever you request, from eggs to oatmeal. The macaws, Barney and Fred, will add their comments. No indoor smoking. Pets and children not permitted. Guests can also have coffee or tea delivered to their rooms in the morning.

A NEARBY PLACE TO STAY & DINE

✪ Langdon Hall. RR #3, Cambridge, ON, N3H 4R8. ☎ **800/268-1898** or 519/740-2100. Fax 519/740-8161. 38 rms, 3 suites. A/C TV TEL. $195–$230 double; from $310 suite. All rates include continental breakfast. AE, DC, ER, MC, V.

The elegant house that stands at the head of the curving, tree-lined drive was completed in 1902 by Eugene Langdon Wilks, youngest son of Matthew and Eliza Astor Langdon, a granddaughter of John Jacob Astor. It remained in the family until 1987, when its transformation into a small country-house hotel was begun. Today its 200 acres of lawns, gardens, and woodlands make for an ideal retreat. The main house, of red brick with classical pediment and Palladian-style windows, has a beautiful symmetry. Inside, a similar harmony is achieved. Throughout, the emphasis is on comfort rather than grandiosity, whether in the conservatory, the veranda where tea is served, or Wilk's Bar, with its comfortable club chairs.

The majority of the rooms are set around the cloister garden. Each room is individually decorated; most have fireplaces. The furnishings consist of handsome antique reproductions, mahogany wardrobes, ginger-jar porcelain lamps, wingbacked chairs and armchairs upholstered with luxurious fabrics, fine Oriental rugs, gilt-framed pictures, and such nice touches as fresh flowers and terry bathrobes. The light and airy dining room overlooking the lily pond offers fine regional cuisine with main courses priced from $22 to $33. Beyond the cloister, down a trellis arcade, and through a latch gate lies the herb and vegetable garden and beyond that the swimming pool (with an attractive pool house), tennis court, and croquet lawn. Other facilities include a whirlpool, sauna, exercise room, billiards room, spa, and cross-country ski trails.

WHERE TO DINE

EXPENSIVE

✪ The Church. Brunswick and Waterloo sts. ☎ **519/273-3424.** Reservations required well in advance. Summer fixed-price dinner $52.20 (discounted 20% 7:30–9pm Tues–Sat and all night Sun.). AE, MC, V. Tues–Sat 11:30am–1am, Sun 11:30am–11pm. Closed Mon, unless there's a special concert or play. CONTINENTAL.

The Church must be one of the few restaurants in Canada where you have to reserve 3 weeks in advance. Still, it's a unique privilege because the food is so good and the decor is incredible. The organ pipes and the altar are still intact, along with the vaulted roof, carved woodwork, and stained-glass windows—you can sit in the nave or the side aisles and dine to the sounds of Bach. Fresh flowers and elegant table settings further enhance the experience.

In summer, there's a special five-course fixed-price dinner and an à la carte luncheon and posttheater menu. Appetizers might include duck confit and caramelized red cabbage with ravigote sauce or blanquette of seafood with cucumber and ginger. Among the entrees might be filet mignon with a sauce of Madeira and truffles, wild mushrooms, roast shallots, and garlic; sauté of ostrich with cranberry and green peppercorn sauce; or salmon wrapped in nori, steamed and served with pickled ginger and dipping sauce. There's also a short vegetarian menu. The pièce de résistance among the desserts might be glazed orange flan with chocolate ice cream, or perhaps the pistachio crème brûlée. This is a very special dining experience.

The upstairs Belfry Bar is a popular pre- and posttheater gathering place for cocktails, snacks, and full lunch, dinner, and posttheater dinner menus.

✪ **The Old Prune.** 151 Albert St. ☎ **519/271-5052.** Reservations recommended. Fixed-price dinner $49.95; main courses $7–$14 at lunch or posttheater. AE, MC, V. Wed–Sun 11:30am–2pm; Tues–Sun 5–9pm; posttheater supper Fri–Sat 9pm–midnight. CONTINENTAL.

Another of my Stratford favorites, the Old Prune is run by two charming, witty women—Marion Isherwood and Eleanor Kane. Set in a lovely Edwardian home, it has three dining rooms and a garden patio. The proprietors have given the place a Québec flair, which is reflected in both the decor and the menu.

The prix fixe menu includes a choice of appetizer, main course, dessert, coffee, and petit fours. The chef uses organically grown meats and vegetables in an imaginative way that creates strong flavorsome dishes, like the roast rack of lamb with a smoked chili-tomatillo sauce, the beef tenderloin in a rich foie gras sauce, or the grilled sea bass with a tomato-basil vinaigrette. Among the appetizers, try the warm goat cheese and potato terrine with local greens, and sweet red-pepper and basil oils; or splurge and pay the supplement on the marvelous beggars purses filled with lobster and Sevruga caviar with a trio of salads and house-smoked salmon. The desserts are classics with a creative twist—raspberry crème brûlée and warm apple tarlette served with sour-cream ice cream. The late-supper menu features lighter entrees, like ravioli filled with duck confit and sweet potato with a jus of oven-dried tomato, or smoked Atlantic salmon on rosti potato with crème fraîche.

✪ **Rundles.** 9 Cobourg St. ☎ **519/271-6442.** Reservations required. Three-course table d'hôte $49.50; gastronomical menus from $56.50 per person. AE, ER, MC, V. Wed and Sat–Sun noon–2:30pm; Tues–Sun dinner hours vary. On Fri–Sat a posttheater menu is available. During the winter the restaurant closes and functions occasionally as a cooking school until theater season resumes. INTERNATIONAL.

Rundles's large windows take advantage of its beautiful setting overlooking Lake Victoria. Its owner, Jim Morris, eats, sleeps, thinks, and dreams food, and chef Neil Baxter delivers exquisite cuisine to the table. The three-course table d'hôte, including appetizer, main course, dessert, and coffee, will always offer some palate-pleasing combinations, like the sweet red-pepper puree soup with eggplant custard, or the warm seared foie gras with caramelized endive, served with garlic-flavored potatoes and sweet yellow pepper and basil oil. Among the six or so main dishes, there might be grilled Atlantic salmon with a light carrot sauce, or grilled tamarind-basted breasts of quail. As for dessert, my choice would be the zesty glazed lemon tart with orange sorbet, but the sherry trifle is also a dream. The dining area is very contemporary with its gray spotlighted tables, good cutlery and crystal, and contemporary art, much of it by Victor Tinkl. The restaurant follows the theater schedule.

Wolfys. 127 Downie St. ☎ **905/271-2991.** Reservations recommended. Main courses $15–$24. AE, MC, V. Tues–Sun 11:30am–2pm; Tues–Sat 5–8:30pm. ECLECTIC.

Wolfys has won a loyal local and visitor following with its well-prepared, flavorful cuisine. It's located in a former fish-and-chips shop and the original decor is still evident—the booths, the counter and stools, and the old fish fryer serving as a display cabinet in one corner. Yet it has a New Wave flavor. The walls are decorated with vibrant art by Kato. On the limited menu, you might find a rice-and-vegetable stir-fry with a pad-Thai coconut sauce, South Indian tiger shrimp curry with ginger and lemongrass, or grilled Angus beef in mustard crème fraîche. Desserts run from tart of the day (peach-nectarine, for example) and a brownie with orange caramel sauce to homemade ice creams.

MODERATE

Bentley's. 107 Ontario St. ☎ **905/271-1121.** Reservations not accepted. Light fare $6–$8; main courses $12–$15. AE, DC, ER, MC, V. Daily 11:30am–1am. CANADIAN/ENGLISH.

For budget dining and fun to boot, go to Bentley's, the local watering hole. In summer, you can sit on the garden terrace. In this atmosphere, you can savor some light fare—deep-fried calamari, grilled shrimp, vegetarian wontons, chicken fingers—along with sandwiches and salads, which are served all day. Dinner items are more substantial, like lamb curry, roast chicken, baked sole, sirloin, or prime rib.

Café Mediterranean. In the Festival Square Building. ☎ **905/271-9590.** Reservations not accepted. Most items under $6. No credit cards. Summer, Mon–Tues 8am–6pm, Wed–Sat 8am–7pm, Sun 10am–2pm; winter, Mon–Sat 9am–5pm. LIGHT FARE.

In the Festival Square Building, the Café Mediterranean is great for made-to-order sandwiches, fruit flans, croissants (cheese, almond, and chocolate), quiches, and pasta dishes like manicotti. Salads, pastries, and crepes are also served. You can order them to go, or dine here while seated on director's chairs.

Keystone Alley Café. 34 Brunswick St. ☎ **905/271-5645.** Reservations recommended. Main courses under $8 at lunch, $15–$20 at dinner. AE, MC, V. Mon–Sat 11am–4pm; Tues–Sat 5–9pm. CONTINENTAL.

Actors often stop in for lunch at the Keystone Alley Café. There are butcher-block tables as well as a counter where you can order a light lunch—soups, salads, burgers, sandwiches, New York cheesecake, and a daily selection of muffins.

At night the atmosphere changes, and there's a full dinner menu featuring eight or so items, such as calves' liver with meaux mustard sauce, sauteed five-spice salmon with oriental vegetables, or roast rack of lamb. Wine and beer are served.

Let Them Eat Cake. 82 Wellington St. ☎ **905/273-4774.** Reservations not accepted. Breakfast and lunch items under $5; desserts $1–$4.50. MC, V. Summer, Mon 7:30am–4pm, Tues–Thurs 7:30am–8pm, Fri–Sun 7:30am–6pm; winter, Mon–Sat 7:30am–5pm, Sun 8:30am–2:30pm. LIGHT FARE.

Let Them Eat Cake is great for breakfast (bagels, scones, and croissants), lunch (soups, salads, sandwiches, quiche, and chicken pot pie), and dinner, but it's best for dessert. There are about 30 desserts and pastries to choose from—everything from pecan pie, orange Bavarian cream, and lemon bars to carrot cake, Black Forest cake, and chocolate cheesecake.

PICNIC FARE & WHERE TO EAT IT

Stratford is really a picnicking place. Take a hamper down to the banks of the river or into the parks: Plenty of places cater to this business. **Rundles** will make you a super sophisticated hamper; **Café Mediterranean** has salads, quiches, crepes, and flaky meat pies and pastries. Or go to **Lindsay's,** 40 Wellington St. (☎ **519/273-6000**), which offers all kinds of salads—pasta, grains, and vegetables—pâtés; fish, chicken, and meat dishes; soups; and breads and pastries. The shop also sells imported specialty foods. Open in summer Tuesday through Friday from 10am to 6pm, Saturday 10am to 4pm (closed 2 weeks in January).

Index

FROMMER'S COMPLETE TRAVEL GUIDES

*(Comprehensive guides to destinations around the world, with
selections in all price ranges—from deluxe to budget)*

FROMMER'S FRUGAL TRAVELER'S GUIDES
(The grown-up guides to budget travel, offering dream vacations at down-to-earth prices)

Australia from $45 a Day

Berlin from $50 a Day

California from $60 a Day

Caribbean from $60 a Day

Costa Rica & Belize from $35 a Day

Eastern Europe from $30 a Day

England from $50 a Day

Europe from $50 a Day

Florida from $50 a Day

Greece from $45 a Day

Hawaii from $60 a Day

India from $40 a Day

Ireland from $45 a Day

Italy from $50 a Day

Israel from $45 a Day

London from $60 a Day

Mexico from $35 a Day

New York from $70 a Day

New Zealand from $45 a Day

Paris from $65 a Day

Washington, D.C. from $50 a Day

FROMMER'S PORTABLE GUIDES
(Pocket-size guides for travelers who want everything in a nutshell)

Charleston & Savannah

Las Vegas

New Orleans

San Francisco

FROMMER'S IRREVERENT GUIDES
(Wickedly honest guides for sophisticated travelers)

Amsterdam

Chicago

London

Manhattan

Miami

New Orleans

Paris

San Francisco

Santa Fe

U.S. Virgin Islands

Walt Disney World

Washington, D.C.

FROMMER'S AMERICA ON WHEELS
(Everything you need for a successful road trip, including full-color road maps and ratings for every hotel)

California & Nevada

Florida

Mid-Atlantic

Midwest & the Great Lakes

New England & New York

Northwest & Great Plains

South Central &Texas

Southeast

Southwest

FROMMER'S BY NIGHT GUIDES
(The series for those who know that life begins after dark)

Amsterdam

Chicago

Las Vegas

London

Los Angeles

Miami

New Orleans

New York

Paris

San Francisco

WHEREVER YOU TRAVEL, *H*ELP IS NEVER FAR AWAY.

From planning your trip to providing travel assistance along the way, American Express® Travel Service Offices are always there to help.

Toronto

American Express Travel Service
Royal York Hotel, #133-134
100 Front Street West
Toronto
416/363-3883

American Express Travel Service
157 Yonge Street
Toronto
416/868-1044

American Express Travel Service
Holt Renfrew Building
50 Bloor Street West
Toronto
416/967-3411

Travel

http://www.americanexpress.com/travel

American Express Travel Service Offices are found in central locations throughout Canada.